SECOND EDITION

PHYSICAL GEOGRAPHY 7

SECOND EDITION

PHYSICAL GEOGRAPHY 7

Graham Draper • Lew French • Jennifer Farrell-Cordon • Pina Sacco

NELSON EDUCATION

NELSON EDUCATION

Physical Geography 7

Authors
Graham Draper, Lew French, Jennifer Farrell-Cordon, Pina Sacco

Director of Publishing
Kevin Martindale

General Manager, Social Studies, Business Studies, and Languages
Carol Stokes

Publisher
Doug Panasis

Managing Editor, Development
Karin Fediw

Interim Product Manager
Doug Morrow

Assistant Editor
Kimberly Murphy

Editorial Assistant
Jessica Fung

Executive Director, Content and Media Production
Renate McCloy

Director, Content and Media Production
Sujata Singh

Production Manager
Helen Jager-Locsin

Senior Production Coordinators
Kathrine Pummell,
Sharon Latta Paterson

Design Director
Ken Phipps

Interior Design
Studio Montage

Cover Design
Rocket Design

Printer
Transcontinental Printing Inc.

Focus Strategic Communications Inc.

Project Manager
Adrianna Edwards

Developmental Editors
Linda Aspen-Baxter,
Adrianna Edwards

Copy Editors and Proofreaders
Linda Szostak, Christine Hobberlin

Index
Ron Edwards

Art Director
Adrianna Edwards

Compositor
Valentino Sanna

Photo Research and Permissions
Elizabeth Kelly

ISBN-13: 978-0-17-635487-9
ISBN-10: 0-17-635487-5

Printed and bound in Canada
1 2 3 4 11 10 09 08

For more information contact Nelson Education Ltd., 1120-Birchmount Road, Toronto, Ontario, M1K 5G4. Or you can visit our Internet site at http://www.nelson.com

Consultants and Reviewers

The authors and the publisher wish to thank the consultants and reviewers for their input—advice, ideas, directions, and suggestions—that helped to make this learning resource more student-friendly and teacher-useful. Their contribution in time, effort, and expertise was invaluable.

Consultants

Tom Conklin
Curriculum Consultant
Student Success Department
Ottawa Catholic School Board

Brenda Davis
Education Consultant
Six Nations of the
Grand River Territory

Patricia Healy
Curriculum Consultant (retired)
York Region District School Board

Karen Iversen
Educational Consultant
Edmonton, Alberta

Reviewers

Heather Chalmers
Teacher
St. Augustine Catholic High School
York Catholic District School Board

Franca Ianni
Teacher
Assumption Catholic Secondary School
Halton Catholic District School Board

Eugene Janssens
Teacher
St. Francis de Sales Elementary School
Catholic District School Board of
Eastern Ontario

Mark Lowry
Instructional Leader for Geography
and Geotechnologies
Toronto District School Board

John MacPhail
Teacher
St. Dominic Catholic Elementary School
Halton Catholic District School Board

Linda Memmo
Teacher
St. Fidelis Catholic School
Toronto Catholic District School Board

Mark Mitchell
Teacher
Hillfield Strathallan College
Conference of Independent Schools

Luci Soncin
Principal (retired)
St. Fidelis Catholic School
Toronto Catholic District School Board

Contents

Features to Help You Use This Book

KEY VOCABULARY

A Key Vocabulary list is found on the first page of each chapter to let you know the terms that are new or difficult in the chapter.

CONNECTIONS TO

Science

These features connect the material you are reading about with other subjects that you study, like science, history, music, and language.

Fact File

Each Fact File is a small piece of information about the topic you are studying. Often, these facts are quite unusual in that they make you look at things from a different angle.

BEFORE READING

Before Reading questions and activities help you to think about what you already know about the topic. Your own experiences can give you some insights into the ideas. You are sometimes asked to share your thoughts with others. This helps you to improve your communication skills.

DURING READING

These questions help you understand key points. They can help you check that you understand what you are reading.

AFTER READING

After Reading activities help you identify main ideas, make conclusions, and apply the ideas you have just learned to new situations.

LITERACY TIP

Helpful Hints

Literacy Tips are helpful hints that will make it easier for you to read, understand, and communicate ideas. These tips are linked to activities or information on or near the page where they are found.

WEB LINK

These margin notes send you to the *Nelson Physical Geography 7* website to learn more about the people, places, and events discussed in this textbook.

GeoSkills

GeoSkills help you learn useful geographic and literacy skills. They show you steps that you can take to practise difficult skills that you will use in everyday life.

Go Geo-Green

Each Go Geo-Green feature lets you know about an interesting action that people have taken to help protect our environment. They show what people can accomplish when they set their minds to it.

Be a Global Citizen

These features are reports about actions that people have taken to help others around the world. They show how we are all connected to the world community.

End-of-Chapter Exercises

At the end of every chapter, there are four types of questions. These questions are designed to let you test yourself on how well you understand the chapter, to get you to stretch your geography skills, and to allow you to demonstrate how ready you are to move on to new material.

Knowledge and Understanding

Inquiry/Research and Communication Skills

Map, Globe, and Graphic Skills

Application

Map Appendix

The Map Appendix, on pages 303 to 327, is a set of maps you will need to help you understand and do the work in this book.

Glossary

The Glossary, on pages 328 to 333, gives meanings for all the words that are printed in **bold** throughout the book. It is like a mini-dictionary.

Index

The Index, on pages 334 to 341, is a list of terms that you can find in the book and on what pages they are found. It is a quick way of finding out on what pages a topic is located.

UNIT 1

The Themes of Geographic Inquiry

IN THIS UNIT

- show that you understand the themes of geography: location/place, environment, region, interaction, and movement
- use the tools of geography to find and organize geographic information, and to share your ideas with others
- use the themes of geography to study environmental problems and events

1 Our blue-green planet is our place in space. Each of us has a place on Earth. What are some other "places" you have in your world?

2 Areas of rock like this along the shores of Georgian Bay in Ontario are found in many regions of the world. This is layered sedimentary rock. It shows that this region used to be covered by a sea for millions of years. Describe the region around your community. Tell about any special physical features.

3 There are large populations of ethnic groups in many large cities of the world. Cultural regions, such as Chinatown in Toronto, Ontario, make cities more interesting places to live. From which countries have immigrants to large Canadian cities come?

4 Until recently, in Beijing, China, bikes got more road lanes than cars in their movement systems. Why do you think this was so?

5 Someday, you will probably want to own a car. What changes do you think will have happened in our traffic patterns?

6 Many introduced species have entered environments around the world because of human activities. This lamprey eel found its way into the Great Lakes through the St. Lawrence Seaway. What problems might introduced species cause to plants and animals?

7 We value magnificent forests, like this one near Temagami, Ontario, for timber, wilderness, and recreation. The effects of our interactions with such precious regions often threaten to ruin them. How can we use such forests now, while making sure that they will be there for our children's children?

8 We all produce garbage. It has to go somewhere. What are some of the problems we face in dealing with this growing mass of waste?

1 Place and Location

IN THIS CHAPTER

- explain the theme of location/place in geography
- create and use maps for different reasons
- use the new terms in this chapter correctly as you investigate the topics
- locate and use helpful information from primary and secondary sources

KEY VOCABULARY

absolute location
eastings
Global Positioning System (GPS)
grid coordinate system
latitude
light year
longitude
mental map
northings
place
relative location
site
specific location

Third Rock from the Sun

BEFORE READING

1. The study of geography is based on place and location. Look at the headings and subheadings on this page and the next page. What do these headings tell you about your place and location? Are "place" and "location" two words that mean the same thing, or do they have different meanings?
2. Geographers want to be able to explain why things are where they are. To begin to think as a geographer, think about where you are on Earth. This is your place on Earth. Why are you and your family living in this particular place on Earth? Think about your surroundings. What are the natural features in the area around you? What have humans made around you? Why are these natural and human-made features where they are? As a geographer, you want to understand these connections.

LITERACY TIP

Using Headings to Predict

It is a good idea to skim a textbook section before you start reading it. The headings and subheadings in the section will give you a general idea of the content you will be reading.

Earth is the **place** in space for all people. Where we are on Earth is our **specific location**. As you read this, you are probably at a desk in a classroom in a school in a community in Ontario. That is your specific location right now.

Our position in our solar system is on the third planet from the Sun, a mere 148 800 000 kilometres away. Our nearest neighbour, Venus, is just 42 000 000 kilometres from us.

Fact File

If you rode in a space shuttle, you would reach Venus in only 2333 hours, or 97 days! Beyond our solar system, the nearest star is Proxima Centauri, 4.22 **light years** away.

The Earth in Space

Pictures taken by astronauts from the *Voyager* spacecraft in 1977 gave us our first views of Earth from space. Those pictures gave us a whole new outlook on our home—planet Earth. We gained a new sense of our place from a different vantage point. For the first time ever, we could

Figure 1.1

Imagine an astronaut's view of Earth against the blackness of space. Close your eyes and picture it. What does the image in your mind make you think about?

look back at Earth and see it as our "lifeboat" in space. We could see that we were part of something much larger than Earth. We realized the awesome connections between humans and other life forms with which we share the planet. That view struck awe in all of the astronauts.

Small but Important

We know that our solar system is part of a galaxy called the Milky Way. There are over 100 billion stars in our Milky Way galaxy and tens of billions of galaxies in the universe. Is it possible to truly understand how enormous our universe is? Where does it start? Where does it end? In the vastness of the universe, how important is one human being? Before you answer, think about it. Each one of us is important on Earth. Each one of us can make a difference to Earth's environment and its well-being. Could Earth's well-being affect the well-being of our solar system? Could the effect of Earth's well-being extend further into the universe?

Your Place on Earth

Your personal position on Earth is your location, and you can identify it with an address. Imagine someone wants to send you a letter. The address that person writes on the envelope is your location. You could expand your address to make it your place on Earth. For example, imagine someone living in Cape Town, South Africa. This person might add Africa, Southern Hemisphere, Planet Earth to their address. Try expanding your address to make it your place on Earth.

Your Place

The place where you live is also called your **site**. A site is a place with specific qualities. Some people choose a hill for the site of their home because of the view. Others prefer to live on a site near a river, on a lake, or sheltered in the woods.

Many of our communities started at a point where important land routes crossed. Other communities began at a river junction where there were good opportunities for trade or beside a natural harbour where ocean-going vessels could come and go. All these sites had special or unique qualities that influenced people's decisions to locate there and not somewhere else.

Fact File

In 1960, there were only 19 cities with over 1 million inhabitants. New York was the largest, with a population of 6 million. In 2007, 120 cities had over 2 million people. The largest was Tokyo, with 33.5 million people. That is more than the entire population of Canada.

DURING READING

1. Based on what you have read, how would you describe your place and location?
2. Are the terms "place" and "location" different words that mean the same thing, or do they mean different things? To help you answer this question, find and list the clues that the text provides. Compare your findings.
3. Why do you think people decided to settle where you are living? What physical characteristics does your place on Earth have that make it a good place to settle?

Figure 1.2

A village clings to the edge of Naervoy Fjord, Norway (62° N, 6° E). Why do you think people decided to settle here?

Web Link

For more information about "your place on Earth," go to **www.nelson.com/phygeo7**.

Literacy Tip

Picturing What You Read

As you read, create mental images, or pictures in your mind. They will help you understand and remember what you read.

Mental Images and Mental Maps

Every day on television, we witness events from around the world. We watch a war as it happens, see a tornado rip through a city, or watch rescuers dig for survivors of an earthquake. The pictures of these events all contribute to our mental images of places in the world. These are the pictures we have in our minds about the shape of our world and the features of different locations we see or hear about.

The more we know about a place, the clearer, more detailed, and precise our mental image of the place becomes. We are most familiar with our immediate neighbourhood, so our mental image of it is usually the clearest. When we sketch a map from memory, using our mental image, this is called a **mental map**. However, mental maps of areas of Earth about which we know little, are not very clear, accurate, or detailed. Studying geography helps us improve our mental images and mental maps of places in the world. As we do, we will be able to better understand daily events, other places, and people from other cultures.

Figure 1.3

This photograph shows the damage that an earthquake caused in Indonesia on April 5, 2005. Natural disasters can affect any place on Earth. However, some places are more affected by natural disasters than others. Can you suggest why? Have you ever experienced a natural disaster?

AFTER READING

1. Think about the address of the place where you are on Earth right now. This is your location. Use an atlas to help you extend your address as far out as the Milky Way galaxy.
2. We build special buildings on sites for specific reasons, often because the site has special or important qualities. Identify three physical characteristics of your school's site that make it a good place for a school. Compare the qualities you identified with a partner. How do they compare?

Getting Precise about Location

BEFORE READING

1. Explain the different ways you can think of to describe your location.
2. What makes some ways of describing location more exact than others?

Fact File

GPS was first used by the military to pinpoint positions and, later, to direct cruise missiles. Now, it is used by sailors, hikers, cartographers, surveyors, farmers, foresters, truck drivers, couriers, golfers, and millions more.

When we study location, we are looking for the answers to two questions:

- Where is it?
- Why is it there?

With new technology, it is quite easy to determine your location very precisely. A **Global Positioning System (GPS)** receives signals from an orbiting satellite. Instantly, you receive your position in **latitude**, **longitude**, and elevation. You know exactly where you are on Earth. Using GPS, it is now possible to know the exact location (within a few metres) of any spot on Earth. GPS is very useful for many things, such as boater safety or hiking. The locational information given by GPS can be stored in computers. Later, this information can be turned into maps. GPS is also used to help towns and cities locate features on maps exactly. This type of locational information has made mapping more precise. Humans have come a long way from the methods of early explorers to find their positions and make maps of areas they encountered.

DURING READING

1. List three people whose jobs would require the use of GPS. How is GPS important to them?

Figure 1.4

Find this boat's position on a map. How do latitude and longitude help you find the exact location of the boat?

Ancient Map of the East Coast of Canada

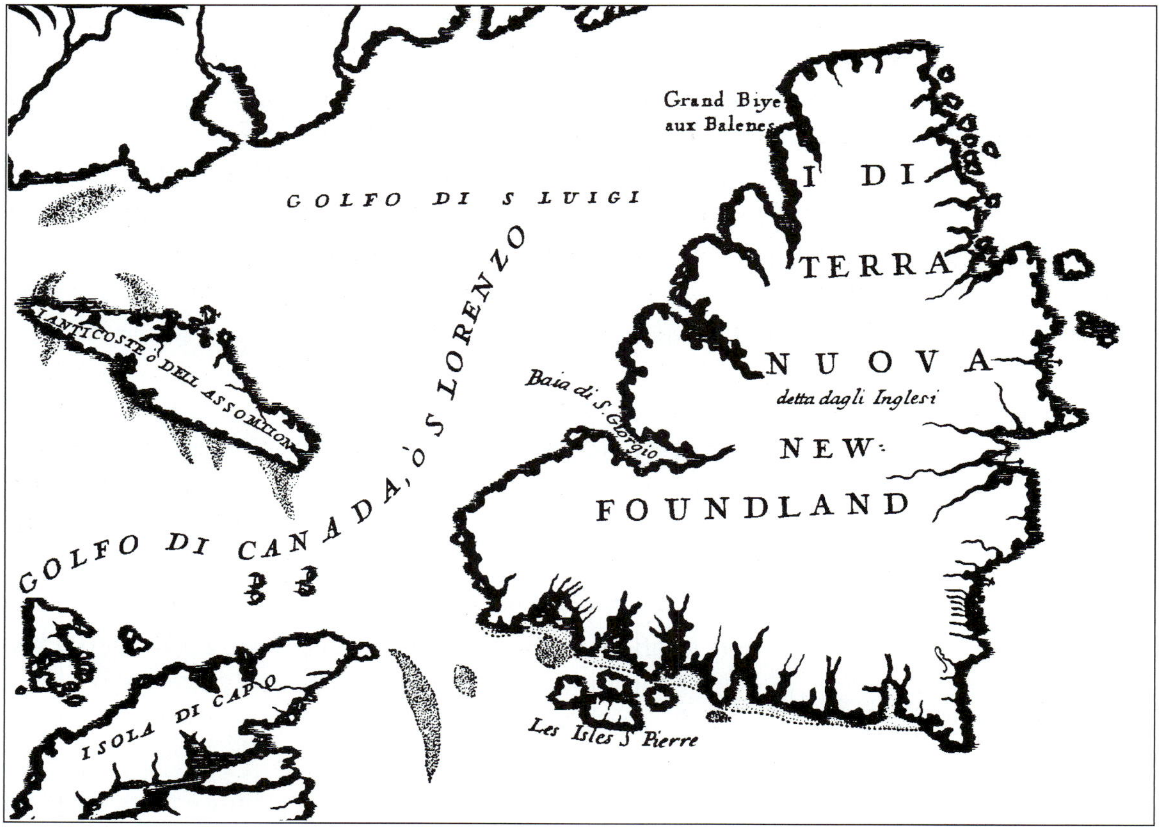

Figure 1.5

Compare this map to a modern map of the east coast of Canada. Where did this mapmaker do a good job? Are there any errors? Why might these errors have occurred?

Where Are You Exactly?

There are many types of maps. Some of the most common are provincial road maps, street maps, and topographic maps that map surface features in great detail.

Different grid systems are used to find the locations of places on maps. A road map usually uses a letter–number system to help you find locations. The maps in an atlas usually use latitude and longitude. Topographic maps are more detailed than maps in an atlas. They use reference systems such as the six-figure **grid coordinate system** of **eastings** and **northings**.

Connections to Math and History

The military uses grid coordinate systems to pinpoint a position or target on a map. By finding a target, the artillery could be aimed and fired on the location. In the grid coordinate system, northings give a location on the *y*-axis and eastings give a location on the *x*-axis. Where they intersect is the absolute location on the map.

DURING READING

1. As you read about the next two types of location, think about the following questions:
   - Which type of location is most exact?
   - When would you use each type of location?

Absolute Location

It is important to be able to locate places precisely. The use of grid systems (for example, latitude and longitude, eastings and northings) help us identify exact locations. We need to be able to give the **absolute location** of a spot on Earth. When natural resources are found, the absolute location must be determined. The absolute location makes the resources the property of one country and not another. Suppose oil is found along the border of two countries with a clearly defined boundary. It is important to know exactly where the oil field lies to determine who owns it.

Oil was discovered in the Gulf of Mexico. Part of the Gulf belongs to the United States, and part belongs to Mexico. It was essential to find out how much of the oil was in the United States and how much was in Mexico. Canada and the United States dispute who has the right to fish for salmon in parts of the Pacific Ocean. Both countries need to know the absolute location of the boundaries between the states of Washington and Alaska with the province of British Columbia. Absolute location affects trade and economic growth. It is also important to help resolve conflict between different groups, companies, and countries.

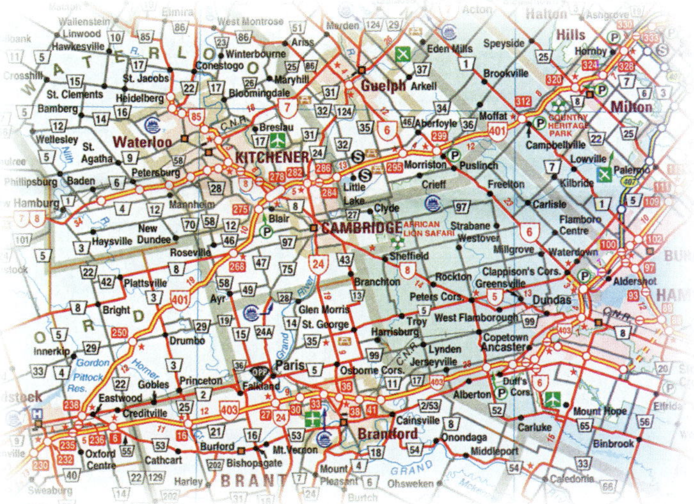

Figure 1.6

This is a map of Kitchener and area. Provincial road maps show travellers which highways and roads to take to get from one location to another. Which highways provide the most direct route between Brantford and Guelph?

Figure 1.7

Find this section of Canada on a full map. What type of map is shown here?

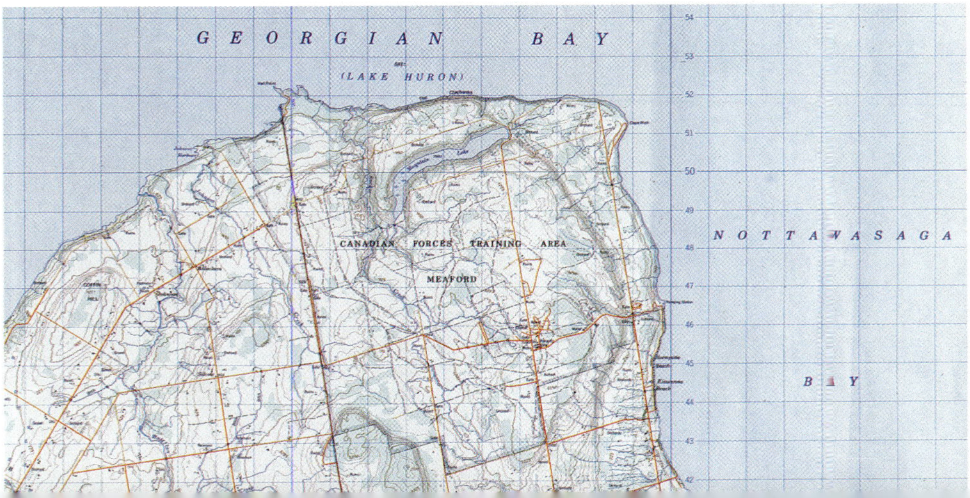

Figure 1.8

The brown lines on this map of the Georgian Bay area represent elevation, or height above sea level. What is the main feature on this map? Look for a label where the contour lines are closest together.

GeoSkills

How to Read a Map—The TLC Method

A map is a drawing that shows the physical features and political boundaries of Earth. It usually includes a title, legend, compass, and scale. Reading a map is not the same as reading a piece of text. Maps combine both visual information and text to create a visual representation. There are many different types of maps, but all of them are created for specific purposes. A transit map allows you to navigate around a city, while a provincial park map may help you locate the best campsite or picnic shelter. The TLC method will teach you the steps that you can use so that you can correctly read and understand maps.

Step One:

Read the *title*. The title will put the map into context for you.

Q: What do you think this map is showing the reader? How do you know this?

Step Two:

Look for and read the *legend*. The legend will explain all the symbols and colours used on the map.

The Lakes of Canada

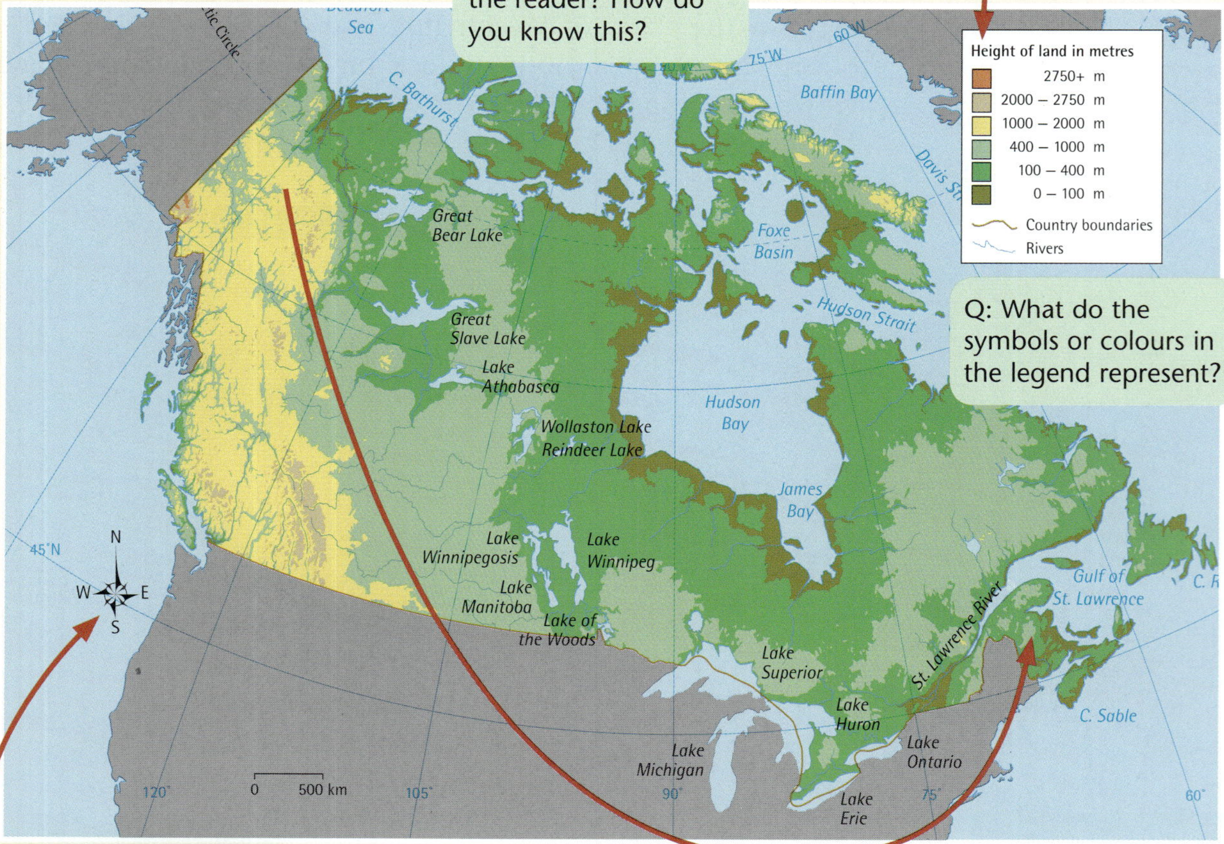

Q: What do the symbols or colours in the legend represent?

Figure 1.9

This map shows the common features of a map.

Step Three:

Find the *compass*. Make sure you can identify the cardinal points of *n*orth, *s*outh, *e*ast, and *w*est.

Step Four:

When reading a map, it is a good idea to read from top to bottom and left to right, as you would read a book. When reading this map, you should look at the *pattern* made by the lakes. Start at Great Bear Lake and follow the arc made by the lakes ending up in the St. Lawrence River.

Literacy Tip

Using Context Clues

If you come across a word that is unfamiliar, read the whole paragraph and look for clues that will help you define the word. These clues can be actual definitions, simpler terms, synonyms, or antonyms.

Relative Location

Relative locations tell us where something is in relation to something else. Have you heard directions such as the following?

- It is about 20 kilometres from here.
- Kitchener is about halfway between London and Toronto.
- New York is about the midpoint between Paris and Los Angeles.

In each example, the location of one site is given in relation to another site or sites. They are relative locations.

Relative location is not exact, but it does help us with more general understandings. For example, the Interior Plains of North America are said to run north to south through the middle of North America. This statement is approximately correct. However, it is far from precise.

Figure 1.10

This is a photograph of Death Valley, California, in the United States. It is part of the Interior Plains of North America. How would you provide a different relative location for the Interior Plains? Use a physical map of North America for ideas. (See Map Appendix.)

AFTER READING

1. Why is it important to have different ways of describing your location? How can you decide when to use absolute location and when to use relative location?
2. Identify the two systems for finding an absolute location.
3. Explain the absolute and relative location of Vancouver Island. Use an atlas for help.
4. Use an atlas to find the latitude and longitude of Toronto (Canada), Calcutta (India), and Sydney (Australia). Check their locations on the classroom globe.
5. Describe the location of your school relative to where you live and two other important places in your area. Explain why you chose those two places as important.

Literacy Tip

Brainstorming

Brainstorming means coming up with as many ideas about a topic as possible. Begin by writing down all your ideas. Then, add to, subtract from, join, or change ideas. Finally, reflect on your ideas, and choose the best ones.

Does the Place Make Sense?

BEFORE READING

1. Why are places located where they are? Look at the headings and subheadings in the next section. Based on these headings, brainstorm reasons why places are located where they are. Record your ideas so that you can compare them with what you read in the next section.

Physical Factors

There are many reasons why places are located where they are. Physical characteristics of the area affect where places are located. It is important to consider the landforms. Are there hills, ridges, or valleys? Bodies of water are also important. Is there a lake or a river nearby? Well-drained soil makes a better location for a place than soil that is poorly drained where flooding might occur. Vegetation, weather, and climate also affect where places are located. Is the area forested, or is it grassland? Is it cold or hot, wet or dry?

Figure 1.11

Why do you think anyone would build a house here? Describe another unique place you have seen people build.

1. Think about the physical characteristics of the area in which you live. Which characteristics do you think influenced the first settlers in this area?
2. Imagine that you want to settle in an area. Which physical characteristics would influence your decision about where to settle? Think about landforms, bodies of water, soil drainage, vegetation, and weather and climate.
3. Check your brainstorming list. Add any additional physical characteristics that you did not have, and remove or change any that do not belong on the list.

Human Factors

Other places were chosen for their location based on human characteristics. People tend to locate where there are other people. Large cities attract people. If there is a river or lake, communities tend to spread along the riverbank or the lakeshore. People tend to live with people of a cultural group similar to their own. Religious reasons can also affect where people choose to live. Some people want to live near the centre of their faith, like Jerusalem or Mecca.

Locations for places like towns, farms, or factories are chosen because of distinctive human and physical characteristics. These different characteristics allow us to distinguish places from each other.

1. Think about the human characteristics of the area in which you live. Which characteristics would influence people to settle in this area?
2. Imagine that you want to settle in an area. Which human characteristics would influence your decision about where to settle?
3. Check your brainstorming list. Add any additional human characteristics that you did not have, and remove or change any that do not belong on the list.

Figure 1.12

The Blue Mosque in Amman, Jordan, is a holy site for Muslims. Why would the followers of Islam want to live close to such mosques?

LITERACY TIP

Picturing What You Read

When you read, slow down and try to picture what you are reading. Creating mental images, or pictures in your mind, will help you understand and remember what you read.

Why Here? Factors of Location

People usually decide to locate a business, an industry, a home, or a park by selecting the best possible combination of "influencing" factors. Often, you must choose between factors. Not all sites will have everything you want. Imagine you want to open a video store. Where would you locate this video store? You would probably want a place that is easy to reach and close to where many people live. When people decide to locate a home, business, or other building, they usually have to think about a combination of physical and human factors.

Basic Needs

When people first roamed Earth, they made decisions about where to locate. They had to find sites that best provided for their basic needs of water, shelter, food, security, and clothing. The physical environment limited places for settlement. The climate may have been too severe, or there may have been too little fresh water. The soil may have been unproductive, or the landscape may have been too rugged. However, because of technology, people now live in or have visited just about every place on Earth. There are very few, if any, new locations to be found.

Figure 1.13

Utilidors connect homes and cover utility lines such as water and sewer, electricity, and telephone in this community in the Northwest Territories. The insulated utilidors keep the utility lines from freezing. How does this show how technology is being used to solve problems?

Change Happens

Over time, many things happen that can cause places to change. Some places become more important and increase in size and population, while other places become less important and decline. Some places flourish and grow, while other places become ghost towns. Many communities needed farmland when they began. Now, these communities need more land for housing and less for farming.

> **Fact File**
>
> Often, land is excellent for many things. For instance, much of the land between Niagara Falls and Hamilton is the best farmland in North America, outside of California, for tender fruits such as grapes and peaches. Now, much of it has been turned into housing developments and industries. The farmland is lost.

Figure 1.14

Which factors do you think influenced the decision to locate each of these places where it is? Put them into two groups: physical factors and human factors.

The Big Picture

At the world level, places can suddenly change in our mental image. Prior to the war against the Taliban in Afghanistan, few Canadians had heard of the city of Kandahar. Now, Kandahar is the centre of our command base, and we hear about it in the news daily. The city of 450 000 people was a quiet trade and market centre for southern

DURING READING

1. In addition to conflict, what other human events can give a city new meaning and importance? Give examples.

Afghanis. Now, jets, tanks, and other military vehicles and equipment are the norm. Bomb blasts occur regularly. Reports of the conflict come from in and around Kandahar as they happen. Suddenly, the city is in the world spotlight because of its position and political importance. Human events have given the city new meaning and importance.

Figure 1.15

Can you name other places in the world that have become well known quickly due to conflict?

Figure 1.16

Canadian troops oversee an observation post in Kandahar, Afghanistan. How might the experiences of Canadian troops change our understanding of places such as Afghanistan?

AFTER READING

1. List three factors that would influence an auto-parts company to locate at a specific site.
2. Explain three reasons why places grow and three reasons why places decline.
3. Identify two places in the world that have made the news lately because of human or physical events. Explain how these events have affected the people and the physical environment of these places.

A Sense of Place

Our world is full of fascinating things to be discovered. We can always observe something new, different, wonderful, or inspiring. There are endless changing patterns and changing habits in our world.

What Makes a Place Special?

Some places may be outstanding human landmarks, like the Eiffel Tower in Paris or the CN Tower in Toronto. Some may be majestic natural features, such as the Grand Canyon in the United States or Mount Kilimanjaro in Tanzania. They may be the homes of famous or important people, like the governor general's home at Rideau Hall in Ottawa or the White House in Washington, DC.

BEFORE READING

1. Think of all you have learned about place and location in this chapter. What do you think it means to have a sense of place?

Figure 1.17

Which of these places do you know, and which ones do you not know? Why? Compare your answers with those of your classmates.

Our Special Places

DURING READING

1. Choose a special place that you have visited, and describe why it is special. Identify the physical and/or human characteristics of this place that make it special to you.

Places have many effects upon us. Each of us has places that are "special" to us for many reasons. We all have places where we would go if we could. It may be a walk to a nearby river or park for some "quiet time" with nature. It may be a trip to a place that excites our imagination and sense of adventure, like travelling by canoe through a wilderness area. In the following news article, a Grade 7 student describes her favourite place, near Tobermory, Ontario, on the Georgian Bay shoreline. Read her description, and think about the physical and human characteristics that she cherishes.

Figure 1.18

What physical factors about the shoreline near Tobermory catch your interest?

My Favourite Place

My family does not have many traditions, but of the ones we do have, my favourite is going to Cyprus Lake in the Bruce Peninsula National Park near Tobermory. Every year, for as long as I can remember, we have gone there.

There is a restaurant in Tobermory. I remember sitting out on its patio eating fish and chips with my family. This is all we ever order from there because it is our favourite.

After eating, we always go to climb the cliffs and look at the islands in Georgian Bay. We have pictures of my brother and sister and me standing there since we were little kids.

When I look at the pictures of us by the cliffs, I am filled with happiness and fond memories of my childhood.

What's in a Place Name?

Everyone sees the world differently. Our local place names reflect our culture. We see many names that show ties to the First Nations peoples who first lived in what is now Ontario. The list includes such names as Algonquin Park, Mohawk Road, and the Lake Iroquois shoreline.

When we see places in other lands, we view them through our own experiences and culture. The way we see such places may be quite different from the way the people who live there see them. When we look at a world map, it nearly always has the Atlantic Ocean near the centre. We are seeing the world from our viewpoint.

Pacific Rim

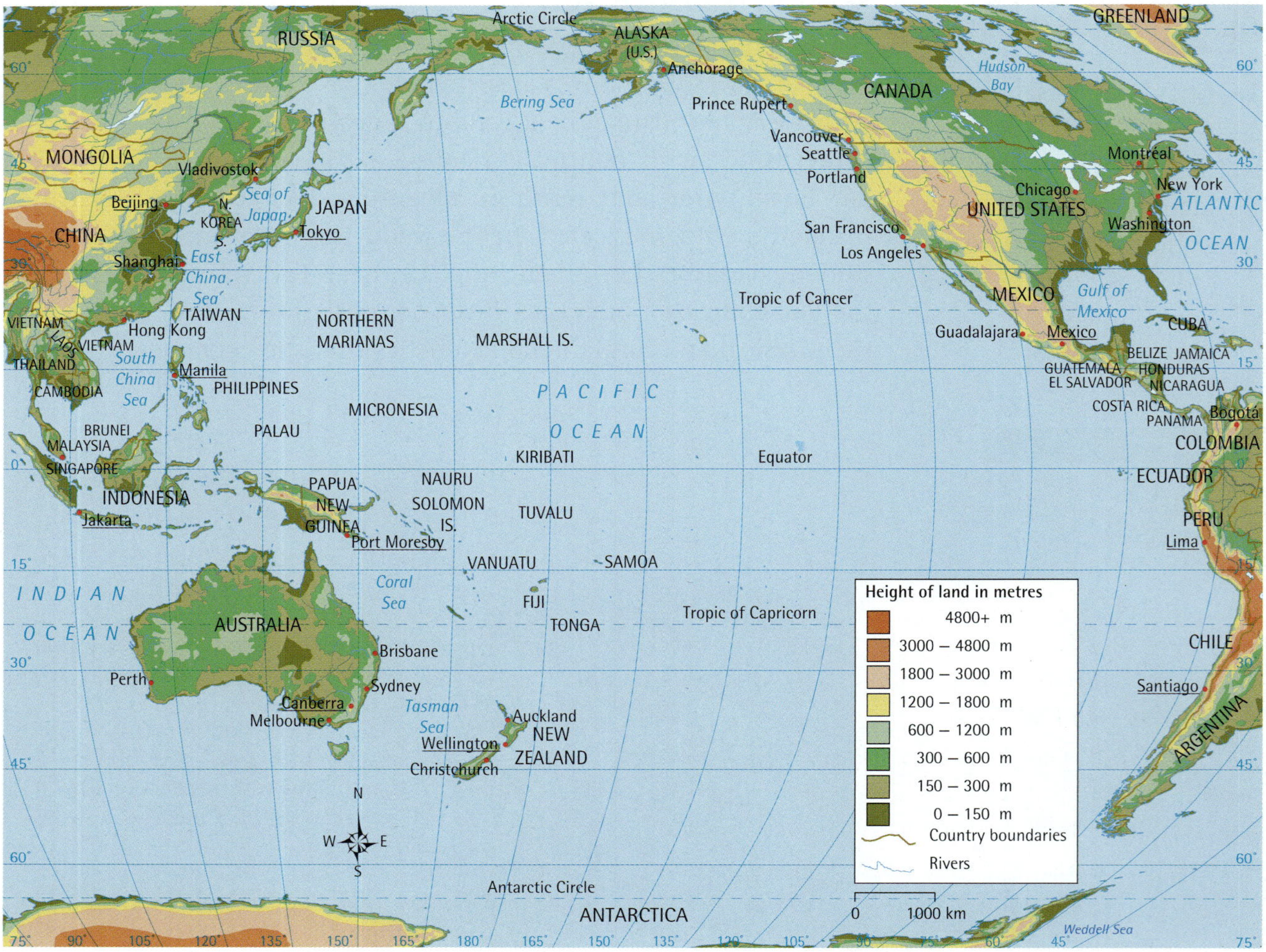

Names such as Darfur, Chernobyl, Auschwitz, Bhopal, and Hiroshima convey sadness, horror, and other intense feelings to many adults. For you, a name like Iraq, Afghanistan, or Amazon rainforest may do the same. On the other hand, places such as the Caribbean, Disney World, or Algonquin Park create positive, pleasant feelings and images in our minds.

Figure 1.19

From the centre of this map, in which direction is North America? How is that different from our "normal" world view?

DURING READING

1. Which place names create sad or upsetting feelings in you, and which create happy feelings?

AFTER READING

1. People may develop great attachments or deep feelings for a place. Identify three special places that would mean a lot to you if they changed or closed. Why are they special to you?

2. No two people see or feel about a place in the same way. Choose one of the following places, and compare and contrast how a person living there and a visitor would see and feel about the place:
   a) Amazon rainforest
   b) Beijing
   c) Greenland
   d) Saudi Arabia
   e) Sahara Desert

BE A GLOBAL CITIZEN

Protecting Special Places

The United Nations Educational, Scientific, and Cultural Organization (UNESCO) has declared 851 sites in the world as World Heritage Sites. These are protected sites because they form part of the cultural and natural heritage of the world. Canada has 14 of these World Heritage Sites. Our most recently appointed World Heritage Site is Canada's Rideau Canal, which was declared in 2007. Our country's sites were selected to protect parts of our natural beauty and cultural heritage.

One of Canada's World Heritage Sites is Head-Smashed-In Buffalo Jump in southern Alberta. It was designated as a World Heritage Site by UNESCO in 1981. It is important because it is an outstanding example of a traditional way of life. First Nations peoples used the site to hunt buffalo for nearly 6000 years. Because of their understanding of the physical geography of the region, they were able to kill buffalo by chasing them over the steep cliff. Then they would carve up the buffalos' remains at the camp below. The Plains First Nations were the last First Nations group to use this buffalo jump. Today, they are keen to preserve their culture, so they are tied closely to the heritage site.

Head-Smashed-In Buffalo Jump offers a number of educational programs. Park interpreters must have strong knowledge of both the Blackfoot language and the history of the First Nations and Métis peoples who lived on the plains. To protect this special site, the Friends of the Head-Smashed-In Buffalo Jump Society work to maintain the area and educate the public. As Alberta grows rapidly, this is a unique and very important site that must be protected for generations to come.

Figure 1.20

Here are two views of Head-Smashed-In Buffalo Jump in Alberta. The top right view is a historic painting showing how the Plains First Nations used the site. The bottom view is a modern day photograph of the site. How is this site being used today?

Knowledge and Understanding

1. Early explorers were able to navigate their ships across the oceans and make maps of the coasts they encountered. What are two major things that would have helped them? To help you recall the facts, go back to the section, Getting Precise About Location. Review the headings, subheadings, and key vocabulary in this section. If you need more help, reread this section, and think about what early explorers had to help them create maps.

2. Ontario has many special places. They are special for different reasons.

   a) Identify three places in Ontario that are special because they are known as "economic places," or places of business.

   b) Identify three places in Ontario that are special because of the happy feelings and images they give people who visit them.

Inquiry/Research and Communication Skills

3. Songwriters often write songs about places. These songs often do two things: they give information about these places, and show how people feel about them. Examples include *New York City* by John Lennon, *Good Morning Britain* by Aztec Camera, or *Canadian Railroad Trilogy* by Gordon Lightfoot. Name one song that is about a place. What place is the focus of the song? What images and/or feelings does the song suggest about the place? If you need research help, try using strings of search terms such as *place names song titles* or *songs place names* in a search engine.

4. **a)** Investigate the beginnings of an interesting place in your community. Consider questions such as the following:

   - When was it created or built?
   - Who named it?
   - Why was it given this name?
   - Does the name relate to the earliest people or settlers there? If so, how?
   - Have the features of this place been changed since its beginnings?

   Where can you look to find answers to these research questions? Try searching your community's website or contacting your community's museum, city or town offices, or library. Try asking senior citizens in your community.

   b) How will you share what you have learned about this interesting place in your community?

   - Will you sketch or draw the place you researched and present it on a poster with what you learned?
   - Will you take digital images of the place you researched and create a collage of visual and text-based information?
   - Will you set up a chart that shows the answers to the questions for the place you researched?
   - Will you take on the role of investigative reporter and videotape a mini documentary about the interesting place you chose?
   - Will you create a PowerPoint presentation? How can you include current and historic photos of the place you chose in your presentation? How can you share what you learned in an interesting way?

Map, Globe, and Graphic Skills

5. Create a mental map of your local community showing local landmarks, major roads, and major physical features such as rivers, lakes, or high hills. Include a compass, a legend, and labels.

6. If you had to give directions from your house to your school, how would you write them? Most people would use a combination of landmarks and directions. Both are used to create and read maps. Visualize your walk to school. Create a t-chart. On one side, write down your directions using only landmarks and the directions of left or right. On the other side, write down your directions using compass directions and distance measurements. Which one is easier to write and follow? Do you think that the best way of giving directions is a combination of the two methods? Explain your answer.

7. Each person in your class has a different idea about how to organize space or estimate distance. Try this.

   a) Consider how far it is from the door of your classroom to the end of the hall.

Have everyone write their "guesstimate" of the distance, in metres, on the board.

b) Measure the distance.

c) Draw a graph to show the distribution of the guesstimates. Follow the instructions below.

- Use these as the basis of your graph:
  - 3.5 to 6 metres over
  - 0.5 to 3 metres over
  - 0.5 metres over or 0.5 metres under
  - 0.5 to 3 metres under
  - 3.5 to 6 metres under
- Plot all estimates on the graph.
- Calculate the percentage for each category (number of estimates in the category divided by the total number of estimates).
- Analyze the results. Look for the following:
  - – Where were the greatest percentages?
  - – Was there a difference between any groups in the class, such as age or gender?
  - – How close were you to the class averages?

d) Did anyone get the distance exactly right? Was anyone out more than triple the distance? What general statement can you make about the ability of you and your classmates to estimate distance?

Application

8 Imagine that you can go anywhere. To what special places would you travel in Ontario, Canada, and the world? Why are these places special to you? In small groups, share your special places, and create a set of reasons that show why places are special.

9 The Ganges River is very important in the Hindu religion. Are there places that are very important to other groups as religious, spiritual, or holy centres? Make a list, and give a short description of the importance of one of the places on your list. If you need to research, try *holy places* as your search term in a search engine.

Figure 1.21

The Ganges River in India is a busy place as a waterway, and it is used heavily for domestic and industrial purposes. It is also sacred to the Hindus. Bathing in the holy waters of the Ganges is important to Hindus, but the practice is becoming increasingly dangerous to their health.

2 Region

IN THIS CHAPTER

- explain the theme of region in geography
- create and use maps for different reasons
- use the new terms in this chapter correctly as you investigate the topics
- locate and use helpful information from primary and secondary sources
- produce a report that applies one or more of the five themes of geography to an environmental event

KEY VOCABULARY

boundary
climate region
criteria
desert
drainage area
drainage basin
drainage divide
ecozone
El Niño
functional characteristic
functional region
geologic region
human characteristic
human region
land-based ecozone
landform region
marine-based ecozone
natural force
physical characteristic
physical region
precipitation
region
rural region
soil region
time zone
urban and regional planning
urban region
user-defined region
vegetation region
wilderness region

What Is a Region?

BEFORE READING

1. How is the word "region" used in the world around you? Scan newspapers and magazines for examples of how this word is used. Share the examples with others.
2. Why do you think we have regions? Give some examples of regions that you know.

We organize the world into spaces and places called **regions**. Any area that has a set of defined characteristics is a region. The characteristics of a region are similar throughout the area of the region and different from the places outside the region. Your neighbourhood is a region. Your schoolyard is a region. Your town or city is a region. Your home has regions in it. It has different spaces where you eat, sleep, relax, and work. Each region is defined by a certain set of shared features or characteristics.

Regions are areas used to examine parts of Earth in the study of geography. They help us understand what, where, how, and why things are like they are. This makes the investigation of physical and human patterns easier and more understandable. Creating regions helps us see and explain relationships and connections more clearly. For example, regions help us plan our cities and communities.

Figure 2.1

This apartment complex is a region. Each apartment is a region within a larger region. What are the common characteristics of each apartment? What are the common characteristics of the apartment complex?

Figure 2.2

Think about the criteria that make your neighbourhood a region. Does this neighbourhood resemble yours? How is it the same? How is it different?

Organizing the World

A region is a space or area defined by similar characteristics, or **criteria**. Some of these criteria are based on what appears naturally in an area. What landforms distinguish one area from another? What grows naturally in different areas? Other criteria are based on the people who live and work in an area. What languages do they speak? How do they earn a living?

A region has definite limits to its size. It also has **boundaries** that outline its area. Your neighbourhood region may have boundaries formed by a road, a river, a rail line, a farm fence, a forest, or a park.

Regions can be very small, like your bedroom. They can be **physical regions** that cover vast areas of the globe, such as the coniferous forest region or the Sahara Desert. Some regions are political, like Canada or Ontario.

Political Regions We Use: Countries, Provinces, Counties, Towns/Cities, Townships

Figure 2.3

This map shows the political regions in Ontario. There are several levels of political regions in Canada. Name the political regions in which you live.

Is Anybody There?

The world can be divided into the following three main types of regions based on where people live:

- **wilderness regions**, where no people live
- **rural regions**, which are farms and countryside
- **urban regions**, which are towns and cities

DURING READING

1. In which type of region do you live: wilderness, rural, or urban?
2. In addition to the population, what are other characteristics that describe the region in which you live?

Wilderness Regions

A wilderness region is an area with no human population. Some wilderness regions cover vast land areas, but they have similar characteristics throughout.

Literacy Tip

Making Jot Notes

When you read text that has lots of information, it is a good idea to use good note-taking skills to help you remember the information. First, think about the purpose of your reading. Then, use jot notes, or point-form notes, to record the information in your own words.

Figure 2.4

What are some of the physical characteristics that define a polar wilderness region, such as this one in Alaska in the United States?

Figure 2.5

The boreal forest is a region that covers much of the northern parts of Canada, Europe, and Asia. Look at the trees in the photo. What types of trees define this region?

Web Link

For more information about protecting wilderness regions, go to **www.nelson.com/phygeo7**.

Fact File

The population of Rwanda is 94 percent rural. In contrast, the island country of Singapore is considered 100 percent urban.

Rural Regions

A rural region has open countryside with few towns. As our population has grown, the number of Canadians living in rural areas has decreased. Urban and rural regions in Canada have changed a lot over the past 100 years. Less than 20 percent of Canadians now live in rural regions. Fewer farmers are needed to supply our food because of technological advances that reduce the need for farm workers.

Urban Regions

An urban region has little open countryside. It has many homes, transportation routes such as roads and railway lines, businesses, and factories. Many urban regions try to create rural areas inside them in the form of parks. In Canada, five people live in towns and cities for every one rural person.

AFTER READING

1. What is the nearest wilderness region to you? Why is it important that this be maintained as a wilderness region?
2. Harvey Locke, President of the Foundation for Canadian Parks and Wilderness, said that "Wilderness parks are the landscape of the soul. They are about beauty, about reflection and quiet contemplation. They are about a society that retains enough humility to leave some part of nature alone."
   a) What does Locke mean by "landscape of the soul"?
   b) What is humility? Why does Locke say we need humility to "leave some part of nature alone"?
3. In 1911, 41 percent of Canadians lived in urban regions. Now, over 80 percent do. Do you think Canada's population will ever become 100 percent urban? Explain your reasons.
4. List two reasons why people would choose to move from urban to rural regions.

Figure 2.6

Identify two characteristics that make this an urban region.

Figure 2.7

Identify two characteristics that make this a rural region.

Figure 2.8

What is the present ratio of urban population to rural population? Predict the ratio of urban population to rural population in 2021.

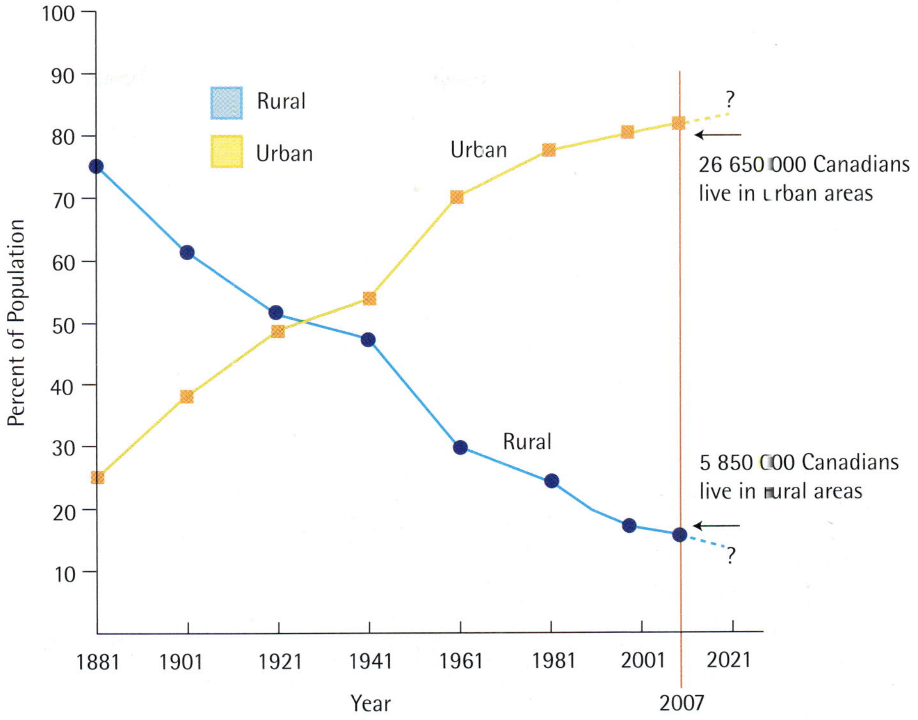

Different Ways of Organizing the World

Before Reading

1. What are some of the regions into which you could organize the world? Record as many as you can. Then, compare your list with a partner.

Literacy Tip

Finding Important Ideas

Pages 27 to 35 have a lot of information about ways to organize the world. Note how it is divided into smaller sections. Each of these sub-sections has a heading that captures its main idea. Make a list of these headings and subheadings to help you understand and remember the important points.

A region can be defined by its **physical characteristics**. This could be type of soil, type of landform, or the amount of **precipitation**. Another way to define a region is by its **human characteristics**—religion, language, or culture. A third way is by its **functional characteristics**. The ways we use a region, such as for farming or for industry, fall into this group.

During Reading

1. You have just read that there are three main ways by which to define regions: physical characteristics, human characteristics, and functional characteristics. As you read the following pages on physical regions, think of the different characteristics of each of the physical regions. Use jot notes to record the characteristics.

Physical Regions

Physical regions, such as the Himalayas (a mountain region) or the Sahara (a desert region), are defined by their physical characteristics. Each physical region has a common characteristic throughout its area.

Literacy Tip

Mapping Important Information

When you have to read and understand text with a lot of factual information, how can you identify and organize important information as you read? One way you can do this is with a web or concept map.

Figure 2.9

What is the most important physical region in your area?

Mountain region

Vegetation region

Maritime region

Sedimentary rock region

Desert Regions

Deserts are regions that receive less than 250 millimetres of precipitation, or rainfall, per year. Look at the map of average precipitation in North Africa. It helps to show us the boundaries of the world's largest hot desert region.

Sahara Desert, North Africa

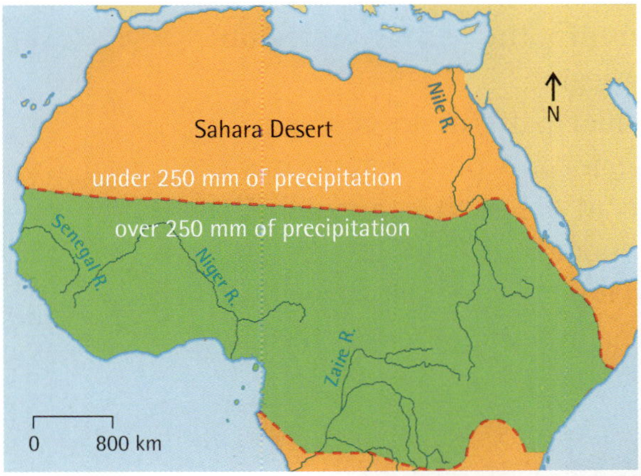

Figure 2.10

The Sahara is the world's largest hot desert region. What other deserts are found in North Africa? Use an atlas.

Fact File

The Canadian Shield is the world's largest rock shield region. It makes up nearly half of Canada. At one time, shield regions were often high mountains.

Figure 2.11

On which continent could this desert region be found? Use an atlas.

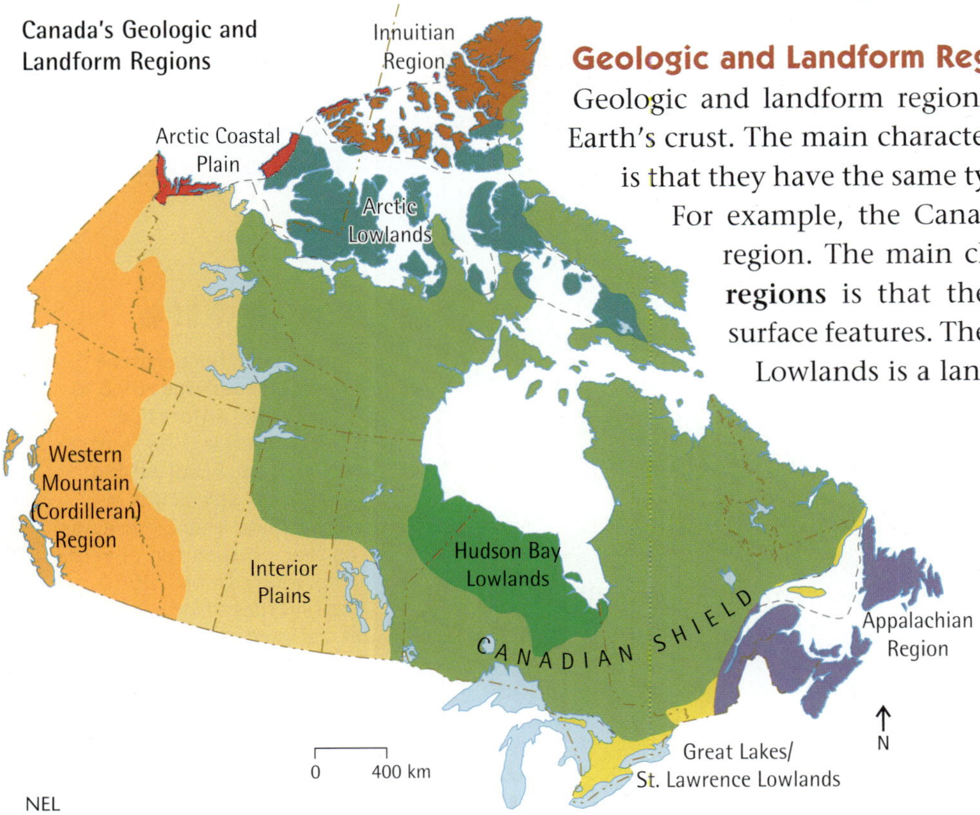

Geologic and Landform Regions

Geologic and landform regions give us a way to study Earth's crust. The main characteristic of **geologic regions** is that they have the same types or structures of rocks. For example, the Canadian Shield is a geologic region. The main characteristic of **landform regions** is that they have the same major surface features. The Great Lakes/St. Lawrence Lowlands is a landform region.

Figure 2.12

Nearly 90 percent of the population of Ontario lives in the Great Lakes/St. Lawrence Lowlands region, which covers only about 25 percent of Ontario's area. In which landform region do you live?

Climate, Vegetation, and Soil Regions

Natural forces define **climate regions**, **vegetation regions**, and **soil regions**. These three types of regions usually have the same boundaries. This is no accident. The climatic conditions of a region affect the types of vegetation that can grow there (for example, cactuses or cattails). The climate and vegetation affect the soils that develop. A specific climatic region will produce a specific vegetation region. In turn, the vegetation region helps make a specific soil region.

Soil regions have similar patterns to geologic, landform, and climate regions. A polar region has a cold, dry climate—a cold desert. It is a region that has little vegetation and very poor soil. A tropical region has a warm, wet climate, which is perfect for plant growth. Thick soil forms rapidly on the gentle slopes in this region.

Range of Vegetation, Climate, and Precipitation across North America

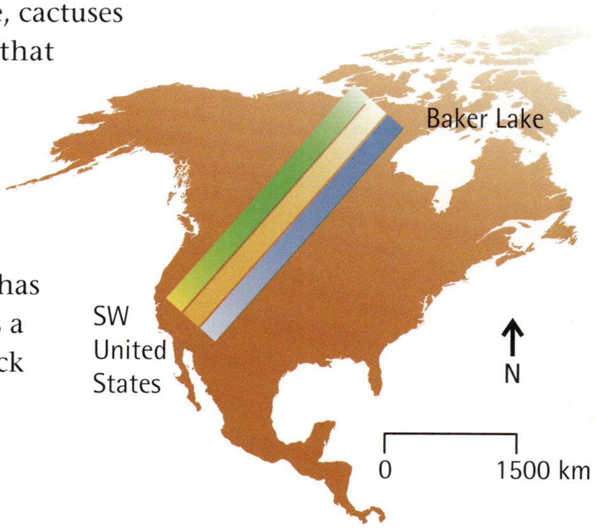

Figure 2.13

The graph below shows the relationship between climate and vegetation. The corresponding band on the map of North America above gives the location. What sort of climate and vegetation does your area have? (See Map Appendix.)

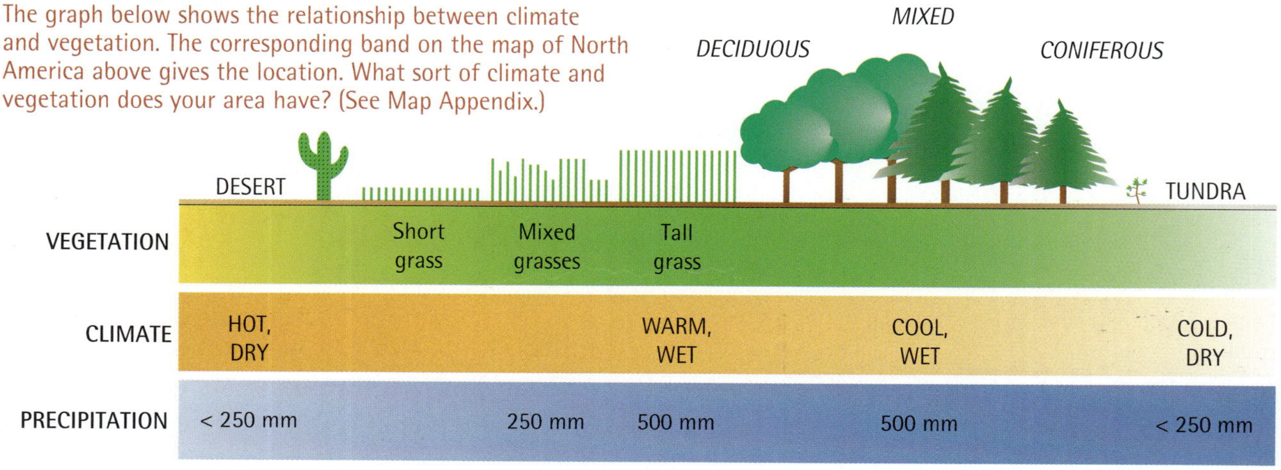

Regions within Regions

There are regions within regions. A coniferous forest is a large vegetation region. It can be divided into many smaller sections where climatic and growing conditions vary. Pine trees prefer sandy soils. Spruce or cedar trees like wet and boggy soil. They will be found in another area of the forest.

Fact File

The coldest temperature ever recorded was –89.6 °C at Vostok, Antarctica. The hottest was 58 °C at Al Azizyah, Saudi Arabia. The driest streak was in Arica, Chile, where there was no precipitation for 14 years! The wettest was 2646 centimetres of precipitation in one year in Cherrapunji, India—7 centimetres a day!

DURING READING

1. Name the different physical regions in which you live. (See Map Appendix.)
2. Explain in your own words how climate, vegetation, and soil regions are connected.

Human Regions

Human regions are defined by human characteristics, such as how many people live closely packed into a region. Cities are regions with a high population density. Rural areas are regions with low population density. Other ways to form human regions include culture (language, religion, customs), political boundaries, or time zones.

A region can be defined in more than one way. For example, the province of Québec has political boundaries, so it is a political region. It is made up of mainly French-speaking people, so it is also a cultural region.

Cultural region

High population density region

Figure 2.14

These regions share some characteristics. Name two shared characteristics of these regions. What characteristics make each region different and unique? Based on the characteristics you can see in each photo, where do you think each of these regions could be found?

Economic region

1. As you read the following pages on human regions, identify the important characteristics of each human region. Use your jot-note skills, and add these notes to your concept map or chart.

Time Zone Regions

We define regions to make things simpler and easier to handle. **Time zones** were developed to help us better communicate with people living in other parts of the world. There are 24 time zones, or regions. Generally, each time zone represents a one-hour difference in time. Time zones start at Greenwich, England, and it is from here that the 24-hour clock is measured. The width of each zone is 15 degrees of longitude. This is based on the earth making one rotation of 360 degrees in 24 hours (360 ÷ 24 = 15).

Connections to History

In 1878, Sir Sandford Fleming, a railway surveyor and construction engineer from Ontario, led the development of the time zone system. His system was adopted worldwide in 1884. Today, with faster transportation and mass communication systems, time zones play an even greater part in our lives. For example, instant messaging with a friend in a different country will have to take place when you are both awake and not in school. If it is midnight in London, England, what time is it in Halifax, Nova Scotia? in Vancouver, British Columbia? in Moscow, Russia? How can these variations affect you? (See Map Appendix.)

Figure 2.15

If it is noon in London, England, what time is it in your area?

Time Zones in the Northern Hemisphere

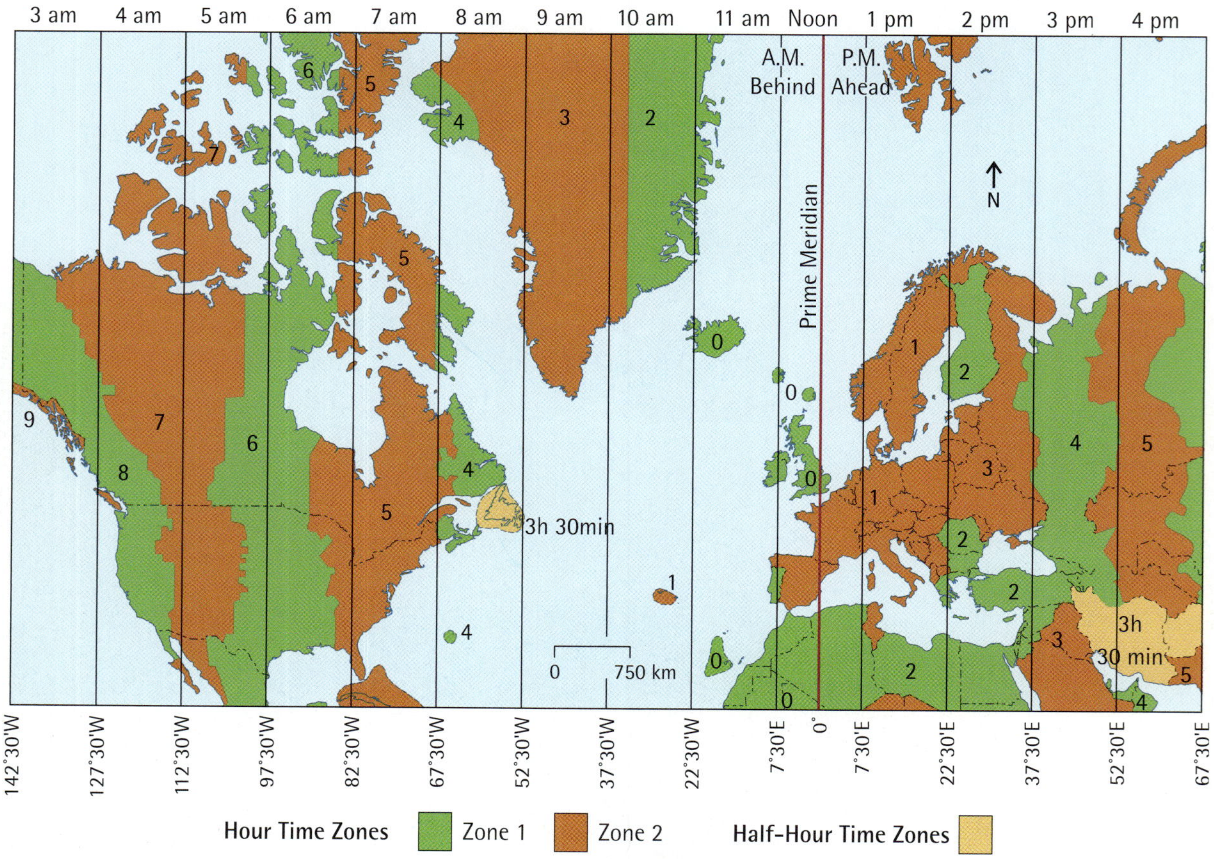

During Reading

1. In which political region do you live?
2. Describe where you live using other human-based characteristics.
3. When you begin your school day in Ontario, what time is it for a student in Italy? (See Map Appendix.)

DURING READING

1. As you read the following pages on functional regions, identify the important characteristics of each region. Use your jot-note skills, and add these notes to your concept map or chart.

Functional Regions

Functional regions are defined by how they are used. They often develop around a centre or focal point. A port can become the centre of a functional region—the region from which people receive products to ship elsewhere. A town or city has a functional region around it from which fresh produce comes. This region is an agricultural region. Functional regions within our towns and cities include industrial areas, residential areas, and business areas.

Making Decisions

Knowing how functional regions relate to each other helps us solve transportation problems, plan cities and towns, and make informed decisions about what should go where. For example, a company wants to build an ice cream plant. This company would be wise to consider the dairy region (farms) and the market region (customers), plus the transportation systems that join everything together.

Figure 2.16

One partner in the ice cream company thinks it would save money if they built the ice cream plant in the dairy region to be closer to the milk supply instead of the market region to be closer to customers who would buy the ice cream. What arguments would you use to change his or her mind?

Regions Are the Same! Regions Are Different!

Regions in one area may be both similar to and different from regions elsewhere. Your neighbourhood has characteristics that are similar to and different from other neighbourhoods. Often, regions not only look different, but they sound, smell, and feel different. Imagine how a region like the Chinese market area in Toronto might look, sound, smell, and feel. Think of how different it is from a park region like Algonquin Park. Likewise, regions within your country have similarities to and differences from regions in other countries. Understanding and comparing regions is a strong geographic tool for understanding our world.

Figure 2.17

Identify three ways your senses would be stimulated if you visited both of these regions.

User-Defined Regions

User-defined regions are defined by a special product or service. They often are inside of, or overlap, other larger physical, human, and functional regions. Your local radio station has a broadcast area or region that is defined by where its listeners are. A newspaper has a circulation region defined by where its readers live. Shopping malls and stores have customer areas, which are market regions based on various products and services. The boundaries for these regions are not clearly defined, like a coastline. They cross many other regions and overlap each other.

DURING READING

1. How would you describe your area as a functional region?
2. Compare and contrast the customer market area of a convenience store and a mall.

London's Newspaper and Radio Regions

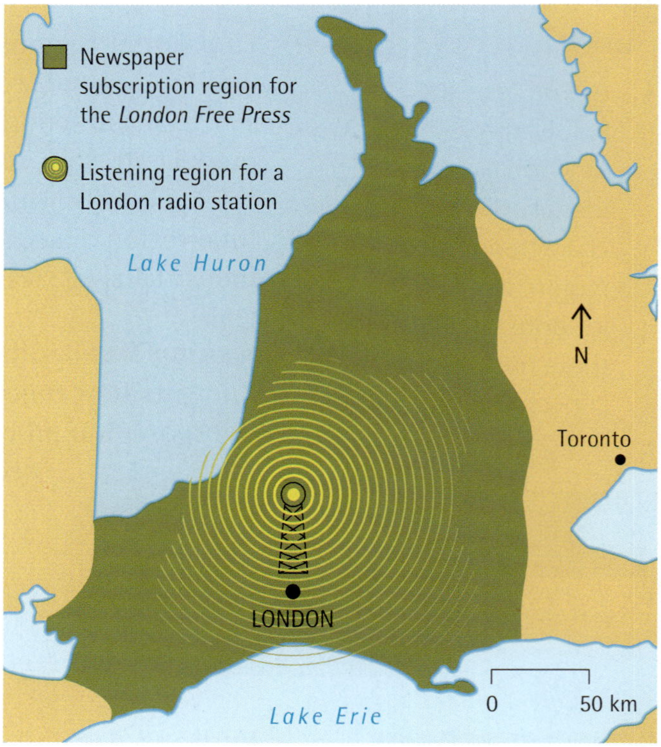

Figure 2.18

Why do you think the broadcast region of the radio station is smaller than the circulation region of the newspaper?

Multi-Factor Regions

Regions can have one main characteristic in common, such as similar vegetation or population. Regions can also be defined by more than one characteristic. They can share physical and human features. A region could be defined by ski resorts (human) and mountains (physical), or it could be defined by farms (human) and plains (physical). When we combine natural features and human activities in a particular area, we create a region called an **ecozone**.

The Riviera region along the north Mediterranean seacoast is an ecozone. It includes parts of several countries (political regions). These parts all have beaches and coastal mountains. They also have a climate that is generally warm and dry all the time (physical region). Similar kinds of crops are grown—grapes and olives (agricultural regions). It has summer year round, so the area has become popular for holidays (human region). All of these things together have made the area a unique ecozone.

DURING READING

1. As you read the following pages on multi-factor regions, identify the important characteristics of ecozones. Use your jot-note skills, and add these notes to your concept map or chart.

Figure 2.19

This is a photograph of Nice, France. Which countries are included in the Riviera region?

DURING READING

1. Using an atlas, identify the ecozone in which you live. What makes your ecozone different from other ecozones?

In Canada, we have 15 distinct **land-based ecozones** and five **marine-based ecozones**. Each of these ecozone regions has similar physical (natural) and human characteristics throughout its area. Defining these regions helps when dealing with problems. Suppose we want to create a national park to protect unique physical features or the habitats of particular animals. We need to know where each ecozone begins and ends. We also need to understand how everything is connected within each ecozone.

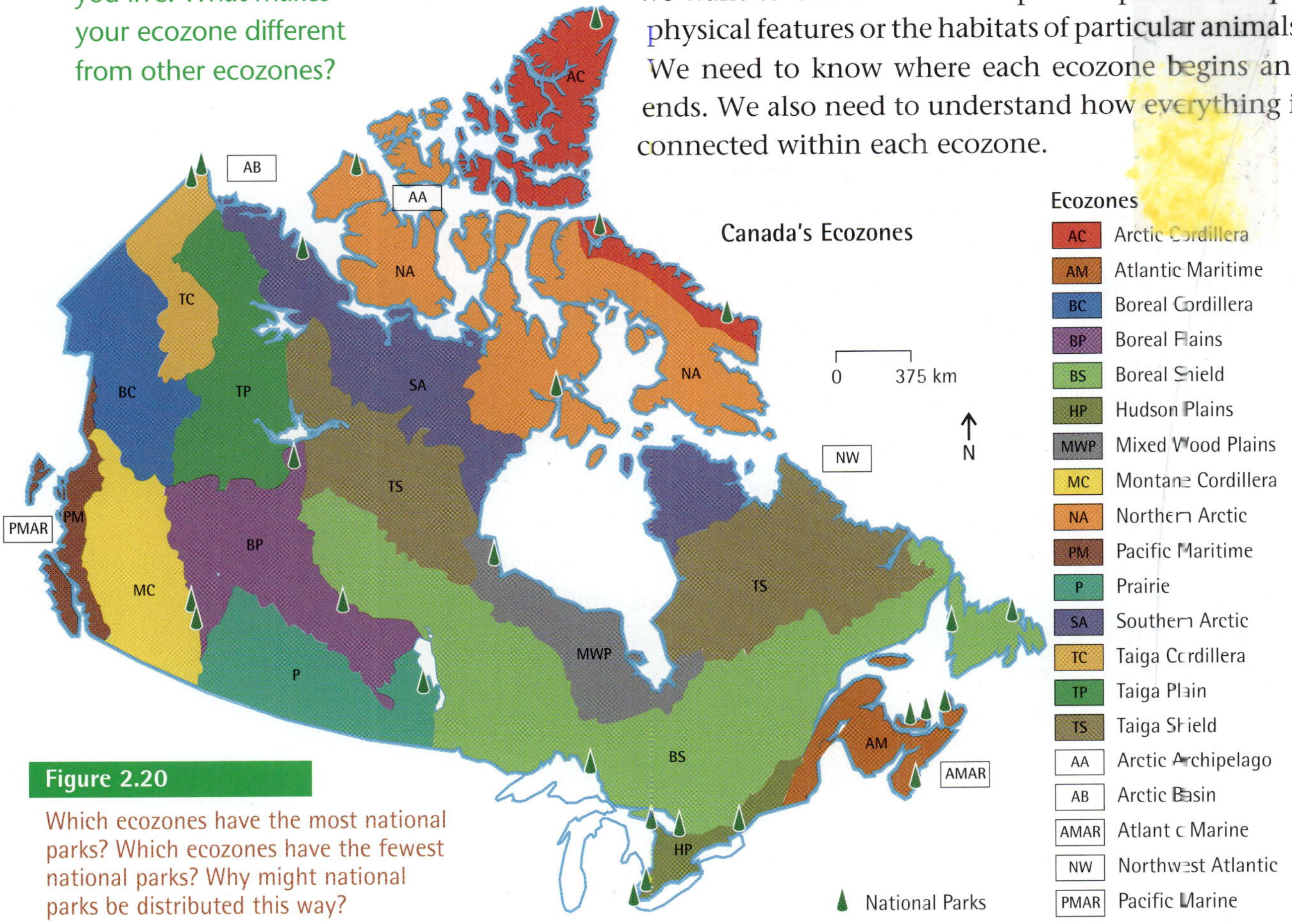

Figure 2.20

Which ecozones have the most national parks? Which ecozones have the fewest national parks? Why might national parks be distributed this way?

GeoSkills

How to Read a Map—Scale and Elevation

When you are reading a map, you should look at the Title, the Legend, and the Compass (TLC) first. These three items will help you determine the purpose of the map. It is also important to know how to read scale and elevation charts because the physical geography of a region has a direct impact on the people living there.

Scale: All maps show Earth from a bird's-eye view. In order to make our drawing of Earth manageable, we shrink that view and use a map scale. The map scale tells you how much the real land has been shrunk to fit on your map. You can use scale to calculate distance between places on a map. A linear scale shows you the relationship between one unit (for example, 1 centimetre) on the scale, and the ground distance (for example, 1 kilometre). Use a ruler to measure the distance in a straight line between two places. Multiply this measurement by the ground distance (represented by one unit on the scale) to calculate the distance "as the crow flies." Use a ruler to measure the distance using roads or streets. Multiply this total measurement by the ground distance (represented by one unit on the scale) to calculate the distance using roads or streets.

Figure 2.21

This is an example of a linear scale. On the maps below, notice how the small-scale map shows less detail, and the large-scale map shows more detail.

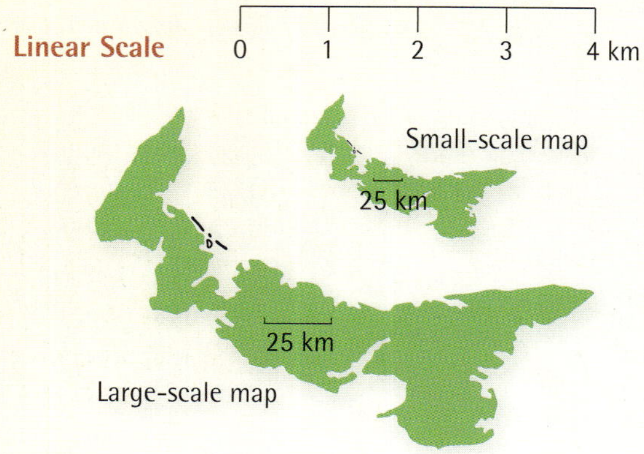

Elevation: When you are reading a legend, some maps will have an elevation chart, which tells you the elevation of the landforms.

Figure 2.22

This map is of the Middle East region. It is a region that is often in the news, but what do we know about that region's physical geography?

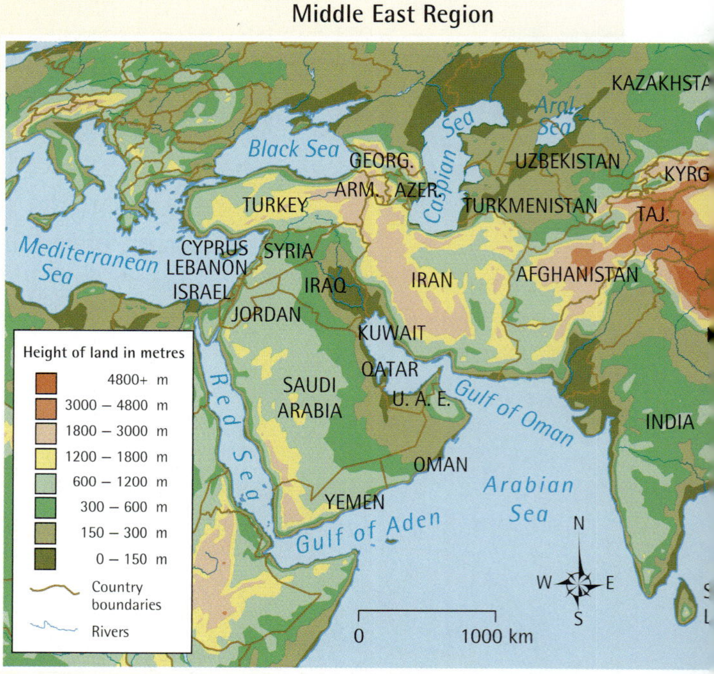

Q: Using the scale found at the bottom of this map, what is the approximate distance between the northern shore of Turkey and the southwestern tip of Yemen?

Q: Which country or countries have the highest elevation in this region? To which mountain chain might these mountains belong?

Go Geo-Green

Saving the Niagara Escarpment

The Niagara Escarpment is a unique natural wonder. You can find its location by looking at the red line on the map below of southern Ontario. The United Nations Educational, Scientific, and Cultural Organization (UNESCO) named the Niagara Ecarpment as one of Canada's 12 World Biosphere Reserves. It is a unique natural wonder that stretches 725 kilometres from Queenston, near Niagara Falls, all the way up to Tobermory, at the tip of the Bruce Peninsula. It is mainly a forested ridge dotted with wetlands, meadows, and waterfalls, the most famous being Niagara Falls. This region is home to many different species of animals and birds.

The escarpment is located in one of the most heavily populated regions in Canada. Since it was rough with thin soils, people did not settle as quickly on the escarpment as in surrounding regions. As Ontario has grown rapidly, the area has become pressured by cottagers, campers, hikers, industries like quarries, farms, and private homes. Special environmental features and natural areas have been lost. The Niagara Escarpment has changed more over the past 100 years than it did during the previous 4.5 million years!

Niagara Escarpment

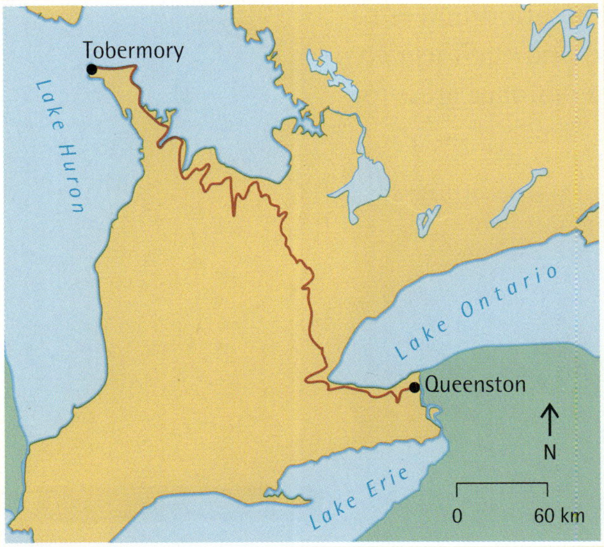

Figure 2.24

The Niagara Escarpment runs from Queenston to Tobermory.

Figure 2.23

This is a side view of the Niagara Escarpment.

Many groups are working to restore the Niagara Escarpment to protect what natural features are left. Staff and volunteers with the Ontario Niagara Escarpment Monitoring Program study the effects of climate change, increased population, and development on the escarpment. Before there was a conservation plan, many parts of the forests were separated from other parts of the forest. Community groups are trying to link these forested areas to increase and protect the habitats for many bird species. People of all ages come on tree-planting days to help restore this incredible region.

Figure 2.25

Tree planting is one way to restore regions such as the Niagara Escarpment.

AFTER READING

1. Look at a population map of Canada and a physical map of Canada. Compare the two maps. Where do most Canadians live? What is the connection between physical regions and where most communities are located?
2. Imagine you are starting a business of your choice. Which functional regions will you need to consider? Which other regions should you also consider for your business?
3. Select one of Canada's ecozones, and explain how its physical characteristics affect its human and functional characteristics.

Regional Boundaries

BEFORE READING

1. What is a boundary? Why are boundaries necessary?
2. Describe the boundaries of Canada. (See Map Appendix.)

Some regional boundaries are natural. They can be rivers, the crests of mountains, coastlines, and bodies of water. Sometimes natural boundaries, such as mountains, act as obstacles or barriers. Others, such as rivers, separate, but they also allow contact and communication.

Figure 2.26

The Alps form a boundary for parts of different countries. Use an atlas to discover which countries are included. The tops of some mountains act as divides for regional drainage basins.

Divides

One type of natural physical region is a **drainage area** of a river, or a **drainage basin**. All the water that falls as precipitation and runs off the land in a basin drains into one main river, and then usually into another body of water. The boundary between drainage areas (or watersheds) is called a **drainage divide**.

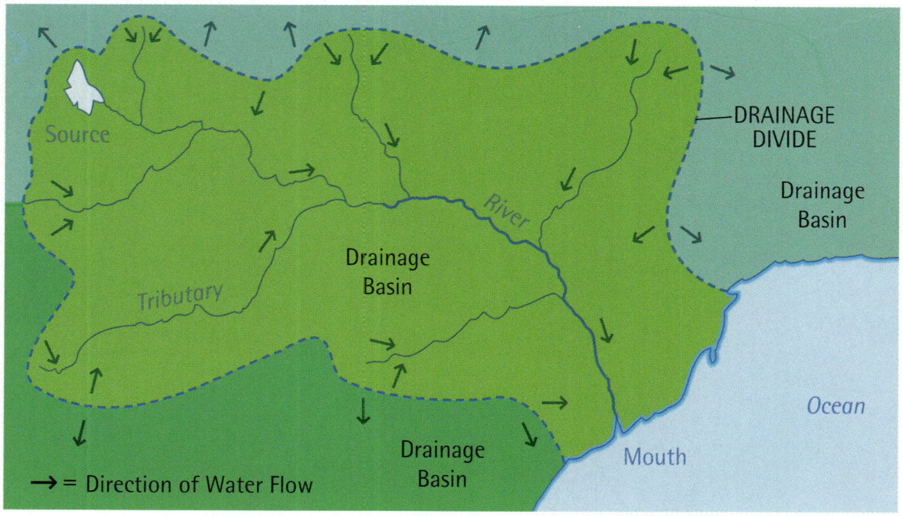

Figure 2.27

In this example, the drainage divide makes the water flow into three different drainage basins. Check to discover where the runoff water drains in your area.

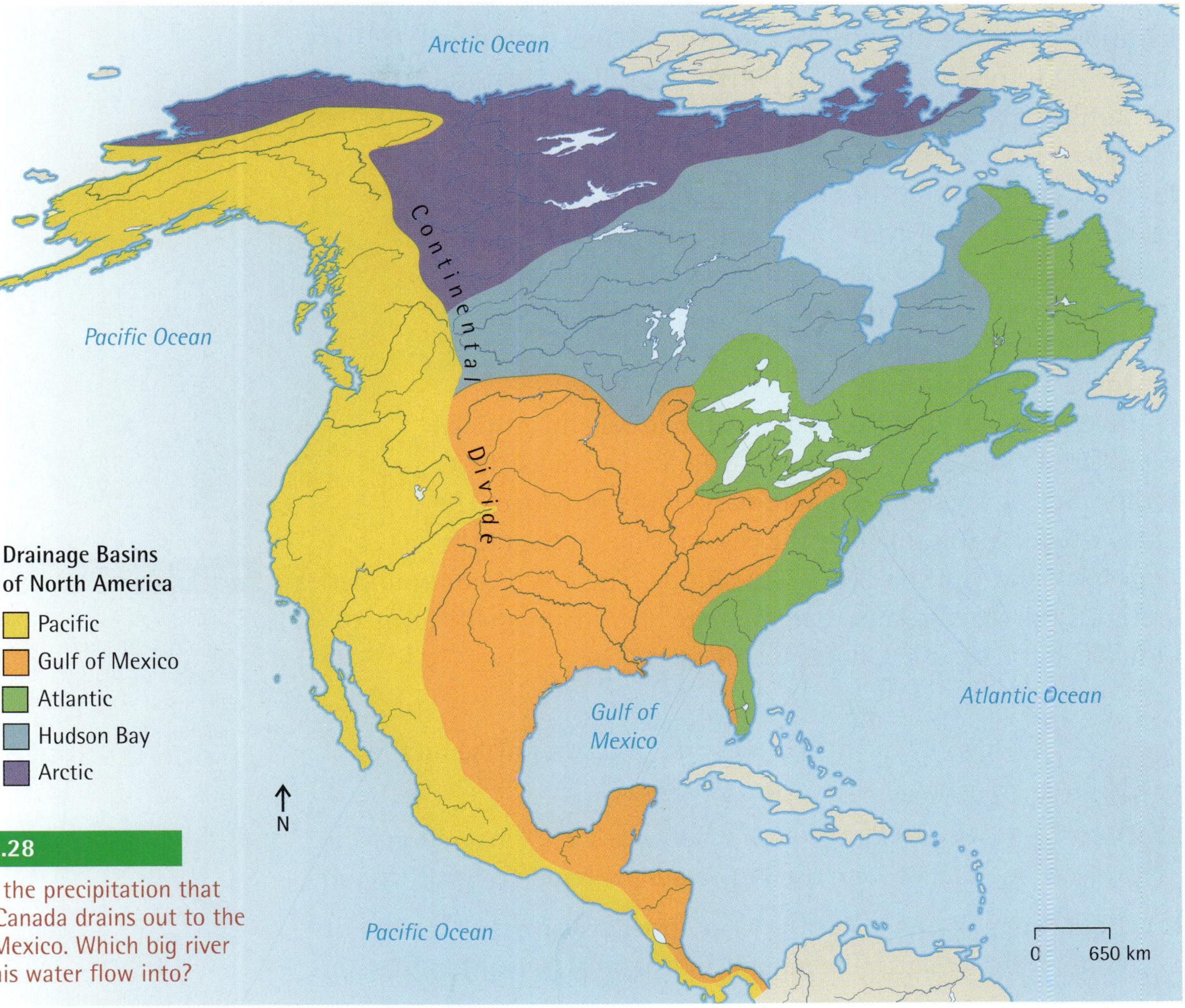

Figure 2.28

Some of the precipitation that falls on Canada drains out to the Gulf of Mexico. Which big river would this water flow into?

Fact File

The greatest drainage boundary on the map is the Continental Divide, or Great Divide. It runs from the Arctic Ocean all the way to the tip of South America. If you were able to stand right on the Divide and dump a pail of water, half would flow toward the Pacific Ocean, and the rest would flow toward the Atlantic Ocean or Arctic Ocean.

Drainage Basins in North America

Drainage basins are natural physical regions. North America has five major drainage basins. Water runs off North America into the Pacific Ocean, the Arctic Ocean, Hudson Bay, the Atlantic Ocean, and the Gulf of Mexico.

DURING READING

1. What are the advantages of using natural features as boundaries?
2. If a chemical were spilled in a river or stream in your region, in which major body of water would the chemical eventually end up? Trace its route.

Figure 2.29

What do you think the sign, near Upsala, Ontario, says on the other side?

Other Regional Boundary Markers

Latitude and longitude are commonly used as boundary lines. Many other features are used as well. Roads and settlement patterns, such as survey lines for county boundaries, act as boundaries. Distance limits from shorelines are used by countries to put boundaries around fisheries. A country will even include the air above it as its fly zone or region, and other countries must ask permission to fly through this air space.

Ontario's Boundaries

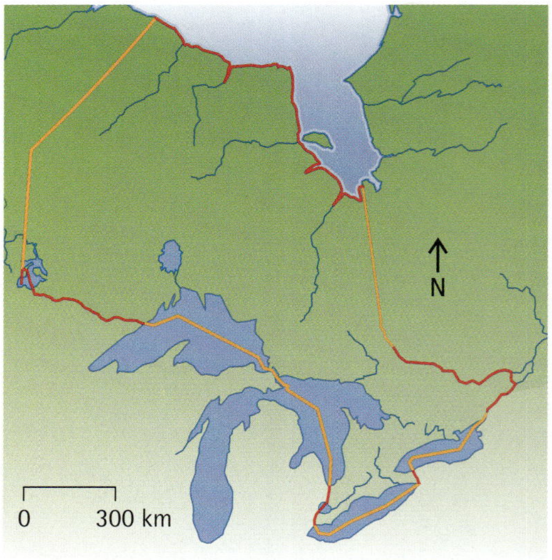

Figure 2.30

Check in an atlas or the Map Appendix to see if there is a province or territory that has only natural boundaries or one that has only lines of latitude or longitude as boundaries.

Ontario's Boundaries

Ontario creates its limits or edges with natural and artificial boundaries. The Great Lakes and the St. Lawrence River form much of the southern boundary of the province. The Ottawa River marks much of the eastern side. In the north, James Bay and Hudson Bay are the limits. The rest of our boundaries are artificial. This means that they are shown on political maps of Ontario, but they cannot actually be seen.

AFTER READING

1. Identify the major lakes and rivers that make up the drainage basin where you live.
2. Describe the boundaries of your school grounds. What natural and artificial boundaries were used to create the region of your school?
3. Using a map of Canada or the Map Appendix, select a province or territory, and describe the natural and/or artificial features used to create its boundaries.

How Regions Change

BEFORE READING

1. What are some reasons why your school-ground boundaries could change?
2. Explain in what ways Canada's boundaries could change in the future.

A region changes because the characteristics that made it a region changed. A new shopping mall may open in your neighbourhood, which changes shopping areas. A new suburb may be built, and people from your neighbourhood may choose to move there. This new suburban area may result in increased or decreased traffic through your area.

Local Regional Planning

We plan for the future growth of our villages, towns, cities, and the land around them. Due to the great size of some regions, the number of people involved, and the interactions that occur over large areas, we must plan and manage very large regions. **Urban and regional planning** involves dealing with systems such as transportation, hydro, water, waste handling, sewers, policing, firefighting, and parklands; protecting special areas; and using the best farmland for agriculture. In order for urban and regional planning to work best, the governments of the municipalities, townships, and counties in these regions must work together.

Connections to History

Think about your community as a region. What are its characteristics? What are its boundaries? Then, do a survey of some of the senior citizens in your area. Develop a set of questions to ask about how your local region has changed during their lives. Consider such things as shopping areas, how people earned a living, the biggest changes, transportation, environmental quality, and the climate.

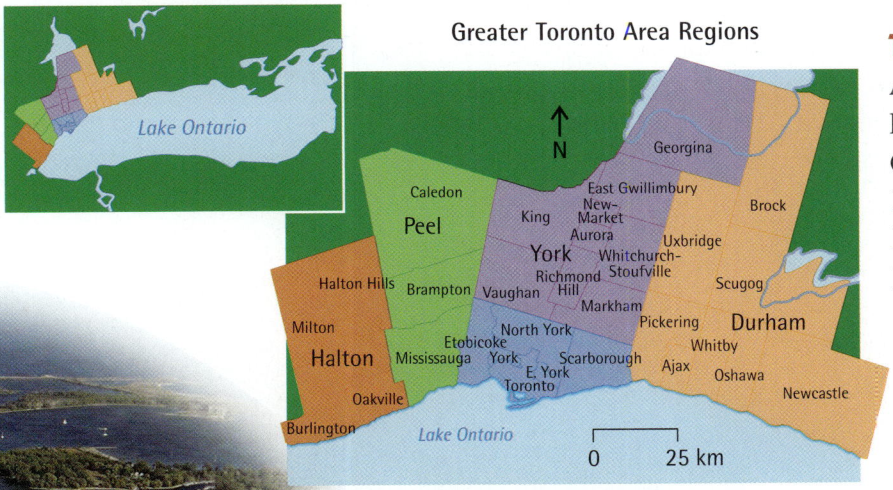

Figure 2.31

If you were in charge of planning, where in the GTA would you put a park, a new highway, or a new shopping mall? Find and use a topographical map of this area to help you answer the question.

The Greater Toronto Area

An example of planning for a large region can be found in the Greater Toronto Area (GTA). In 2007, over 6 million people lived in this region, within an hour's drive of the CN Tower. Many of these people worked in Toronto but lived in areas well beyond the city limits. These people and their families travelled into downtown Toronto to shop; to go to a Raptors, Jays, Argos, or Leafs game; and to visit such places as the Canadian National Exhibition, Ontario Place, or the Royal Ontario Museum.

Others lived within the city and travelled into the surrounding region for work or for recreation at the ski hills, lakes, golf courses, and conservation areas. The area is alive with agricultural, industrial, and commercial activities. The Greater Toronto Area planners must understand the interactions between these regions to plan wisely for the GTA's future.

Figure 2.32

This is a photograph of the GTA. How do people use Lake Ontario? How would this variety of uses affect the planning for functional regions within the GTA?

Large Regional Planning

Decisions made in one part of a region will affect all parts of it, and probably parts of other regions as well. People may decide to build a dam to prevent flooding along a river that flows through your region. That decision causes changes in other areas upstream and downstream—all along the river. The dam itself backs up water in a reservoir, which drowns previously exposed areas. The flow of the river below the dam is changed and usually controlled.

Better or Worse?

Activities in the region may change. It may be possible to use the reservoir for recreational activities like boating, swimming, and camping. The dam may permit a power facility to be constructed for hydro power. Formerly flooded open areas below the dam become safer and dry, and they may now be used for residential or other uses.

The entire ecological system will also change. It may become impossible for some existing species of plants and animals to survive, while new ones may thrive. There are many interconnections that are involved in any change to a region. All must be considered before changing one aspect of one region.

Literacy Tip

Checking Comprehension as You Read

While you are reading, it is a good idea to stop and think about what you have read, by doing the following:

- Ask a question.
- Clarify something.
- Make a comment.
- Make a connection.
- Make a prediction.

Interrupting your reading to think aloud helps you check your understanding of the text.

DURING READING

1. Think about the region where you live. What changes have occurred? Why have these changes occurred?

Figure 2.33

A huge project in China called the Three Gorges Project is nearly complete. It is now providing much-needed electrical power. It is also having dramatic effects on the surrounding region. Over 3 million people have been forced to move away from their homes to other areas. Large land areas have been flooded, and entire towns and cities have been moved. Why do you think some people are opposed to such large regional changes? How is it an example of large-scale regional planning?

Weather Changes Regions

Sometimes changes in the weather patterns in another area of the world can cause changes in our regions. Amazingly, the pattern of ocean currents over 8000 kilometres away affects our lives here in Ontario. **El Niño** is a huge mass of very warm water. It appears frequently off the coast of northern South America. Since 1985, such episodes have happened in 1986, 1991, 1993, 1994, 1997–98, and 2002.

It is difficult to predict what effect an "El Niño year" will have on the weather in North America. However, these episodes can result in more storms, higher precipitation, and more extreme seasonal temperatures.

Hurricane Increase

In the past decade, more frequent and more intense hurricanes and tropical storms have affected North America and the Caribbean. Many people believe that global warming and effects like El Niño are to blame. In 2005, Hurricane Katrina brought great devastation to the Gulf of Mexico coast in the United States, especially to New Orleans. By 2007, New Orleans still needed more reconstruction despite the tremendous efforts of governments and citizens.

Figure 2.34

This is a photograph of Hurricane Frances, which struck the coast of Florida in September 2004. The strongest El Niño on record was in 1997–98. In that winter, western Canada was unusually warm, and the southern and western parts of the United States suffered many storms. How do you think El Niños have affected Ontario?

Figure 2.35

This is what a neighbourhood in New Orleans, Louisiana, looked like shortly after Hurricane Katrina. Although billions of dollars have been spent to provide protection from future storms and to rebuild, the future effects of climate change are still hard to predict accurately.

Figure 2.36

Hurricane Felix, which struck coastal Central America on September 4, 2007, was a devastating category-five hurricane. The "tightly wound" counterclockwise spiral is characteristic of such storms. Can you see the calm eye of the hurricane in the centre of the spiral?

Fact File

2007 marked the first time in history that two category-five (the strongest) hurricanes struck in the same year. Both Felix and Dean struck Central America in August and September. Also, on September 4, 2007, two hurricanes, Felix and Henriette, hit on the same day—one on the Atlantic Ocean side, and the other on the Pacific.

Figure 2.37

This table shows that the frequency of hurricanes is increasing, but the greatest concern is the occurrence of more major storms like Hurricanes Dean, Felix, and Katrina.

Years	Avg. Number of Named Storms	Avg. Total Hurricanes	Major Hurricanes
1985–1994	8.5	5	1.5
1995–2005	13	7.7	3.6

1. Under the title Dams: Why or Why Not, create a t-chart. Label one column Advantages, and the other Disadvantages. Brainstorm with a partner the advantages and disadvantages of constructing dams and reservoirs on rivers. Be sure to consider the positive and negative effects on people, nature, and wildlife. In your opinion, do the advantages outweigh the disadvantages of building dams?
2. Think about a change in your region. Using a t-chart, list the positive and negative effects of this change. Overall, is your region better or worse because of the change?

Literacy Tip

Using T-Charts

These questions ask you to list opposing points and views on a topic. A simple way of presenting two sides of a topic is by using a t-chart. A t-chart is a type of graphic organizer with two columns, one for each of the two different sides. Using t-charts and concise jot notes will help you clearly see opposing views and arrive at a conclusion.

Knowledge and Understanding

1. Compare your neighbourhood to another in your community. List the physical and human similarities and differences in a chart.

Inquiry/Research and Communication Skills

2. Describe how humans adapt to meet the physical characteristics of a region. For example, in southern Ontario, people grew hedges and trees around sides of their fields or homes to block winds. Use one of the following regions: the Polar Region, the Great Plains of North America, or the desert regions in Australia. Compare your findings with those of a classmate. If you need to find out more about the physical characteristics of your chosen region, use an encyclopedia for quick results.

Figure 2.38

Identify two adaptations people would make to their homes in a region like this one in Australia.

3. Choose one country from two of the following world regions:
   - the Caribbean: Cuba, Jamaica, Haiti, Dominican Republic, Puerto Rico, Trinidad and Tobago, the Bahamas, St. Kitts and Nevis, Antigua and Barbuda, Barbados, Guadeloupe, Martinique, St. Lucia
   - Middle East: Saudi Arabia, Yemen, Oman, Qatar, United Arab Emirates, Jordan, Israel, Iraq, Iran, Lebanon, Palestine, Syria, Bahrain, Turkey, Kuwait
   - Central America: Guatemala, Belize, El Salvador, Honduras, Nicaragua, Costa Rica, Panama
   - Southeast Asia: Burma (Myanmar), Thailand, Laos, Cambodia, Vietnam, Philippines, Malaysia, Singapore, Indonesia

   Compare the language, customs, and religions of the people who live in these regions. Use an encyclopedia or a search engine on the Internet to help you find the information you need. If you use a search engine, use keywords in your search string, such as *Saudi Arabia language religion customs*. Make jot notes of important information as you read. Organize your jot notes into similarities and differences for each of the areas for research: language, customs, and religion. You may wish to use a chart format such as the following:

	Similarities	Differences
Language		
Customs		
Religion		

4. Using a software program such as PC Globe, select a country in Europe, Asia, or Africa, and compare it to Canada under the topics of population, economy, culture, and services (education, health). Report on the similarities and differences between the two countries.

5. Investigate the Three Gorges Project in China. Find answers to the following questions:

   a) What is the Three Gorges Project? In which region in China is it located? (See Map Appendix.)

   b) What are the goals of this project?

   c) How is the Three Gorges Project having an impact on, or affecting, the region?

   If you want to use a search engine to research this project on the Internet, use the following search string: *Three Gorges Dam*. You can narrow your results by adding to your search string terms such as *Three Gorges Dam impact environment people*.

Map, Globe, and Graphic Skills

6 Different regions at the same latitude have many physical characteristics in common. For example, there are fjord regions in British Columbia, Greenland, Norway, and Newfoundland. Can you find another set of regions that share the same latitude? Use a physical map of the world in an atlas or the Map Appendix to help in your search.

Figure 2.39

Use your atlas to determine the length of some long fjords in Norway.

7 Use an atlas or the Map Appendix and find maps that show global landforms, ecosystems, and climate regions. Use these maps to make comparisons of these regions.

a) Find two landform regions and two climate regions that almost match. Name the regions and the continents they are on.

b) Study the maps of global ecosystems and global climate regions. Find two ecosystems and two climate regions that almost match. Name the regions and the continents they are on.

c) Study the maps of global landforms and global ecosystems. Find two landform regions and two ecosystems that almost match. Name the regions and the continents they are on.

d) Look again at the maps of climate regions and global ecosystems. Explain how climate regions and vegetation regions are connected.

e) Look again at the maps of global landforms and ecosystems. Explain how landform regions and vegetation regions are connected.

f) In two or three sentences, summarize how landforms, climate, and vegetation are related or connected.

8 Canada is divided into postal regions to make mail delivery faster. Every address has a postal code, such as N6A 3X4. The first letter in your postal code indicates the largest region that your address is part of (your province or part of it). The last number tells the smallest part of your postal region (your section of a street or rural road). Write to Canada Post for a detailed explanation of the postal codes they use. Find their contact information at their website.

a) Get a map of the area around your school. Plot the location of each student's home by placing a dot and the last three characters of the code on the map.

b) Postal regions help us find addresses and speed up mail service. Pizza delivery zones are based on address and telephone numbers. Sports teams draw players from areas based on their addresses. List two other regions that have been created to provide services.

Application

9 Prepare a visual display, including maps, graphs, and pictures, to compare ways in which people work to earn a living in two different regions of the world.

10 As North Americans, we think of certain regions as having special characteristics. Make a chart with two headings: Characteristics and Place. Write the following characteristics on your chart:

- region with many earthquakes
- highest populated region
- lowest populated region
- most undisturbed environment
- highest snowfall region
- region with lots of crime
- region with many lakes

- apple-growing region
- wheat-growing region
- government region
- sunbelt region

Now put in a place name for each (for example, for "many earthquakes," you might put in "California").

11 Predict one change in your activities that may occur as a result of each of the following happening in the region in which you live or in your community:

a) an increase in population density

b) a decrease in population density

c) a series of very severe winters

d) the opening of a new shopping mall

12 Use an atlas to create your own geographic region, as follows:

a) Map at least one physical and one human characteristic on a world outline map. For example, you could map areas of greatest precipitation and population, or different soil types and major industries. When you plot the two sets of data on your map, you will see that some areas will overlap. These will be your new regions. Show boundaries around the overlapping areas by colouring, shading, striping, or using some other technique.

b) Create a unique title for your map that captures the physical and human characteristics of your chosen region. For example, you could map "number of tourists" and "highest sunlight hours" and call the map "Regions for Fun in the Sun."

Figure 2.40

Which concerns are making scenes such as this in Sauble Beach, Ontario, less "fun in the sun"?

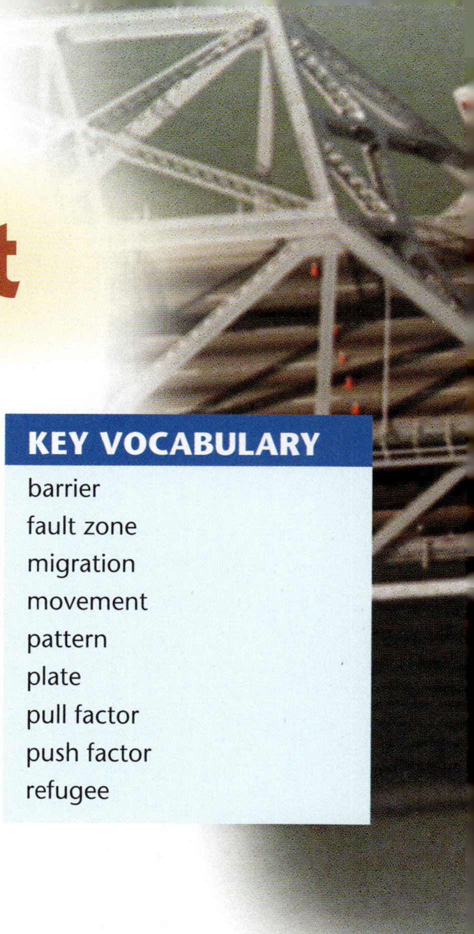

3 Movement

IN THIS CHAPTER

- explain the theme of movement in geography
- create and use maps for different reasons
- use the new terms in this chapter correctly as you investigate the topics
- locate helpful information from primary and secondary sources
- produce a report that applies one or more of the five themes of geography to an environmental event

KEY VOCABULARY

barrier
fault zone
migration
movement
pattern
plate
pull factor
push factor
refugee

Everything Is in Motion

BEFORE READING

1. Name 10 things that move.
2. Which ones do not require fuel power to move?
3. Name five things that move naturally.

Our world is full of **movement**. Earth moves. The land, water, and air move. We move from place to place and change our locations. Goods are shipped from places of production to markets. They are moved from region to region. Information passes from one person to another.

Under Your Feet

Planet Earth moves around the Sun once every year, creating our seasons. It also spins around on its axis once every 24 hours, giving us night and day. Below Earth's surface, movement can be a hazard, in the form of earthquakes.

Fact File

As Earth moves around the Sun, it moves at about 100 000 kilometres per hour—and so do you!

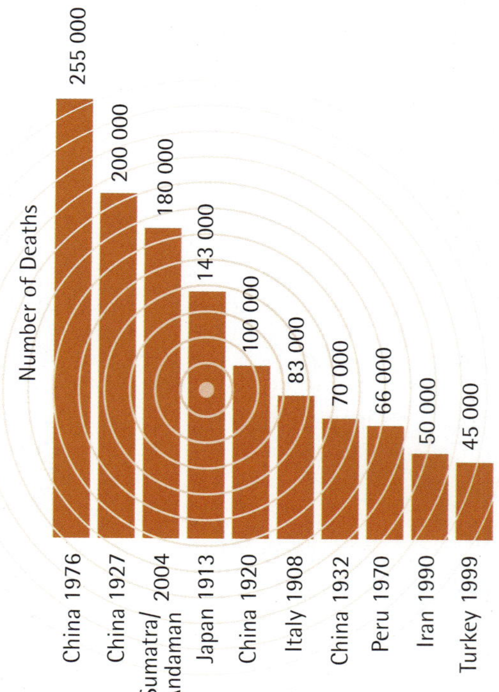

Figure 3.1

This bar graph shows some of the world's major earthquakes and the resulting deaths. According to the graph, in which part of the world have most deaths occurred as a result of earthquakes?

Figure 3.2

In 1989, 27 people died on this Bay Bridge in Oakland near San Francisco, California, after an earthquake struck. Why are earthquakes more dangerous in a city than in the country?

Fact File

Canada has over 1000 earthquakes annually. British Columbia has about 200 earthquakes, and coastal British Columbia is expected to be the location of a major earthquake soon.

The San Andreas Fault

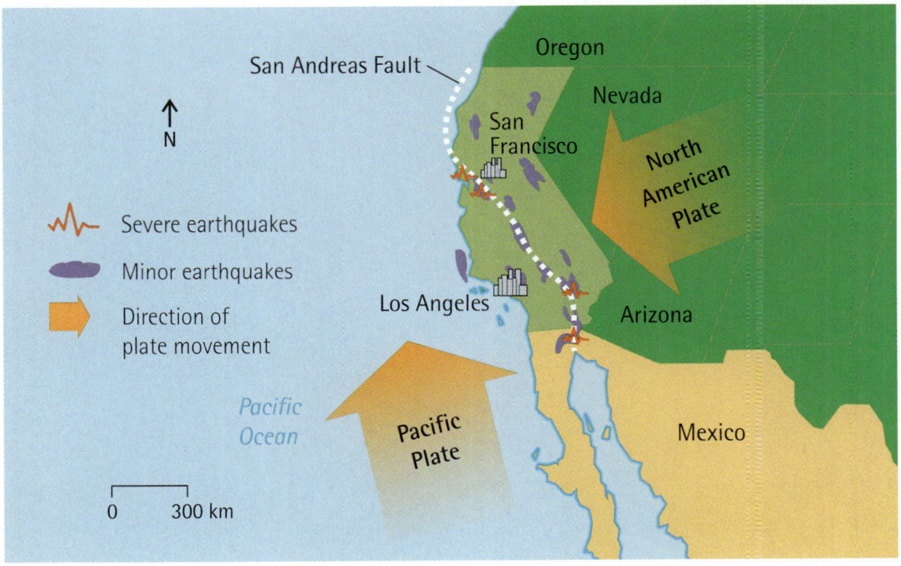

Figure 3.3

Los Angeles is slowly moving northward toward San Francisco because these cities are on different plates. Los Angeles will pass San Francisco to the northwest in about 10 million years.

Earthquakes

Have you ever felt an earthquake? An earthquake occurs when parts of Earth move. Most people in Ontario have had experiences with earthquakes, but only minor ones. Windows shake and dishes rattle, but no real damage occurs. Many people live in places where there are earthquakes every day!

Earthquakes happen when sections of Earth's crust shift. These shifting parts are called **plates**. They are actually pieces of the crust floating on Earth's hot, molten interior. Most earthquakes happen along the edges of these plates and along weak areas of the crust called **fault zones**. (See Map Appendix.) In California, along the San Andreas Fault, earthquakes occur in a clear pattern.

Literacy Tip

Making Connections

Ask yourself what experiences you have had or what you already know that connects to what you are reading. Thinking of how you can relate to what you are reading makes the text more meaningful.

The Power of Movement

Natural movement can be caused by the following forces:

- gravity
- moving air and water
- heat and cold (expansion and contraction)

DURING READING

1. Look carefully at the photographs on pages 50 and 51. Before you read the captions, try to identify the natural movement shown in each photograph. Which of these movements match those you identified at the beginning of this section?

Figure 3.4

Mount Etna, in Sicily, Italy, erupted on July 24, 1998. As volcanoes erupt, Earth's materials move. What do you think happens to all the dust and smoke that flies into the air, along with molten rock called lava, during a volcanic eruption?

Figure 3.5

This glacier is located near Jasper, Alberta. As snow and ice accumulate over time in great quantity, the weight of the glacier creates extreme pressure on the layers of ice. This pressure plus heat from Earth cause the glacier to slide downward. The pressure changes and the pull of gravity on downward slopes cause these tiny ice crystals to move. All of the motions combined propel the glacier forward. How fast do you think glaciers move? Estimate and then research to find out how close your guess is.

Figure 3.6

This rock formation is located on Flowerpot Island in Georgian Bay. The force of water moves Earth's materials and shapes them into features. The tops of these rocks are harder than their bottoms and so they wear down more slowly. What do you think will happen to these strange rock formations over time?

Figure 3.7

In January 2005, this mudslide in California destroyed or damaged 28 homes. As land that is steeply sloped becomes wet and heavy, it falls away due to the force of gravity, and a landslide happens. As mountains are worn, pieces break off and tumble down the slopes due to gravity. How do these movements of Earth affect people?

Figure 3.8

The force of the moving air (wind) can move ground materials such as sand and help shape landforms. Why do you think sand is constantly changing shape?

Literacy Tip

Viewing Photographs

When viewing a photograph, ask yourself the following questions:

- What is the main idea in this photograph?
- What was the first image that caught my eye? Why?
- What other details stand out?
- What is the purpose of this photograph?
- Is there a title or caption?
- How does this photograph make me feel?

Figure 3.9

The wind and the oceans move heat away from the equator to other parts of the world. This movement of heat northwards makes the climate livable in places even farther north than Stavanger, Norway. Use an atlas or the Map Appendix to find out which ocean current brings warmer water to Norway.

Web Link

For more information about natural hazards, particularly volcanoes, go to **www.nelson.com/phygeo7**.

AFTER READING

1. Choose one way that parts of Earth move. Explain two dangers that can result because of the movement.
2. In your opinion, which is more powerful: natural movements, or human-created movements? Give examples to support your answer.

People on the Move

The movement of people to new areas is called **migration**. People move more now than ever before. Personal mobility is a characteristic of our modern society. Over the past 250 years, the most common movement of people has been from the country to the city. That is, people have moved from rural to urban regions.

People move within communities and to new communities and provinces. People also move to new countries. There are many different reasons for people to move. Some reasons are quite exciting, like opening up a new frontier or starting a new life in a new place. Other reasons are tragic, such as moving to escape hunger or war. Sometimes, large numbers of people are forced to move. This creates a flow of **refugees**.

BEFORE READING

1. What are some of the reasons why people move to new areas?
2. Imagine you were moving to another city. How would you feel? Why?

Percentage of Foreign Born, by Region

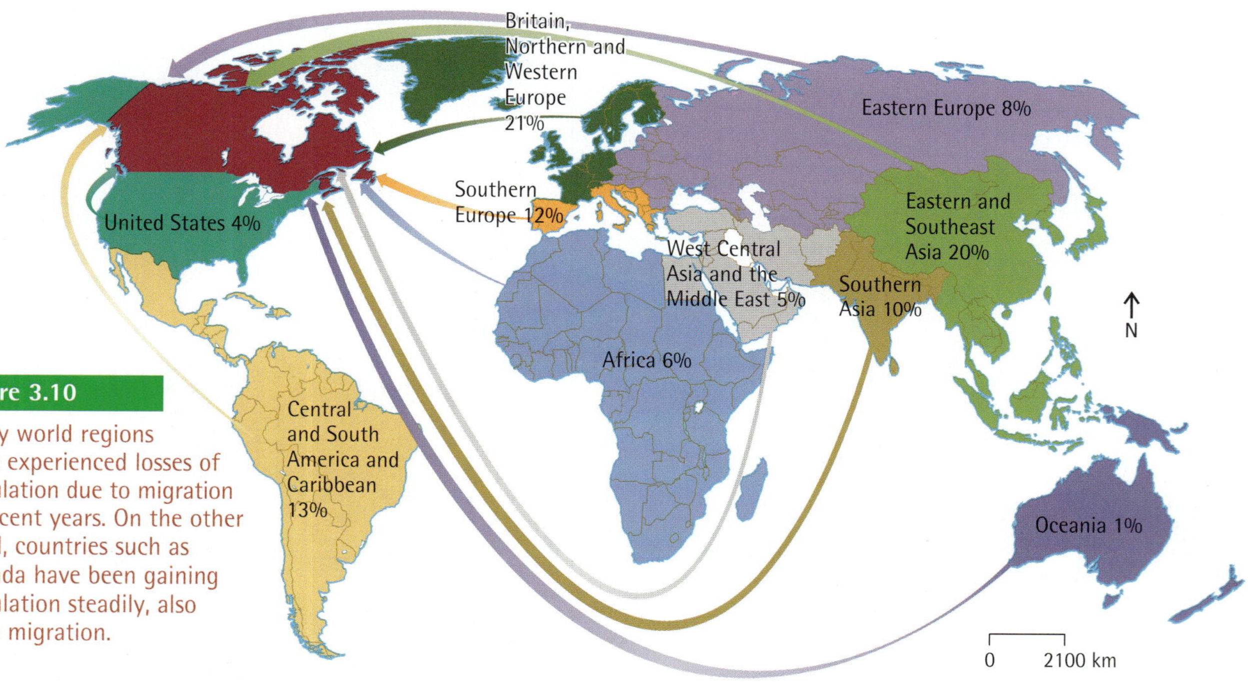

Figure 3.10

Many world regions have experienced losses of population due to migration in recent years. On the other hand, countries such as Canada have been gaining population steadily, also from migration.

New Canadians—Immigration 1997–2005

Figure 3.11

In the past decade, the number of people immigrating to Canada has been rising. What reasons might there be for this increase?

Fact File

One of the largest single migrations of people in the 1900s involved the move of 8 million Muslims into East Pakistan (now Bangladesh) and West Pakistan (now Pakistan) in 1948 from India. Over 3 million Hindus moved from East and West Pakistan into India.

GeoSkills

Reading a Map—Latitude and Longitude

Lines of latitude measure distance north and south of the equator. Latitude is given in degrees because it measures the angle from the equator to Earth's centre, then to a location on Earth's surface. There are 180 degrees of latitude: 90° north and 90° south.

Lines of longitude measure distance east and west of the prime meridian. Longitude is given in degrees because it measures the angle from the prime meridian to Earth's centre, then to a location on Earth's surface. There are 360 degrees of longitude: 180° east and 180° west.

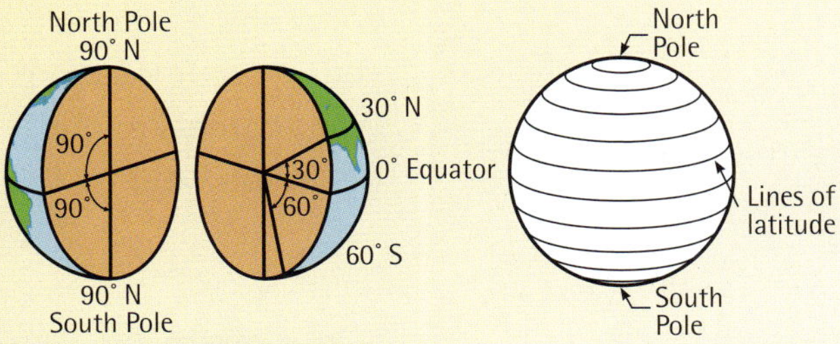

Figure 3.12

These illustrations demonstrate how lines of latitude measure distance north and south of the equator.

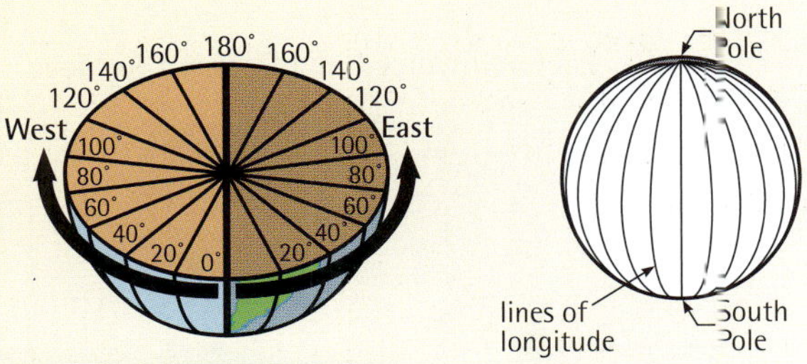

Figure 3.13

These illustrations demonstrate how lines of longitude measure distance east and west of the Prime Meridian.

How to Read and Use Latitude and Longitude

What is the latitude and longitude of Toronto, Ontario? In order to answer this question, you need to remember to find degrees of latitude first and longitude second. Think of it this way: if you are going to a classroom on the second floor of a school, you enter the building and then go up the stairs. This is the same way to read and use latitude and longitude coordinates. Always remember to go *in the door and up the stairs.*

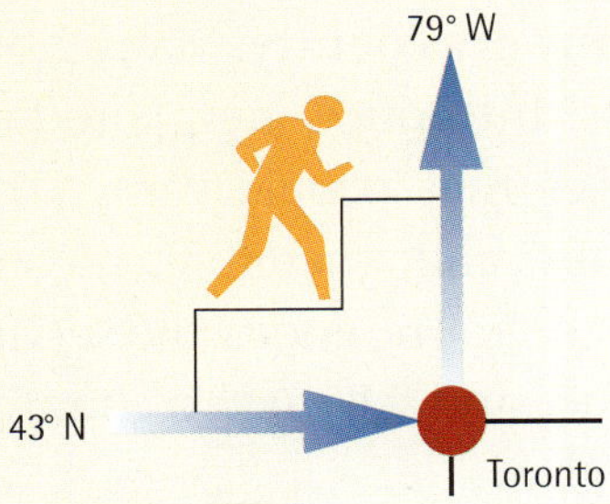

Figure 3.15

Remember to go in the door (find the degrees of latitude) first, and then go up the stairs (find the degrees of longitude).

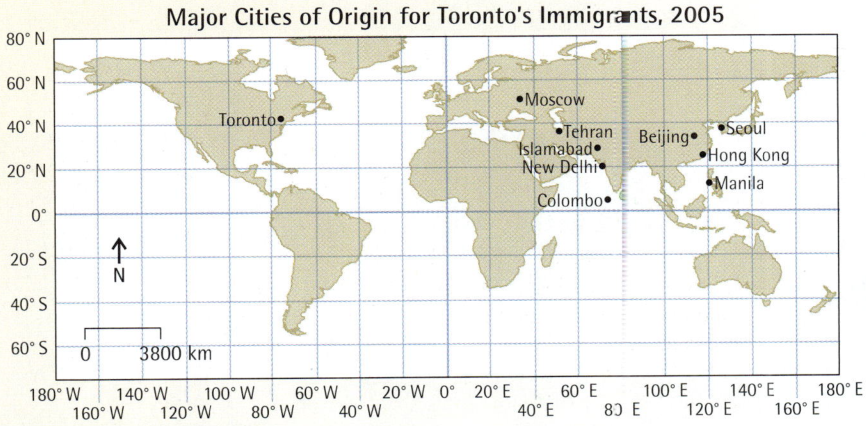

Figure 3.14

Do you know someone who has immigrated from one of these cities?

Q: What is the purpose of this map? How do you know that?

Q: What cities are found at the following latitude and longitude coordinates?
- 35° N, 51° E
- 37° N, 126° E
- 55° N, 37° E

Q: Find the latitude and longitude for the following cities:
- Beijing
- Manila
- Islamabad
- Colombo
- your own community

Q: By reading this map, which continent do most of Toronto's immigrants come from?

Factors in Deciding to Move

There are many factors that influence a person's decision to move. Forces that encourage people to leave a place are called **push factors**. These could be poor living conditions or war. Forces that draw you to another place are called **pull factors**. Good jobs, good education for children, or better living conditions can pull people to a different place. Despite these pushes and pulls, many people experience **barriers** that make it difficult to move. Family ties, travel costs, and qualifying procedures can get in the way of people's desire to move.

DURING READING

1. Imagine that you could move anywhere in the world. Where would you move? What are the factors that are pulling you to this location? What are the factors that are pushing you from your present location? What barriers might get in the way?

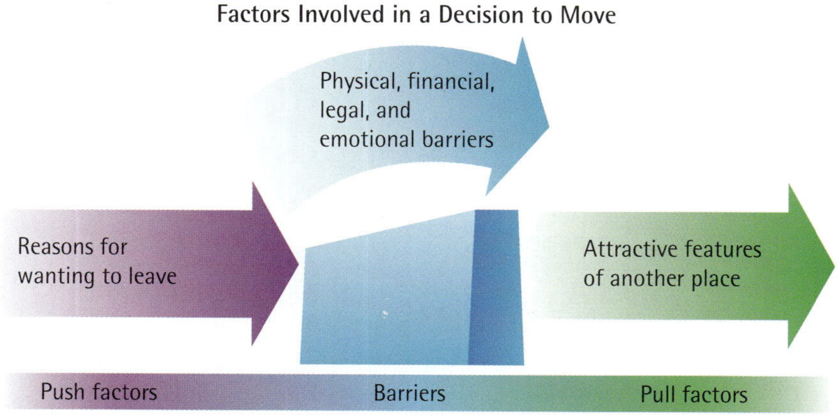

Figure 3.16

Which do you think is generally stronger—push or pull? Why?

Goods to Go

It is not just people that are on the move. Goods and information also move all over the globe. Clothes made in China or Thailand are sold in North America and Europe. People can be seen drinking American pop in India, Argentina, Australia, or Sweden. Large corporations have a great impact on the economy of a country. Many global companies introduce new products and services that people want. They provide jobs, and, therefore, income, to many people. The goods and services they produce and sell make a country's economy grow.

Figure 3.17

This boy is from Bhutan, in South Asia. Many North American products and businesses are becoming more global.

BE A GLOBAL CITIZEN

Movement of Products and People

How can we make choices in what we buy and how we travel that will make a positive difference to our world? One thing we can do is check labels and try to ensure that the products we buy are not made by companies that take advantage of workers, particularly children. There have been cases of 10-year-old children being forced to work 10 to 14 hours a day in order to produce items such as clothing and sporting goods that we may buy. Also, many farmers and small producers get very little profit from the products they sell because they must compete with large international companies. The products made through exploiting workers and by large multinational companies are less expensive and are imported into our stores every day. In order to be a thoughtful consumer, we should look for a "Fair Trade" sign or label on the item or the store in which we are shopping. This sign tells us that the people who made the item are getting a fair share of the profits.

Figure 3.18

Fair-trade stores, such as this one in California, allow us to buy fair-trade products. Check a label on another student's clothes. Then, survey the class to get an idea from which countries most clothing and types of clothing come. Which countries stand out in your survey?

Another way we can make a difference is in our choice of transportation. Estimates show that 25 to 40 percent of our greenhouse emissions come from cars and trucks on our roads. We are addicted to the use of vehicles. We need to find ways to use more energy-efficient vehicles, use vehicles less, and use alternative fuels. Some companies have chosen to do long-distance haulage only by train, a decision that lessens the number of trucks on our roads. Some people have already chosen to buy hybrid cars, small two-seater cars, scooters, and electric bikes. At some schools, students have helped organize monthly car-free days. On these days, students are encouraged to carpool, walk, bike, or take mass transit to get to school. One school in Toronto has a walking school-bus program that students can participate in once a week. Your class could help by organizing car-free days for your school, starting an environment club to organize and run events to raise environmental awareness, and beginning a campaign to make people aware of fair-trade shops and products in your neighbourhood.

Figure 3.19

These children from Morton Way Public School in Brampton, Ontario, participate in a walking school-bus program.

Figure 3.20

The solar car is powered by energy from the Sun. Solar cells convert solar energy to electrical energy to power the car.

AFTER READING

1. Canada has always been a land of immigrants and continues to accept immigrants from all over the world. Why does Canada need immigrants?
2. Using a Venn diagram, show how some factors can be both push and pull factors.

Literacy Tip

Venn Diagrams

A Venn diagram is a circle diagram that can help show how information or ideas are related. Overlapping circles are used to indicate the areas where ideas or information are the same.

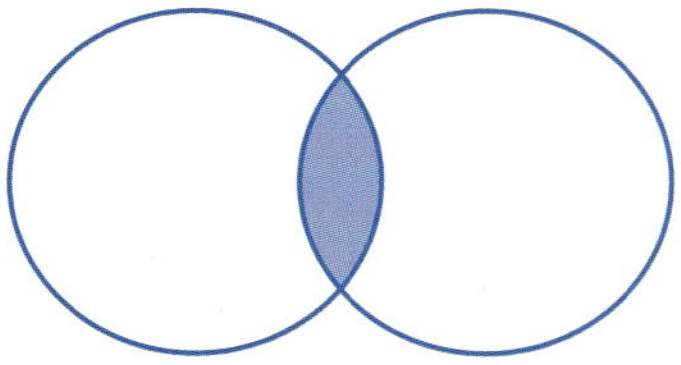

Transportation Movements

BEFORE READING

1. Consider the forms of transport you and your family use each week. Which two do you rely on most? Why do you rely on these two forms?

We have created a number of ways to move ourselves and send products all over the world. There are many kinds of transportation available.

A lot of people still depend on walking and using animals for transport. In time, we may all be whisked along on moving sidewalks. However, right now, bicycles, cars, trucks, buses, subways, trains, ships, planes, and pipelines are the major people and/or product movers.

Bikes to Go!

In some parts of the world, the bicycle is the main means of transportation. Millions of people use bicycles to travel to work and other places. Bicycles create movement patterns that are high in volume, but short in range. That is, there are a lot of them, but people cannot travel far.

Bicycles have many advantages. They require no fuel except pedal power. They are relatively cheap transport. They give the rider good exercise. They do not pollute. They can take many paths other vehicles cannot.

Figure 3.21

In Beijing, China, millions of bicycles are in use every day. Many people still cannot afford cars, but the number of cars there has increased rapidly.

Figure 3.22

Some cities in Europe, such as Paris, France, provide bicycles for people to use and then leave for others. This reduces the amount of pollution produced in the cities by cars. How can we get more people in our community to use bicycles?

Figure 3.23

Some new ideas have possibilities, too! How would you use these methods of transportation?

Figure 3.24

The car is a powerful moving force, in more ways than one. Imagine the effort and cost involved in building road tunnels through mountains like the Swiss Alps.

Cars and More Cars

The car has become the most commonly used form of transportation in the Western world. It has both short- and long-range capability. In response to this invention, roads have been built over farmland, across deserts, over (and through) mountains, through forests, and over plains.

Figure 3.25

No matter how awkward the shape of the land, such as this valley in Switzerland, a road can be built over it. Do you think there are places where no roads should be built? Why?

Figure 3.26

Even remote areas, such as this game reserve in South Africa, have been made accessible to cars. What problems might this cause?

Cars Change Cities

The designs of our urban places have been greatly affected by roads. Ring roads have been built to form a circle pattern around some cities, such as Paris and Boston. Ring roads are built to move people rapidly. They prevent traffic congestion in inner-city cores because they tend to keep people out of the downtown area. Some interior road patterns are designed with curves, crescents, and dead ends. These designs discourage traffic from residential neighbourhoods. Many people who live in quiet areas of the city do not want major roads built near them.

DURING READING

1. Why do you think cars are the most commonly used form of transportation in North America?
2. What effects do cars have on cities?

The 18 Wheeler

For both short and long trips, huge amounts of freight are moved by trucks. The 18 wheeler is now almost as common on North American highways as the car. Companies building these trucks (like those in Chatham and St. Thomas, Ontario) have become around-the-clock operations. They have to work 24 hours a day to try to keep up with the demand. Some trucks pull two trailers. Other trucks are outfitted with more axles to carry greater loads. As rail service declines, trucking fills the gap. Trains move goods more cheaply over long hauls, but they require goods to be transferred from train stations to trucks to get them to the buyers. This increases the time taken and the cost. Trucks bring goods door to door.

Fact File

Highway 401 through the Toronto region is the second busiest highway in North America.

Figure 3.27

Around large urban areas, such as Oshawa, Ontario, trucks make up a large percentage of traffic. What problems are created by this large number of trucks? What might happen if more goods were transported by railway? What changes would we have to make in our daily lives?

Road Systems

A wide range of road systems exists to accommodate the various vehicles we use. Roads range from narrow dirt lanes to complex networks of expressways. The scale and quality of the road system in a place depends on its nearness to areas of high population, markets, and other large centres.

Figure 3.28

In old towns and cities of the world, such as Paris, France, the road systems do not suit large, modern transport.

Figure 3.29

This highway is in Anaheim, California. We use a huge amount of land for our highway systems. Why should that be a concern?

The Iron Wheeler

Trains can move people and huge loads long distances. Therefore, they are an efficient mode of transportation. The development of railway systems has been very important in the spread of settlement and growth in many countries. In Canada, transcontinental railways moved large numbers of people and great quantities of materials across the continent. This helped to open up new areas and build our nation.

Today, most Canadian rail traffic is freight, not passenger trains. Our large cities use subways, a form of rail transport, to move millions of people daily. They work well over rather short distances where population density is high.

As trucking by 18 wheelers increases, rail faces high competition.

Figure 3.30

Some regions of the world depend heavily on trains. Why might trains be used more in some regions of the world than others?

Map of Europe with Railway Lines

Figure 3.31

In the Swiss Alps, a new 34 kilometre train tunnel (Lötschberg) will cut travel times by a third. How will this tunnel help reduce the 4000 trucks crossing into and out of Italy daily? A second 60 kilometre tunnel (Gotthard) will be complete in 2015. What effects will the building and use of these train tunnels have on the environment?

Figure 3.32

Fewer passenger trains are taking people across Canada today. Why do you think that is? If more people decided to use passenger trains to travel from place to place, how would our environment benefit?

Literacy Tip

Using Context Clues

If you read terms that you do not know, try the following:

- Look for clues in the sentence.
- Read the whole text to get the gist of the word.
- Look for clues in the pictures or diagrams.
- Use a dictionary, an encyclopedia, or the Internet, or ask someone to help you understand.

DURING READING

1. Think about the different types of regions in Canada. How would road building be affected by physical, human, and functional characteristics of these regions? (See Map Appendix.)
2. Should more land be used to develop better road systems in all regions? Why or why not?
3. If trains move people and huge loads long distances, why do you think 18 wheelers are such stiff competition for trains?

Across the Water

Ships have the ability to move great quantities long distances at low cost. This makes them the cheapest way to move bulky products like cars, wheat, or iron ore all over the globe.

Thousands of ships travel the world's major shipping routes daily. Ship traffic occurs on the oceans. It also occurs on inland waterways, such as rivers and lakes. To shorten distances and increase traffic, several major canals were built to permit ship traffic from one ocean to another. The Panama Canal joins the Atlantic and Pacific Oceans. The Suez Canal joins the Indian Ocean to the Mediterranean Sea.

Figure 3.33

The Panama Canal was a difficult engineering project. What would make it so difficult to build? Today, many new large ships like some container ships and supertankers will not fit the canals and locks.

Bigger Ships, Big Problem

Ships have been increasing in size every year. The newer container ships have become so large that they are too big to pass through the Panama Canal. They do not fit in many harbours. Some giant oil supertankers travelling at maximum speed take 10 kilometres to stop. Check your library or the Internet to discover just how big some of these newer passenger ships and freighters are.

Connections to Technology

Ship technology is being revolutionized to become greener to protect the natural environment. In 2005, the E/S Orcelle was shown to be the innovative, sustainable cargo ship of the future. It may hit the water in 2020. Already in service is the green ferry, Solar Sailor, that whisks 100 passengers a trip across Sydney Harbour, Australia. This hybrid ferry is solar and wind powered.

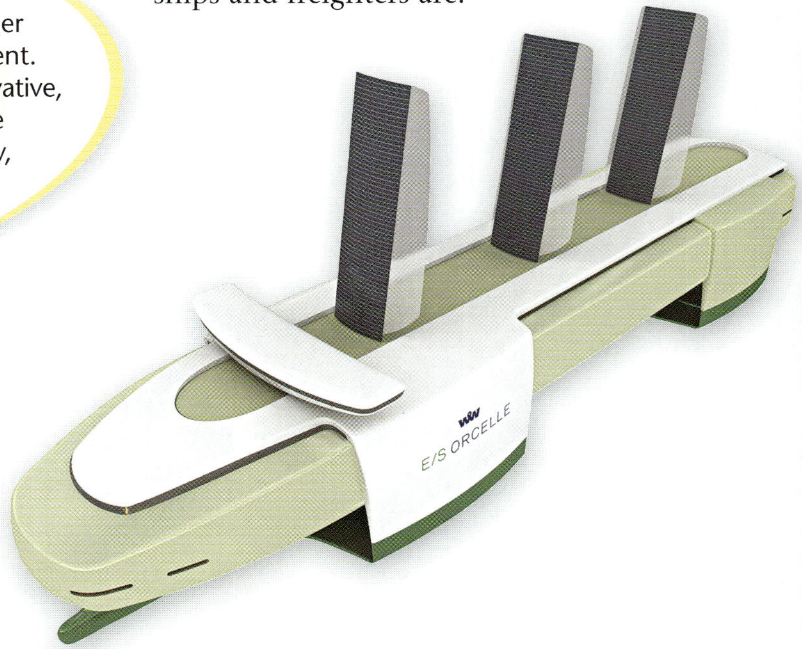

Figure 3.34

The Orcelle will combine at least three alternative power sources. It will run on wind, Sun, and wave power.

Figure 3.35

Note the large solar panels on the Solar Sailor ferry. They power the vessel over 90 percent of the time.

By Air

Several thousand aircraft are flying at any moment during a normal day in the air space above North America. Many types of aircraft carry people, mail, and cargo to all points around the globe.

Figure 3.36

The Airbus 380 is the largest commercial plane in the world. It can carry 580 passengers. This is about three to four times what normal commercial jets carry. The Airbus 380 will make per-person costs lower because it can carry more people each time it flies. The competition by Boeing is a smaller but lighter plane that will cut fuel costs by 20 percent. Which do you want to see in our skies? Why?

Some Regional Air Routes

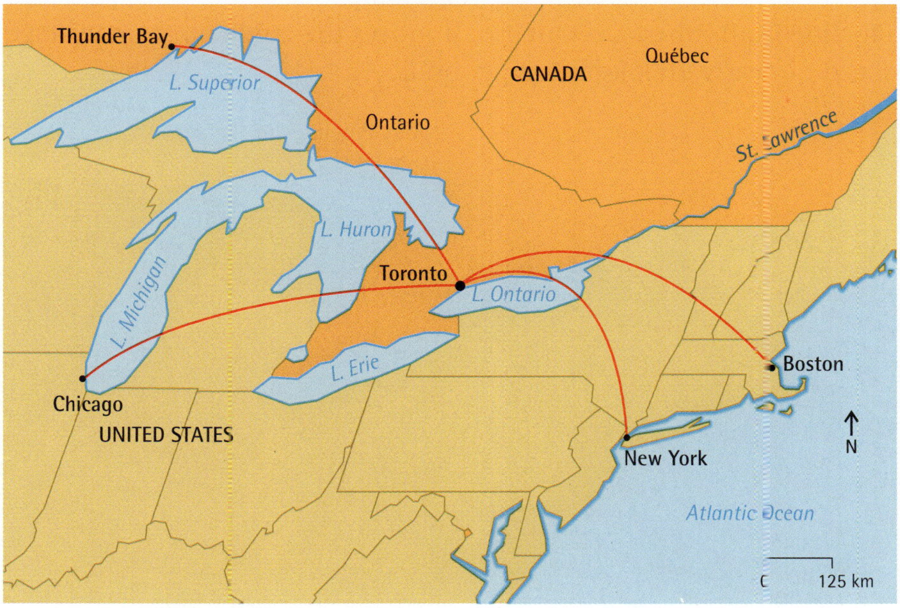

Figure 3.37

Some of our airports are so busy that planes are either arriving or departing at a rate of two per minute. In an 18-hour day, that is 2160 planes. Our friendly skies may soon have traffic jams, too!

DURING READING

1. Imagine that you are the captain of a large container ship, and you need to transport your freight from Toronto, Canada to Tokyo, Japan. Travelling by inland waterways and then by ocean, which is the best route? What could shorten the distance? (See Map Appendix.)
2. Planes consider winds, weather, and the shortest route possible to cut time and cost. Long flights follow the Great Circle routes, which travel in a circle around Earth's circumference. Using a globe, follow the Great Circle routes from Toronto to Tokyo. Why is the Great Circle route a shorter route?

Fact File

A few space tourists have paid several million dollars to fly in space. Seats on the shuttle spacecraft are being sold to people who want to become the world's first space tourists. One company has even sold seats on a Moon flight. When do you think tourism will actually begin in outer space?

Pipe It On Through

Most of us are unaware of how much we rely on pipelines. Every time you get water from a drinking fountain or flush a toilet, you use a pipeline. We use pipelines to move water, waste, oil, gas, chemicals, and coal. Foods such as grains (mixed with a liquid) can be pumped through pipelines.

Pipelines have several advantages. Materials move continuously with little labour involved. The movements are direct from point to point and require little maintenance. The big problem is the cost of installation.

Large pipelines (up to 120 centimetres in diameter) move oil in huge quantities. In Canada, our largest pipeline is the Interprovincial Pipeline from Alberta to Ontario. It moves the crude oil at an average speed of nearly 16 kilometres per hour.

Figure 3.38

These are the pipelines that carry just one resource to us —natural gas.

Gas Pipelines in Canada

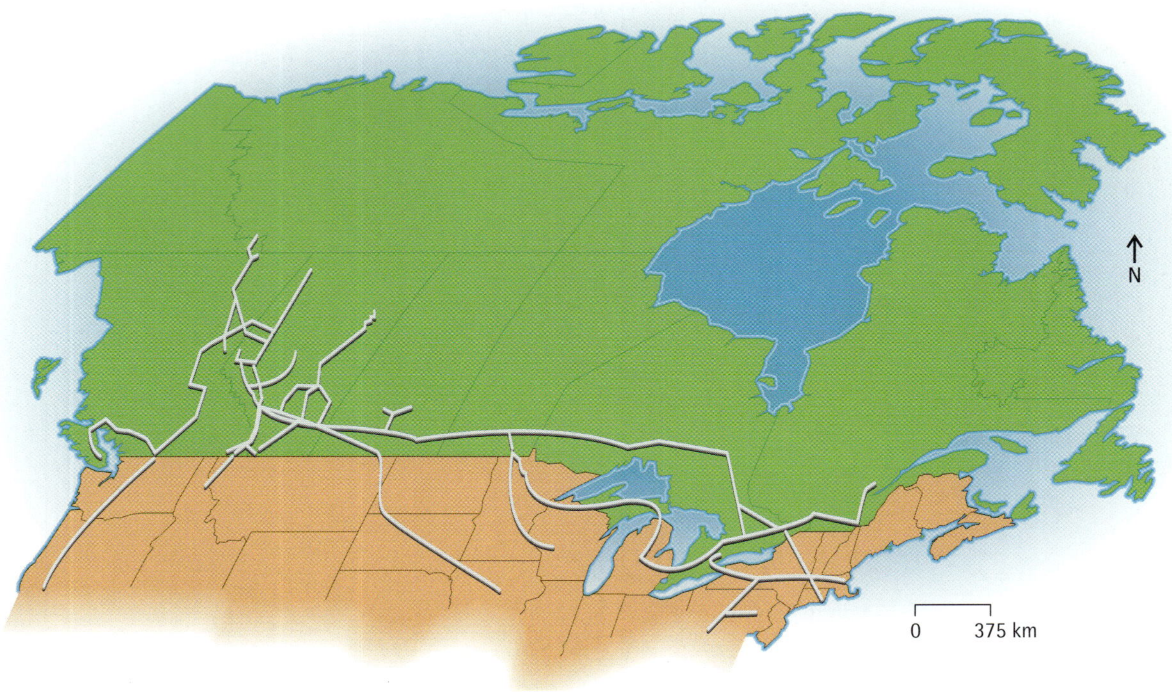

The Underground Network

Many different types of pipelines are arranged within our urban areas. There are networks of water pipes, storm sewers, and sanitary sewers running under our cities. Commercial enterprises supply our homes with piped natural gas.

Figure 3.39

This oil pipeline is being built in Alberta, from Edmonton to Fort McMurray. How does the use of pipelines affect the environment? Overall, could pipelines be considered a green choice for transporting products?

Figure 3.40

We seldom think about the millions of kilometres of pipes beneath us. However, they are critical to many services we receive.

DURING READING

1. What could be transported through pipelines in the future?
2. How could pipelines be changed to increase their possible uses?

Needs Drive Movement

We do not grow all our own food. Much of it comes to a grocery store from many different sources throughout the world. Thus, food moves from its source of production to reach us. To do this, food often moves across large distances.

We do not produce the electricity that runs our lights and appliances. It is moved or transmitted to us through a power grid or system. The same is true for other resources that become the products that we use.

From Wood to Woodwind

A high-quality clarinet is made from granadilla. This tropical, dark wood grows in the rainforests of Central America. From felling the tree, the wood begins the first of many moves. It is taken out of the forest to a mill and cut to size. From the mill, it is trucked to a port and loaded onto a ship. Then, it is moved north along the Pacific Ocean coast to Los Angeles. From there, it is sent by rail to Indiana where a clarinet manufacturer makes clarinets. The instruments are shipped by truck from the company to music stores all across North America. You (or your school) may buy one. Its final move is to you.

1. Many resources and products are moved to us from their source of production. How many can you list? Compare your list with a partner. Can you add to your list?
2. How has the movement of resources, products, money, and ideas improved our quality of life?

Figure 3.41

Trace the movement from a rainforest to you.

Making a Clarinet

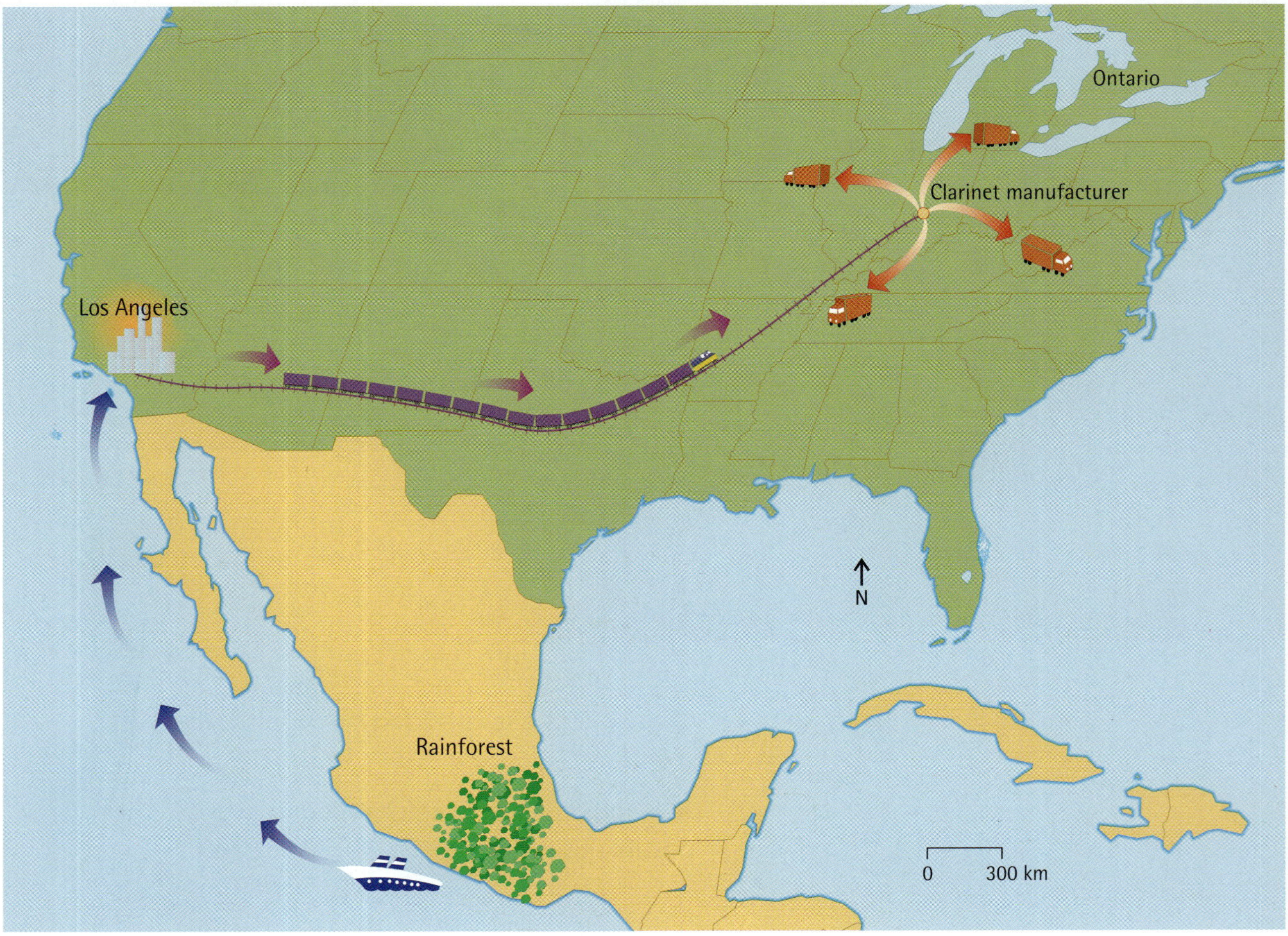

Trading around the World

Resources are not equally distributed around the world. For example, Australia has a lot of bauxite (aluminum ore). Canada has no bauxite, but it has a lot of hydro power to make the bauxite into aluminum. This establishes a basis for trade. We import bauxite, use our hydro power to make it into aluminum, and then export aluminum. Once a basis for trade is established, movement of products will occur.

Figure 3.42

An employee works inside the Alcan plant in Alma, Québec. Canada is number one in world aluminum production. How is that possible without Canada having any bauxite? How does Canada benefit from unequal resource distribution?

Figure 3.43

This world's largest bauxite mine in Huntly, Western Australia, sells its bauxite to Canada. How does Australia benefit?

Electronic Movement

Money moves, ideas move, information and messages move. Technology—the Internet and other telecommunication systems—has made it possible for these things to happen in an instant. Putting satellites in orbit allows us to relay signals and transmit information. We can receive or send information in electronic format to any place on Earth. Ideas and information once took centuries to spread across the world. They now can move around the world in less than a second.

Figure 3.44

Satellites like this Landsat can be used to produce images of Earth's surface. Geographers use these images to monitor and survey the environment. What else could such a satellite be used for?

Connections to Technology

Many Canadian info-tech companies are world leaders, especially when it comes to new devices such as the Blackberry, developed by Research in Motion in Kitchener-Waterloo, Ontario. Companies must spend large budget amounts on research and development to keep their market edge.

After Reading

1. Examine the photos showing roads on page 57. What are three physical characteristics that would help with building roads in a region? What are three physical characteristics that would limit or interfere with road building in a region?
2. Three critical factors that affect choice of transportation type are time, distance, and environmental impact. Create a chart to show which is the best choice in the following situations:
   - coal being moved 2000 kilometres
   - an important parcel going 700 kilometres
   - cars made in Italy to sell in Canada
   - students going to school 3 kilometres away
3. Today, you can see events such as floods, battles, or spacecraft launches as they are happening. A hundred years ago, this would not have been possible. How do you think modern technology (TV, computers, the Internet) makes you think differently about this kind of event than people who lived 100 years ago did?

Fact File

Over half of Canadians either use e-mail or browse the Internet daily. The top five world languages used on the Internet are English (35 percent), Chinese (14 percent), Spanish (9 percent), Japanese (9 percent), and German (7 percent).

Movement Creates Patterns

BEFORE READING

1. Create a mental image of your neighbourhood or community. Imagine the roads, houses, public buildings, and so on. Describe how the roads, homes, and public buildings are arranged.

Figure 3.45

Geographers describe pattern using the terms "point," "line," "area," and "volume." Find all of these features in this sketch.

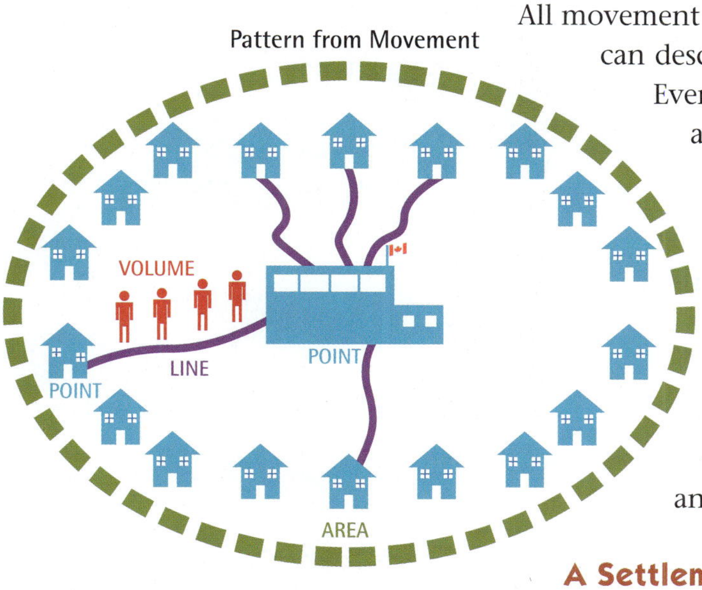

All movement creates a **pattern**. Using geographic methods, we can describe these patterns and try to account for them. Every pattern has four components: points, lines, areas, and volume. Your school and where you live are two points. The two points are connected by a road or line. Your place is in a neighbourhood or area. The number of students moving along the lines is a volume.

Patterns for Planning

Recognizing, analyzing, and explaining patterns is important in understanding relationships and planning for the future.

A Settlement Pattern

River valleys encourage people to settle along the river banks. This pattern involves the houses (points), the river (line), the river valley (area), and the number of settlers living there (volume). Town planners must take the settlement pattern into account to maintain the health of the ecosystem that is dependent upon the river.

DURING READING

1. Using the mental map of your neighbourhood or community that you created in the Before Reading above, identify patterns of points, lines, areas, and volume.

Figure 3.46

Find examples of point, line, area, and volume in this picture of Charlevoix, Québec.

Figure 3.47

What might happen to the volume if a new community is built close to the migration line?

A Migration Pattern

Many animals and birds migrate, or move for feeding and mating. In North America, many migrations follow a seasonal pattern. Caribou migrate across vast distances in the Arctic tundra. The four components of a pattern in caribou migration are as follows:

- the points (the caribou feeding grounds and mating grounds)
- the line (the migration path)
- the area (the tundra)
- the volume (the number of caribou in the herd)

It is important to know this migration pattern before any changes can be planned. Companies and governments want to extract natural resources from the area. They want to build communities there and lay pipelines across the tundra. To maintain the health of the caribou herd, the migration pattern must be studied and taken into account before any activity takes place in the area.

Figure 3.48

Picture your community. Think of examples of each of these kinds of arrangement.

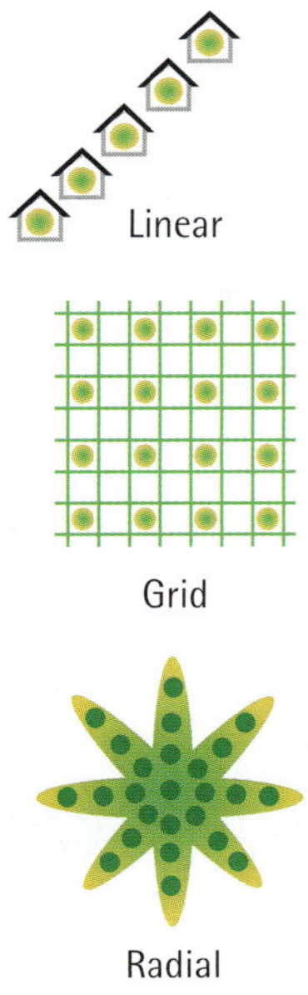

What Kind of Pattern Is It?

Geographers use other qualities to describe patterns. Patterns can show quantity by using descriptive terms such as dense (very thick), as in a dense forest; or sparse (very thin), as in a sparsely populated area.

Arrangements are given descriptive terms such as in linear (in a line), as in a row of houses; grid (like graph paper), as streets in a city; or radial (as in the radius of a circle), like the arrangement of petals on a flower.

AFTER READING

1. Sketch the pattern of halls and classrooms in your school. Label the four pattern components of point, line, area, and volume on your sketch.
2. Select two animals or birds that migrate. Imagine their migration patterns. How would their migration patterns differ?

Knowledge and Understanding

1. Create an organizer that shows five types of natural movements and five types of human-related movements. For each movement, state the main cause (for example, for earthquakes, the cause is plate movement). You can organize information about the types of movements and their causes in a web, diagram, or a chart.

Inquiry/Research and Communication Skills

2. Choose a manufacturing industry that makes products from raw materials (for example, a steel plant uses iron ore to make steel; a pulp and paper company converts logs into paper products). Research to find out the following:

   a) Where do these manufacturing companies get their raw materials?

   b) What form or forms of transportation are used to bring them to the company from the source area?

   c) What products does this company manufacture from the raw materials?

   d) Where do the products go next? How are they transported during this step?

Figure 3.49

How were trees cut down before such technology?

3. **a)** Trace a tomato's journey to the tomato sauce on your pizza (or to a fast-food outlet) from a source outside Ontario in winter. If you want to show your tomato's journey on a map, look back at Figure 3.41 to see how it is done. You will need to find answers to the following questions in order to discover your tomato's journey:

   - Where are tomatoes grown outside of Canada during the winter months?
   - Where are tomatoes processed into tomato sauce?
   - Where does your grocery store (or choice of fast-food outlet) get its tomato sauce?

   b) This journey has hidden costs along the way. There are costs to people and to the environment. List three.

4. Trucking has had an enormous effect on the decline of rail traffic. What would be two positive effects of encouraging more rail traffic? What would be two negative effects?

5. Use a map of your local area to track your movements for three days. Include all activities where you move to a place outside your home (for example, going to school, going to hockey, or visiting friends).

   a) Plot the movement lines on your map. Make the line wider if you travel the same path more than once. What kind of pattern do the movement lines create?

   b) Do you notice that there are large areas of the map where you would seldom travel? These areas are the parts of your community you know the least. Think about how well you know Ontario. How is the pattern of your movements similar to the patterns related to your understanding of Ontario? Why might the patterns be similar?

6. Here in Canada, we have had major landslides and avalanches (snowslides) that have been disastrous. They include the following:

   - the Frank slide in Alberta in 1903
   - the St. Jean de Vianney slide in Québec in 1971
   - the avalanche on Baffin Island in 1999, which buried a school

a) Research one of these disasters. Find answers to the following questions:

- Where did it happen?
- Who was affected?
- How big was the slide or avalanche?
- What was the extent of the damage?
- Why did it happen?
- What happened in the hours and days that followed the slide or avalanche?
- What rescue efforts were made?
- How could this slide or avalanche have been made less disastrous?

b) How will you share what you have learned from your research? Choose from one of the following options:

- Write a news report of the disaster. Then, create an audio or video recording of your news report.
- Write a front-page news story about the disaster. Remember to include a gripping headline and to answer all the research questions in your news story.
- Create a three-dimensional model to show the disaster area, and present your model and what you have learned from your research in an oral presentation.
- Create a PowerPoint presentation about your chosen slide or avalanche.
- Create an informative poster that answers all the research questions about your chosen disaster.

7. What new ways of moving people and goods do you think will have developed 100 years from now? Describe one new way in detail. How do you think it will work? What special features will it have? What type of energy will it use? Which natural resources will it use?

8. Imagine you are a journalist. You are assigned to investigate the building of either the Panama Canal or the Suez Canal.

a) Sketch a map of the canal you have chosen.

b) Find the answers to the following questions:

- When was it built?
- Why was it built?
- How does it work?
- What physical obstacles were faced?
- How long did it take to build?
- How many people were involved?
- Who controls these canals today?

c) How will you report your findings? You could choose one of the following:

- Write the results of your investigation in a news story or magazine article.
- Write and create an audio recording of your report for radio or the Internet.
- Write and create a video recording of your report for television or the Internet.

Map, Globe, and Graphic Skills

9. **a)** Some communities in central and northern Canada, Greenland, and parts of Asia and Africa have no road links to other communities. Check out an atlas to find these and other areas of the world without road links between communities.

b) On an outline map of the world, create regions that show continental areas as one of the following:

- no roads (sparse or void)
- some roads (medium density)
- many roads (high density)

c) Can you find another theme map in your atlas that has a similar pattern?

10. Many commercial jets fly to one centre, then to another, and then return to their base. This pattern creates a flight triangle.

a) Create a possible flight path, like the one described, for jets flying to major North American cities. Use an atlas to measure the distance of the first flight and the second. Calculate the distance of the return flight.

b) Flights from Toronto to Moscow may sometimes fly over the North Pole. Why?

Application

11 Consider your breakfast.

a) Plot the locations of the source countries for the food you ate. Make a map of the routes taken by these foods in reaching your table.

b) Compile all the countries identified by you and others in your class onto a master map for the whole class. This map shows some of the world connections to your global breakfast.

12 Draw a cartoon to show some growing concerns about increasing air traffic or road traffic. Remember that cartoons tell their story by the action shown in the illustration in each frame and by what characters say in speech balloons.

13 Choose one piece of clothing, such as your jeans or a T-shirt.

a) Where did the material come from that was used to make it?

b) How did this material get to the factory that manufactured it?

c) How did it get from the factory to you?

Figure 3.50

The next time you buy a piece of clothing, think about where it was made and how it got to the store.

4 Environment

IN THIS CHAPTER

- explain the theme of environment in geography
- use the new terms in this chapter correctly as you investigate the topics
- construct questions to help guide and connect your research on an environmental issue
- locate and use helpful information from primary and secondary sources
- share the results of research about different points of view on an issue using options such as computer slide shows, videos, websites, oral presentations, written notes and reports, drawings, tables, charts, diagrams, maps, models, and graphs

KEY VOCABULARY

atmosphere
balance of nature
biome
biosphere
carbon dioxide
desalination
ecology
ecosystem
endangered
extinct
finite
greenhouse effect
habitat
hydrosphere
introduced species
lithosphere
mantle
nitrogen cycle
oxygen
ozone layer
photosynthesis
steward
sustainable

The Environment

BEFORE READING

1. What do you think of when you hear the word "environment"?
2. In one minute, list all the words you can think of that have something to do with the environment.
3. Compile a class list of words related to the environment that you can check off/add to as you work through the chapter.

Our environment is everything that is on, in, or surrounding Earth. We are part of the environment, and we have an effect on it. At this moment, you are changing the environment. As you breathe in, you are taking **oxygen** out of the air. As you breathe out, you are putting **carbon dioxide** into the air.

People are becoming more concerned about the environment. They are noticing that Earth is changing. Our activities are affecting Earth in many ways, from polluting our water to warming the atmosphere.

Figure 4.1

When we look at the sky during daytime, the atmosphere appears to be of different colours. For instance, at sunset, the atmosphere may look red or orange due to the Sun's rays being scattered by dust, water vapour, and smoke.

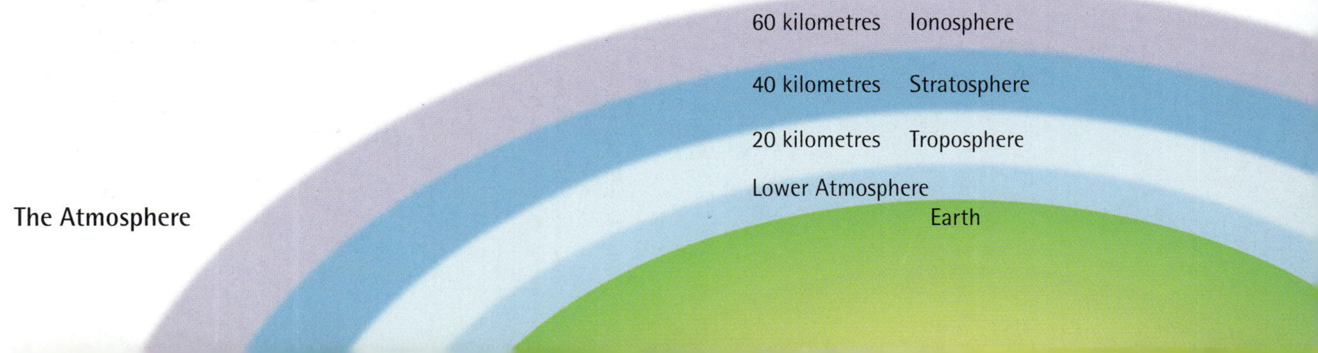

Everything we do affects the environment in some way—we change it as we use it. We cut down trees, mine for minerals, catch fish, use water, and walk on the grass. Every one of our actions is an interaction with the environment. We must have a good understanding of our environment and how it works. Our very survival depends on it!

The Components of the Environment

The environment has four parts to it. They are

- the **atmosphere**: air
- the **hydrosphere**: water
- the **lithosphere**: Earth's surface (rocky crust)
- the **biosphere**: living things; plants and animals, including people

The Atmosphere

Our atmosphere is made up of gases: nitrogen (76 percent), oxygen (21 percent), carbon dioxide (0.6 percent), and other gases. It has four layers: the ionosphere, the stratosphere, the troposphere, and the lower atmosphere. All life on Earth depends on the atmosphere. It allows us to breathe. It shields us from the direct rays of the Sun. It supplies water for the land. The nitrogen and carbon dioxide that plants need to grow come from the atmosphere.

Connections to Music

R. Murray Schafer, a Canadian composer, said, "A mountain stream is like a chord of many notes." He even wrote a special set of songs called "Music for a Mountain Stream." Many of the early explorers wrote and sang songs to ease the hard work of paddling their canoes. Use your library to find other music related to water.

The Hydrosphere

The hydrosphere includes all the water on the surface of Earth: oceans, lakes, rivers, and the frozen ice of the polar caps. The surface of Earth is about 70 percent water and only about 30 percent land. Maybe our planet should have been called Water instead of Earth! Just one ocean, the Pacific Ocean, takes up almost half of Earth's entire surface. Our oceans supply most of the precipitation that falls on the land. They are our giant reservoirs.

Figure 4.2

This illustration shows the world's water supply. What does the small blue dot suggest to you about how we treat and use fresh water?

The World's Water Supply

95 percent of all the water on Earth is salt water.

5 percent of the water is fresh water, but most of that is either frozen or underground.

- All the water on Earth
- Fresh water on Earth
- Fresh water that is not ice or underground

That little blue dot represents the tiny amount of fresh water that is not frozen or underground.

The Lithosphere

The lithosphere is the crust (the surface) of Earth. It is the layer, about 5 kilometres to 50 kilometres thick, sitting on top of Earth's **mantle**. The lithosphere is composed of different rocks and is the least dense of Earth's layers. Soils and other loose materials form a thin skin-like covering over most of the crust. The lithosphere provides us with the nutrients needed to grow crops, and with natural resources like metals, oil, and natural gas.

LITERACY TIP

Using Word Parts

When you come across a word that you do not understand, look to see if the word has a "root." New words are often created by adding beginnings (prefixes) or endings (suffixes) to a root word. Keeping a list of common root words, prefixes, and suffixes in your notebook can help you figure out the meaning of unfamiliar words.

Figure 4.3

Note the different layers of Earth. The deepest hole we have drilled into Earth has not penetrated the upper mantle. The thinnest parts of the crust are found under the oceans. These parts are about 3 kilometres thick. Why might the crust be thinnest under the oceans?

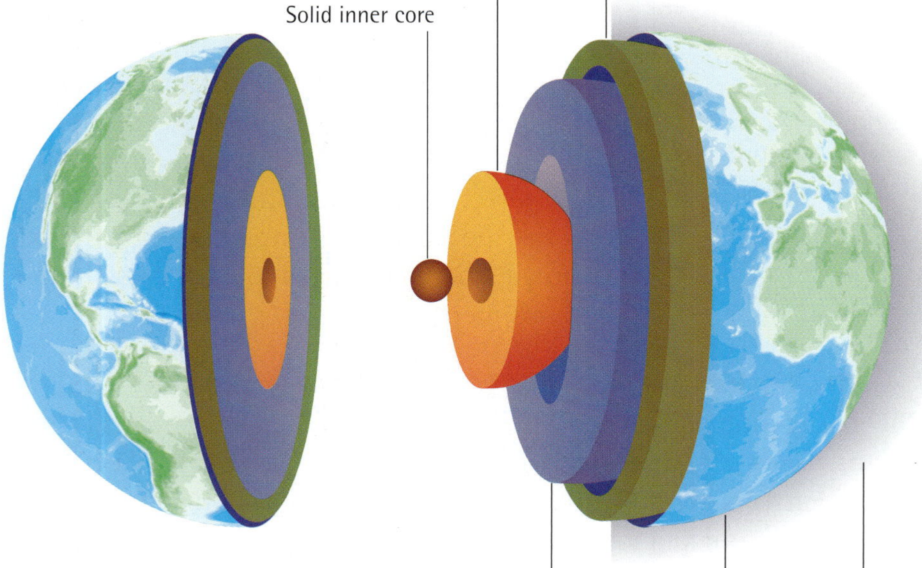

Fact File

Scientists estimate that there are over 50 million species of plants and animals! Nearly all the larger species have been found and identified. However, each year, we find nearly 5000 more in remote areas of land and sea. To speed up the search process dramatically, the University of Guelph has a new genetic bar-code system for cataloguing and identifying new species.

The Biosphere

The biosphere is the life zone of Earth. It is the part of Earth where plants and animals live. This zone overlaps with the other three spheres: the lower layers of the atmosphere, the first few metres of the lithosphere, and all of the hydrosphere. Millions of living species are found in these spheres all over Earth.

DURING READING

1. Why does life exist only on the biosphere and not in the upper layers of the atmosphere or in the different layers of the lithosphere?

The Nitrogen Cycle

Figure 4.4

People have affected the nitrogen cycle by burning fossil fuels, like coal, gas, and oil. This puts extra nitrogen into the atmosphere. As well, we are using large amounts of fertilizers. These add nitrogen to the soil. From the soil, it seeps into the water supply and causes pollution there. Examine the diagram closely. Can you explain how this extra nitrogen could cause acid rain?

The connections among the parts of the environment are well shown by the **nitrogen cycle**. Plants need nitrogen to grow. The atmosphere is composed mainly of nitrogen. Large amounts are released into the air from Earth by volcanic action. More is stored in volcanic rocks. Plants cannot take in nitrogen in its gas state from the air. They need to take nitrogen in through their roots from the soil. Bacteria, and some crops like peas and alfalfa, change the nitrogen they find in the soil. When plants die, their nitrogen goes back into the atmosphere. Our oceans also have nitrogen, mainly in algae. That nitrogen is also used and eventually recycled to the atmosphere.

Nitrogen Cycle

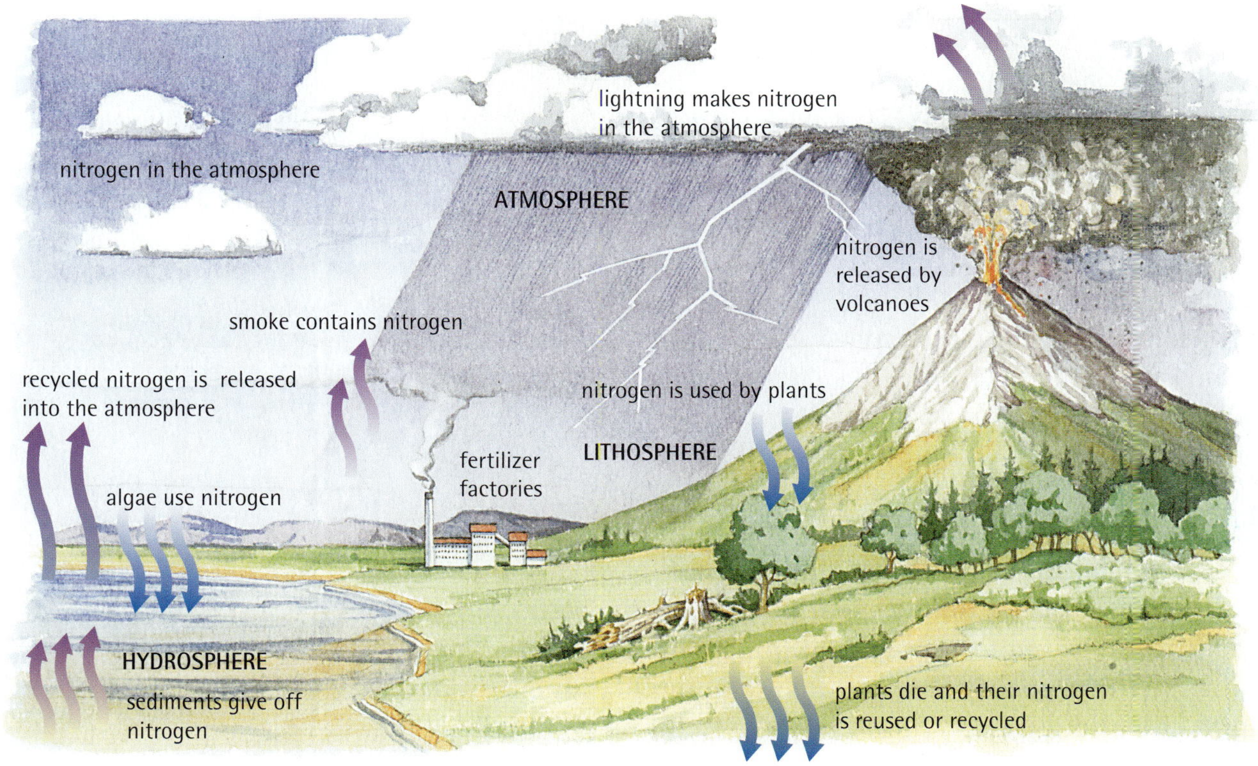

AFTER READING

1. a) Identify two ways in which humans have affected the nitrogen cycle.

   b) What two actions could humans take to reduce the amount of nitrogen they add to the environment?

2. The name of each of the four spheres is made up of a prefix added to the root word "sphere."

   a) Use your dictionary to find the meaning of the root word "sphere." Then, find the meanings of the four prefixes: "atmo," "hydro," "litho," and "bio." Make sure that you use the prefix definition if more than one meaning is defined.

   b) Now add the meaning of each prefix to the meaning of the root word "sphere." Is the combined meaning similar to the definition of each of these spheres? For example: "atmo" (steam or vapour) + "sphere" (a globe-shaped body) = "atmosphere" (the mass of air surrounding Earth).

Our Environment— The Storehouse of Resources

BEFORE READING

1. What does the word "resource" mean to you?
2. In your opinion, what are some of the most important resources that humans need to survive? In which spheres of Earth do you find these resources? Compare your answer with a partner.

Our world is **finite**. That means that there is only so much air, water, rock, plant, and animal material on Earth. Earth is like a spaceship with only so many resources on board. There are no supply ships to drop in and give us a refill. This makes us **stewards** or caretakers aboard this spaceship. We must preserve and wisely use what we have.

Resources from the Atmosphere

To stay healthy and work well, there must be clean air for us and other living things. The major components of the air—nitrogen, oxygen, and carbon dioxide—are essential for all life.

High up in the stratosphere (about 25 kilometres high) is the **ozone layer**. This layer of ozone gases blocks out much of the harmful ultraviolet (UV) light from the Sun. Ultraviolet light can cause skin cancer and eye problems in people, and it harms trees, plants, and animals.

Ozone Depletion

Recent studies have shown that the ozone layer of the atmosphere has become thinner over various parts of Earth, particularly over Antarctica. Our protection is weakening. Humans are the greatest threat to the ozone layer. When we use things like air conditioners, spray cans, refrigerators, and some manufacturing processes, we put ozone-destroying chemicals like chlorine, fluorine, and hydrocarbons into the atmosphere. Worldwide co-operation is needed to stop the damage.

Global Warming

Our activities affect the atmosphere in another way. Burning fossil fuels like oil and gas is causing the release of more and more carbon dioxide and other gases into the atmosphere. This is causing higher average temperatures and other changes to Earth systems. This **greenhouse effect** in the atmosphere is now a major concern due to the impacts seen in recent years.

DURING READING

1. As you read through the following sections, you will notice that there are several problems found on Earth's different spheres. Use your note-taking skills to identify and summarize what each problem is, what causes it, and what effect or effects result from each problem.

LITERACY TIP

Cause and Effect

To understand why things happen, we need to look for cause/effect relationships. A cause is an action, event, or problem that makes something happen. The effect is the result of that action, event, or problem. Often an action, event, or problem can have many causes and many effects that are both positive and negative.

Cause(s) Problem Effect(s)

Fact File

The Environmental Protection Agency (EPA) in the United States has predicted there will be 153 million cases of skin cancer worldwide by 2075 unless we act to stop ozone depletion. In Australia, children in many areas may not attend school without wearing hats and sunscreen.

Figure 4.5

Carbon dioxide concentrations have dramatically increased since the middle of the twentieth century. Why does the graph show such a jump after 1950?

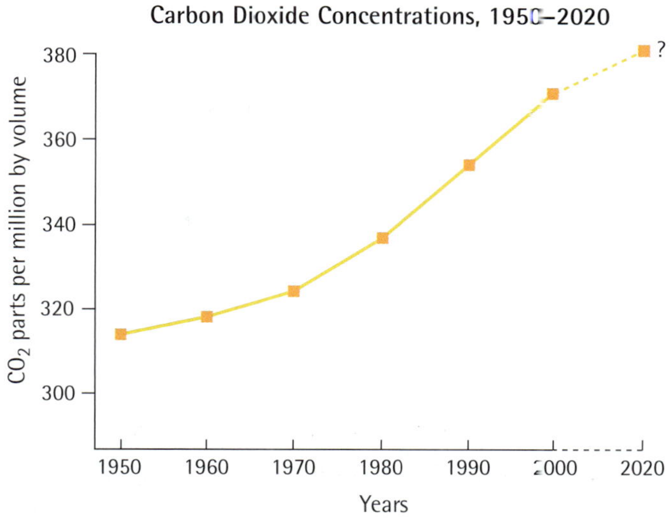

GEOSKILLS

Reading a Graph

Line graphs are a combination of numerical data and visual information. Learning how to read and create a line graph can become easy if you remember TAPP: Title, Axes, Pattern, and Purpose.

Let us read the graph below:

1. Read the *title*—Canada's Greenhouse Gas Emissions, 1990–2004. This title tells you that you are reading the amount of CO_2 (carbon dioxide) gas Canada has released into the atmosphere over a 15-year period.
2. Read the two *axes*. The *x*-axis (horizontal) is labelled "Years." The *y*-axis (vertical) is labelled "Kilotonnes (in thousands) CO_2 ^{eq}." At this point, if you are unsure of a term, it is important to look it up or ask a teacher for help.
3. Look for a *pattern* in the graph. This graph shows a line steadily increasing over the years.
4. Now let us determine *purpose*. You need to ask yourself this question: What is this graph telling me about Canada's greenhouse gas emissions? This graph shows that Canada's greenhouse gas emissions have continued to rise. Now, as a reader, it is up to you to relate what this graph shows to information you already know about greenhouse gas and climate change. Connecting what you already know with what the graph shows will help you draw a final conclusion about the purpose of this graph.

Figure 4.6

This graph shows Canada's greenhouse gas emissions for the years 1990 to 2004.

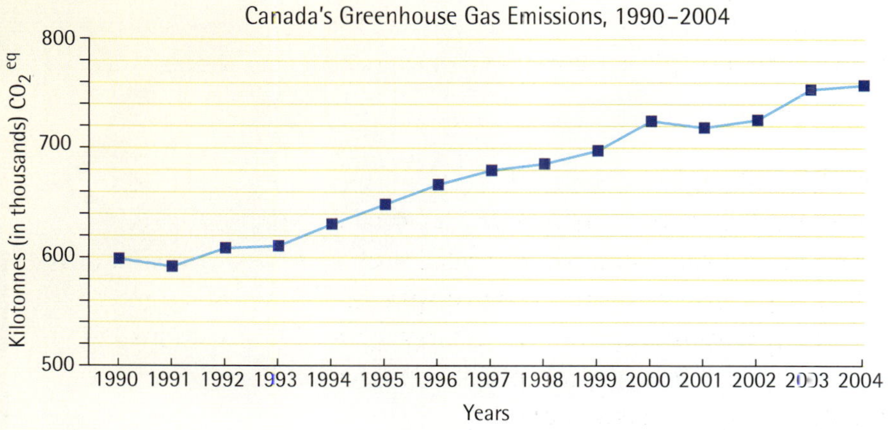

Resources from the Hydrosphere

Fresh water is critical to all life on Earth. Farmers need fresh water to grow crops. Industry uses water. We need water for all of our domestic uses. We now have ways to make fresh water from the salt water in the oceans (**desalination**), but the technology is complicated and very expensive.

Figure 4.7

This desalination plant is located in Spain. It costs over 40 times more money to make desalinated water than to deliver fresh water in southern Ontario. Some desert nations in the Middle East like Kuwait use desalinated water.

Freshwater Problem

From 1900 to 1950, the Great Lakes, particularly Lake Huron and Lake Superior, had large lake trout fisheries. The opening of the St. Lawrence Seaway in 1954 changed all that. A type of eel, the lamprey eel, made its way through the Seaway and into the Great Lakes. The lamprey eel was not a natural species to the Great Lakes ecosystem. It became an **introduced species**. It attacked the lake trout and no natural predators stopped it from multiplying. The rapid growth of the lamprey eel meant the rapid decline of the lake trout. Once a major industry, the fishing industry is now disappearing.

Figure 4.8

The lamprey eel attaches itself to the lake trout with its mouth. Then, it feeds on the blood and flesh of the fish. There are many other species affecting our lakes and land. Can you name an introduced species of insect that is causing problems for southern Ontario's trees?

A close-up of a lamprey eel's mouth

Fact File

Zebra mussels, round goby, ruffe, and purple loosestrife are just four of the 87 known introduced species increasing quickly in number and causing a variety of problems in the Great Lakes region. Research to find out how one of these introduced species got into the Great Lakes region and to find out what is being done to control it.

Resources of the Lithosphere

We use the top layer of soil at the surface of the lithosphere for farming. We quarry rock, sand, and gravel from it to build homes, buildings, roads, and other structures. We mine the lithosphere for useful metals and non-metallic minerals. We extract coal, oil, and gas for our energy.

When we take resources from the lithosphere, that is it! They are gone forever. It took millions of years for oil to form. When the world's supply of oil runs out, it runs out. There will be no more. We must be very mindful about wise use. Resources that cannot be renewed are not **sustainable**. However, they can and must be managed wisely.

AFTER READING

1. a) Why is it important to reduce ozone depletion? What are two ways you can reduce ozone depletion?

   b) Why is it important to reduce global warming? What are two ways you can reduce global warming?

2. For each sphere, construct a chart with these headings: Resource Type (living/non-living), Major Uses, and Renewability (high/low/none). List two resources from each sphere.

Ecosystems

BEFORE READING

1. If "eco" refers to the environment, and a "system" is a group of things or parts that work together and combine to form a whole, how could you use these word parts to explain what an "ecosystem" is? How close is your definition to what you learn in the next section?

An **ecosystem** is a balanced arrangement of plants and animals and their surrounding physical environment. All parts of an ecosystem are related to each other, and all parts depend on each other. The biosphere contains many different ecosystems. They can be very small like a pond ecosystem, or they can be large, like a desert ecosystem. We must understand these systems and how they work in order to make good planning decisions and manage our resources wisely.

Literacy Tip

Vocabulary Trees

Visual cues, like a vocabulary tree, are good ways to remember words with common "roots." Draw a tree with several branches. Write the common root word in the root area of the tree. Record the definition in the trunk of the tree. Write words that have the same root on each tree branch. Then, write a definition and a sentence for each word.

Ecosystems contain both biotic (living) elements like people, plants, and animals; and abiotic (non-living) elements like water and rock. The place where living things survive is their **habitat**. A combination of ecosystems and other factors like weather and temperature make up the environment of a particular area.

Some of the world's largest land ecosystems are also our largest vegetation regions, or **biomes** (see Map Appendix). The tropical rain forest, the coniferous forest, and the tundra are all biomes. Larger ecosystems tend to have a wide range of species. The study of ecosystems is called **ecology**.

Give and Take

The plants and animals of an ecosystem are all struggling to survive. To be successful, each plant or animal makes use of special features that allow it to take what it needs from the ecosystem. Plants use their roots and leaves to get nutrients, while animals and birds use their legs, talons, or teeth.

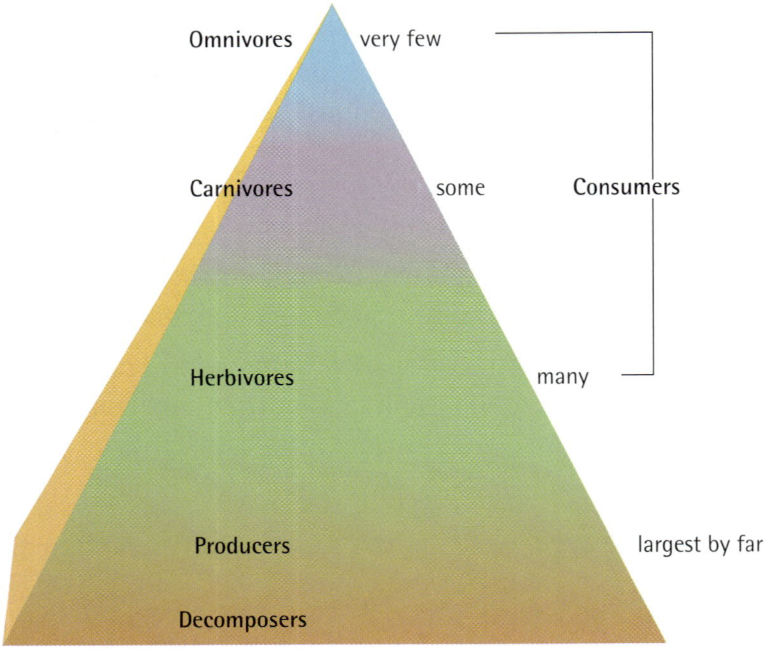

Figure 4.9

All the life forms in an ecosystem form a food pyramid. At the base of the pyramid are the decomposers. These life forms break down dead plant and animal matter and return nutrients to the soil. Plants, or producers, make up the next level of the food pyramid. Plants are the only living things that can make their own food. Above these producers are the consumers. This group is composed of herbivores (plant eaters) like rabbits, carnivores (flesh eaters) like wolves or hawks, and omnivores (plant and animal eaters) like human beings.

Each member of an ecosystem also adds something to the system. Small animals are the food source for larger animals. Some organisms such as earthworms loosen soil by burrowing through the layers. The decay of all organisms adds to the soil's fertility. A rotten, hollow tree becomes a home for squirrels and raccoons. Beaver dams make better environments for fish by creating natural ponds. This give-and-take is vital to the health of the ecosystem. Changing any one part of an ecosystem changes the whole. No matter how small, any change causes a ripple effect that impacts the entire ecosystem.

Food Pyramids and Webs

The key to all life on Earth is the Sun. The Sun provides warmth. It gives the energy used by plants to make their food. Plants use solar energy to change water and carbon dioxide into a kind of sugar that they use as food for growth. This process, called **photosynthesis**, produces oxygen as a by-product. Since most animals need oxygen to survive, they are dependent on plants.

Figure 4.10

Within an ecosystem, the cycle of producing, consuming, and decomposing links all living things together. At each stage in this cycle, some energy is being used, and some is being stored by the living things. Where do humans fit into this cycle?

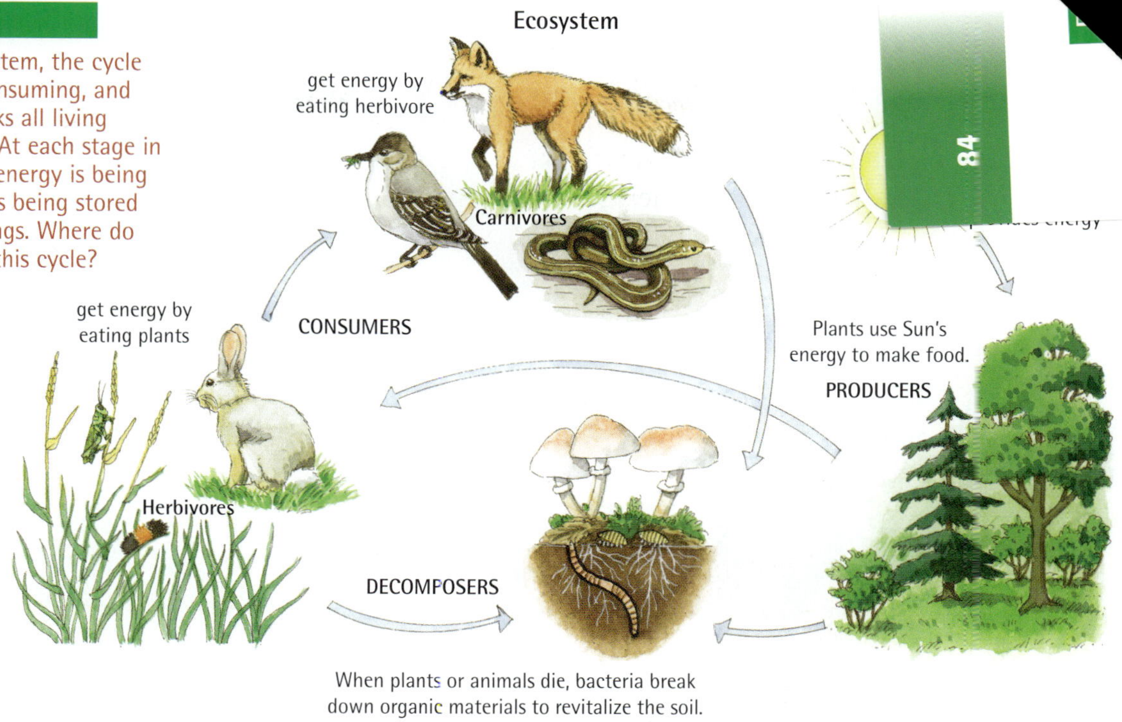

Figure 4.11

A food web is a complicated feeding relationship between producers, herbivores, carnivores, and omnivores. Nearly all species feed on more than one type of food. This makes the food web very complicated. Any toxic (deadly) chemicals eaten by one species will be passed along to the others. The higher on the food pyramid a species is, the more of these toxic chemicals it eats. That is why bald eagles and beluga whales are now threatened with birth defects and disease. These animals are high up in their food pyramid.

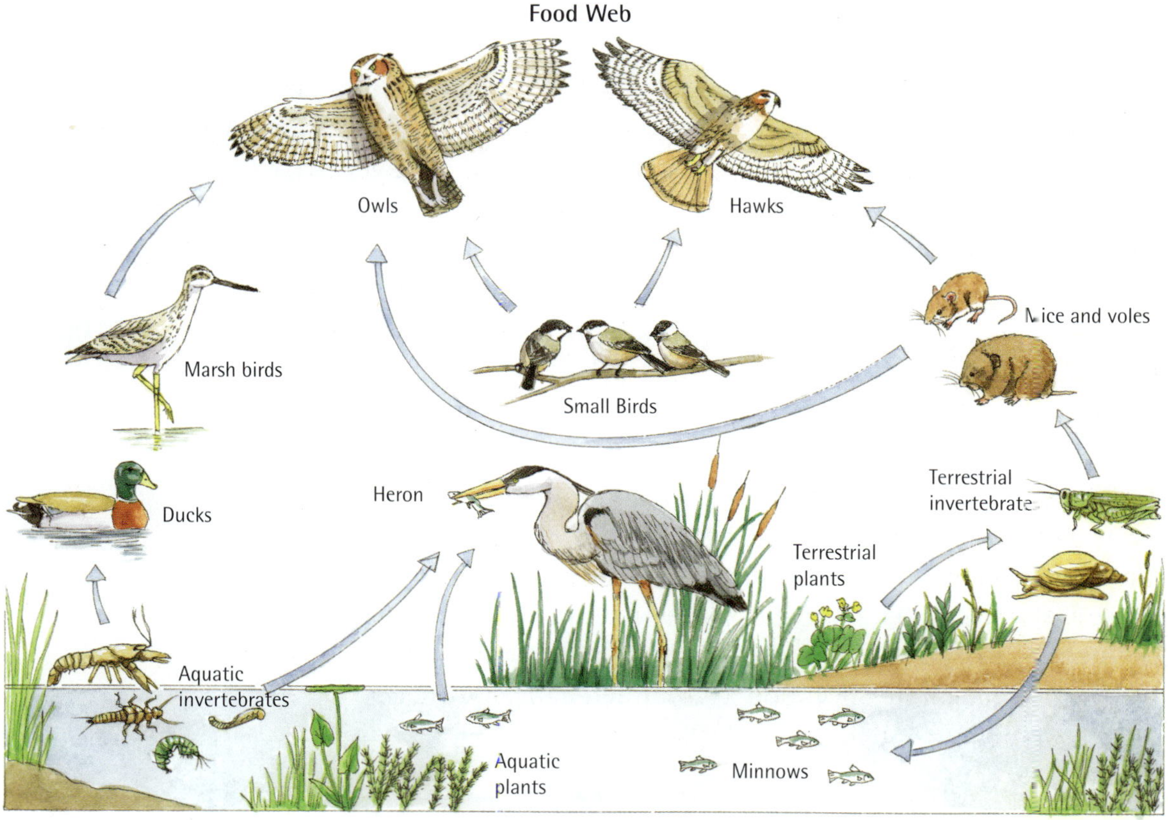

Figure 4.12

These beluga whales in the St. Lawrence River have ingested so many harmful chemicals that their bodies are considered toxic waste hazards. How could you discover what chemicals are being dumped into the St. Lawrence River?

Figure 4.13

Note the misshapen beak of this cormorant, which was found on an island in Lake Erie. Chemicals called PCBs (polychlorinated biphenyls) were the likely cause of this deformity. PCBs are now banned from use in Canada, and we try to store them safely. What were PCBs used for?

The Balance of Nature

Each ecosystem can support only a limited number of plants and animals in a close relationship. A good example of this can be found in wolf-management plans. If wolves are removed, the deer population rises. The deer then overeat the local plants, especially young and low-growing trees. Soon, even that food source is gone. Weakened by the lack of food, the deer are more likely to die from disease, from exposure to cold, or by being eaten by predators. Some deer might move to another area with a better food supply. Over time, predators, disease, and migration reduce the size of the deer herd. Changes to any part of the system can upset the delicate **balance of nature**.

Humans are a huge part of many food webs. There are so many people on Earth that our needs for food and other resources have seriously affected many food webs. The result is that many life species have become **extinct**. That is, they no longer exist anywhere on Earth. As well, many species are **endangered**, or at risk of becoming extinct.

Figure 4.14

A deer stays alert to guard against a predator like a wolf. What would be a predator of a wolf?

DURING READING

1. Retell how deer and wolf populations can show balance of nature.
2. Think of a slogan that captures why it is important that humans do not upset the delicate balance of nature.

Literacy Tip

Creating Slogans

A slogan is a short phrase that captures an important idea. It is a saying that clearly communicates a message and that gives people a reason to remember it. Effective slogans are simple, but they contain keywords that use emotions, present benefits, or call people to action (for example, "Canada's Forests, A Fine Balance").

Figure 4.15

These four animals are on the endangered list from around the world. Can you name three animals in Canada that are endangered?

The Case for Protecting Species

You might think of some species in Ontario as nuisances or pests that we could do without, such as mosquitoes, black flies, gophers, or mice. Do you ever wish we could get rid of them? Before you respond, consider the following values of protecting species:

Value 1—Ecosystem Effect

In an ecosystem, every species has value. All life is related to other life. Ecologists are trying to find out what the impact of the loss of a species may be. They think that losing one species may threaten the health of the whole ecosystem. We still have a lot to learn about how creatures interact within an ecosystem.

Connections to Science

The Green Revolution promoted new types of high-yield crops that were genetically changed. These new crops were supposed to save the world in the 1960s and 1970s. Such crops were said to yield 5 to 20 times more food per hectare. The effort failed. Today, many companies want to market foods that have been genetically changed. Use newspapers or the Internet (search for *genetically changed foods*) to find foods that have been genetically changed and are being sold (for example, milk). What are the advantages of genetically altered foods? What are the disadvantages?

Value 2—Genetic Loss

Every time a species is lost, we lose it as a genetic resource. It is our genes that we pass on to the next generation. Characteristics such as the colour of your eyes and hair, freckles, athletic ability, left-handedness, and intelligence are all passed on through your genes. If we lose a species, its genetic materials are lost for all time. People have discovered that we can take some important genetic quality from one species and mix it with another. This can create a type of wheat that does better in drought conditions, or an apple that is redder and has harder fruit. Work with animals has been done to breed cows that produce more milk and chickens that grow faster.

Fact File

In 1870, there were 7098 different varieties of apples in North America. Today, there are fewer than 1000. What do you think happened?

Value 3—Loss of Present or Potential Use

Would it not be a shame to lose a species that may hold the cure for cancer, AIDS, or the common cold? There are so many species yet to study, or even to find. It is possible that a species is lost before we discover its value. The rosy periwinkle is found in the tropical rainforest. It is able to help fight leukemia, a deadly form of blood cancer. Quinine is a drug that fights malaria. It was also discovered in the tropical rainforest. Often species have been found with the help of the Aboriginal peoples, who knew how to use them for many different purposes.

Web Link

For more information about endangered species, go to www.nelson.com/phygeo7.

Value 4—Intrinsic Value

We are amazed by the creatures that surround us. We have pets. We create zoos, aquariums, and special gardens to visit and enjoy. Many people camp, canoe, and hike for leisure and recreation. Obviously, we care about plants, birds, insects, fish, and other animals (and their habitats) apart from any use they may have for humans.

Fragile Ecosystems

Ecosystems are constantly changing. As the climate changes, an ecosystem may get drier and drier. Vegetation that prefers drier conditions will do well and gradually become dominant. Trees and plants that need more water will die off. Wildlife that can stand a drier environment will increase.

Some ecosystems can handle change better than others. Ecosystems that are drier and cold tend to be more fragile than others. They have more difficulty handling changes. These ecosystems have fewer species. When a change occurs, they have fewer choices to fall back on.

The tundra is a good example of a fragile ecosystem. It is both cold and dry, with a very limited number of species. Suppose a predator has only two animals on which it feeds. If one of these is drastically reduced in number, many of the predators will starve. This kind of change is much less likely in a warm, wet environment, where there are far more species and very complex food webs.

Figure 4.16

What carnivore do you think is at the top of the food pyramid in this polar ecosystem? What does it eat?

Figure 4.17

Plants and animals in deserts, such as this one in Arizona in the United States, have special ways of surviving the harsh climate. What special things do cacti do to help them survive in the desert?

Go Geo-Green

Saving Endangered Species

Throughout the world, many governments, organizations, and individuals are working to save endangered species. In Africa, over 310 species are getting a lot of attention.

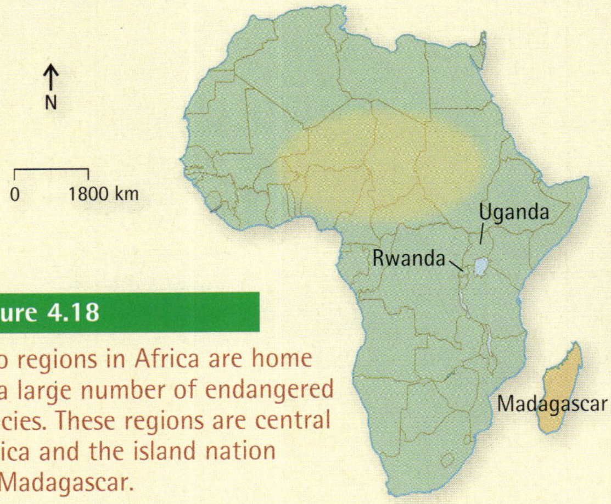

Figure 4.18

Two regions in Africa are home to a large number of endangered species. These regions are central Africa and the island nation of Madagascar.

Mountain gorillas were unknown to science until 1902. They are the largest primates, and they have massive muscles. However, they are gentle, shy animals that live in family groups. Their natural lifespan is 40 to 50 years. Only about 720 mountain gorillas remain in the wild, and they are confined to national parks in the central African countries of Uganda and Rwanda. The island nation of Madagascar has some of the rarest animals in the world. In fact, 98 percent of the land mammals and 92 percent of the reptiles found on this island are found nowhere else on Earth.

Figure 4.19

The number of mountain gorillas living in the wild, such as these in Rwanda, Africa, is decreasing steadily.

Figure 4.20

Madagascar's most famous species is the lemur, of which there are 50 different types.

Today, the main threats to these animals are clearing of the forest and habitat degradation due to human activities. By some estimates, 80 percent of Madagascar is now heavily eroded. As settlement and development spread in these regions, threats to these animals increase.

Figure 4.21

After every heavy rain, the bright red soils of Madagascar are washed from the hillsides into the streams and rivers out to the coast. Astronauts have described their view of Madagascar as "bleeding into the ocean."

International groups like the World Wildlife Fund and the African Wildlife Fund have many programs that need help from caring people like you. One program is called Adopt an Animal. Your class or school could adopt an endangered animal, like a gorilla or a lemur, and help save these species for future generations to enjoy.

Figure 4.23

Majestic, inspirational, genetic treasure—these are three terms people use to describe this old-growth forest in Temagami, Ontario. This may be the last stand of old pine forest in the world. Do we have a responsibility to protect it? Why or why not?

How People See the Environment Differently

Have you ever seen ads on TV of someone driving a dune buggy or jeep through a desert or over sand dunes? The message of those ads is that those environments are there just for our pleasure and that it does not matter if we destroy some parts of these areas either knowingly or unknowingly. Many people will never believe that. They know that a sand dune is a special, delicate environment that can be easily destroyed. They understand that deserts and sand dunes are homes to fragile ecosystems. Many animals live within a sand dune, including fringe-toed lizards and sand snakes.

Figure 4.22

Should we be encouraging such activities? What might be done to limit damage from such activities?

Take Care

In Ontario, there is an old-growth forest near Temagami. Some people want to cut down the trees for lumber. Others want to keep it as it is. They believe it is unique and must be protected for coming generations. Many people are somewhere in the middle. They want some use and some protection.

Most people are in favour of using our resources wisely. They want to help make our resources sustainable. That is, we should use our resources wisely now so we still have more for the future. We are all responsible for looking after the environment. We can learn from Aboriginal peoples who have known for centuries how important it is to preserve the environment for future generations. What you inherited and live with will become the inheritance of future generations. We know the environment is complex and changing. How humans interact with the environment is crucial to our well-being now, and in the future.

AFTER READING

1. Draw a diagram of an ecosystem that is real or made up by you. Use arrows to show how everything interconnects in your ecosystem. Use a legend of colours to distinguish between biotic and abiotic things. If you need help, look back at Figure 4.10.
2. a) With a partner, create a list of as many herbivores, carnivores, and omnivores in your local area as you can within a two-minute time limit.

   b) Has your local area changed greatly in the number and variety of life forms within it? Search in your library to find information about what your area was like before settlement. What are four major changes that have taken place over the past 100 or 200 years that have had an effect on your local ecosystem?
3. Why should humans consider themselves a part of nature as opposed to apart from nature? Give examples to support your answer.
4. Name one local area that you would not want to see changed. Describe it in words or pictures. Explain why you want to preserve it.

Knowledge and Understanding

1. Sunlight provides you with light and heat. How does sunlight provide energy for you?

2. Parks Canada has a slogan: "Take only pictures, leave only footprints." What do you think this slogan means? How does the quote help us understand how Parks Canada wants us to behave when we visit a park? Create two other slogans that our parks could use to attract visitors, care for campsites, or help with some other aspect of our parks.

3. List two advantages and two disadvantages of keeping animals in captivity in zoos.

Figure 4.24

The Toronto Zoo has over 5000 animals.

4. **a)** Make two lists about the things on Earth that you inherited from your parents' generation, like the air quality, the condition of your water supply, the transportation system, and health care. On one list, record four positive things, and on the other list, record four negative things. Now note beside each item on your lists how you can preserve the good and improve the bad.

   b) Make two lists about the things on Earth that your children will inherit from your generation. On one list, record four positive things, and on the other list, record four negative things. Note beside each item on your lists how you can strengthen the good and improve the bad as you mature and become an adult.

Inquiry/Research and Communication Skills

5. Find a map of global ecosystems in an atlas or the Map Appendix. Choose two ecosystems on one continent between 30° N and 30° S latitude. You might select a desert and a rainforest or mountains and tropical grasslands. Use an encyclopedia or a search engine on the Internet to find information on the climates and the landforms of your chosen ecosystems. How does the location of the ecosystems you chose explain the differing climates and landforms?

6. Search in magazines like *Canadian Geographic* and *National Geographic* on the Internet or in the library for articles on life in tidal zones. Make a presentation that shows the variety of the life (plants, fish, other sea creatures) and their relationships to the tides (obtaining food, exposure to air and water environments). Use these relationships to show how changing one thing (cause) can destroy the whole ecosystem (effect). The following are possible ways to present the connections within this ecosystem:
   - Create a three-dimensional model to show the life forms and the environment of the tidal zone. Present your model and the relationships between the life forms and the tides in an oral presentation.
   - Create a poster that shows the relationships between the life forms in a tidal zone and the tides (refer to Figure 4.10 for ideas). Present your poster and the relationships in an oral presentation.
   - Create a PowerPoint presentation to show the life forms in tidal zones and their relationships to the tides.

   Whether you choose a model, a poster, or a PowerPoint presentation, make sure that you show what can happen in this ecosystem if one thing is changed.

7. Choose one of the world's largest ecosystems (see Map Appendix) and write descriptions with sketches (or find pictures) to show its major plants and animals, and the ways they adapt to the natural conditions in that ecosystem.

8 Select an introduced species, such as purple loosestrife, zebra mussels, or Asian beetles, and research to find out how it is a threat to Ontario's wetlands, stream valleys, or lakes. Before you begin to research, it is important to think about what you want to know. What questions do you have about the introduced species you chose? (for example, How did this introduced species get into Ontario? Where is it a natural life form? When was this species first introduced in Ontario?) Record as many questions as you can. These questions will guide your research. If you are using a search engine on the Internet to look for answers to your research questions, try using search strings such as *purple loosestrife introduced species Ontario* or *introduced species Ontario Asian beetles* or *zebra mussels Ontario*.

9 **a)** Conduct research to create a list of species that we once used as food and have been lost or threatened in the past 30 years. Consider seeds, grains, fruits, and/or animals. To begin, think about what you want to find out, and record questions to guide your search. If you use the Internet to search for answers, use keywords from your questions as possible search strings. A KWHL organizer can help you plan your research and make notes. Focusing on these questions will keep you on task and your research notes organized.

K	W	H	L
What do I **K**now about this topic?	What do I **W**ant to find out about this topic?	**H**ow can I find this additional information?	What did I **L**earn?
• • •	• • •	• • •	• • •

b) Create a chart that shows what kinds of species we have already lost and/or those that are threatened, and suggest how these losses affect or will affect us.

Map, Globe, and Graphic Skills

10 **a)** Using an atlas or the Map Appendix as a reference, outline and lightly shade the world's tropical rainforests on a base map of the world. These areas have the greatest diversity of plant and animal life on Earth.

b) Label the countries that share the rainforest. Count the number of countries you have labelled.

c) List some of the current threats to these areas. How would local farmers, native forest dwellers, developers, and government resource management officials see the tropical rainforest differently? Research to find out about each group's point of view regarding the tropical rainforest. To begin, think about what you want to find out and record questions to guide your search. If you use the Internet to search for answers, use key words from your questions as possible search strings. To communicate what you learn from your research, present the different points of view about the tropical rainforest using an organizer, such as a chart or a web.

d) Suggest why it is very difficult to protect tropical rainforests.

Application

11 **a)** In your local ecosystem, list five ways that humans have caused changes by their activities (for example, expanding farming into wooded areas, draining a wetland, building apartments or a mall).

b) Select one of the changes from 11a), and evaluate the positive and/or negative impacts of the change on your local ecosystem. Use an organizer to help you decide whether the changes caused by human activity have had a positive or negative impact overall on your local ecosystem.

12 A city has been described as an artificial ecosystem. New sets of environmental conditions have been created in cities. There are new habitats for all the life forms. Think about what was there before and what is there now. Which parts of the city ecosystem are completely artificial, and which are at least partly natural? Can you suggest three changes that cities could make to help them be more natural?

5 Interaction

IN THIS CHAPTER

- explain the theme of interaction in geography
- use the new terms in this chapter correctly as you investigate the topics
- create and use maps for different reasons
- select an environmental issue that illustrates one geographic theme, and explain why some people/groups have different points of view on the issue
- locate and use helpful information from primary and secondary sources
- use a visual presentation to show how the five themes of geography can be demonstrated by conditions in and around your school

KEY VOCABULARY

acidic precipitation
chlorofluorocarbon (CFC)
geothermal spring
groundwater
Mid-Atlantic Ridge
monsoon
non-point pollution
permafrost
point pollution
sea level
smog
wetland

How the Environment Affects People

BEFORE READING

1. Think of five different ways the weather affects you and how you live. Compare your ideas with a partner. Can you add to the ways in which weather affects you?

Our physical environment—weather and landforms—affects what we do and how we live. We interact with it.

The Weather and You

When we wake up, the first thing many of us do is check the weather. If it is cold, we put on warm clothing. If it is warm, we wear shorts. The weather dictates what we wear. It also controls our activities. The weather can rain out your baseball game. Wind and snow can close roads and schools.

Long stretches of dull, wet weather make some people depressed. Changes in the weather can cause changes in people's attitudes, energy levels, and health.

Figure 5.1

All weather affects us, but severe weather can also cause considerable damage.

Fact File

The growing season can be the number of days from the last frost in spring to the first frost in fall. It can also be the total number of days when the temperature is above 6 °C.

Agriculture: What Grows Where

Climate affects where and what we can grow. The amount of heat and moisture, along with its distribution throughout the growing season, sets the limits for agriculture. In Ontario, the area around Windsor is called the Sun Parlour. This area has the longest growing season (over 200 days) and receives the most heat. The far north of Ontario, along Hudson Bay, has a short growing season (fewer than 80 days) and receives the least heat of any part of Ontario.

Figure 5.2

Corn is a major product in Ontario. What products are made from corn? Glue and starch are two examples to help get you started.

Connections to Science

Prior to 1960, corn was grown almost entirely in the southwest part of the province (mainly west and south of London and Woodstock). Through research, new corn types were found that would grow in shorter seasons and with less heat. Their use spread rapidly, and corn is now grown throughout southern Ontario, as far north as the Bruce Peninsula and near Algonquin Park. Write to an agricultural seed company to learn the different types of corn now being grown in Ontario.

Extreme Climates and Agriculture

In other parts of the world, the climate affects agriculture in many different ways. Most areas between 30° N and 30° S latitude have year-round growing seasons. If these areas are well watered, agriculture continues throughout the year. However, if the areas are either very wet or very dry, people must adapt to those conditions and use different methods of agriculture. In a very dry area, raising livestock may be the only major alternative to growing crops. In very wet areas, people may have to wait for a dry season to grow crops, or they may grow crops like rice that thrive in water.

Where it is too cold, agriculture is not possible. **Permafrost** covers a very large part of Earth, particularly across northern Asia, Europe, and North America. In these areas, the subsoil is permanently frozen, and only a thin surface layer thaws in summer. Until recently, people who lived in these areas got their food mainly from herding reindeer, fishing, and hunting caribou, seals, walruses, and whales.

Figure 5.3

The Masai have adapted to the dry grassland regions of Tanzania by raising cattle. What other animals are herded in east Africa?

Figure 5.4

These farm workers are planting rice in northern Philippines. Rice is the main crop of this region. Often three crops a year can be grown. Do we grow rice in Canada?

Extreme Climates and Shelter

The climate of an area affects the nature of the agriculture. It also influences the kind of shelter people need. For example, homes in areas covered by permafrost must be built on gravel pads or other insulators. The gravel pads prevent thawing of the ground because of heat from the buildings. Thawing softens the ground and causes homes to shift or sink. In northern communities, the utilities (water pipes and electrical wires) often run above ground from building to building. Insulated pipes, called utilidors, keep the pipes and wires from freezing.

Figure 5.5

High winds, extreme cold, and long, dark winters are characteristic of tundra regions. How is this settlement in Nunavut built with these characteristics in mind?

Fact File

Pingos have been tunnelled into and used as natural freezers.

Figure 5.6

Pingos are ice-cored mounds that rise up in permafrost zones like the Mackenzie Delta in the Northwest Territories. Some are 20 to 25 metres high.

Environmental Limits on Human Activity

People usually do not settle on lands that are too rough or steeply sloped. People prefer to settle in areas that have flat plains, gently sloping river valleys, or wide coastlines. There were many such areas in Ontario when European settlers first arrived. The land was mostly covered by forest. This was cleared, providing good soil for building or agriculture. In contrast, landforms like mountains, cliffs, canyons, ridges, and wetlands can hinder or even block people from moving from one area to another in search of a good place to live.

CONNECTIONS TO History

In Canada, finding a way through the Rocky Mountains to the coast was a challenge. Finding and building routes for the railway was an even greater challenge. View the video *The National Dream—The Western Mountains*, which can be ordered from the National Film Board. See the obstacles the workers faced on this daunting project. Watch how they overcame these challenges.

Mountain Barriers

Mountains forced people to move along them until they found a pass—a way over them—like the Khyber Pass in the Hindu Kush mountains north of India.

In North America, mountains once blocked the flow of European settlers from east to west. The Appalachians were the first barriers to movement inland. Then came the Canadian Shield. Further west was the Western Cordillera, or the Rocky Mountains.

DURING READING

1. Identify the physical features in your local region. How can these physical features present problems for settlement or movement from place to place?

Figure 5.7

This road in the Khyber Pass is situated between Afghanistan and Pakistan. Over centuries, the Khyber Pass area has been a major battleground for the many groups who tried to control it. What makes it fairly easy to defend?

Today, mountains still obstruct human movements. It is difficult to construct railways or roads through them. Some mountains are active volcanoes, which present even more challenges. Volcanic ash enriches the soil, but volcanic eruptions can be a constant threat. Iceland is actually the top of a volcanic mountain area, which is part of the **Mid-Atlantic Ridge**. Iceland has many volcanoes. Most of the heat and hot water needed by residents comes from the underground **geothermal springs**. The people use the inner heat of the volcanoes to meet their needs for heat. However, if the volcanoes erupt, homes, fields, and communities may be buried in lava or ash.

Figure 5.8

These are the remains of a citizen of Pompeii, who was buried in ashes when Mount Vesuvius erupted suddenly and violently in 79 CE. Could a similar disaster happen today? In 2006, some smaller eruptions occurred!

Water Barriers

There are many types of **wetlands**. Five common ones are listed here:

- river deltas
- lagoons
- swamps
- bogs
- marshes

These areas are very rich in plant and animal species. However, wetlands forced settlers and settlement to go around them. In the southern parts of North America, huge swamplands, like the Okefenokee or the Everglades in Florida, kept people on their perimeters, or outer edges.

Figure 5.9

This is a photograph of the Everglades in Florida. Swamp and wetland areas are drained for human activities. How is the wildlife affected? Find out how groups like Ducks Unlimited or the World Wildlife Fund help protect wetlands.

Hazardous Building Sites

Some areas are not stable enough to build on. Where there is no solid bedrock for foundations, the land becomes waterlogged. It will not support heavy buildings. In other areas, regular and seasonal flooding forces people to live high above ground in houses built on stilts. These types of homes are found in the Amazon River basin in South America and in Bangladesh in Asia. Nearly all of Bangladesh, with its 120 million people, is only a few metres above **sea level**. Two large rivers, the Ganges and the Brahmaputra, flow from the northern hill country and flood regularly. The flooding has destroyed many communities. It has also drowned hundreds of thousands of people over the years.

The summer **monsoon** winds blast Bangladesh and bring heavy rains. They increase the height of the Indian Ocean's waves and tides. This pushes water farther inland, drowning many fields and homes. Many people in Bangladesh have rebuilt their homes completely 10 to 20 times!

Fact File

At Cherrapunji, India, north of Bangladesh, it rained continuously for over two years!

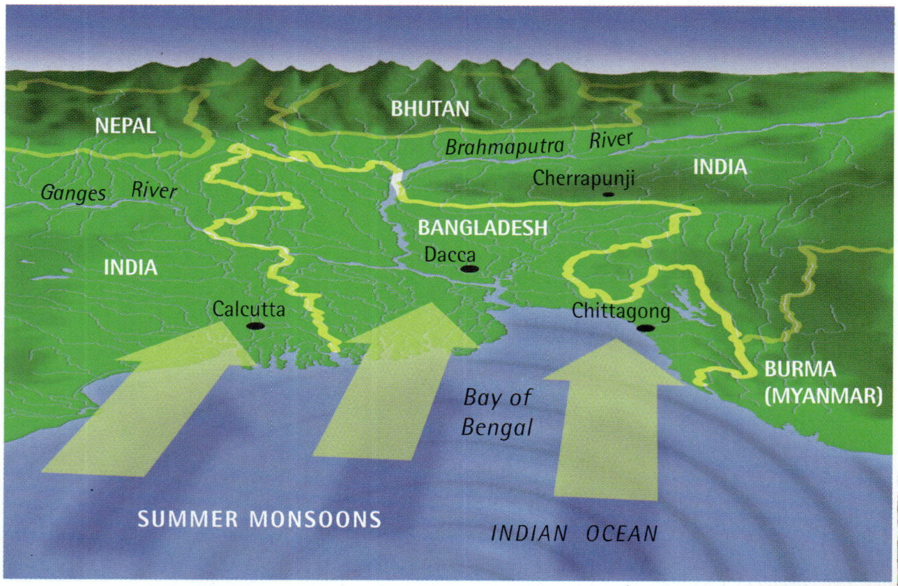

Figure 5.10

Before widespread logging in the mountain and hill country, severe floods happened only once every 50 years or so. After the trees were removed, the land lay open and bare to the rains. Nothing was left to slow the flow of water. Now, floods happen every second year.

Figure 5.11

Disastrous floods wash away homes, kill livestock, and ruin crops. These people of Bangladesh have few resources and little wealth. They have almost no control over what is decided about land use. Many families have lost their homes and belongings several times. What two things can you suggest to help change the situation?

The Physical Environment—Challenge and Opportunity

People display an amazing ability to adapt to the physical environment. People use what the environment offers in these ways:

- Some people build snow houses, sod houses, leaf and thatch houses, houses made from animal skins, log houses, and even homes inside natural caves or cliff sides.
- Some people use trees to make canoes. Others use animals and vegetation for going across snow and ice, or for moving settlements.
- People adapt their surroundings to get food. Some people build stone weirs, or fence traps in the water, to catch fish. Others move water to irrigate farmland.

Figure 5.12

As times change, people's methods of living change as well. What changes do you see in this photo of a trapper in Nunavut?

Conflicting Viewpoints

Not every group of people sees the environment in the same way. When Europeans entered North America, they placed a value on furs that First Nations peoples and Inuit would have considered foolish. First Nations peoples and Inuit used the furs they needed for survival. The Europeans used the environment for its riches. First Nations peoples lived with the environment. They used what they needed, but they did not exhaust the resources.

In North Africa, local peoples lived more or less in balance with their environment. They grew grains and raised animals. The Europeans saw a chance to grow cash crops like peanuts. These crops had high value, but growing them made the soil less fertile and more easily eroded. Drought affected the soil more easily. The price of growing cash crops became the environment.

BE A GLOBAL CITIZEN

Traditional Ecological Knowledge

Many people believe we should be paying more attention to Traditional Ecological Knowledge, or TEK. This means the ways that Aboriginal peoples learn and make use of what they know about their local ecosystems. For generations, they have learned about and experienced their land, waters, fish, plants, and wildlife.

In 1992, the Earth Summit was held in Rio de Janeiro, Brazil. Efforts were made to make TEK part of resource management programs. More countries are recognizing and using TEK. Here in Canada, TEK is used and supported by the UNESCO Canada Man and the Biosphere program, Environment Canada's Species at Risk Act (SARA), and the Canadian Environmental Assessment Research Council. Preserving TEK is also important for social and cultural reasons.

Teachers and students in all schools can find ways of including TEK in their classes and assignments. It is one way to ensure that this knowledge is around for many generations.

Figure 5.13

Young Aboriginal students are now involved in programs at school to learn more about traditional knowledge. The purpose of these programs is to make Aboriginal youth independent, increase respect for their groups' cultural past, present, and future, and increase self-confidence and skills.

Natural Hazards

Volcanoes, earthquakes, and flooding are only three of many natural hazards. Cyclones (hurricanes, typhoons), tornadoes, blizzards, ice storms, drought, landslides, snowslides, sandstorms, tsunamis (tidal waves), and plagues of insects (locusts or grasshoppers) also seriously affect us. As more and more people live closer and closer together, natural hazards become an increasing threat to life and property. One hundred years ago, a tornado could have passed through an area unseen and unfelt, far away from any community. A similar tornado today would probably cause damage to some community simply because there are now more communities.

Web Link

For more information about natural hazards, go to **www.nelson.com/phygeo7**.

Preparation Is Needed

We can take steps to prepare for some of these hazards and to reduce their effects. Hurricanes are now tracked on weather maps, and warnings are provided. Shelters against hurricanes have been set up in areas that have frequent storms, like the southeastern part of North America and the western Pacific islands. Emergency evacuation routes have been set up to move people out of a threatened area quickly and safely. With warning, property can be protected by boarding up windows, moving boats up and away from the shore, and tying things down.

Figure 5.14

This is a photograph of Florida City, Florida, following a tornado. Tornadoes and hurricanes kill people and cause billions of dollars in property damage every year. Have there ever been any tornadoes or hurricanes in your area? What were their results? What steps could have been taken in advance?

Figure 5.15

A system like this can water huge areas in a day. What are some of the advantages of using large irrigation systems? What problems could this type of system cause?

People in some parts of the world deal better with natural hazards than others. From time to time, serious drought affects much of the central and southern United States. However, people can keep farming because of large-scale irrigation equipment and dry-farming practices. A drought in Ethiopia or Sudan in Africa can cause famine or starvation, and forced migration.

The same natural hazards can occur around the world, but people in different areas of the world experience them differently. What causes people in one part of the world to deal with a hazard successfully, while people in another part of the world experience disaster? Great gaps in levels of technology, development, and wealth cause these different results to similar natural hazards. Some areas of the world have the technology and money to prepare for and respond to natural hazards successfully; other areas do not.

Figure 5.16

Vast areas of Africa, such as Namibia, are experiencing drought at present.

1. a) Explain two physical factors that affect agriculture in southern Ontario.

   b) How does the latitude of the Sun Parlour region compare to California? Look it up in an atlas. How might this explain why this region of Ontario has the longest growing season in the province?

2. What natural hazard has made the news lately? Collect information about this natural hazard, and write an informational paragraph that explains how it has affected the lives of people. Use the following tips as a guide to writing an effective informational paragraph:

- Decide what categories of information you want to collect about your topic (for example, casualties and fatalities, property damage, economic devastation, prevention measures, and so on). Collect three pieces of information for each category.
- Write a topic sentence that identifies the main idea of your informational paragraph. This sentence should introduce your topic.
- Write the information you collected under the first category in sentence form. This will be your first supporting sentence. Do the same for the information under the other categories. Sequence your supporting sentences so they flow logically.
- Write a concluding sentence that restates your topic sentence in a different way. This sentence should leave the reader with something to think about.
- Reread your informational paragraph, and check that the flow of information is logical, or makes sense. Transition words such as *also, likewise, therefore,* and *finally* can help make your sentences flow more naturally. Also, check that you have used words correctly and that your spelling and punctuation are correct.

How People Affect the Environment

1. List five different ways your daily activities affect the environment. Compare your list with a partner. Determine which activities on your lists affect the environment in a negative way, and which ones have a positive effect on the environment. In general, are your daily activities good or bad for the environment?

We interact with the environment all the time. We take from the environment, and we change it. Imagine that we walk in a forest, pick a flower, and enjoy what we see. We have taken from the environment. We have also changed and related to the environment. Our footprints change the ground under our feet. The picked flower is gone, and the plant's cycle of life is changed. We have experienced the forest, and that experience has become a part of us. All parts of the interaction are important.

CONNECTIONS TO Literature The story *A Sound of Thunder* by Ray Bradbury is a science fiction tale about similar issues. Search for it in your library and enjoy it.

Creating a Built Environment

Human beings are inventive. This inventiveness has made it possible for many amazing things to occur. We link areas by building bridges. We also link areas by tunnelling great distances under water or through mountains.

Figure 5.17

This is the Golden Gate Bridge in San Francisco, California. As technology has developed new materials and new construction techniques, the length and shape of the bridges we build has changed. What are some advantages to being able to span huge bodies of water with bridges? What are some of the environmental problems we could cause with such bridges?

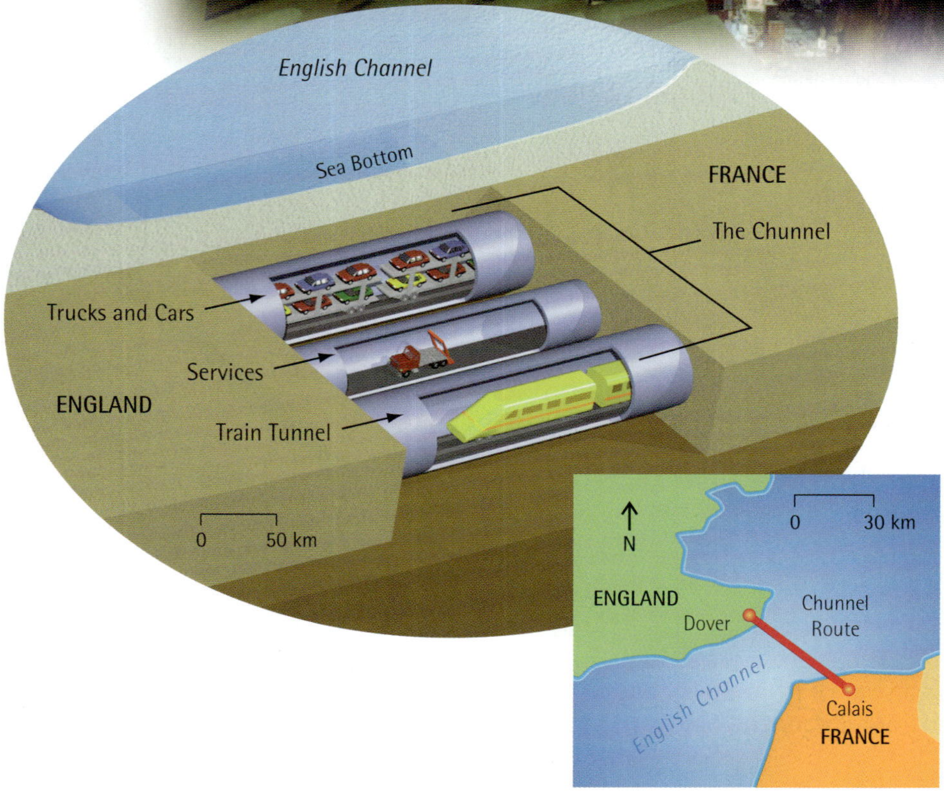

Figure 5.18

This tunnel (called the Chunnel because it is a tunnel under the English Channel) runs between England and France. It handles cars, trucks, and trains. Research to find out more about it. How long is it? How long did it take to build? How was the Chunnel constructed under water?

Figure 5.19

Windmill farms vary in scale, both in the size of the wind towers and blades, and the number of units built in an area. Some wind towers being built are nearly 100 metres tall with 40- to 60-metre blades! Could every community have at least one wind tower?

Figure 5.20

The power in these lines was generated from three major source types. Can you name them?

Literacy Tip

Reading Complex Webs

In a complex idea web, look for titles or captions that will help you identify the main topic. Then, find the main web (often in the centre), and follow the arrows to the smaller webs (subwebs). Then, follow the arrows from the subwebs to the outside bubbles. These bubbles contain specific information related to ideas in the subwebs. Finally, in your own words, summarize all the information in the idea web.

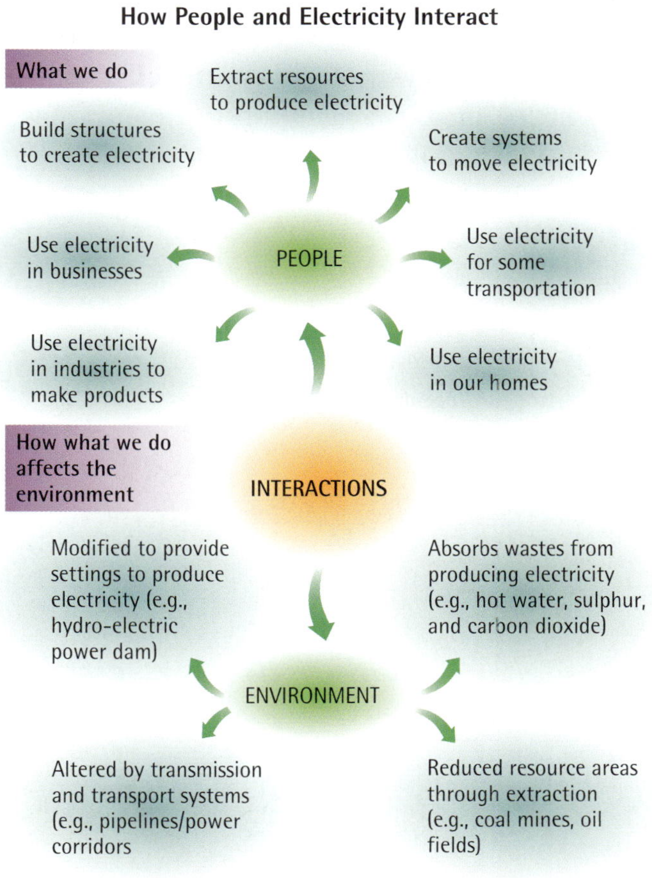

Figure 5.21

Examine this web to learn how the ways in which we obtain and use electricity affect the environment.

We control our local environments through engineering and technology. We add heat or cold to our buildings and homes when we need it. We use resources such as oil, natural gas, and coal to produce electricity. We have learned to take advantage of the Sun, moving water, the tides, and the wind to provide power.

Big urban areas use up a lot of energy. We have built power lines to move energy from the power sources to cities and towns.

Figure 5.22

What do you think we should do with all the garbage we produce?

Waste Management

The artificial environments in our cities waste a lot of energy. In recent years, we have tried to use more energy-saving methods such as better insulation, windows, heating systems, and lighting. In spite of this, Canada is a world leader in energy consumption. This is not a "number one" that we want. We can all reduce the amount of electricity we use. Just remembering to turn off the lights will help a lot!

How Much Garbage Do We Produce?

When we use resources, we also generate waste products—leftover, unwanted resources. Some societies generate very little waste of this kind. Others, like ours, create huge amounts. North America has a major problem storing and disposing of its waste products.

Figure 5.23

Compare how much garbage we trash to how much we recycle.

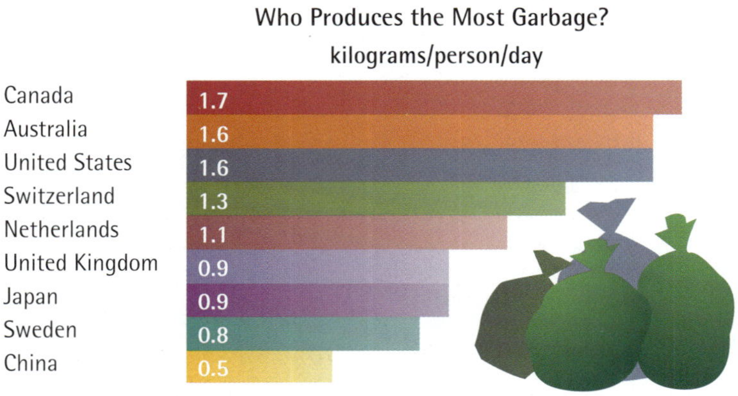

➡Sweden produces less than half the garbage per person that Canada does. Why do you think Canada produces the most garbage per person?

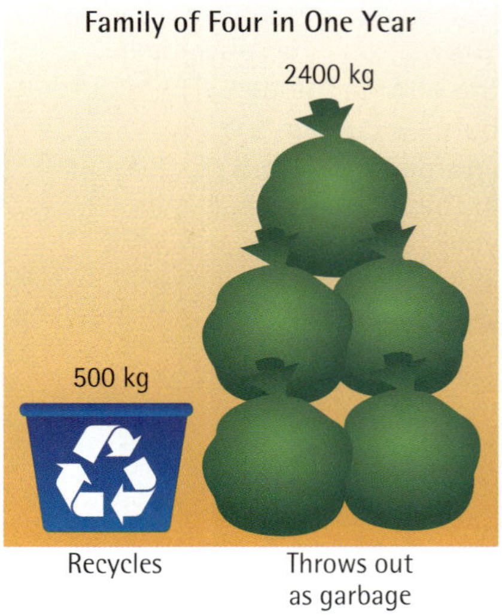

GeoSkills

Creating a Bar Graph

In order to create a graph, it is important to remember TAPP—Title, Axes, Pattern, and Purpose. By following these steps, you will be able to create a bar graph using the data below.

Step 1: Read the *title* and the data in Figure 5.24 so you begin to understand what you are going to graph.

Figure 5.24

Use the data in this chart to create a graph.

Residential Solid Waste Generated by Province and Territory, 2002

Province/Territory	Kilograms per capita*
Newfoundland and Labrador	445
Prince Edward Island	X
Nova Scotia	270
New Brunswick	342
Québec	466
Ontario	363
Manitoba	428
Saskatchewan	323
Alberta	372
British Columbia	329
Yukon, Northwest, and Nunavut Territories	X

*per person in that province or territory
X—insufficient data

Step 2: Using graph paper and a ruler, create your two *axes*, and label them accordingly.

- The *x*-axis (horizontal) should be labelled with the names of all of the provinces and territories. Each province/territory bar should be two squares wide on your graph paper. Leave one space before you begin your next province/territory bar. You will need 33 squares.
- The *y*-axis (vertical) should be labelled Kilograms per capita*. Start with 0 at the bottom, and go up by 25s—0, 25, 50, 75, and so on. You will need 18 squares.

Step 3: Place a title at the top of your graph.

Step 4: Look at the data set, and begin to create your *pattern*. Start with Newfoundland and Labrador, and draw a horizontal line at approximately 445 on the *y*-axis. Use your ruler to draw two vertical lines down to the bottom of your graph. Colour in your first bar. Follow Step 4 for all of the remaining provinces and territories.

Figure 5.25

Use the data in Figure 5.24 to begin creating your graph.

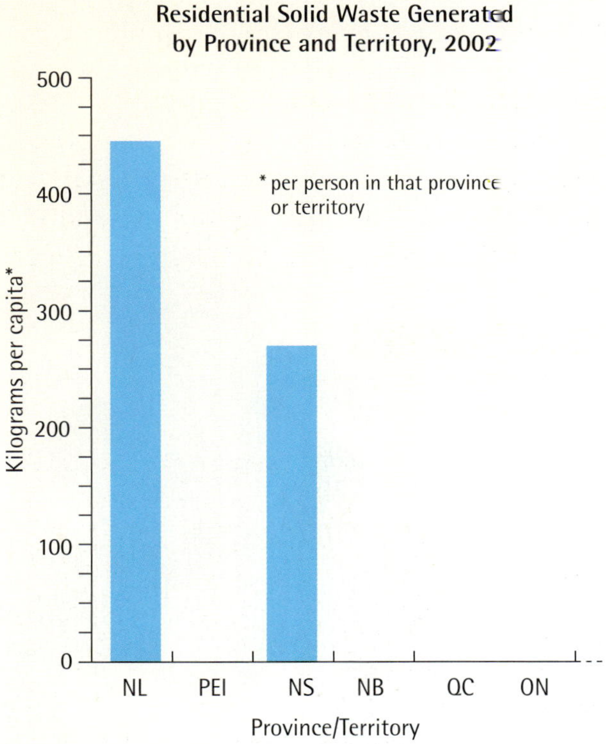

Step 5: Determine *purpose*. Ask yourself: What is this graph telling me about residential waste in Canada?

CONNECTIONS TO **Language**

We use the saying, "Out of sight, out of mind." Another such saying is, "What you don't know can't hurt you." Both these sayings seem to tell us that as long as we cannot see the problem, it does not exist. Can you think of another similar saying? How are these sayings wrong when it comes to the environment and our garbage?

Figure 5.26

Cities and towns can construct safe dumping areas, that is, sanitary landfill sites. Harmful substances are contained or removed to prevent them from entering the surrounding area.

Where Do We Put Our Garbage?

Finding places to put our garbage is a hot topic. We have dumped garbage in oceans, lakes, rivers and streams, old quarries, and in many other places. Our environment has been damaged by our garbage dumping. The piles of trash smell terrible and look ugly. Over time, leaks from the dumps cause many serious problems, such as contaminated water and disease.

DURING READING

1. NIMBY is an acronym. The letters in the acronym stand for Not In My BackYard. NIMBY is often associated with waste issues. In your opinion, why would it apply to waste issues?

Figure 5.27

In 2006, waste removal experts worked to get rid of more than 6000 tons of toxic waste from garbage dumps in Abidjan, the largest city in Africa's Ivory Coast. Dozens of people died or were hospitalized. Why do you think cleaning up these sites is so difficult and costly?

LITERACY TIP

Creating Word Puzzles

Creating word puzzles can help you remember vocabulary or information. "Acronyms" are words formed from the first letter of other words (for example, GPS: Global Positioning System). "Mnemonics" are arrangements of words to help you remember vocabulary, names, spelling, concepts, or sequence (for example, <u>N</u>ever <u>E</u>at <u>S</u>oggy <u>W</u>afers: North, East, South, West). Create your own word puzzles to help you remember geography vocabulary and concepts.

What Happens When We Dump Chemicals?

There are many problem sites around the world. Close to home, we have many toxic "hot spots" in the Great Lakes region. A toxic hot spot is a place where chemical poison has been dumped into the water and has not yet been cleaned up. It could have happened many years ago, or the dumping may still be occurring.

Figure 5.28

Note where these hot spots are found around the Great Lakes. The distribution of these hot spots is directly related to two major factors. What do you think they are?

Toxic Hot Spots in the Great Lakes Region

AFTER READING

1. For one week, keep track of what garbage you are putting out. What are three ways you could reduce the amount of this garbage?
2. Where does the garbage go in your community? Contact your local municipality offices to find out. Draw a diagram showing how the garbage gets from your front door to its last stop. Identify any environmental problems you see and explain them.
3. Discover how the electricity you use is produced, where it comes from, and how it is moved to your community. List any environmental problems you can identify.
4. What could big cities do to conserve the amount of energy they use? Would turning off every second light in a big city be a practical and safe solution? Why or why not?
5. Why is conservation such an important topic? Why do you think individuals and governments have a hard time with conservation?

People and the Four "Spheres"

The artificial environments we create have many large-scale effects. These effects involve all four parts of the environment.

BEFORE READING

1. Think back to Chapter 4, and name the four spheres. If you cannot remember them, create a word puzzle for future use. List some environmental problems that you think affect each sphere. Compare your list to what you read in the following section, and add any problems that are not on your list.

People and the Atmosphere

We pollute our atmosphere. The result is a thinning ozone layer, **acidic precipitation** (rain or snow that is contaminated by acids from industrial pollutants, especially sulphur dioxide and nitrogen), and **smog** (polluted air that is made up of fog and smoke or other chemical fumes).

Holes in the Ozone Layer

The thinning ozone layer is a fairly new and very complex situation. Chemical compounds, called **chlorofluorocarbons (CFCs)**, are used in such things as air conditioners and aerosol spray cans. CFCs cause most of the thinning of Earth's atmosphere. Efforts have been made to get rid of CFCs worldwide, but these efforts are not complete. Damage continues to be made to the ozone layer. Predictions are that the decade 2003 to 2013 will be the world's worst period for the ozone layer.

Fact File

In the southern half of Norway, 80 percent of the lakes and streams are either technically dead, which means nothing can live in them, or they are dying.

Acid Rain

Acid rain has become a major problem in several areas of the world. Cars, trucks, planes, trains, power plants, and industry spew sulphur and nitrogen into the air. These combine with sunlight, water vapour, and oxygen to make acids and other toxins, which fall to Earth as acid rain. This increases the acid level of lakes. It makes the water environments unfit for life. Acid rain kills vegetation. It eats away buildings and even makes car paint fade. Areas like the Canadian Shield are the hardest hit. The bedrock cannot make the acids neutral so they do not cause damage.

Figure 5.29

The acid rain that killed this lake and these trees in Petroglyphs Provincial Park near Peterborough, Ontario, can be controlled. What law would you pass to help stop acid rain?

> **Fact File**
>
> - Beijing, the capital of China, sometimes has been so covered in smog that it could not be seen on satellite photos for days.
> - The city of Santiago in Chile has rules that keep 30 percent of all cars off the roads each day.

Smog

Local weather reports, especially in southern Ontario, carry smog warnings. Imagine—breathing in a big city can be hazardous to your health. Breathing in Mexico City on a hot summer day has been compared to smoking two packs of cigarettes a day!

Technology: Problem and Solution

Technology has helped create these problems. It has also given us some ways to reduce the problems. It is easiest to deal with pollution problems when they come from a single point source, called **point pollution**. When environmental damage is caused by a single source, like the smokestacks on a power plant, things like scrubbers can be added to them.

Figure 5.30

Many cities all over the world, such as Mexico City, Mexico, have major smog problems. How do you get governments to clean up the air? How do we get people to change their behaviour so the air will be cleaner?

When the pollution is non-point, environmental damage is caused by sources spread over a wide area, like the millions of cars and trucks spread over the world. **Non-point pollution** is far harder to treat. In the short term, we can help by developing better emission control systems. The only way to eliminate harmful emissions completely is to have vehicles that do not produce harmful emissions at all. Electric-powered or hydrogen-powered vehicles look like good future choices since they are non-polluting.

Figure 5.31

Can you think of ways that would convince people to leave their cars at home and use public transportation, a carpool, or maybe even a bicycle?

Fact File

At least two companies have small fleets of hydrogen cars being tested in several countries. Hydrogen cars have a problem with systems for storing enough fuel for long trips.

People and the Hydrosphere

In the past, we thought oceans were great places to dump things. We felt they were so large that there could never be a problem. Today, we know that is not so.

Our Oceans

With so many people living in coastal regions dumping their sewage and garbage into the oceans, there are big problems for the water life (the fish we eat!) and for us. People have used the seas to hide other things (out of sight, out of mind). Non-detonated explosives, toxic industrial wastes, and even nuclear wastes have been dumped in ocean waters. It is no wonder that world fisheries have declined.

DURING READING

1. As land is taken up for living space, many more people live on the water. Some people even consider living under the water. What do you think are the advantages and disadvantages of living on the water?

Figure 5.32

Already, a few million people live on the water, as here in Hong Kong, China. Do you know of any North American examples?

Our Fresh Water

Our inland waters have not escaped this kind of treatment. Lake Ontario has been called a chemical soup because of what has been dumped into it by all the industries around it. Untreated human wastes make their way into our Great Lakes. What we put into our rivers and streams pollutes the water we need for life.

Chemicals—fertilizers, herbicides, and pesticides—spread onto the land find their way into our water systems. They can also affect our **groundwater** quality. Eventually, chemicals affect the quality of all water. As these chemicals are circulated by natural systems, they become potential silent killers.

Figure 5.33

Ontario has strong regulations on water quality. However, enforcing the regulations is a difficult problem. Why do you think that is?

People and the Lithosphere

We clear woods for farming. We plough fields. We quarry rock, sand, and gravel. Each action changes the environment. Clearing land can cause more erosion and runoff. This process creates landforms like gullies or increases flooding. Using the land for agriculture can deplete its minerals and make it too acidic, waterlogged, or too salty. Quarrying and mining remove some landforms and change others.

Fact File

In 2006, we used over 165 million tonnes of sand and gravel for roads and buildings in Ontario.

Figure 5.34

Most quarries end up looking quite attractive when the owners are finished with them. However, some remain ugly scars on the landscape. Many people make their living working at quarries or in other construction jobs that depend on quarries.

Figure 5.35

Many municipalities and provinces have laws about what happens to pits and quarries when they are no longer mined. Often, old quarries become new parks, golf courses, or other recreation facilities, as this one in Milton, Ontario. Do you have any examples near you?

People and the Biosphere

Our interactions with the environment cause major changes in the biosphere. Many of the concerns mentioned regarding the other spheres also apply to this sphere. The activities of people threaten all forms of life. We know that many animal, bird, and fish species have been wiped out. Many others are endangered. Our plants and trees are also threatened by our activities. Our cities are growing, which means there are fewer places left where some plants can grow. For example, in North America, we have many kinds of beautiful orchids. One such orchid is the calypso. It now only grows on Flowerpot Island in Georgian Bay, Ontario. People go there from all over North America just to see one!

Figure 5.36

How can we prevent the further loss of the tiny calypso? Is there one thing each of us could do?

AFTER READING

1. a) Compile a list of sources of pollution. Classify them as *point pollution* or *non-point pollution*. Choose two sources you think would be the most difficult to manage. For each source, explain why.

   b) Pollution knows no borders or boundaries. Pollution produced in one part of the world, say North America, causes problems in other parts of the world, like Europe. Pollution in someone else's town could cause problems for your area. Is there a major cause of air pollution in your area? Is anything being done about it? How can you find out?

2. Scientist and broadcaster David Suzuki commented, "If all humans disappeared today, the Earth would start improving tomorrow. If all the ants disappeared today, the Earth would start dying tomorrow." Explain why David Suzuki's comment is true.

3. Explain how the saying "For every action, there is a reaction" applies to people and the environment.

4. Find the names of three animals that are now extinct. Find three that are now endangered, that is, close to becoming extinct.

Knowledge and Understanding

1. How does the physical environment limit your activities on a seasonal basis? For example, how does the winter weather change what you can do and how you can do it? Present your answer in a chart with a section for each season. List three activities for each season. Explain any changes you have to make in terms of how you do activities because of the seasonal changes in weather.
2. Describe how you and your family prepare yourselves and your home for the different severe weather patterns in your area. Present your information under two headings: My Home; Me.
3. What are the advantages of having a flower bed or garden area on school grounds? Are there any disadvantages? If so, what are they? How would having a flower bed or garden on school grounds affect the biosphere?

Inquiry/Research and Communication Skills

4. Where does the sewage from your house go? Contact your local municipality offices to find out. Draw a diagram showing its route. Mark any possible or real environmental danger spots. What are two ways to make sewage disposal safer in your community?
5. Research to find areas of the world, besides Iceland, that are able to use geothermal heat for energy or hot water heating. Obtain a map showing active volcanoes by searching for *active volcanoes* using a search engine on the Internet. Plot the areas with geothermal energy.
6. Research websites or books about the Niagara region. List five different ways people use the Niagara region. Find pictures that show people using the natural and built environments. Describe each of the ways you chose. Do any of them conflict with each other? How?

Figure 5.37

This is a photograph of the Horseshoe Falls, which is on the Canadian side of Niagara Falls. People use the region of Niagara Falls in many ways.

7. Commercial forestry, mining, and hydro-electric development are not allowed in protected areas of Ontario. People cannot take any usable resources from these protected areas. Sometimes, people become concerned about other areas they feel should be protected from development and industrial activity. They try to make their concerns known so that they can stop the development.

   a) Use the Internet to find one news story that shows how people have tried to make their concerns known about the development and industrial use of land they feel should be protected.

   b) Do you agree or disagree with the way in which the people in this news story tried to make their concerns known? Explain why.

   c) How would you voice your concerns over an area you feel should be protected? Explain why.

8. Contact Environment Canada and ask for details about the toxic hot spots around the Great Lakes and what is being done about them.

9. Research the whooping crane. Find answers to the following questions:
   - How did it almost become extinct?
   - What steps were taken to save it?
   - How well did these steps work?
   - What is the status of the whooping crane today?

   Use what you learn to write a short story. Make the hero of your story a young whooping crane.

10. Select and research an environmental issue. In one paragraph, describe what the issue is all about. (One example might be the concern about tourist trips to the Galapagos Islands, why the islands are special, and what is at issue.) Then, in point form, identify the groups involved in the issue, and how each group views the issue.

Map, Globe, and Graphic Skills

11. **a)** Use a world base map to track natural hazard events for a week. Create a symbol for each hazard shown, and plot uniformly sized symbols in the correct locations during the week. Colour-code the symbols for each type of natural hazard, and explain your symbols in a legend. Note how severe each natural hazard is. Watch for any patterns of movement or where these natural hazards occur.

    b) Display your map. Identify the natural hazards, and describe where they happened. Explain the pattern for the week.

    c) How should people prepare for a natural hazard? Canada Public Safety has a website titled Is Your Family Prepared? This website provides family emergency and disaster planning. Learn about the risks of natural hazards in your area, and prepare an emergency planning kit for your family.

Application

12. Write to one or two of the different organizations in Ontario that are concerned with conservation and our natural habitat. Find out how students your age can get involved.

13. Design the ideal residential community. Show how the land will be used in different and responsible ways to preserve the environment.

14. **a)** Create a visual presentation to show what positive changes you can make to your school environment to promote a healthy ecosystem. Make sure that your presentation illustrates how the five themes of geographic inquiry—place and location, region, movement, environment, and interaction—are shown in the improvements to your school environment.

    b) Explain why you feel these changes are important. Outline the steps you will need to take to have these changes put into place.

UNIT 2

Patterns in Physical Geography

IN THIS UNIT

- find patterns in physical geography, and explain how they were created
- use a variety of resources and tools to find, organize, and share geographic information about Earth's physical patterns
- point out ways that physical geography affects human activities

1 Describe the landform in this photograph taken in Banff, Alberta. What processes created this landform?

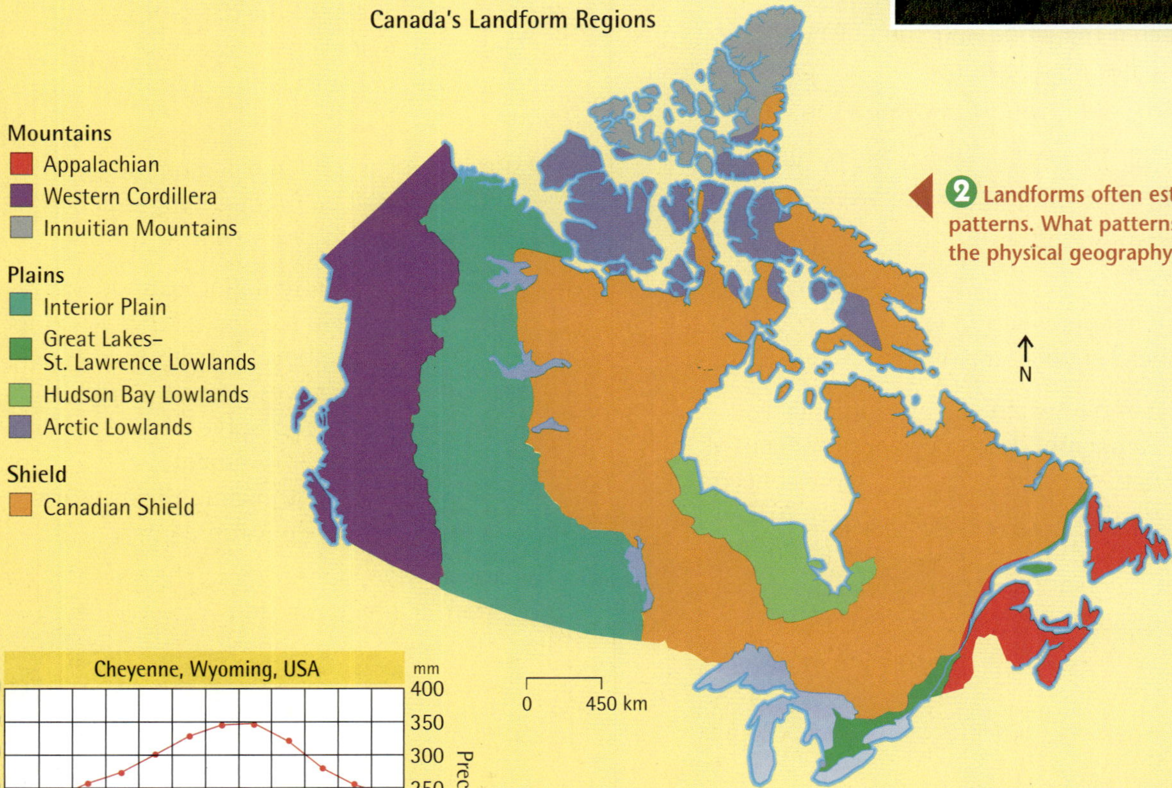

2 Landforms often establish large patterns. What patterns do you see in the physical geography of Canada?

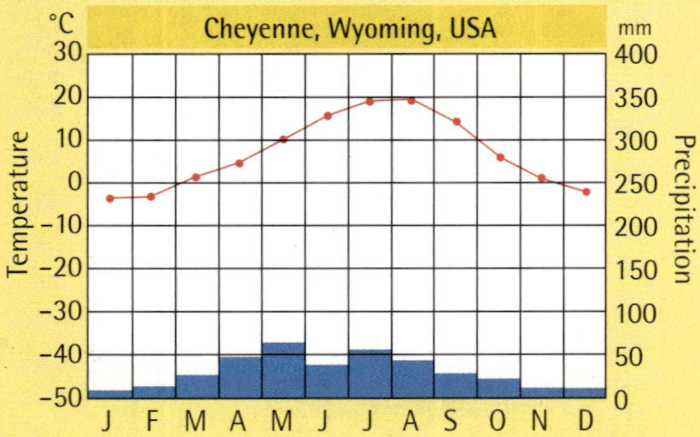

3 This is a climate graph for Cheyenne, Wyoming, in the United States. It shows the average precipitation and temperature by month for one year. What do you think are some of the factors that create climate?

4 In what ways do landforms affect other physical patterns, such as the shape of rivers? Is there a major river near or in your community? Describe it.

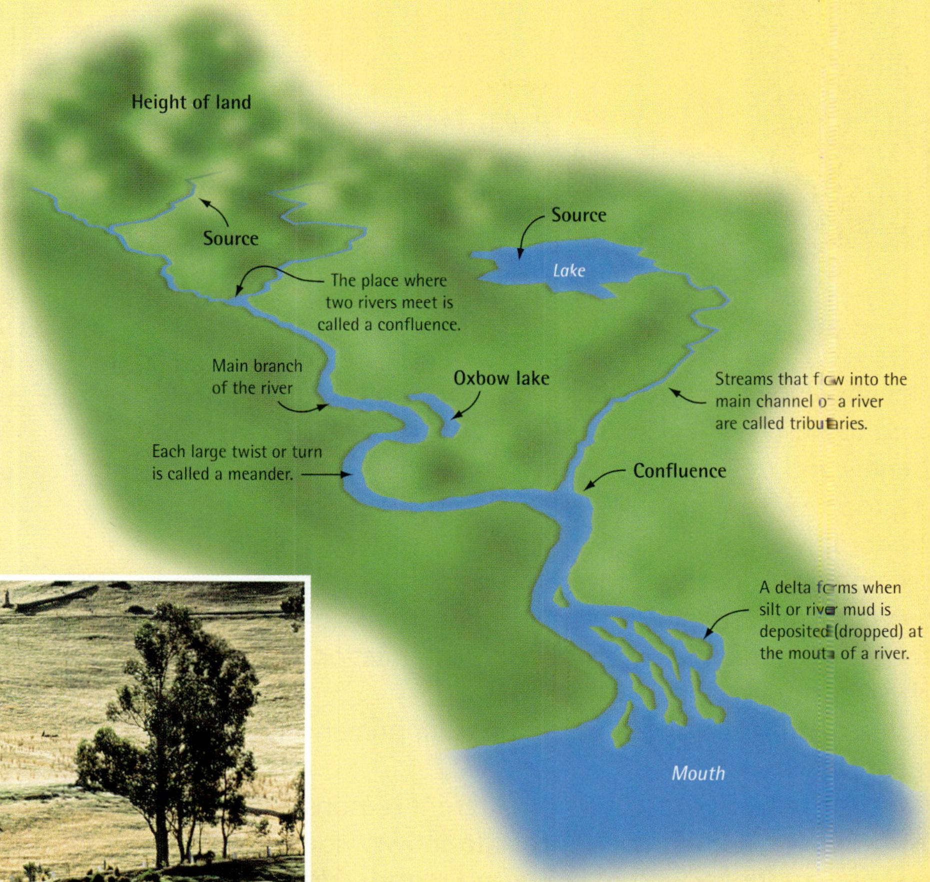

5 How does the climate and natural vegetation of an area, such as here in Australia, influence the food people eat? Is there a special food grown or raised in your area? What is it? Where is it sold outside of your community?

6 How has agriculture stayed the same over time in places such as Vietnam? What are two major changes in agriculture that have occurred in the past 100 years?

6 Patterns in Natural Systems: Landforms

IN THIS CHAPTER

- identify various types of landforms, and explain how they are used to describe regions
- identify and describe world landform patterns
- use the new terms in this chapter correctly as you investigate the topics
- use contour lines to represent elevation on maps
- draw cross-sectional diagrams from topographic maps
- construct questions to help you find information to compare physical patterns
- locate and use helpful information from primary and secondary sources
- share the results of research for different reasons and audiences using options such as computer slide shows, videos, websites, oral presentations, written notes and reports, drawings, tables, charts, diagrams, maps, models, and graphs

KEY VOCABULARY

Appalachian Mountains
continental drift
contour line
fold mountain
Innuitian Mountains
Interior Plain
island arc
landform
magma
mountain chain
mountain range
plain
plateau
Ring of Fire
topographic map
valley
volcano
Western Cordillera

This Not-So-Solid Earth

BEFORE READING

1. What do you think is meant by the heading above—This Not-So-Solid Earth? What evidence is there that Earth's crust is not one solid slab of rock?

What does Earth look like from outer space? Its surface appears to be relatively smooth with large bodies of water between the continents. However, we know that there are huge mountains, flat plains, and deep valleys on each of the large land masses. Some of the mountains are so high that very few people have ever reached their summits. If we were to drain the oceans, we would find great trenches—some deeper than the height of the highest mountains.

Humans have inhabited almost every landform on Earth's surface. They have discovered the patterns that exist in them. In fact, patterns are all around us. Geographers study the patterns made by nature, and by people, to help us understand our world.

LITERACY TIP

Making Connections

Before you start reading a text or answering a question, always connect the topic with what you already know about it. Think about what you have already read, seen, or heard about the topic. For example, what do you already know about Earth's crust?

Fact File

Earth is not round. Instead, it is a sphere flattened at the poles, or an oblate spheroid. The distance around the globe at the equator is 40 074 kilometres. The distance around the globe at the poles is 40 007 kilometres.

Figure 6.1

Everything looks different when viewed from different heights. Imagine you could meet someone from 200 years ago. This person would know nothing of space exploration and satellite images. How would you describe this image of Earth to that person?

Earth's Crust

When we look at the great mountains, the seashores, and the deserts, we just assume that they have been there forever. It is logical to think that North America has always been thousands of kilometres from Europe. However, if you jumped into a time machine and went back 100 million years, you might not recognize the land and water patterns. They would be different from what you see on maps or globes today.

The Continental Drift Theory

A German scientist, named Alfred Wegener, developed a theory known as **continental drift**. He suggested that, at one time, all the continents that we know today were one supercontinent, which began to split up over 100 million years ago. The continents have slowly moved apart over millions of years. Look at a map of the world today. Can you see how the continents might have once fit together?

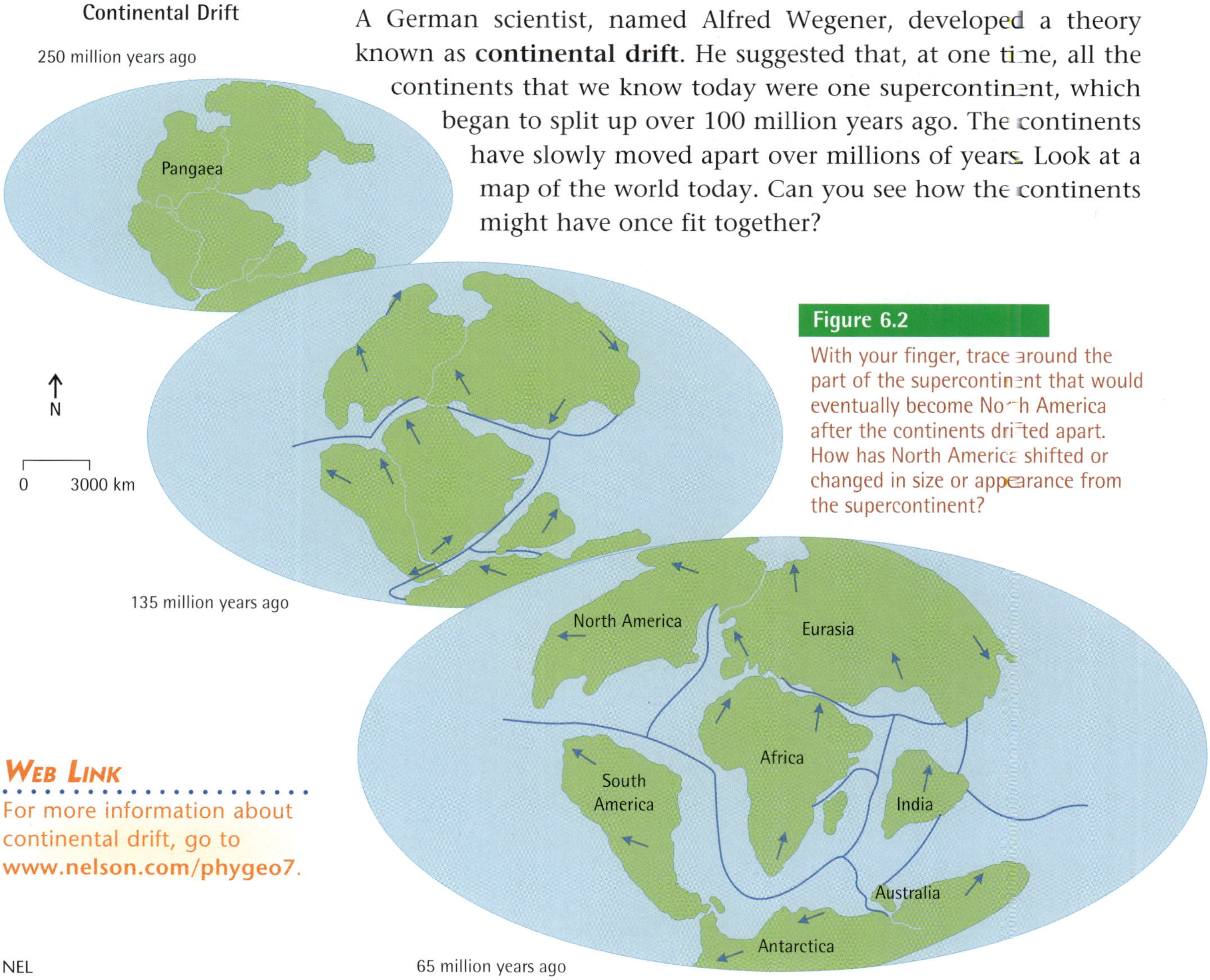

Figure 6.2

With your finger, trace around the part of the supercontinent that would eventually become North America after the continents drifted apart. How has North America shifted or changed in size or appearance from the supercontinent?

WEB LINK

For more information about continental drift, go to **www.nelson.com/phygeo7**.

1. What evidence exists to support the theory of continental drift? As you read the next two sections, find and record the proof of continental drift found in mountains, rock, and fossils.

Landform Evidence of Continental Drift

The easiest pattern to see occurs when we shift South America east across the Atlantic to meet Africa. The coastlines tend to fit together.

In North America, the Appalachian Mountain range ends abruptly at the Newfoundland coastline. However, mountains of the same age and form occur in eastern Greenland, Ireland, Great Britain, and Norway. That is strong evidence that they were once joined together!

There is evidence here in Ontario, too. A type of limestone known as corallian limestone can form only in tropical waters. Corallian limestone can be found on Manitoulin Island, a large island in Lake Huron. This fact suggests that North America must have drifted northward from somewhere warmer, closer to the equator.

Fossil Evidence of Continental Drift

Fossils found at different places around the world provide more evidence that the continents were at one time linked into one large continent. Some fossil ferns are found on all southern land masses.

Plates

The continental drift theory suggests that Earth's crust is divided up into large pieces called plates. These plates are floating on the hot, plastic-like top layer of the mantle, which is the large middle layer of Earth.

Fact File

One of the world's most famous volcanoes, Krakatoa, is on the island of Java. The eruption of Krakatoa in 1883 was so great that it was heard in Australia! Check the scale on an atlas map to find out how far the sound of that eruption travelled. Compare that distance to the same distance from Toronto. Tsunamis that resulted from the eruption killed more than 35 000 people. There was so much volcanic dust that the sky was dark for days. The dust floated in the air for long distances and produced remarkable sunsets for many weeks after the eruption.

Figure 6.3

This map shows the plate boundaries.

World's Plate Boundaries

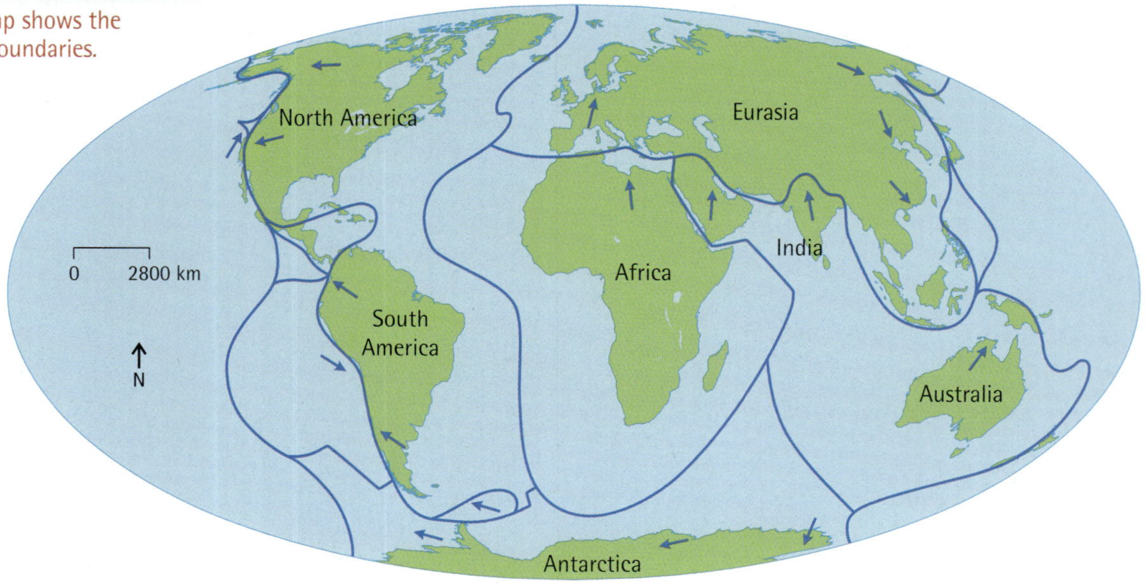

Figure 6.4

The crustal plates produce enormous heat when they slide over one another. Try rubbing one hand against the other to feel the heat effect of friction.

When Plates Meet

When two crustal plates come together, one is forced up over the other. The top plate folds, cracks, and breaks. As the plates slide over each other, the friction creates extremely high temperatures. Molten rock, or **magma**, is formed below Earth's crust. It explodes up through the cracks and breaks in the plates to Earth's surface to form volcanoes. Volcanic islands are common where the continental plates collide. These islands often form a curved line, or arc. This pattern in ocean volcanoes is known as an **island arc**. The Japanese islands form a volcanic island arc in the Pacific Ocean.

DURING READING

1. Why is the Pacific Ring of Fire a fitting name for the pattern of volcanoes that exists along the Pacific plate?

The tectonic plate that lies below the Pacific Ocean is called the Pacific plate. Along the boundary of this plate, volcanoes have formed on the continents and on the ocean floor. The pattern of volcanoes along the border of the Pacific plate is known as the Pacific **Ring of Fire**.

World's Volcanic Regions

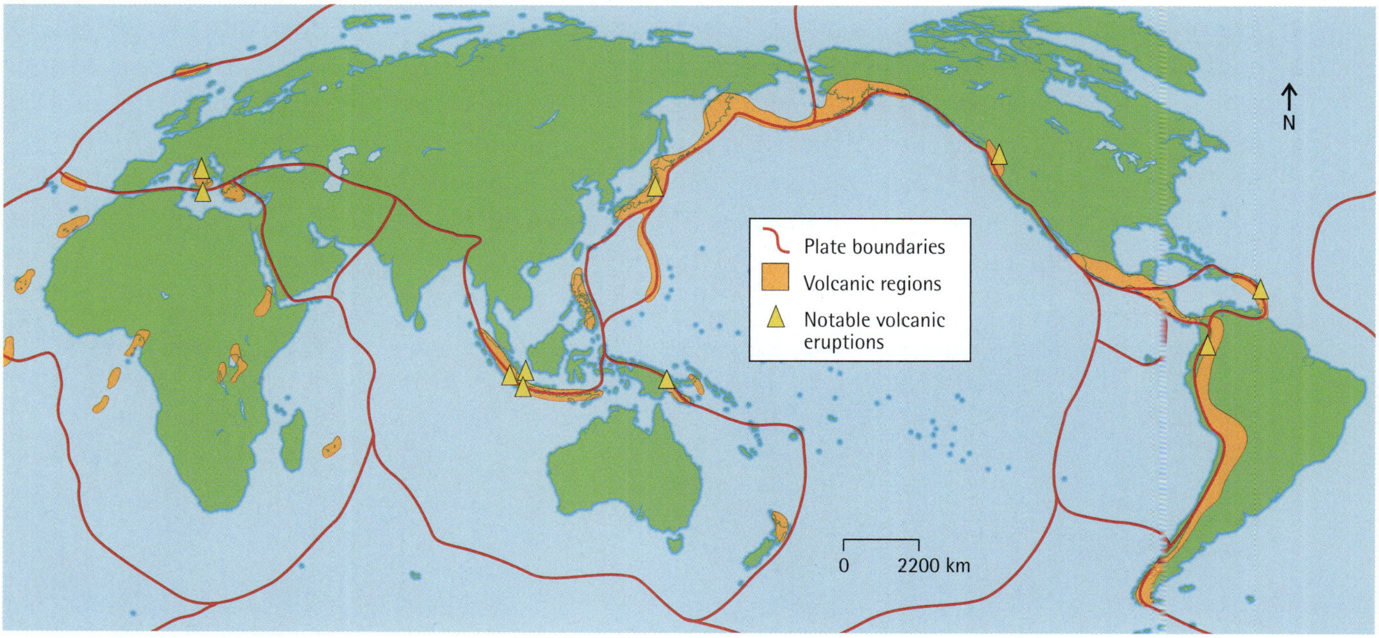

Figure 6.5

This map shows Earth's volcanic regions. What characteristics do these regions share that define them as volcanic regions?

BE A GLOBAL CITIZEN

Responding to a Natural Disaster

Floods, hurricanes, tsunamis, drought, and earthquakes are natural disasters that are becoming all too common in today's news stories. Some of these recent natural disasters are tied to global warming. Others are a reminder to all people that we do not and cannot control the natural environment.

The Pacific Ocean's coast is known as the Ring of Fire. It is an area where earthquakes and volcanic activity are common. Some earthquakes are focused on the ocean floor. These earthquakes cause tsunamis, or tidal waves, that can cause unexpected disaster. Such was the case on December 26, 2004. A huge tsunami wave struck southern Asia. Thailand, southern India, and the east coast of Sri Lanka were affected the most.

The city of New Orleans and the counties on the north shore of the Gulf of Mexico continue to recover from Hurricane Katrina, which struck in August 2005. In August 2007, massive monsoon rains devastated northern India and Bangladesh. These monsoon rains are vital to farmers, but they are both a blessing and a curse. The floods of 2007 caused the death of more than 2000 people and displaced millions. People died not only by drowning, but also from hunger and water-borne diseases. Others were crushed to death or electrocuted when these monsoon floods submerged these regions.

It is easy to feel overwhelmed when you read these stories. You may feel as if there is little one can do to help. However, there are many ways people can help these ravaged regions. Large multinational organizations like UNESCO, the Red Cross, and Red Crescent organize fundraising drives as soon as they realize an area is in a state of emergency and needs immediate aid. There are medical relief groups, such as Doctors Without Borders, that will send medical professionals directly into the disaster region to help with the aid efforts.

As a class, you could investigate current relief efforts that are being carried out around the world. You could become part of the disaster relief effort by telling students in your school about these disasters and organizing school or class-based fundraising events.

Fact File

Before the 2004 tsunami struck a resort area in Thailand, a 10-year-old British girl proved that geography matters when she warned people of the disaster that was about to happen. As she was playing on the beach, she recalled her geography teacher's lesson about the tide going out rapidly ahead of a tsunami. The resort managers took her and her mother's information seriously. They evacuated people from ground level and saved countless lives.

Figure 6.6

Many people were affected by the recent monsoon floods in Bangladesh. How would so much water affect your daily activities?

Figure 6.7

Students can help in many ways with tsunami or other disaster relief efforts.

Landforms

We live on **landforms**, which are the natural physical features of the land. Most humans live on the flattest or gently rolling areas of Earth. Our landforms are changing all the time due to forces on and within Earth.

Volcanoes

Volcanoes are landforms created by magma escaping from below Earth's surface. Volcanoes are erupting regularly and building new land on our continents and in the oceans. There are over 900 active volcanoes in the world.

Figure 6.8

Located in Hawaii in the United States, Kilauea is the most active volcano on Earth. It has been erupting almost continuously for the past 25 years. Check an atlas or the Map Appendix to find the volcano that is closest to where you live.

Fold Mountains

Moving plates buckle, bend, and fold rock layers upward to create **fold mountains**. When plates collide, the resulting pressure forces the rock to bend and rise up.

Figure 6.9

These fold mountains are located in Banff, Alberta. The Canadian Rockies and the Himalayas in south Asia are fold mountains. Can you see the bending in the rock layers? These mountain ranges were once relatively flat layers of rock that built up on ancient sea bottoms.

Fact File

The Appalachian Mountains of eastern North America are examples of old fold mountains. They extend over 3200 kilometres, from Newfoundland in the north to Alabama in the south. (See Map Appendix.)

Plateaus

A **plateau** region is formed when a fairly flat area in a mountain region has been uplifted by plate movement. Plateaus are typically flat high areas with steep sides.

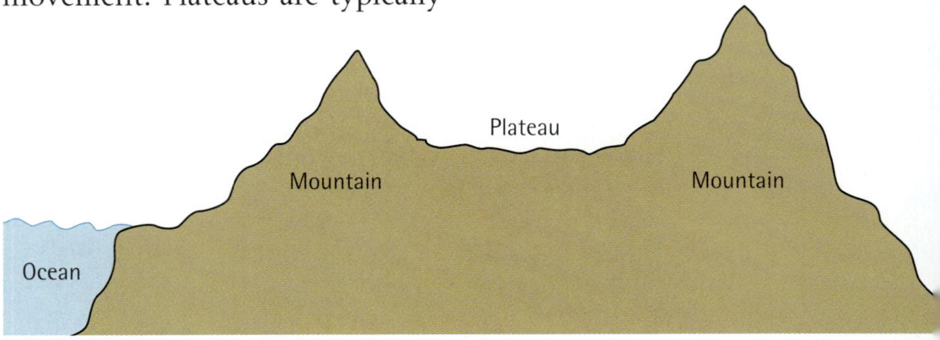

Figure 6.10

The central portion of the Western Cordillera is a plateau. Plateaus are usually quite high and flat with steep sides. One of the world's highest large plateaus is in central Bolivia. Use an atlas and find La Paz, Bolivia. What is that capital's elevation above sea level?

Shields

Shields are the original foundations for our continents. Other landforms were built upon them. Major world shields include the Brazilian Shield, the Central Massif of France, and the Canadian Shield.

Figure 6.11

A shield is the base of an ancient mountain region. The mountains have been worn away leaving a rocky, rugged landform.

Plains

Large **plains** regions are found on every continent. They are mainly former sea bottoms that became exposed after the water disappeared.

Connections to History

Historically, we think of First Nations people hunting buffalo on the plains with horses. However, there were no horses in North America until the arrival of the Europeans in the late 1600s. Prior to having horses, First Nations people would often stampede buffalo over the edge of steep cliffs by running on foot.

Figure 6.12

Plains like North America's Great Plains (or Interior Plain), the Eastern European Plain, or the Pampas of Argentina provide wide open spaces where horizons seem to go on forever! Check an atlas or the Map Appendix to see how these regions are used today.

Fact File

Some of the surface rocks found on the Canadian Shield in the Northwest Territories are over 3.8 billion years old. The Shield has been worn down by Earth's forces. This includes the bulldozing action of moving glaciers.

Valleys

Valleys vary greatly in size and shape. Some are broad and gently sloping. Others are very narrow with high steep walls. Key factors in valley formation include the following:

- time—The longer the time, the more weathering will occur, and valleys will be broader and more gently sloped.
- local geology—Softer rocks like shale will erode away faster than harder rocks like granite.
- degree of slope of the valley walls
- agents of erosion like moving ice or running water
- the movement of land areas along faults

Figure 6.13

The Elora Gorge, in Elora, Ontario, is a classic example of a gorge. This deep, narrow valley is created by water running through a limestone area. Why are the sides of the gorge so steep?

Figure 6.14

Valleys like Africa's Rift Valley are formed when the valley sides are pushed up along fault lines. Africa's Rift Valley extends from central Africa to Israel. Can you see the walls or sides of the valley in the distance?

1. a) Look back at Figure 6.5, and explain how plate boundaries and volcanoes are related.

   b) Some volcanoes occur at places on Earth's crust called "hot spots." Find out how these volcanoes form using a search engine and search strings such as Hawaiian volcanoes or *Mauna Loa*.

2. Choose a landform from a continent of your choice from this section (see Map Appendix), and research to find out more about it. To begin, think about what you want to learn about this landform on this continent, and record at least three questions to guide your search (for example, How are different types of valleys formed on this continent? What are the features of the mountains found on this continent? How are the plains used on this continent? Where are plateaus found on this continent? How have the valleys on this continent changed over time?). If you are using a search engine on the Internet to search for answers, use key words from your questions as possible search strings (for example, *valley types formation Africa,* or *mountain features South America,* or *plateau location Asia*).

3. Copy and complete the chart below into your workbook.

Landform	Description	Location and Name of One Example
Volcano		
Fold mountain		
Plateau		
Shield		
Plain		
Valley		

BEFORE READING

1. Use what you already know about Canada's landforms to create a mental image of Canada. Try to picture different landforms. Make a list of the landforms that you can picture, and describe where they are found.

Landform Regions

You already know that a region is a large area of land that has a major characteristic that is similar throughout its area. Regions described by one special landform, like mountains or plains, are called landform regions. Landform regions are generally one of the three following types: mountains, plains, shields.

Canada's Landform Regions

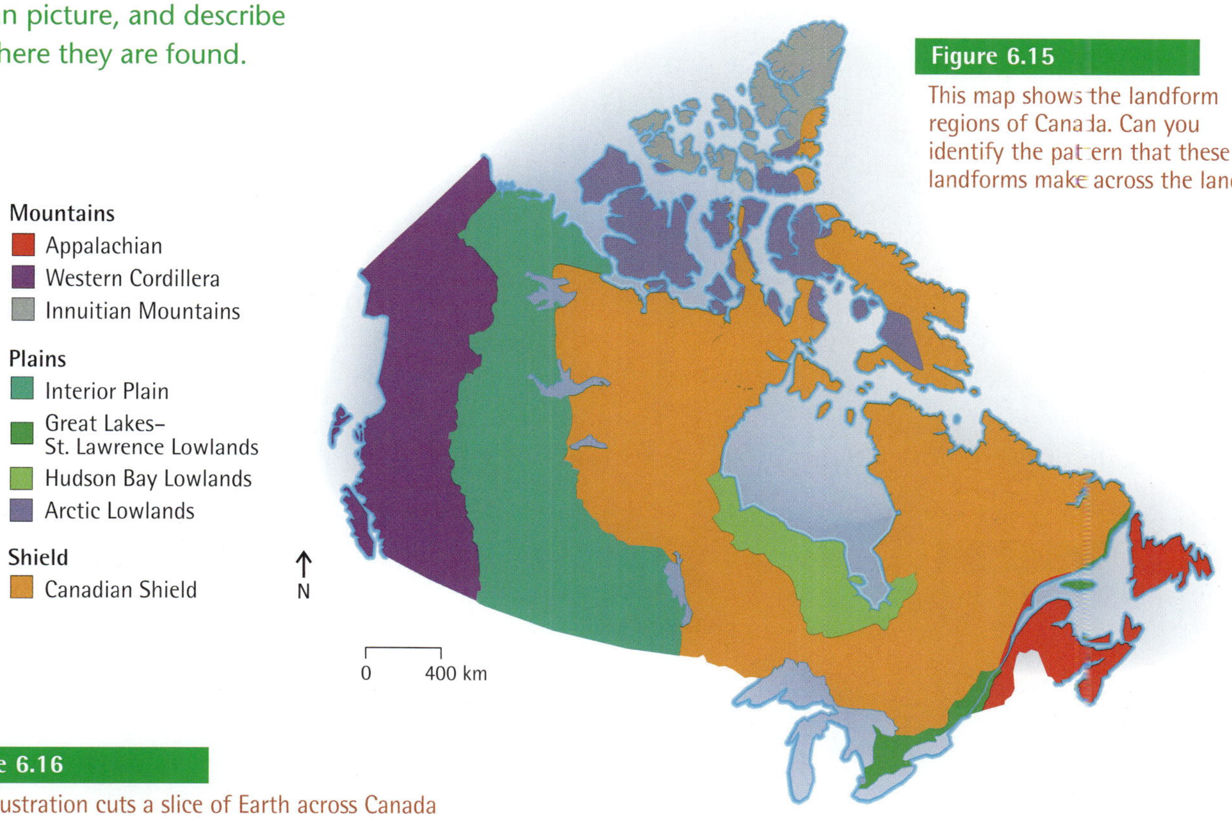

Figure 6.15
This map shows the landform regions of Canada. Can you identify the pattern that these landforms make across the land?

Figure 6.16
This illustration cuts a slice of Earth across Canada to view a profile of Canada's landforms.

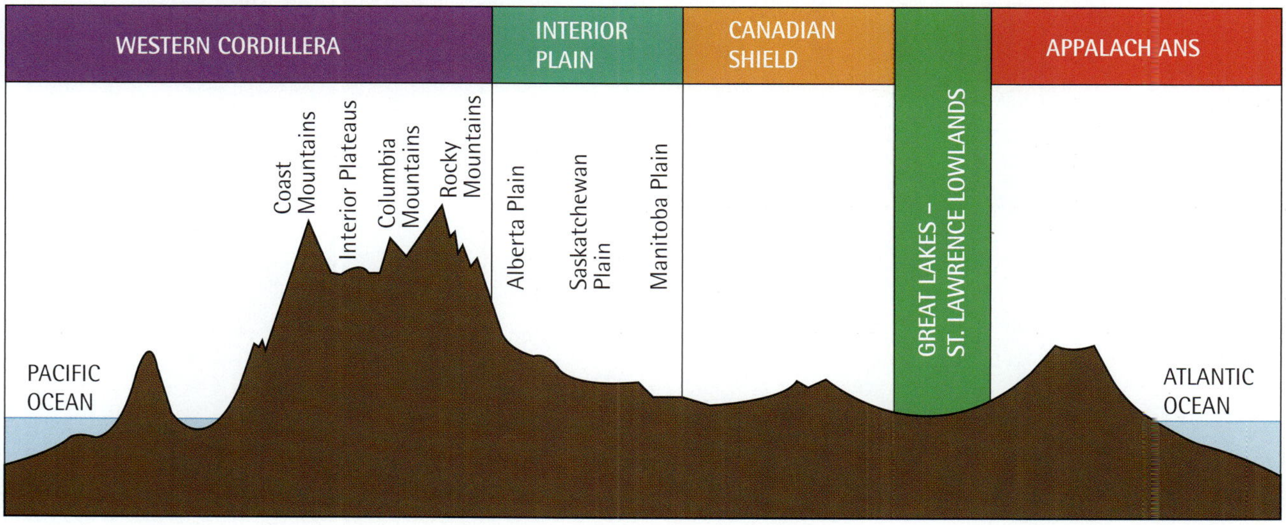

Mountains

Anything over 600 metres is generally considered to be a mountain. Mountains present challenges to people in the following ways:

- It is difficult for people to settle on land that is so rough and rugged.
- Transportation is a challenge. People must find a way between the steep mountains.
- The harsher climate and the limited amount of topsoil in most mountain regions make agriculture very difficult.

Several mountains clustered together as a group are called a **mountain range**. When several ranges are grouped together, they are called a **mountain chain**. The Himalayas and the Western Cordillera are two of the largest and longest mountain chains in the world. Mount Everest, in the Himalayas, is the highest peak in the world at 8848 metres high.

The Andes in South America continue from the Rocky Mountains, which are part of the Western Cordillera. The Andes and the Rockies are mountain chains that extend along the west coast of two continents. The southern side of Europe and south central Asia are also mountainous. The most famous mountains in Europe are the Alps.

Figure 6.17

This map shows the mountain regions of the world.

DURING READING

1. As you read the next section, compare and contrast the three major mountain areas in Canada. Use a graphic organizer, like a matrix.

Literacy Tip

Using a Matrix

A matrix is a good visual tool. It helps you remember how things are alike or different. To create a matrix, list the mountain regions that you are comparing along the left side. Across the top of the matrix, list the characteristics. As you read about each different mountain region, identify its characteristics by putting an X in the correct box.

North American Mountains

North America has the following major mountain regions:

- the Western Cordillera
- the Appalachian Mountains
- the Innuitian Mountains

The Western Cordillera

British Columbia promotes tourism in the province by calling itself "Supernatural BC." Perhaps the most spectacular part of British Columbia is the highland region known as the **Western Cordillera**. This highland region contains three distinct mountain ranges. The Coast Mountains, as the name suggests, follow Canada's West Coast along the Pacific Ocean. The Interior Plateaus and Mountain Ranges are in the middle of the Cordillera. The Rocky Mountains are further east. People often refer to the whole Western Cordillera as the Rockies, but only a portion of the Western Cordillera is actually the Rocky Mountains.

The mountains of the Western Cordillera are much younger than the Appalachian Mountains. Because they are younger, they are higher, sharper-peaked, and more spectacular than the Appalachian Mountains, which are older, "soft," rounded mountains. Many of the mountains in the Western Cordillera region are over 3000 metres high. Some of the highest peaks remain snow covered even during the summer months.

Figure 6.18

This illustration shows the profile of the Western Cordillera and its mountain ranges.

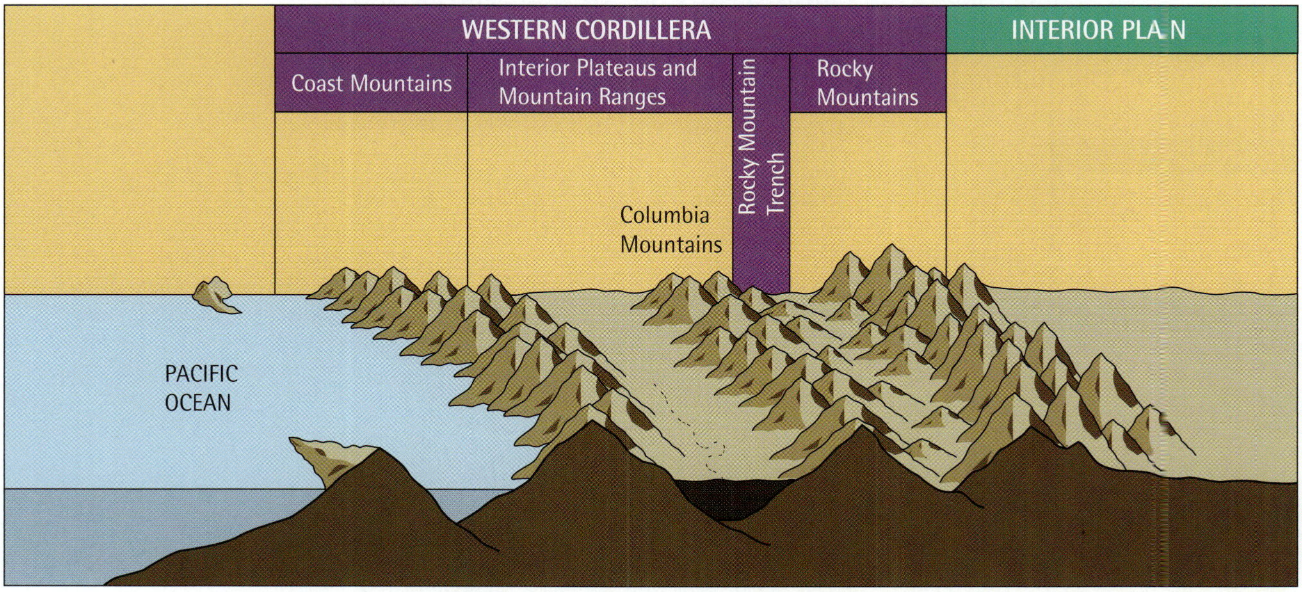

Figure 6.19

This is a photograph of Lobster Cove Head in Newfoundland. Mountains of this type are typical of those found on Canada's East Coast. They are part of the Appalachians. Use an atlas or the Map Appendix to find where this mountain region starts and ends. You could hike the Appalachian Trail's 1600 kilometres!

The Appalachian Mountains

The **Appalachian Mountains** are located on North America's East Coast. Over the past 300 million years, erosion has worn down the peaks of these mountains, making them smooth looking. They are considered old mountains. Today, wide valleys and rolling hills make up the landscape of this region.

Innuitian Mountains

The third mountain region in North America is not as well known because of its remote northern location. The **Innuitian Mountains** are found in some of the northern Arctic islands, specifically Ellesmere Island. Like the Western Cordillera, the mountains in this region are young. Erosion has not reduced them to hills. Extremely cold weather creates a very short growing season, so there are no trees. A very small number of Inuit live in small villages such as Taloyoak and Qausuittuq in the territory of Nunavut.

Literacy Tip

Viewing Photographs

Photographs are often used to provide more information and to support what you are reading. Look at the photographs of Canada's landform regions and think about the following:

- Where do you look first in the photograph?
- How does this part of the photo relate to the text?
- What else in the photo relates to the text?
- What new information can you learn about the topic from this photo?

Figure 6.20

This is a photograph of Ellesmere Island in Nunavut. The arctic climate and harsh, mountainous landscape make the Innuitian Mountains an extremely difficult place to live. Why do you think there is no vegetation here?

Fact File

One of the largest deserts in North America is the Eureka Upland. It is located on Ellesmere Island in Canada's Arctic. It is a very cold desert!

DURING READING

1. As you read the next section, compare and contrast the three major plains (lowlands) in Canada. Use a graphic organizer, like a matrix.

Plains

Plains are large areas of level or gently rolling land. The northern portion of Europe and Asia is a mix of plains and plateaus. The grasslands of Eurasia are large, mainly treeless plains known as the Steppes. The plains in southern Argentina are known as the Pampas.

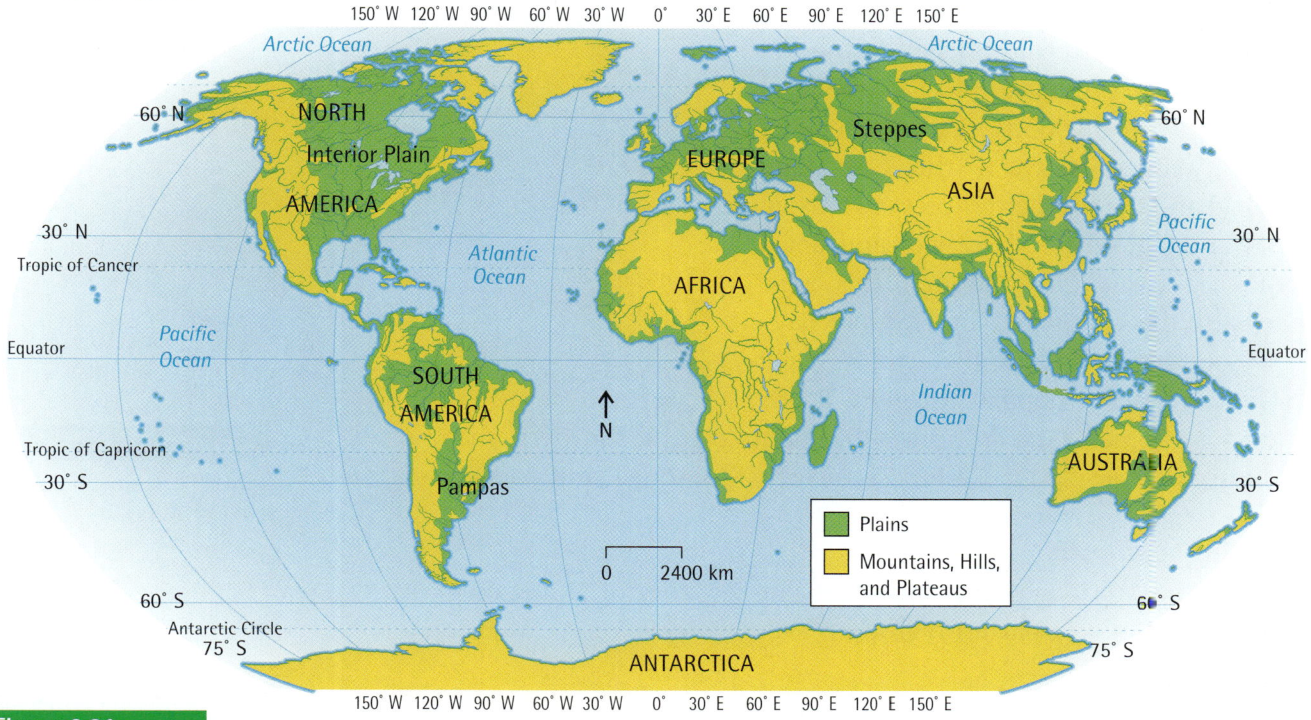

Figure 6.21

This map shows the plains of the world.

Figure 6.22

Notice the flat appearance of this area of the Interior Plain in Saskatchewan. Some of the largest farms in Canada are found on the Interior Plain. Many of them are wheat farms. Why do think such large farms developed in this region?

In North America, there is a large, flat or gently rolling **Interior Plain**. It begins at the Arctic Ocean and extends south all the way to Mexico. The Interior Plain includes the following:

- the Great Plains of the United States
- the Prairie grasslands
- the Mackenzie valley

This region is well suited to farming from central Canada to Texas. Because of the huge wheat and other grain farms found throughout the Interior Plain, it is often called "The Bread Basket of North America."

Canadian Plains

The major plains in Canada include the Hudson Bay Lowlands, the Great Lakes–St. Lawrence Lowlands, the Arctic Lowlands, and part of the North American Interior Plain.

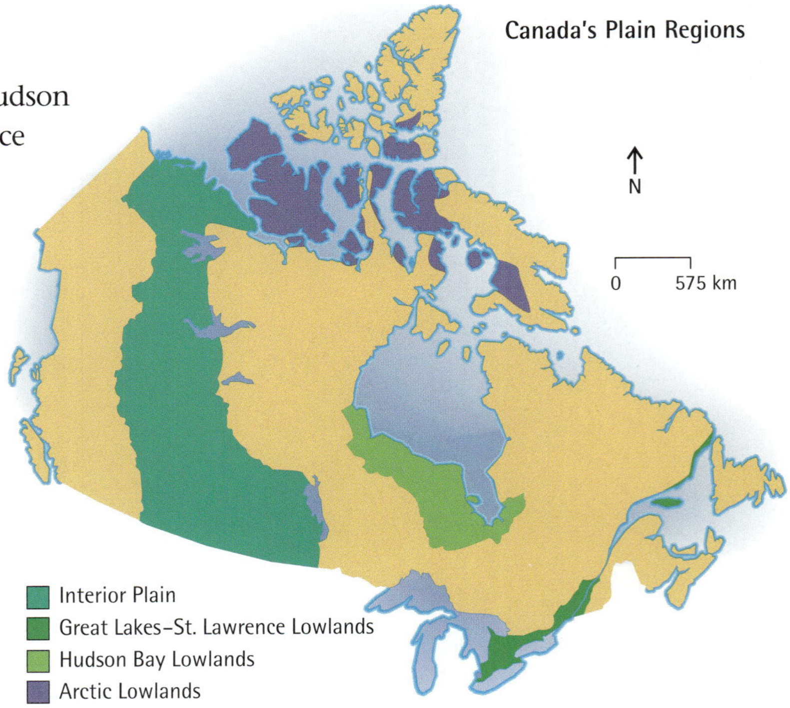

Figure 6.23
This map shows the Canadian plains.

Hudson Bay Lowlands

Just as the Innuitian Mountains are not well known, the Hudson Bay Lowlands are also not familiar to most Canadians. This is a small, poorly drained piece of land wedged between the Canadian Shield and the southern shores of Hudson Bay and James Bay. Many wide and slow-moving rivers flow through this area toward the salt water of Hudson Bay. Mosquitoes and black flies thrive here. This is a sparsely populated region. There are a few small First Nations settlements on the southern shore of Hudson Bay at places like Moose Factory, Moosonee, and Fort Severn.

Arctic Lowlands

The Arctic region is mostly in the territory of Nunavut. It is a flat and barren region.

CONNECTIONS TO History

Henry Hudson wanted to find a passage from the Atlantic Ocean to the east through North America. In 1610, he sailed into and explored the huge saltwater bay now called Hudson Bay. That winter, supplies ran low, and his crew mutinied. They set him, his teenage son, and eight loyal crew members adrift in a small boat on the icy waters of the bay. Captain Hudson and that small band were never heard from again. Eight of the mutineers survived the winter and returned to England.

Figure 6.24
Inuit who live in Nunavut, Canada's newest territory, have survived for thousands of years in this harsh, cold climate, with its long winter nights.

GEOSKILLS

Reading a Topographic Map

A **topographic map** is a representation of a three-dimensional surface on a flat piece of paper. Reading one of these maps is still based on the Title, Legend, and Compass (TLC) process. The **contour lines** are the main element that is added to topographic maps. These lines are used to join points of equal elevation. The closer the lines appear on a topographic map, the steeper the slope. Topographic maps have a variety of uses. They can be used for planning the best route for a bike ride or a hike. They can also be used to figure out the location of a new school or local sports field.

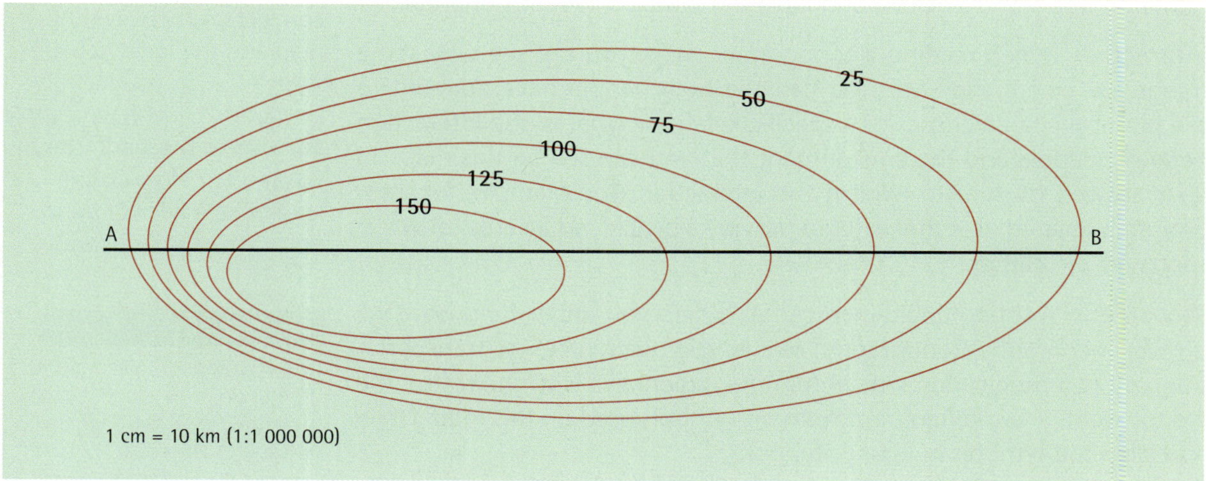

Figure 6.25

This landform sketch uses contour lines to join points of equal elevation. What is represented when the contour lines are close together? What is represented when the contour lines are farther apart?

Draw a cross-section along the line A–B. Such a line makes use of the contours and map information to draw a representation of the ups and downs of the land surface. To make a cross-section, complete the following steps:

1. Place the edge of a piece of paper along the line A–B.
2. Mark where each contour meets the paper, and number each contour's elevation.
3. Place your marked paper edge along a line on another sheet of paper.
4. Draw an *x*-axis and *y*-axis. Let point A begin at the *x*-axis, and let point B be at the appropriate point along the *y*-axis.
5. Assign a vertical scale up the *x*-axis, such as 1 cm = 25 m.
6. Transfer the points from your paper edge accurately to the graph by drawing tiny dots at the correct elevation.
7. Join the dots with a fine pencil line. Make sure that you mark the starting and ending points correctly.
8. Title your cross-section "Cross-Section along A–B on Sketch Map."
9. Label the words "hilltop," "steepest slope," and "gradual slope" in the correct spots along the cross-section profile line.
10. Label the scales: "Vertical Scale 1 cm = 25 m"; "Map Scale 1 cm = 10 km."

continues...

GEOSKILLS

Reading a Topographic Map *(continued)*

Topographic maps can be used to look at location and place, and interactions and movement within an area.

Location and Place: These maps can give you a clear picture of the physical and human-made characteristics of a location. You can begin to see physical features such as swamps, canyons, and orchards. Using the topographic map (Figure 6.26), locate two physical features and two human-made features. Draw and label the symbols in your notebook.

Interaction: When reading a topographic map, you can see why some things are where they are. You can see how people have adapted to the physical characteristics of a specific location. What is one interaction between people and the environment that you can see on this map? In your answer, be sure to explain the interaction (for example, a campground is located near the water to provide a beach and an area for water sports for the campers).

Movement: A topographic map can also help you understand how the physical geography (topography) of a location can influence transportation and communication links within the region and with the rest of the world. Identify two different movement symbols used on this map. Draw and label the symbols in your notebook.

LITERACY TIP

Reading Maps

When reading a map, use the TLC method you learned about in Chapter 1. Also, examine the map for patterns of points, lines, areas, and volume. Then, look for connections between the map and the ideas you are studying. Can you identify landforms? How have people adapted to the landforms in this region? How do the landforms influence transportation in this region?

Topographic Map of Vineland, Ontario

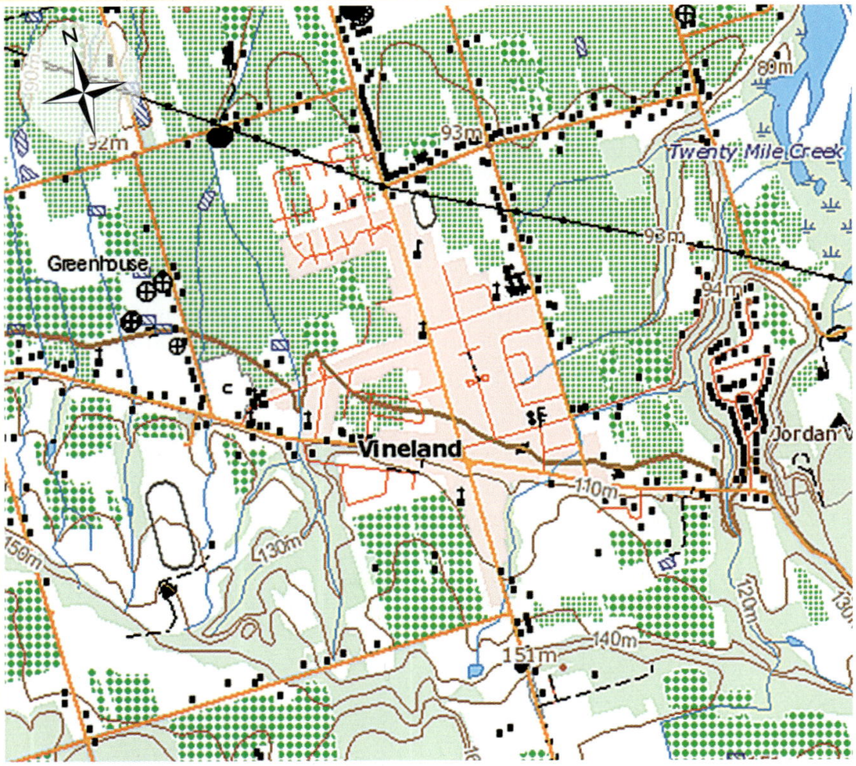

0 0.25 0.5 0.75 1.0 km

Map Scale 1:11 430

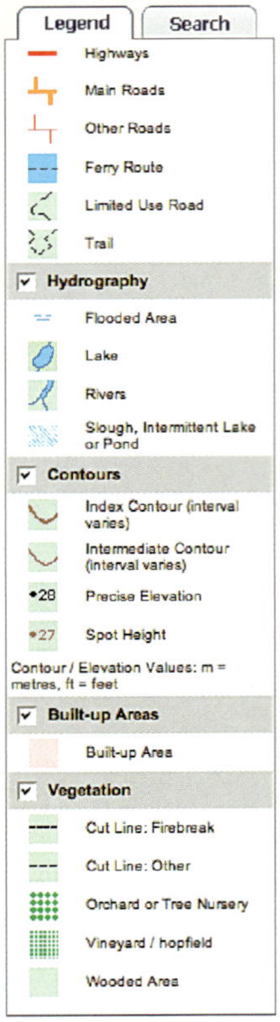

Figure 6.26

This is a topographic map for the town of Vineland, Ontario. This town is in the Niagara Region of Ontario.

Great Lakes–St. Lawrence Lowlands

The third and smallest of Canada's plains is the Great Lakes–St. Lawrence Lowlands. It is the most densely populated part of Canada. This small lowland region includes the southern portion of Ontario between Georgian Bay and Kingston, and an area in southern Québec along the St. Lawrence River. It is a relatively flat and easily farmed region—a very prosperous area. The rivers in this area drain into the Great Lakes and the Atlantic Ocean. These rivers have played an important role in the development of settlement and industry.

Figure 6.27

The St. Lawrence Lowlands, mainly east and northeast of Montreal, were flooded by the sea after the last Ice Age. When the sea moved back, the St. Lawrence River gradually established its course.

Shields

Most shields are very rocky. They contain some of the oldest rocks on Earth. Some are over 3.8 billion years old. Shields exist on every continent around the world. In fact, shields are the foundations of our continents.

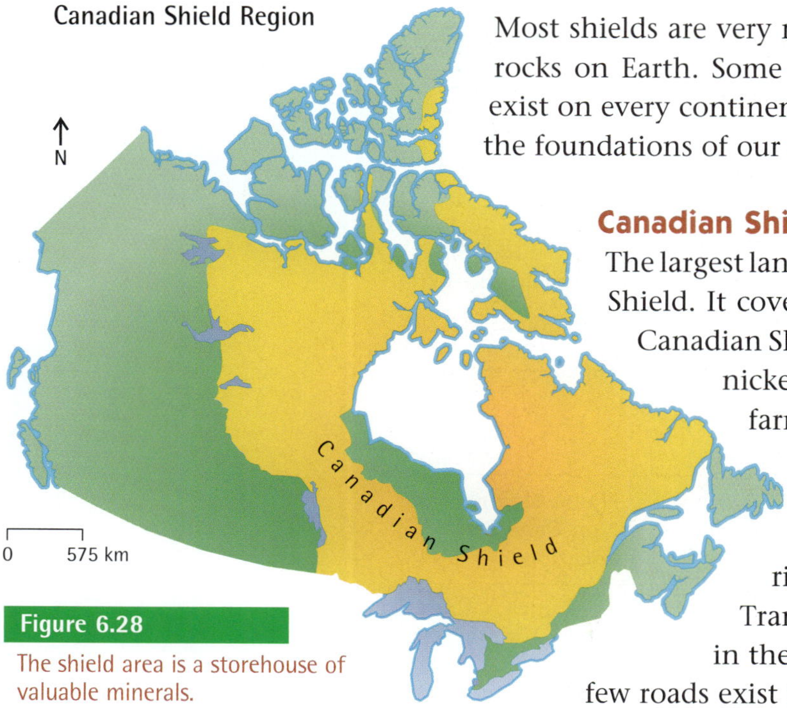

Figure 6.28

The shield area is a storehouse of valuable minerals.

Canadian Shield

The largest landform region in Canada is the Canadian Shield. It covers over half of the country's area. The Canadian Shield is rich in mineral resources such as nickel, copper, zinc, and lead. Most types of farming and settlement are very difficult on the Shield because of poor soil, the rocky landscape, and harsh weather. Vast stretches are covered in lakes, rivers, and swamp areas. Except for the Trans-Canada Highway, and logging roads in the southern part of the Canadian Shield, few roads exist in this huge area.

Figure 6.29

This is Arthur Lismer's Isles of Spruce, Hart House, University of Toronto Permanent Collection. It depicts the Canadian Shield.

CONNECTIONS TO Art

Often, artists give us their "sense of place" in their work. We can understand a great deal about a place by studying artwork that depicts it. Look at the landscape shown in Figure 6.29. What characteristics of the land were special to the artist? Does it create any feelings or moods for you? What aspect of the place do you think the artist captures best?

The southern part of the Canadian Shield, in Ontario, is often referred to as cottage country—the Muskokas, Kawartha Lakes, and the Haliburton Highlands. These three areas are on the border between the Great Lakes–St. Lawrence Lowlands and the Canadian Shield.

AFTER READING

1. Look at a world population map in the Map Appendix. Compare it to the map of mountain regions on page 130. Describe and explain the pattern you discover.
2. Copy and complete the chart comparing Canada's different regions to other world regions.

Type of Landform Region	Physical Characteristics	Name of One Canadian Location	Name of One Non-Canadian Location

Knowledge and Understanding

1. **a)** What is a landform region? Give examples to make your explanation clear to someone who has not studied this part of geography yet.

   b) In which landform region do you live? How do you know?

2. **a)** If you flew above the border between Canada and the United States from the Pacific coast to the Atlantic coast, what landform regions would you fly over? Identify and describe the landforms you would see as you flew over these regions (see Map Appendix).

   b) If you flew from Toronto to the North Pole, what landform regions would you see as you flew? Identify and describe the landforms you would see as you flew over these regions (see Map Appendix).

3. In Chapter 5, you learned about using word puzzles, like acronyms, to remember information. Create an acronym to help you recall the seven Canadian landform regions.

Inquiry/Research and Communication Skills

4. A brochure is a pamphlet that is used to inform people about a specific topic. A brochure uses both written and visual text to communicate information in a detailed but concise way. Design and produce a brochure intended to make people want to visit a very dangerous and perhaps remote landform region. You want to excite the tourists with the possible danger, but you also want to reassure them of their safety. Add drawings, maps, and/or photos cut out of magazines. Ask some of your classmates to pretend they have visited this landform region, and record their comments about their adventure tour with your company as quotes for your brochure.

5. Make up new names for the landform regions of Canada. The new names should be as descriptive of the landforms as possible. For example, instead of the Western Cordillera, you might call them the Mighty High Western Mountains.

Map, Globe, and Graphic Skills

6. **a)** Look at a physical map of North and South America (see Map Appendix). Find and list at least four ways in which these two continents are similar. Consider landforms, rivers, oceans, coastlines, and other characteristics.

   b) Think of three questions that would help other students understand the similarities and differences of landform patterns between North and South America (for example, Which continent has the highest mountains?).

7. Design a reasonably large island (roughly 10 kilometres by 20 kilometres) on which you would love to live. Suggested scale is 1 cm = 1 km.

   a) Show the locations of at least three different landforms on your island. Remember, landforms will affect the kind of activities you can do (skiing, swimming, canoeing, and so on). Be sure to have someplace on your island that allows you to build a dock or an airport.

   b) Draw contour lines on your map. Assume your island is in an ocean, so start at sea level. Remember the rules for contour lines:

   - Contours never cross.
   - Contours are drawn at a constant chosen contour interval.
   - Closed-in contours are hills.
   - The closer the contours, the steeper the slope.
   - Contours bend upstream when crossing a river or stream.

   c) Draw a cross-sectional diagram of your island. See GeoSkills on page 135 for help.

Application

8. Read newspapers, watch television news, or read current Canadian magazines to find a story that concerns a major Canadian landform. The story may be about a flood on the Prairies, a lost hiker on a mountain, an avalanche in the Rockies, or some other event. Explain how the characteristics of the landform are an important part of the story.

9. Take a virtual tour of the Group of Seven artists by using the search string *Group of Seven art*. Find a piece of art that you feel displays the characteristics of any four landform regions in Canada. Briefly explain why you feel each choice represents its landform region well.

7 Patterns in Natural Systems: Climate and Vegetation

IN THIS CHAPTER

- explain how world climate patterns are caused by many factors working together
- draw and understand climate graphs, and use them to compare different climates
- explain how natural vegetation is shaped by factors like climate, landforms, and soils
- identify ways that natural events affect people and the environment
- use the new terms in this chapter correctly as you investigate the topics
- use a variety of maps to identify patterns on the surface of Earth
- locate and use helpful information from primary and secondary sources
- share the results of research for different reasons and audiences using options such as computer slide shows, videos, websites, oral presentations, written notes and reports, drawings, tables, charts, diagrams, maps, models, and graphs
- use climate and physical features to make a decision about the ideal locations for tourist destinations

KEY VOCABULARY

air mass
altitude
chinook
climate
greenhouse gas
humus
low-pressure area
natural vegetation
ocean current
orographic precipitation
prevailing wind
weather
wind

Weather or Climate?

BEFORE READING

1. How much does the weather affect your life? Make a list of the ways that the weather affects your behaviour (for example, you may put a coat on before you leave for school in the morning).

What is the weather for today? Is it hot or cold? Is it raining? This daily change in outdoor conditions is called **weather**. When we talk about weather, we usually describe the following:

- the temperature
- whether the Sun is shining or not
- if there is any precipitation

Figure 7.1
Does this photograph show weather conditions or climate conditions?

People may confuse weather with **climate**. Weather deals only with short-term changes, while climate is long term. Climate refers to the yearly patterns of precipitation and temperature that emerge when all the daily weather patterns are combined.

Geographers look for patterns in the way temperatures and precipitation change over the year. Geographers study climate because its patterns tell a great deal about places. Climate is one of the most important factors influencing the vegetation found in a place. Together, climate and vegetation shape the soils. The climate, vegetation, and soils of a place influence people and their activities.

Seasonal Changes

In Ontario, the seasons are spring, summer, fall, and winter. However, in the north, there are really only two seasons—a long winter and a short summer. In the tropics, the temperature is fairly constant throughout the year, but there is a rainy season and a dry season.

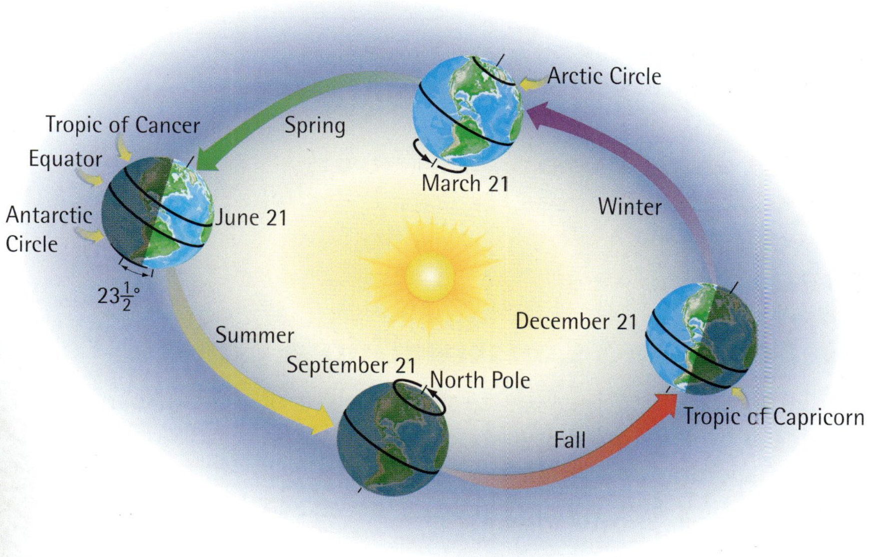

Figure 7.2

The shape of Earth and the tilt of its axis result in seasonal differences in different parts of the world. This diagram shows seasons in the northern hemisphere. What would be different if the diagram was showing seasons in the southern hemisphere?

DURING READING

1. What words would you use to describe the climate of your area?
2. We need to give details about both temperatures and amounts of precipitation over an entire year to describe the climate of a place. What are two good ways of doing this?
3. How are climate and weather different?

Climate Graphs

To describe the climate where you live may seem like a difficult task, but there is a simple and effective method. Climates can be studied and compared by analyzing climate graphs. A climate graph makes it easier to identify patterns because it combines two graphs. Temperature is displayed using a line graph, and precipitation is shown using a bar graph.

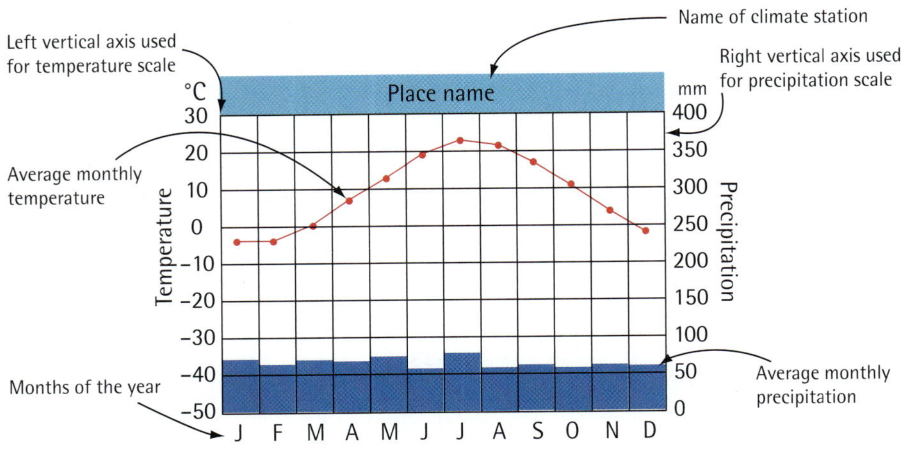

Figure 7.3

This is the way we show climate information in a graph. The GeoSkills feature on this page explains how to construct a climate graph.

GeoSkills

Reading and Constructing a Climate Graph

A climate graph is a visual way to show two sets of data: the average monthly temperature, and the average monthly precipitation for a place. You still use TAPP (Title, Axes, Pattern, Purpose) to read and construct climate graphs.

Let us begin with constructing a climate graph for Saskatoon, Saskatchewan. Figure 7.4 below shows the data you will need to construct your climate graph.

	Jan	Feb	Mar	Apr	May	June	Jul	Aug	Sept	Oct	Nov	Dec
Average monthly temperature (°C)	−17	−13	−6	4	12	16	19	17	11	5	−5	−14
Average monthly precipitation (mm)	16	13	16	20	44	63	58	37	32	17	14	17

Figure 7.4

Use this data to construct your climate graph.

continues…

GEOSKILLS

Reading and Constructing a Climate Graph *(continued)*

Step One: Create the axes for the climate graph using graph paper and a ruler. You will need two *y*-axes (vertical), one on the left side of your graph and one on the right side of your graph. The *y*-axis on the right should be labelled "Precipitation" (mm). Start with 0 at the bottom right corner, and go up by 50 for each line up to 400. Your left *y*-axis should be labelled "Temperature" (°C). The scale for this axis should begin with –50 °C at the bottom left corner of your graph. Every line should increase at 10 °C up to 30 °C. Label the *x*-axis (horizontal) with the initials of the months.

Step Two: Draw a temperature line graph. For each month, put a red dot at the correct location using the left *y*-axis. Look at the example in Figure 7.5. January's temperature has been completed for you. You can see that there is a red dot at –17 °C. For February, you would place the dot at –13 °C, and so on, until all 12 months are complete. Place the dot at the centre of each month's section on the graph. Join all of the red dots together to create a temperature line graph.

Step Three: Draw a precipitation bar graph. Start with January, and draw a horizontal line at 16 millimetres, making sure to use the right *y*-axis (precipitation). Use your ruler to draw two vertical lines down to the bottom of your graph. Follow this process for all 12 months. When all bars are complete, colour them blue.

Step Four: Give your climate graph a title.

Step Five: Read the climate graph, and ask yourself questions about climate patterns such as the following:

- Which months have the least precipitation? Which have the most precipitation? What patterns can you see in precipitation?
- Which months are coldest? Which months are warmest? How many degrees are there between the warmest and coldest months? For example, does more precipitation seem to fall during certain months of the year?
- How would the information on this climate graph be useful to a farmer? To a resort operator?

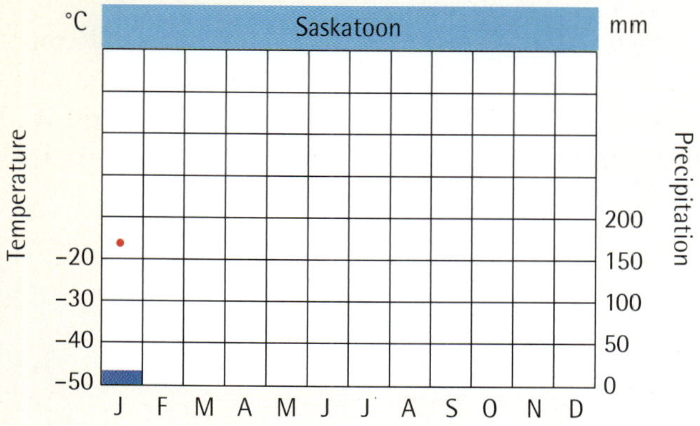

Figure 7.5

These are the first steps in constructing a climate graph.

Global Climate Patterns

Many different climates exist around the world. No two places in the world have exactly the same climates, but some areas have similar characteristics. Areas that are alike can be grouped together into climatic regions. When you look at these regions on a map, patterns begin to emerge. Geographers describe these climate patterns and look for explanations for them.

Figure 7.6

Look closely at the global climate regions. Can you see a pattern? Where are the tropical regions situated? Where are the dry regions? Where are the wet regions? Think about what you know about lines of latitude.

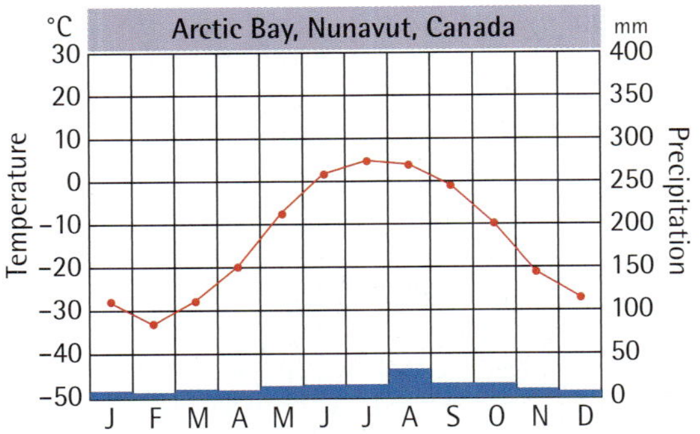

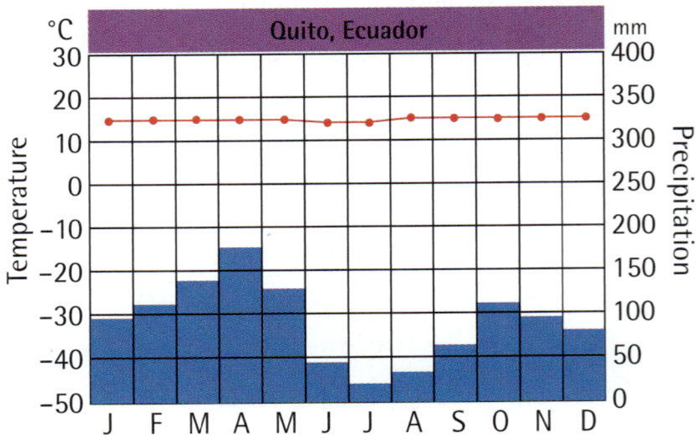

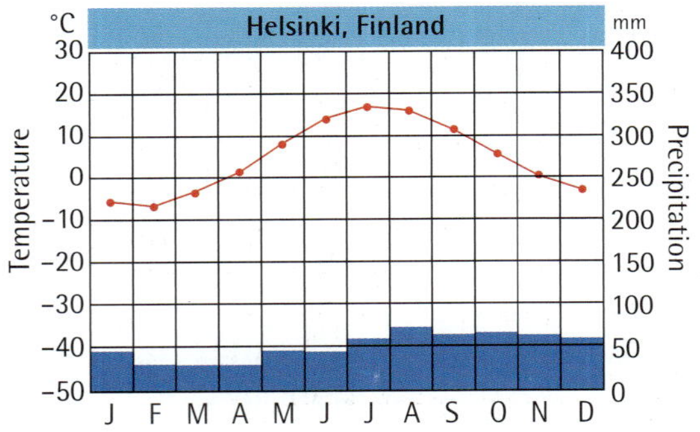

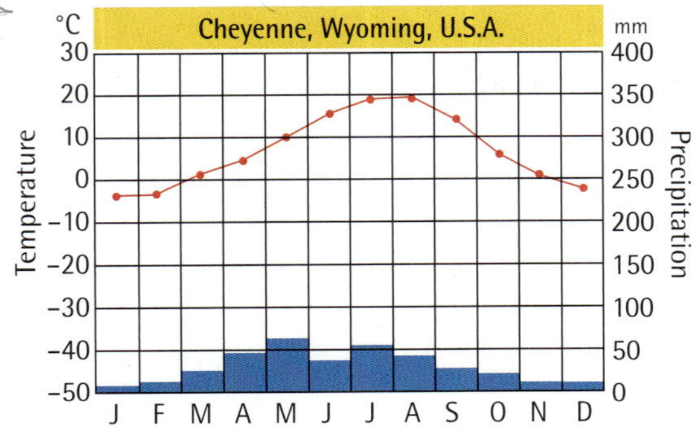

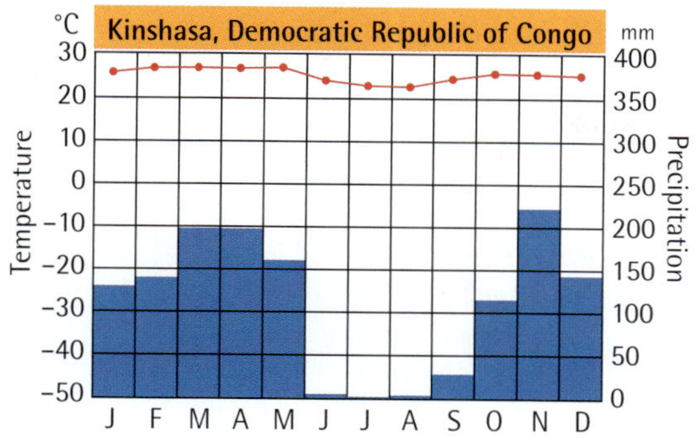

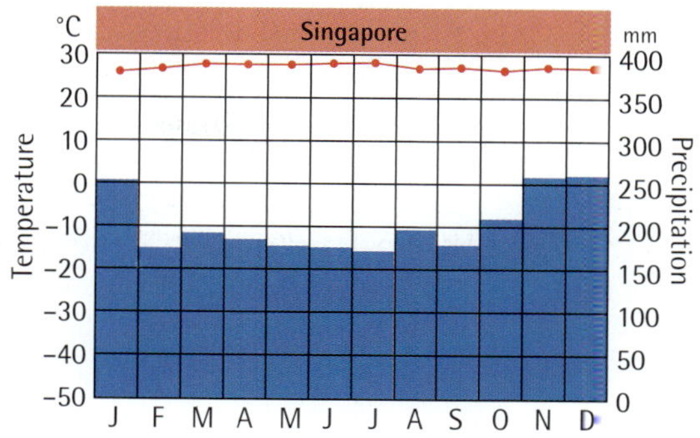

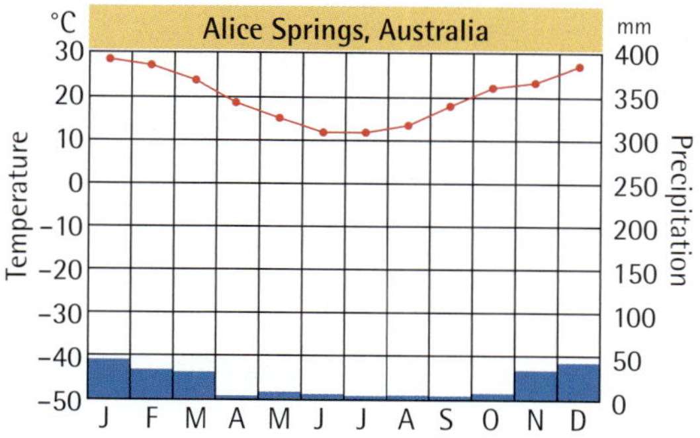

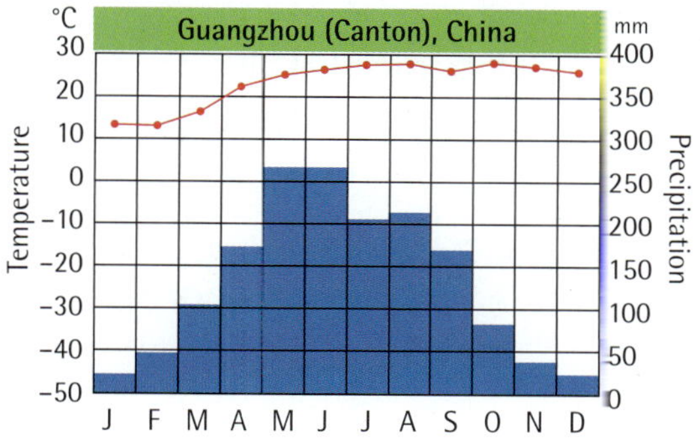

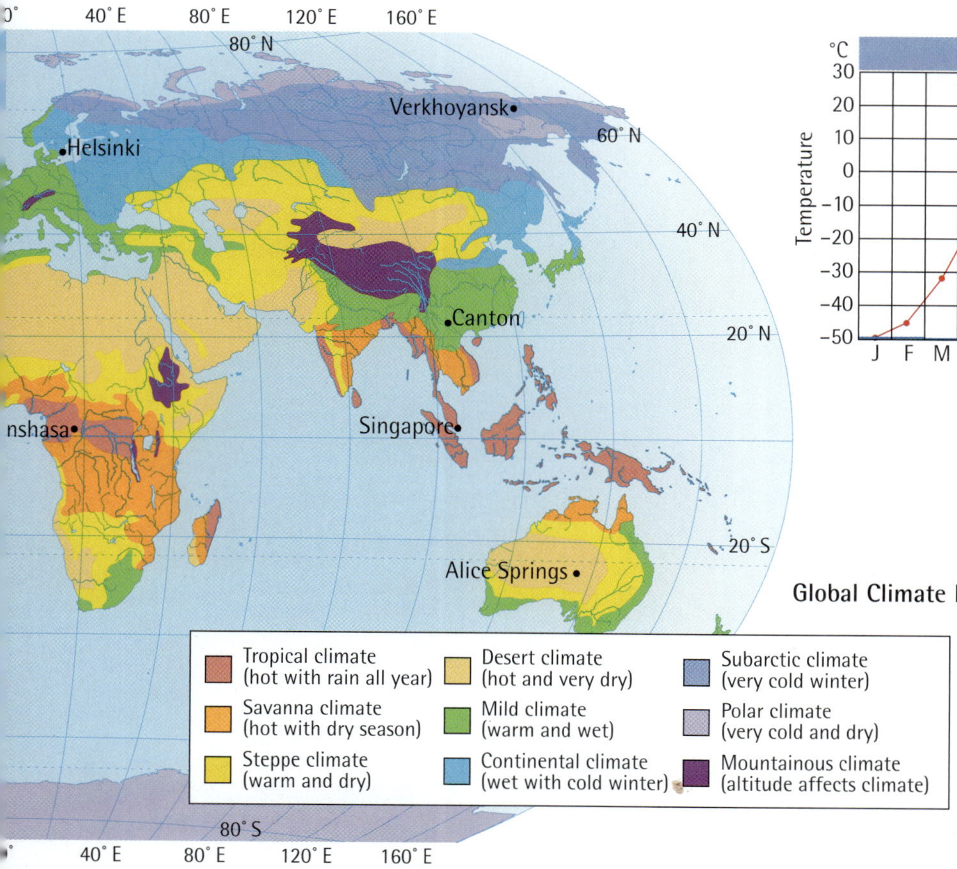

Global Climate Regions

AFTER READING

1. a) Follow the instructions in GeoSkills on page 143, and construct a climate graph for Mexico City, Mexico. Use the data below.

	Jan	Feb	Mar	Apr	May	June	Jul	Aug	Sept	Oct	Nov	Dec
Average monthly temperature (°C)	12	13	16	18	19	19	17	18	18	16	14	13
Average monthly precipitation (mm)	13	5	10	20	53	119	170	152	130	51	18	8

Make sure that all of the labels are added to your climate graph.

b) Read your completed climate graph, and note the patterns that you see. Make three statements about the climate of Mexico City.

2. a) Choose three of the climate graphs shown in Figure 7.6. In your notebook, complete a chart with the following headings:

	Location 1	Location 2	Location 3
Average annual temperature (Add the temperatures and divide by 12.)			
Annual temperature range (Subtract the coolest month from the warmest month.)			
Annual precipitation (Add the monthly precipitation totals.)			

b) Which location has a climate most similar to the climate in your community? Explain why you made this choice.

3. a) The three climate graphs below show different precipitation patterns. Look back at the climate graphs in Figure 7.6, and find one example that is close to each of these patterns.

b) Make up a sentence to describe the pattern of precipitation in Toronto, and another sentence to compare the pattern of precipitation in Vancouver.

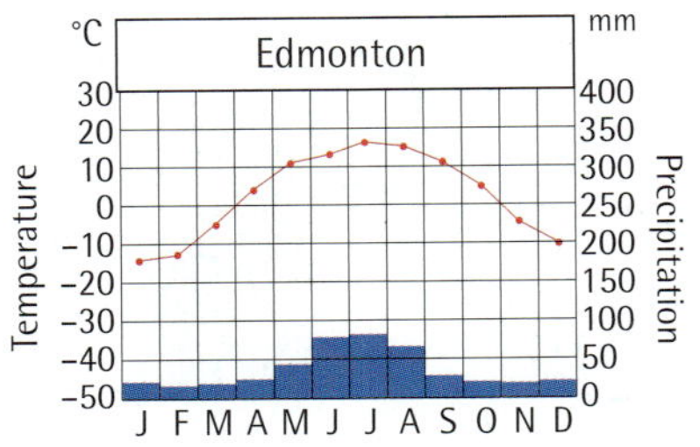

Summer Maximum

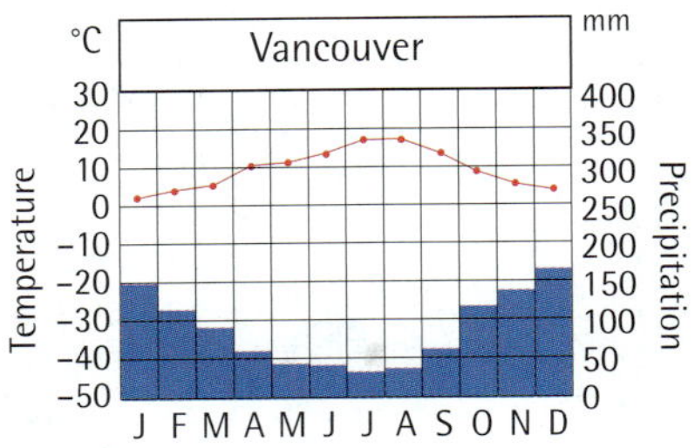

Winter Maximum

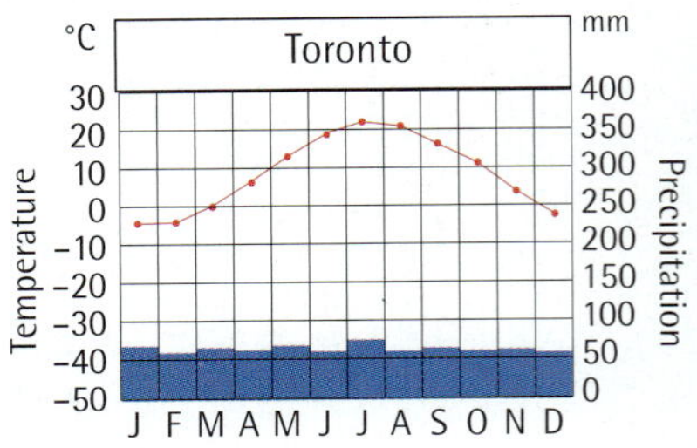

Evenly Distributed

BEFORE READING

1. Without reading ahead, what conditions shape or affect the climate of the area where you live in Canada?

Climate Factors

Climate factors are those conditions that shape or affect the climate that we find in any place in the world over the long term. Many factors can affect the climate of a place. Each place has a different climate because these factors are found in different combinations and strengths. Some of these factors are global conditions. They influence all parts of Earth. Other factors are local and affect small parts of Earth's surface. Let us look first at global climate factors, and then at local ones.

Global Climate Factor: Latitude

The hottest areas on Earth are those located closest to the equator. The coolest areas are those located closest to the poles. This is due to Earth's shape. The places close to the equator receive the most direct rays of the Sun. Regions farther from the equator receive rays that hit Earth's surface on a slant. Therefore, the Sun's energy is spread over a larger area of Earth.

This unequal heating of Earth's surface causes air to move from one place to another, creating winds in the atmosphere and currents in the oceans.

WEB LINK

For more information about climate and climate patterns, go to **www.nelson.com/phygeo7**.

Figure 7.7

As you move away from the equator, the Sun's energy has to pass through more of the atmosphere. Less heat reaches Earth's surface.

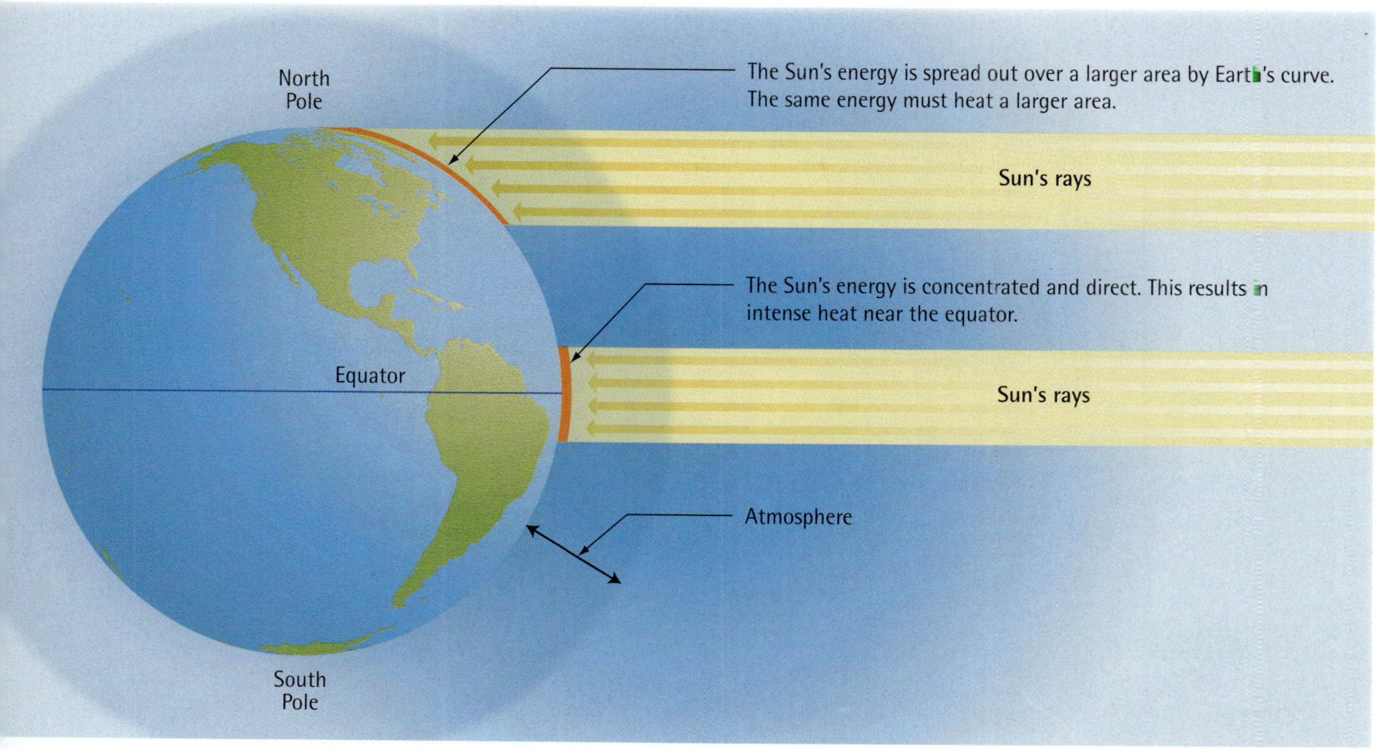

Global Climate Factor: Wind Systems

The air over the hotter parts of Earth is warmed by the heat from the surface of the land or water. A heated **air mass** rises because it expands as it warms. Cooler air slides in below and under the rising air. These movements of air across Earth's surface are called **winds**.

Since the equatorial areas are hot and the polar areas are cold, would you expect the winds to always move along Earth's surface from the poles to the equator? This does not happen for two main reasons: Earth rotates, and land and water are distributed unequally around Earth's surface.

Earth's rotation on its axis from west to east creates a force that causes the winds in the northern hemisphere to seem to swerve to the right, and winds in the southern hemisphere to swerve to the left.

The unequal distribution of land and water around Earth's surface (for example, water at the North Pole and land at the South Pole) means that the pattern of hot and cold is not uniform. These two forces working together give a global circulation pattern of rising and falling air masses.

Winds are the air movements that bring daily weather to your area. The **prevailing winds** in an area are the winds that blow most commonly for that particular area. Winds across Canada generally blow from west to east, so we call these winds the prevailing westerlies.

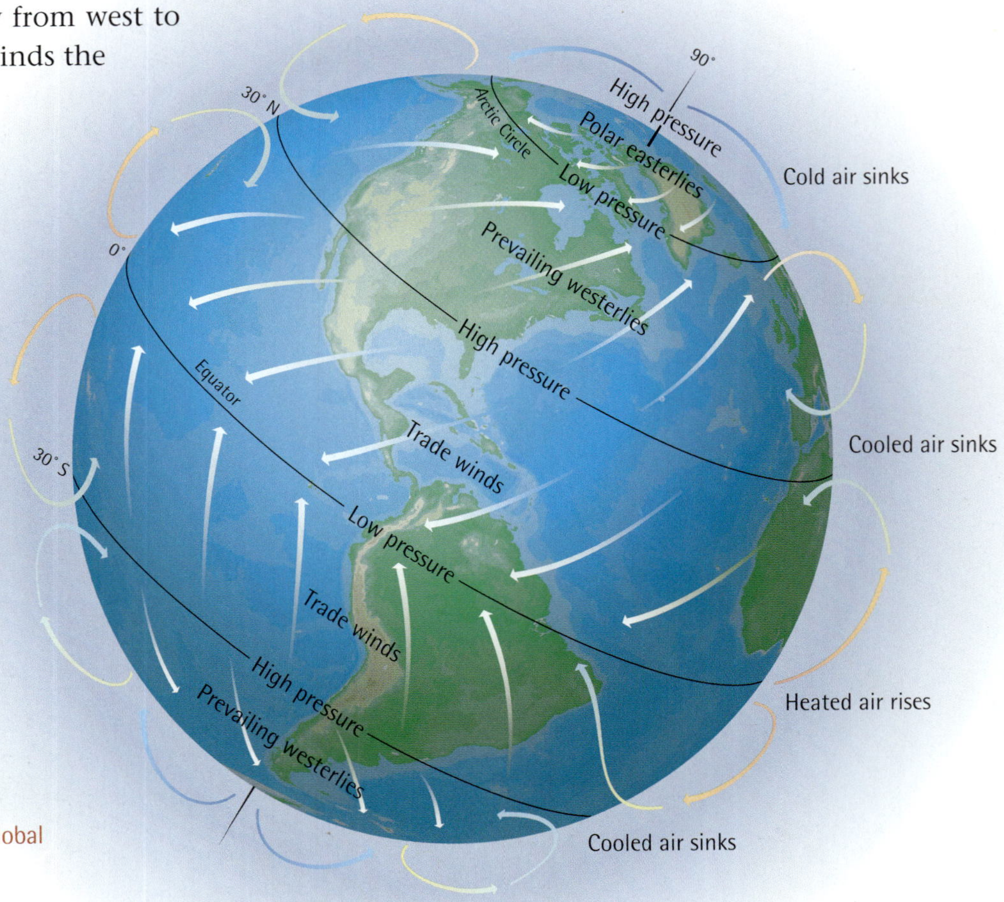

Figure 7.8

Notice the patterns in the global wind systems. What are the prevailing winds in Mexico?

Movement of North America's Air Masses

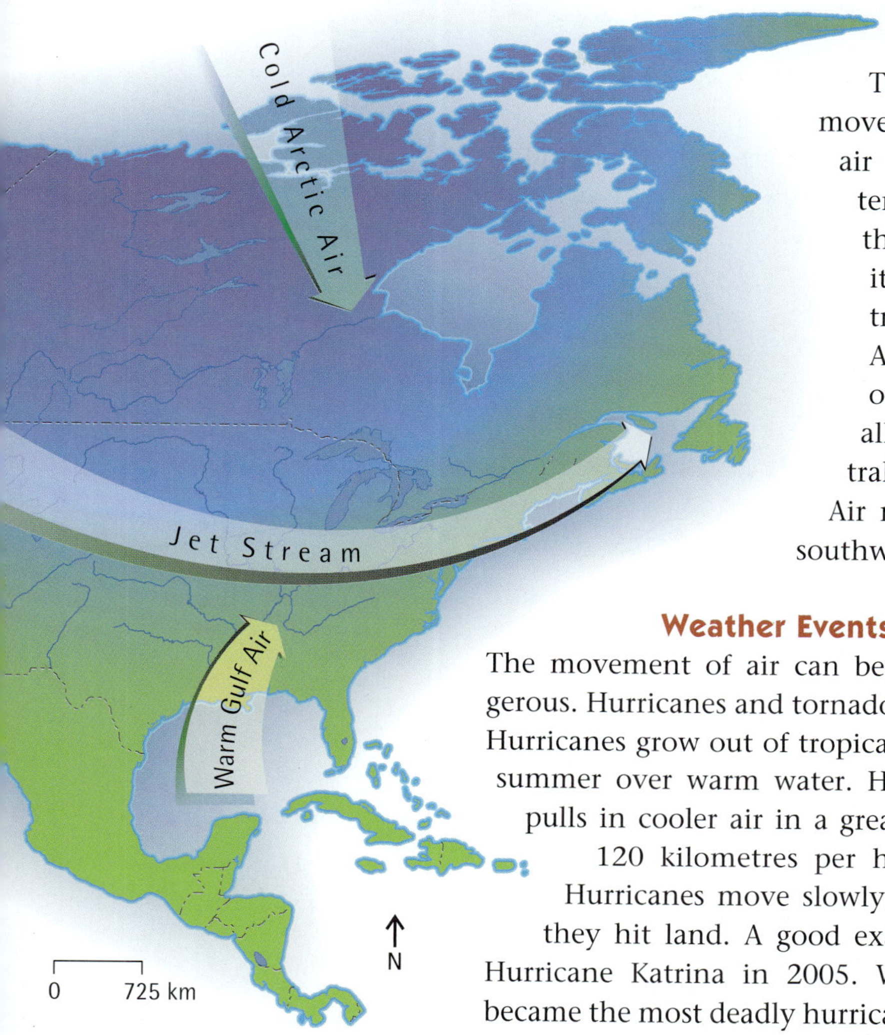

Figure 7.9

Air masses have their origins in the cold Arctic or the warm Gulf of Mexico. The jet stream is a fast-moving current of air in the upper levels of the atmosphere marking the boundary between the cold and warm air masses.

Global Climate Factor: Air Masses

The unequal heating of Earth causes the movement of huge volumes of air called air masses. Each air mass has the same temperature and moisture conditions throughout. If it formed over a cold area, it will be cold and dry. If it formed in a tropical area, it will be warm and moist. An air mass affects the weather of areas over which it travels. For example, usually a few times each winter the central part of Canada has long cold spells. Air masses form in the Arctic and move southward, bringing in cold, dry weather.

Weather Events: Dangerous Winds

The movement of air can become so rapid that it becomes dangerous. Hurricanes and tornadoes are two examples of violent winds. Hurricanes grow out of tropical storms. Tropical storms form in late summer over warm water. Heat causes air to rise, which rapidly pulls in cooler air in a great spiral. When wind speeds are over 120 kilometres per hour, a storm becomes a hurricane. Hurricanes move slowly, but they are very destructive when they hit land. A good example of a dangerous hurricane was Hurricane Katrina in 2005. When it smashed into Louisiana, it became the most deadly hurricane in the history of the United States. Over 1800 people lost their lives, and damage was estimated at $81 billion.

Tornadoes form over land in the spring or early summer. They are created by winds rushing into a **low-pressure area** that is connected to a thunderstorm. Wind speeds in the centre of a tornado can reach up to 500 kilometres per hour. Tornadoes rarely last more than an hour, but they move quickly and wildly. The strongest tornado recorded in Canada occurred in June 2007 at Elie, Manitoba. Wind speeds were estimated at between 420 and 510 kilometres per hour. Fortunately, no one was killed during this weather event.

Fact File

- Tornado Alley is an area of the United States that runs from northwest Texas across Oklahoma and through Kansas. The area receives an average of 200 tornadoes each year.
- Canada has an average of 75 tornadoes per year. A third of them are in Ontario.
- June is the peak month for tornadoes.

Figure 7.10

This is a photograph of a tornado that struck northern Texas in June 1995. A tornado's path of destruction is usually confined to a small area less than 25 kilometres long.

Global Climate Factor: Ocean Currents

The ocean's water is moving constantly, pushed by prevailing winds. The winds create **ocean currents**, that is, water moving in one direction. When ocean currents are traced on a map of the world, they flow in circular patterns. In the northern hemisphere, currents move in a clockwise direction. In the southern hemisphere, they move in a counterclockwise direction.

The temperature of a current depends on where it comes from. Warm currents start in the tropics and bring warm water into cooler regions. Cold currents begin in the polar regions and bring cool water toward the equator. These currents either warm or cool the climates of land areas nearby. A good illustration of this is the United Kingdom. Located on the western edge of Europe, the United Kingdom is at the same latitude as northern Labrador. Labrador is cold in the winter, but Britain remains quite mild. This is due to the Gulf Stream, a warm ocean current that begins in the tropical Gulf of Mexico. It flows northward across the Atlantic Ocean to warm the coast of Europe.

1. Four global climate factors have been discussed so far. Recording jot notes is a good strategy to help you understand and remember the main points about these factors. Use point-form notes to summarize how each factor affects climate.
2. Review your jot notes for each climate factor. Can you capture in one sentence how each factor affects global climate? Summarize the main idea of each climate factor.
3. Based on what you have learned about these global climate factors, can you describe how each of these factors affects the climate in your part of Canada?

Fact File

Coral brought from the Caribbean Sea by the Gulf Stream is found on beaches along the west coast of Scotland in the United Kingdom.

Literacy Tip

Summarizing

Summarizing means choosing the most important ideas in a text. Follow these guidelines:

- Read a section of the text to get a general understanding.
- Read the first paragraph and look for the main ideas.
- Look away and identify the main ideas. If you cannot remember, reread the text.
- Record these ideas in your own words.
- Follow the same guidelines for the rest of the paragraphs in the section.

Local Climate Factor: Altitude

Mount Fuji is the highest mountain (3776 metres) in Japan. If you were to climb from the base of Mount Fuji to its summit, you would feel the temperature getting colder and colder. Why does the temperature decrease as you approach the summit of the mountain? The reason is its altitude.

Figure 7.11

You can see from the cherry blossoms that the temperature at the foot of Mount Fuji in Japan is higher than the temperature at the summit, where there is still snow.

Altitude refers to the vertical height of land. It is measured in metres above sea level. Air is less dense at higher altitudes than at sea level. Air pressure decreases the higher up you go because there is a lower gravitational pull on molecules of air. With less pressure, air expands and loses heat. Temperature drops approximately 6 °C for every 1000 metres increase in altitude. Communities located on a mountain will have lower average temperatures than places located at the foot of the mountain.

Fact File

The snow cap on the top of Mount Fuji is getting smaller with each year that passes. A rising global temperature means that more melting takes place each spring, and the snow cap shrinks.

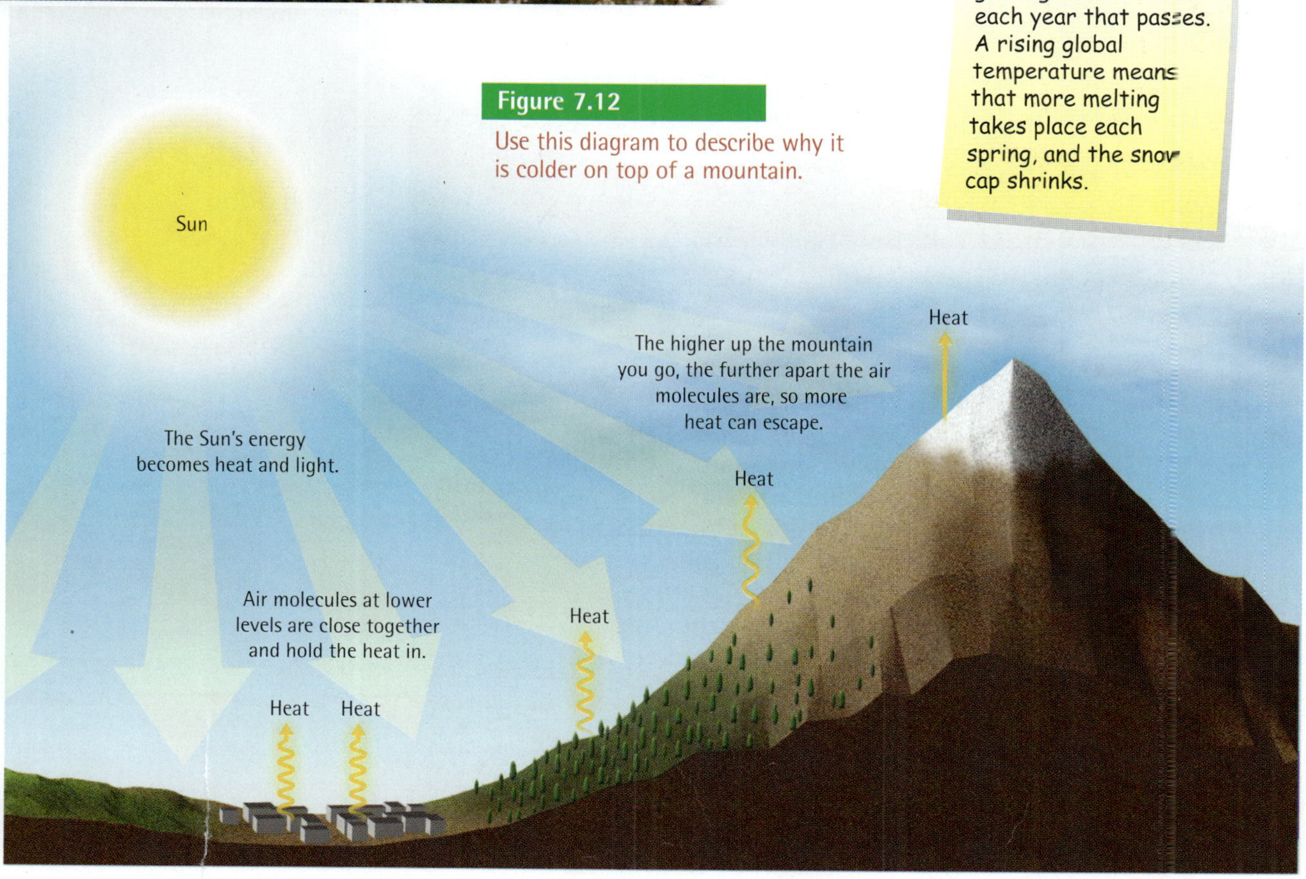

Figure 7.12

Use this diagram to describe why it is colder on top of a mountain.

Local Climate Factor: Mountain Barriers

Mountain barriers influence climate patterns. When moisture-bearing winds meet mountains, they move up the windward sides of these barriers. As the air rises, the reduction in air pressure causes the air to cool. The cooler temperatures cause the moisture to condense. This condensation produces clouds, and then rain. By the time the air reaches the tops of the mountains, it has released most of its moisture. This type of rainfall is sometimes known as relief precipitation, or **orographic precipitation**.

Parts of the west side of British Columbia's Coast Mountains receive over 2000 millimetres of rain every year due to orographic precipitation. As the air mass comes down the east side of the mountain—the leeward side away from the wind—the air becomes warmer and drier. The east side of these mountains remains dry. This side may get as little as 300 millimetres of precipitation annually.

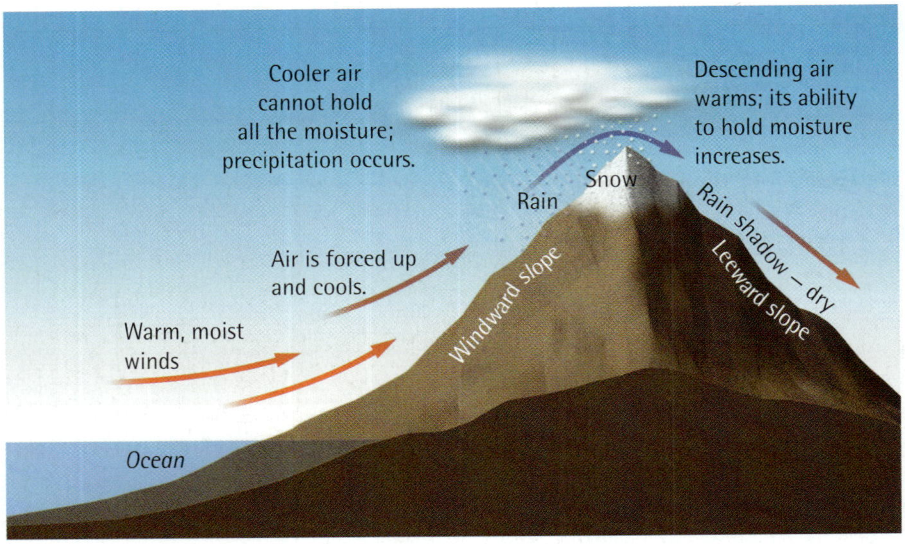

Figure 7.13

Places on the windward side of mountains have more rainfall than those on the leeward side.

Connections to Science

Sometimes in January and February, the warm air that has travelled up the windward slopes of the mountains of British Columbia crosses over and moves down the leeward side of the Rocky Mountains. As this warm air descends into Alberta, it can raise the temperature as much as 24 °C in as little as 15 minutes. This warming wind is called a **chinook**. This unique temperature change creates some very interesting winter and early spring days in Calgary. Piles of snow can melt in a matter of hours.

Local Climate Factor: Bodies of Water

Large bodies of water, such as oceans or lakes, take a long time to heat up or cool down compared to the land around them. This is best seen in the early winter when the ground is covered with snow, but lakes and ponds are not yet frozen over. Temperatures in large bodies of water are cooler in summer than the land nearby and warmer in winter.

A lake's temperature affects the temperature of the land around it. Temperatures in the Toronto area are warmer than the surrounding areas in the winter because of the heat held in the lake. The Toronto area is also cooler in the summer. Overall, the temperatures are more moderate, or less extreme, than they would be without the lake.

Figure 7.14

Large bodies of water hold heat longer than the surrounding land does. How does that show up in this photograph of the shoreline of Lake Ontario?

Figure 7.15

Lake Ontario moderates the climate of the Greater Toronto Area.

Connections to Science

Years ago, the old Canadian National Exhibition stadium in Toronto hosted many of the events that are now held in the Rogers Centre. As the spectators sat in the open stadium, the temperature often dropped considerably. The winds that blew across Lake Ontario would bring in cold air. These cold winds cooled the air so that it could not hold all the water vapor it contained. These condensed water droplets formed a cloud at ground level. On several occasions, fog blew into the stadium. One Grey Cup game actually became known as "The Fog Bowl." These nasty weather conditions caused the stadium to be known as "The Mistake by the Lake."

Fact File

These are the foggiest cities in Canada.

Average days with fog:

St. John's, NF	119
Halifax, NS	100
Saint John, NB	98
Gander, NF	77
Truro, NS	76

If you do not like fog, live in Penticton, BC. It has an average of only 1.5 days of fog per year.

Raindrops Keep Falling

Large bodies of water have an additional effect on climate. As an air mass passes over a large body of water, it picks up moisture. When the air crosses land, it may lose that moisture in the form of snow or rain. Areas near large bodies of water often have more precipitation than places not near water.

After Reading

1. Here are 10 terms that relate to local climate factors. Group the terms according to the three main local climate factors, and create a concept web, with Local Climate Factors at the centre: moderate temperatures, orographic precipitation, altitude, condensation, increased precipitation, chinook, 6°C per 1000 metres, gravitational pull, large bodies of water, and leeward. Add additional terms to your concept web to make sure that it explains local climate factors.
2. In your notebook, complete a chart with the headings below. Identify each local climate factor and how it affects climate. The first entry has been started for you.

Local Factors that Influence Climate	Influence on Climate
Nearness to large bodies of water	Climate of surrounding area is warmer during cooler months and cooler during warmer months.

BEFORE READING

1. Would you like to see the climate of your part of Canada changed? Why or why not?
2. Why do you think that people might be concerned if the climate is changing?

Global Climate Change

So far, this chapter has identified natural factors that shape climate. However, humans are another powerful force that can affect climate. People are causing the world's climate to get warmer.

Causes of Global Climate Change

Human activities have produced extra amounts of **greenhouse gases** that stay in the atmosphere. These greenhouse gases trap and hold heat in the atmosphere and stop it from escaping back out to space. Greenhouse gases have a similar effect to the glass in a greenhouse that you might see in a garden centre or on a farm. Because of the extra greenhouse gases, the average temperature of the planet is rising.

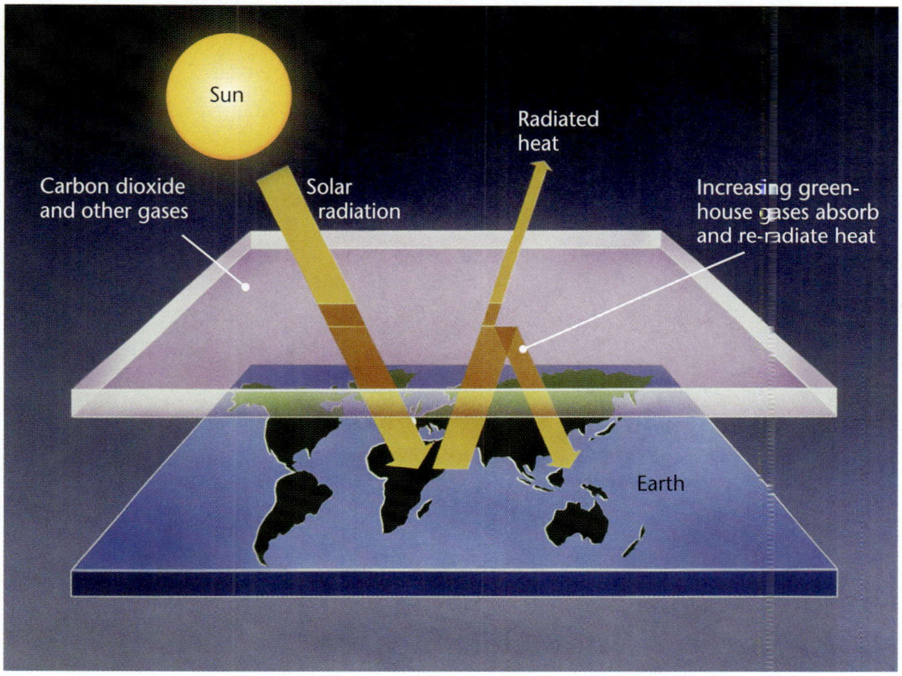

Figure 7.16

Greenhouse gases occur naturally and help to keep the average temperature of the planet at around 15 °C, so that life is possible. Human-produced greenhouse gases are causing temperatures to rise rapidly. Plants and animals cannot evolve fast enough to keep up. Humans will feel the impacts in many ways.

Most of the extra greenhouse gases are produced by burning fuels, including coal, gasoline, and natural gas. These fuels are consumed in vehicles, homes, factories, and stores. We rely on these fuels to live modern lives with lots of comfort. Smaller amounts of greenhouse gases are produced by activities such as the following:

- cutting and burning forests, especially tropical rainforests that are being cleared to create farmland
- raising livestock like cows and pigs (their digestive systems produce greenhouse gases)
- growing rice in paddies where the decaying plant material produces greenhouse gases

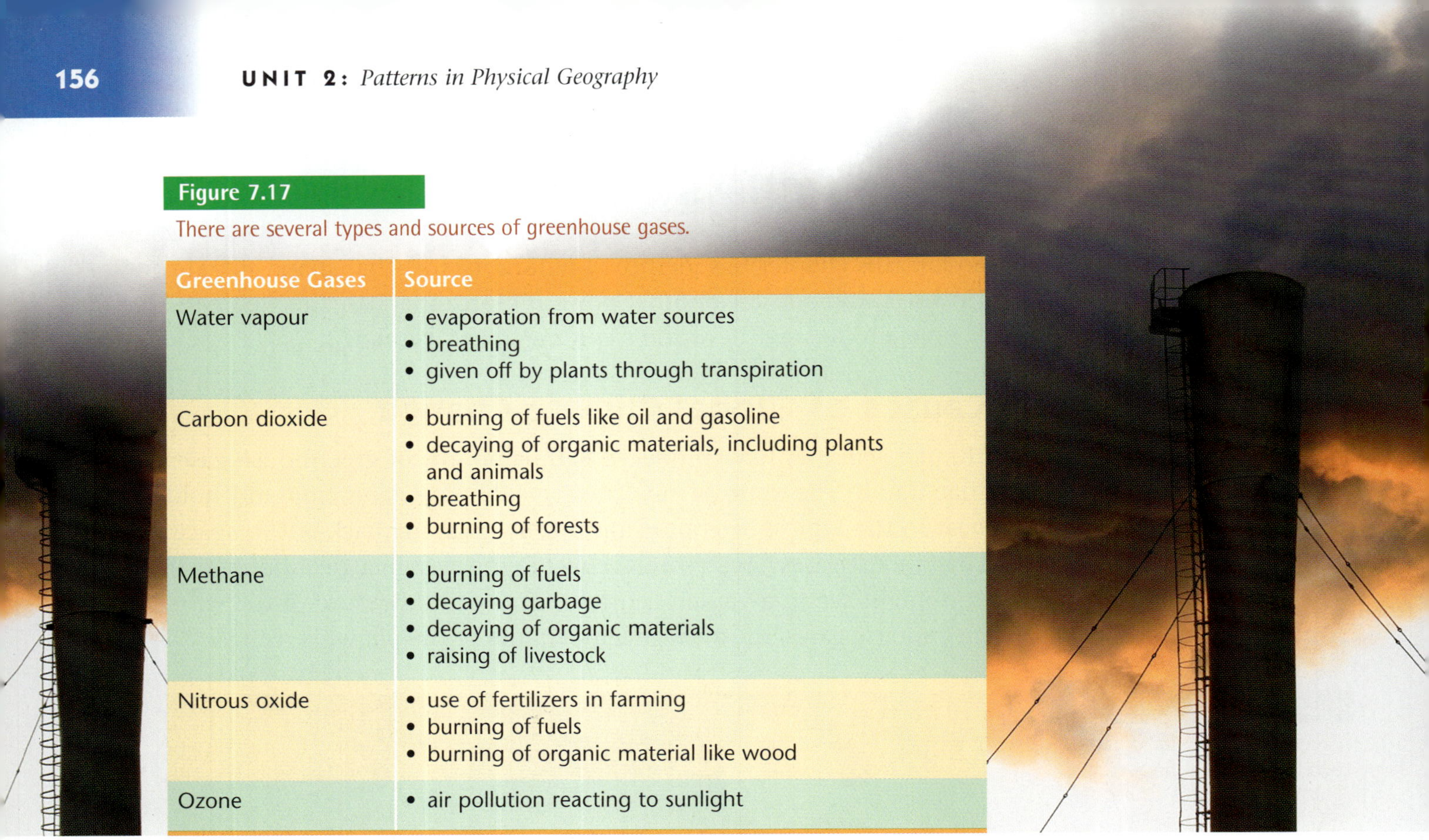

Figure 7.17

There are several types and sources of greenhouse gases.

Greenhouse Gases	Source
Water vapour	• evaporation from water sources • breathing • given off by plants through transpiration
Carbon dioxide	• burning of fuels like oil and gasoline • decaying of organic materials, including plants and animals • breathing • burning of forests
Methane	• burning of fuels • decaying garbage • decaying of organic materials • raising of livestock
Nitrous oxide	• use of fertilizers in farming • burning of fuels • burning of organic material like wood
Ozone	• air pollution reacting to sunlight

Consequences of Global Climate Change

DURING READING

1. What are some ways that global climate change might affect you and how you will live your life?

2. Think about the world's population. Who in the world will feel the harmful effects of global climate change the most? Why?

The whole world will be affected by rising temperatures, but the effects will be quite different across the globe. Some regions will become drier. Others will receive more rainfall. Some locations may actually see their temperatures cool as winds and ocean currents change. One thing is clear—the extra heat will mean more severe weather conditions such as droughts, floods, and tornadoes.

Global climate change will bring high economic costs such as the following:

- Insurance costs will go up because of the extreme weather.
- Forest fires will destroy valuable forests.
- Higher rates of disease will mean more medical costs.
- Farms in parts of Canada that are already dry could be forced out of business by drought.
- While winter heating costs might be reduced, summer cooling costs will jump.

There will be other unexpected costs as well, costs we will discover over the coming decades.

Literacy Tip

Making Connections

Sometimes answers to questions are not stated clearly in the reading. You have to go beyond what is stated on the page and read between the lines. Connecting what you read and what you already know about the topic will help you answer question 2.

Fact File

During the past 100 years, the average global temperature increased by 0.6 °C, while the levels of the oceans rose by 10 to 20 centimetres. In the next 100 years, temperatures are predicted to rise by up to 6 °C.

Figure 7.18

Global climate change will have serious consequences for the world.

Global Impacts of Climate Change	Impacts of Climate Change for Canada
• More heat means more severe weather events such as tornadoes, hurricanes, and floods. • The higher temperatures are melting ice caps in the Arctic and Antarctic. • Glaciers and ice caps are shrinking. • Ocean levels are rising, with increases of up to 95 centimetres predicted by the year 2100. • Many parts of the world will face severe water shortages, while other areas will struggle with floods. • Changes in temperatures will ruin habitats for some species. • The world's coral reefs are being threatened by the warmer ocean temperatures. • People may be forced to leave some areas and migrate to places with less severe impacts, creating overcrowding.	• Rising temperatures may mean that farming is possible in more northern parts of the country. • Drier conditions will result in more forest fires. • Droughts will occur in many parts of the country. • Arctic ice is getting thinner, and polar bears, at the top of the food chain, are finding it harder to live. • Wetlands (swamps and bogs) will dry up. • Warmer temperatures will lead to the spread of tropical diseases like malaria into Canada. • More frequent heat waves will threaten the health of people. • Water levels in the Great Lakes and St. Lawrence River are expected to drop, making shipping more difficult.

Figure 7.19

Canadians are lucky because we are rich enough to be able to deal with some of the problems created by global climate change. Many people in other parts of the world, such as northeastern Kenya, in Africa, are not so fortunate. Their lives will be filled with hardship as a result of climate change.

Go Geo-Green

Cochrane High School Sustainable Development Project

In June 2000, a group of students and teachers in Cochrane, Alberta, started a project to reduce the school's use of fuels that contribute to global climate change. Their plan was to install solar panels and a wind turbine on the roof of the school. To buy the equipment, they needed to raise about $50 000. The panels and generator were in place by 2004. However, the group did not stop there and continued to raise money to install even more solar panels.

The real payoff for the school was the enthusiasm that their efforts generated for alternative energy. Local businesses became interested, and the town government began exploring ways to use wind and solar energy in their own buildings. One of the big highlights for the school was that David Suzuki, environmentalist and broadcaster, was the guest speaker at the dedication ceremony for the energy project in 2005.

Figure 7.20

In 2007, new solar panels were added to the roof of Cochrane High School in Cochrane, Alberta.

AFTER READING

1. What is the most important cause of climate change?
2. Some people have given the name "global warming" to this problem. Explain why the name "global climate change" is a better label to use.
3. What do you think will be the biggest consequence of global climate change in your part of Canada? Explain your answer using information from this section of the chapter.

Vegetation and Soils

BEFORE READING

1. How would you describe the natural vegetation in your area? How is it different than that found in tropical regions?

2. Why do you think the natural vegetation in your area is so different than that found in tropical regions?

To survive, people have basic needs: food, water, and shelter. Green plants have basic needs as well: light, moisture, nutrients, and heat. The availability of these raw materials for plants determines the type of vegetation that exists in a particular area. Vegetation refers to plants that grow in an area. **Natural vegetation** is the term used for plants that are native to the area—plants that grow there naturally without human interference.

Very few areas in the world are left with completely natural vegetation. This is because humans have changed the physical environment. We have destroyed species, introduced new species, and changed the habitat of many places. Humans must be considered one of the most powerful, and dangerous, factors affecting vegetation.

CONNECTIONS TO **Science**

If you could examine the growth rings of a spruce tree from a northern area, you would notice that the rings were quite small and close together. The tree itself would be short. The growth rings and diameter of a tree that grew in a southern location would be much larger. This difference can be explained by the length of the growing season. The growing season is much longer in southern locations because of the additional heat in locations closer to the equator. Use an encyclopedia and your science books to discover how and why the rings in a tree are there.

Figure 7.21

Climate sets controls on vegetation.

Light	Sunlight is essential for photosynthesis. This is the process of changing carbon dioxide and water into food. Green plants cannot survive in an area where there is no light.
Moisture	All plants need water to carry the nutrients from the environment to plant cells. Plants cannot survive without water.
Heat	Plants adapt to growing conditions within certain temperature ranges. They do not grow well or cannot survive outside of this range.

Canada's Tree Line

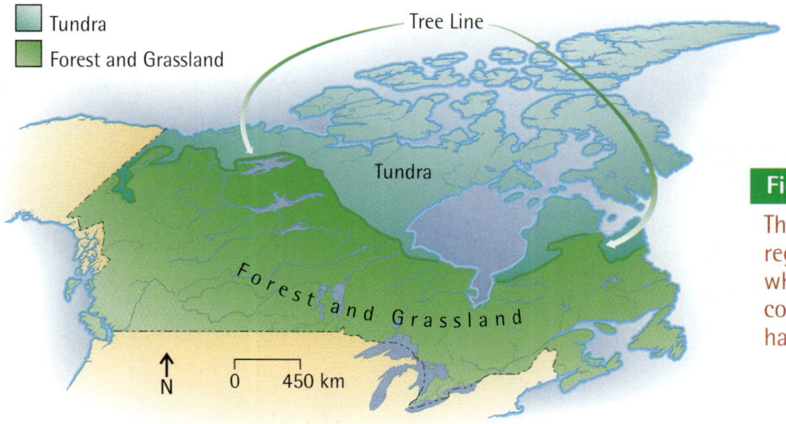

Figure 7.22

There are no trees in either of Earth's polar regions. The tree line is the line beyond which trees will not grow because of the cold. Small, low-lying bushes, which are very hardy plants, do grow beyond the tree line.

Factors Affecting Vegetation

Vegetation is determined mainly by climate. Three of the four raw materials plants must have—light, moisture, and heat—are directly tied to climate.

Figure 7.23

Look closely at the global natural vegetation regions. Which type of region has the most natural vegetation? Which has the least?

1

2

3

4

5

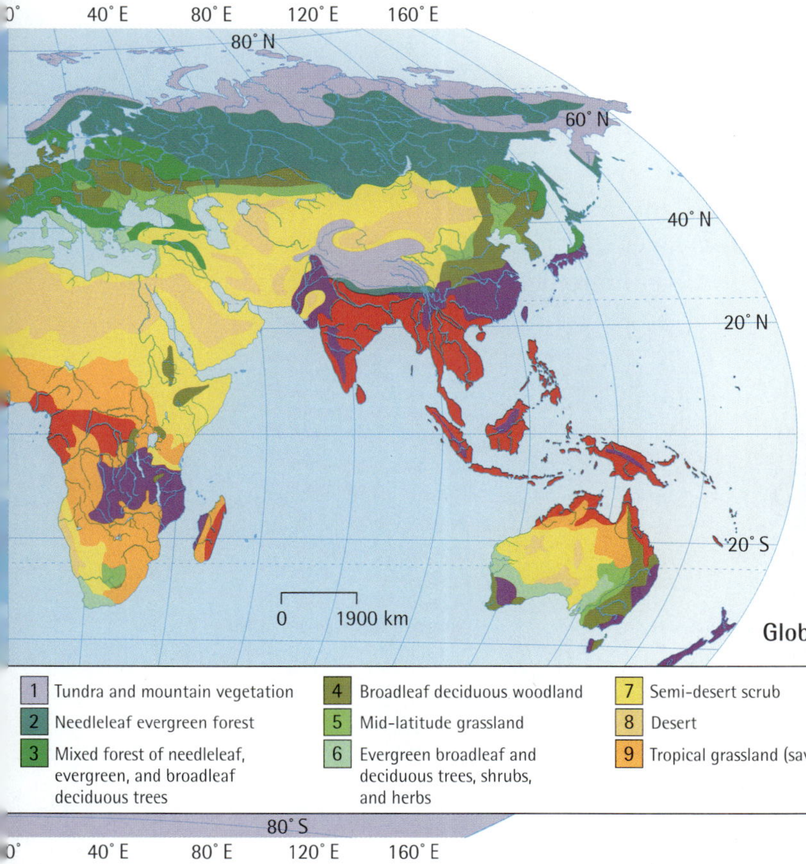

Global Natural Vegetation Regions

1. Study global climate regions in Figure 7.6 and global natural vegetation regions in Figure 7.23. What are the connections between climate and vegetation regions?
2. What would the world be like if there were no soils? How would your life change if all the soils in the world were used up and useless?

Soils

The type of soil in an area will help to determine the type of natural vegetation and how well it grows. Soil contains moisture, air, and organic material. It also contains vital minerals such as phosphorous, potassium, and calcium that are necessary for plant growth. To meet daily requirements, vegetation relies on the minerals contained in the soil. Unfortunately, not all soils are really productive. Desert soils are often sandy and lack nutrients. The sand is unable to hold water and lacks organic material.

Figure 7.24

Desert vegetation in places such as Arizona in the United States must be extremely hardy and adapted to the poor growing conditions.

Topsoil Really Is Tops

To an extent, vegetation creates the soil in which it grows. The plants die, and the decaying plant material—**humus**—builds up in the top layer. Nutrients are released slowly, to be captured by growing plants. Soils also get nutrients from the weathered rock of the area. As the rock is broken down, nutrients are made available to plants. Over long periods of time, layers build up in the soil. The top layer, the topsoil, has the most nutrients. It is this layer that gives food to the world. Unfortunately, it is the layer most vulnerable to human misuse and neglect.

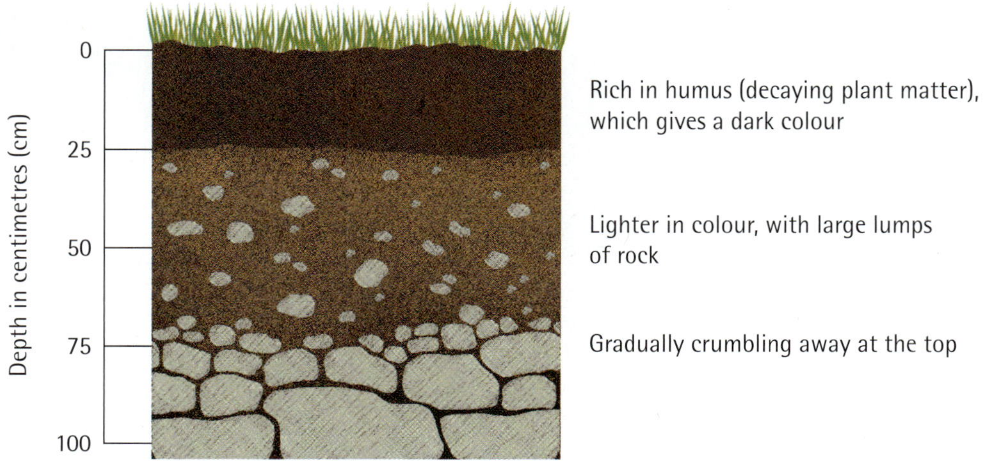

Figure 7.25

A typical soil profile shows the soil layers. The top layer of topsoil is affected by the natural forces of erosion and human activities.

Figure 7.26

The soil in the Holland Marsh in southern Ontario appears to be dark and rich in nutrients. However, fertilizers and constant irrigation are needed to keep the soil productive. The soil is light, so root crops like carrots and onions grow well.

1. Explain how natural vegetation is different from the plants that people grow.
2. a) Explain why temperature is a factor that influences the natural vegetation in a place.

   b) Explain why precipitation is a factor that influences the natural vegetation in a place.
3. Give two reasons to explain why it is important to protect soils and to keep them in good shape.

Knowledge and Understanding

1. a) Edmonton and Calgary get less precipitation than Vancouver and Victoria. Explain why.

   b) In which type of climate would you prefer to live? Why?

Figure 7.27

This is a photograph of Vancouver.

2. Seven climate factors were identified in this chapter. Think about the climate of the place where you live.

   a) Rank (put in order from most important to least important) the influence of the climate factors for your area.

   b) Write a paragraph in which you give reasons for your ranking. Begin with a topic sentence that states the main idea of your paragraph. (Hint: Think about the purpose for writing this paragraph.) Continue with supporting sentences that provide evidence and reasons for your ranking. End your paragraph with a concluding statement that sums up the main idea of your paragraph, but restates it in a different way than your topic sentence.

3. Why is June a peak month for tornadoes in Canada?

4. Suppose you are the environment reporter for the local newspaper. You have just written an article about the importance of soil to vegetation. Make up three possible titles that you might give your article, so that your editor can choose the best one. Remember that a title captures the main idea of your article in an interesting and inviting way so that readers will want to read your article.

Inquiry/Research and Communication Skills

5. Use the Internet and classroom resources to find three ways that each of these industries makes use of climate data:

   a) tourism

   b) farming

   c) airlines

   Make up a poster to display your research findings.

6. Many people have said that Canada's climate has been important in shaping Canada's culture. Create a cartoon or cartoon strip that says something funny about the Canadian way of life and how climate is connected to it. To get you started, think about these comments on climate:

   - "Everyone talks about the weather, but nobody does anything about it."
   - "Canada has 10 months of winter and two months of bad sledding!"

   Use your imagination to make up your cartoon.

7. Compare the vegetation and soil conditions in two parts of Canada. Start by identifying a place that could be described as cold and dry. Then, identify a place that is warm and wet. Compare the climates, natural vegetation, and soils of these two places by doing research. Organize your information in a comparison chart.

8. What is being done in Canada to deal with global climate change? Use the Internet and library or classroom resources to find out about three programs or actions to help reduce greenhouse gases and global warming. Write a paragraph about each in which you identify the following:

   - goal of the program or action
   - who is responsible
   - what is being done

Map, Globe, and Graphic Skills

9. Use the Internet to find a source that gives weather information for places around the world.

a) Write down the forecast high temperature for 20 cities from around the world.

b) On an outline map, locate these cities. Label both the name of the place and the high temperature.

c) Try to determine three temperature zones on the map: hot, warm, and cold. Shade these zones using three different colours.

d) What can you conclude from your map?

Application

10 Where is the best place to build a major new tourist facility? Climate and physical features of a place are often important considerations. They are sometimes part of the attraction of a place (for example, people go to locations like Victoria, British Columbia, to enjoy the mild temperatures). Climate and physical features may pose challenges for new tourist facilities (for example, "The Fog Bowl" on page 154).

a) Climate statistics for five places in North America are given in the statistical table below. Look at the information, and rank the places from

- wettest to driest
- hottest to coldest
- most seasonal variation to least seasonal variation

b) The following three different tourist facilities are being planned:

- a major new amusement park that features the latest technology in water rides
- a five-star skiing resort that offers heli-skiing and extreme slopes
- an ecotourism resort where visitors can learn about the yearly changes in physical environments

Describe the climate characteristics that each of these tourist facilities would find most desirable.

c) Decide which of these places would be best for each of the planned tourist facilities. Explain in a sentence or two why you matched the facility to the location.

d) The five locations given in the statistical table are actually the following:

- Banff, Alberta
- Boulder, Colorado
- Orlando, Florida
- Ottawa, Ontario
- San Francisco, California

Use the statistics to match the location number to the actual places.

	Jan	Feb	Mar	Apr	May	Jun	Jul	Aug	Sep	Oct	Nov	Dec	Year
Location 1													
Temp. (°C)	–11	–9	–3	6	13	18	21	19	14	8	1	–8	5.7
Precip. (mm)	58	58	66	69	76	76	89	91	84	74	86	84	911
Location 2													
Temp. (°C)	16	17	19	22	25	27	28	28	27	24	21	17	22.6
Precip. (mm)	62	60	90	61	95	187	182	159	146	69	59	59	1229
Location 3													
Temp. (°C)	0	2	6	9	14	19	22	21	17	11	4	1	10.5
Precip. (mm)	18	19	45	73	77	51	48	41	45	33	36	20	506
Location 4													
Temp. (°C)	9	11	12	13	15	16	17	18	18	16	13	10	14.0
Precip. (mm)	113	102	83	30	10	3	1	2	5	26	63	73	511
Location 5													
Temp. (°C)	–10	–6	–2	3	8	12	15	14	9	4	–4	–9	2.8
Precip. (mm)	30	23	20	33	58	61	51	51	43	30	30	36	466

8 Patterns in Natural Systems: Rivers

IN THIS CHAPTER

- identify ways that natural events affect people and the environment
- find out about the major river systems of the world, and describe their patterns
- use a variety of maps to identify patterns on the surface of Earth
- use the new terms in this chapter correctly as you investigate the topics
- locate and use helpful information from primary and secondary sources
- share the results of research for different reasons and audiences using options such as computer slide shows, videos, websites, oral presentations, written notes and reports, drawings, tables, charts, diagrams, maps, models, and graphs

KEY VOCABULARY

aquifer
cut-off slope
dendritic drainage pattern
headwater
meander
moraine
oxbow lake
slip-off slope
trellis drainage pattern
tributary

Gateways to the Continents

BEFORE READING

1. Why were rivers very important to Canada's development and history?
2. What rivers run near to where you live? How are they important to you?

Rivers are one of the most important physical features because they play a huge role in shaping our world. They have cut channels between mountains and created deep valleys. They have flooded large areas of land. They have provided us with transportation, food, and sources of fresh water. Rivers influence how land is used around them, and they are continually changing the landscape.

The St. Lawrence River played a vital role in the settlement of Canada. Early settlers followed the St. Lawrence River and continued through the Great Lakes system to reach Canada's interior.

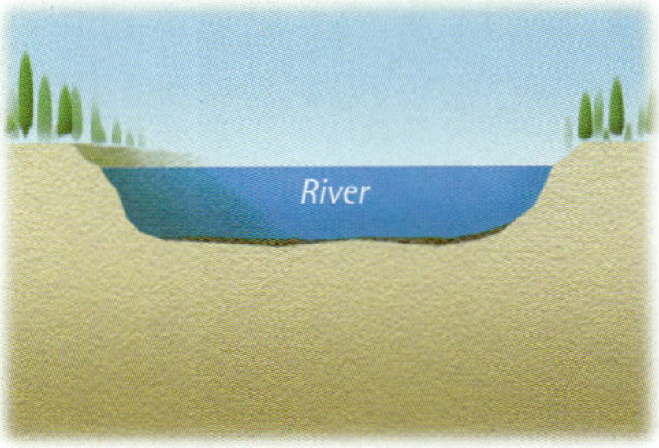

Broad, shallow channel

Narrow, deep channel

Semicircular channel

Figure 8.1

River channels come in many shapes. The materials that make up the land over which the rivers flow help to shape their channels. Imagine the water of a fast-flowing river moving over the land. Now imagine the water of a slow-flowing river moving over the land. What other factor might help to shape a river's channel?

Literacy Tip

Reading Diagrams

Geographers often use diagrams to illustrate important information. When reading diagrams, look for and read titles, captions, labels, and phrases. Also, look for use of colours, symbols, arrows, and lines to help you find important information. Follow all arrows and lines because they will lead to the key points.

Large cities and many smaller cities and towns are located on rivers. Winnipeg, Montréal, Vancouver, London, and Moscow were all built on the banks of rivers. Why would people choose to build settlements on the banks of rivers? Each continent has at least one major river (see Map Appendix). Why are major rivers important to the development and history of any continent?

River Profile

The water in a river seems to flow continuously, but it has a beginning and an ending. The source, or **headwaters**, is the location where the river begins. This is often a series of underground springs or melting glaciers. Most of the water in a river comes from surface run-off due to rain or snow. In some areas, springs bring groundwater to the surface, and this water is also added to the river.

Figure 8.2

Rivers may have more than one source. Small streams called tributaries flow into progressively larger streams until a river is formed.

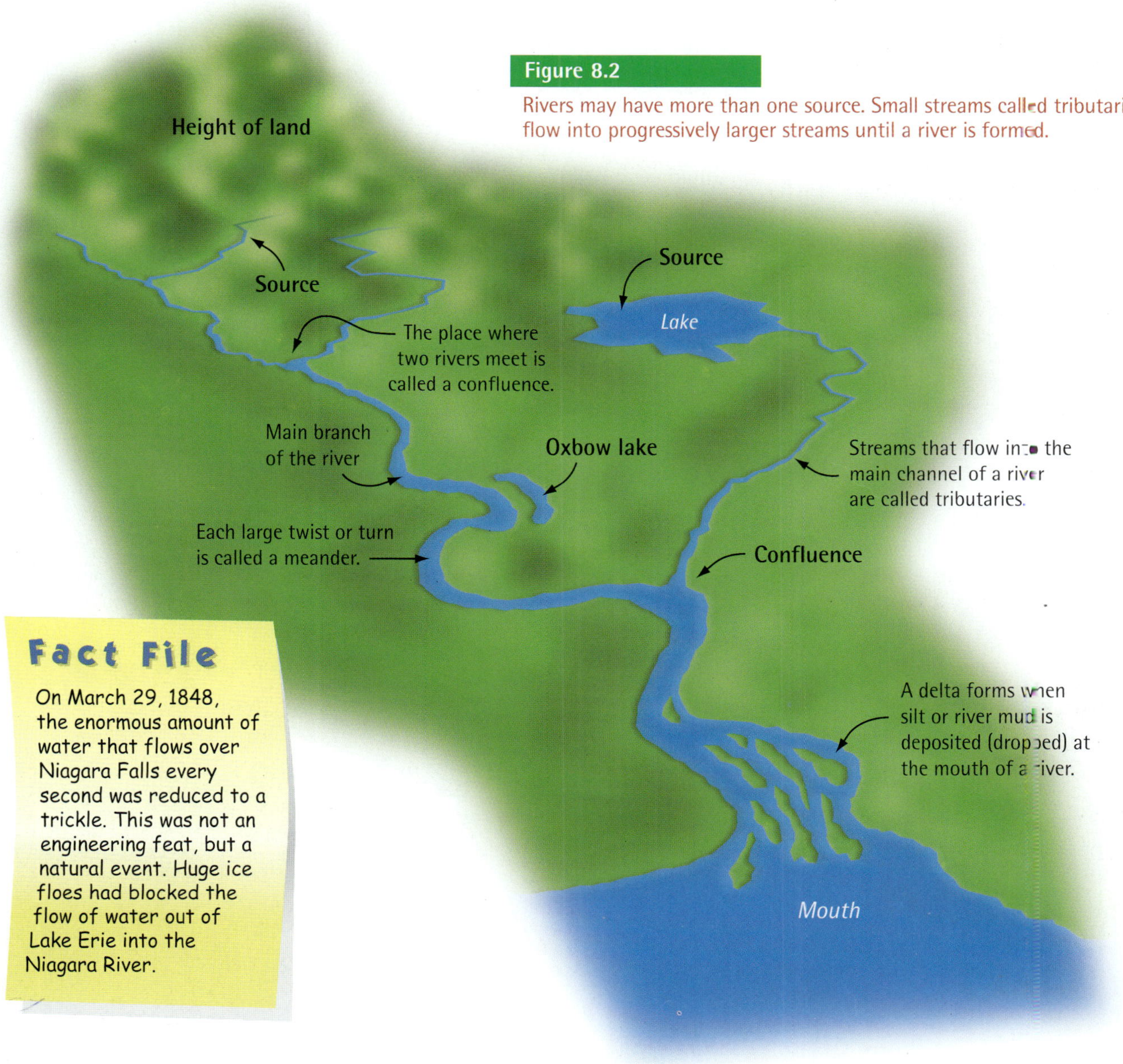

Fact File

On March 29, 1848, the enormous amount of water that flows over Niagara Falls every second was reduced to a trickle. This was not an engineering feat, but a natural event. Huge ice floes had blocked the flow of water out of Lake Erie into the Niagara River.

Drainage

Water drains from the highest point of land in an area to the lowest. Rivers flow from the high ground to the low. Look at the map in Figure 8.3. Can you see that rivers can flow downhill in different directions? Some flow north, while others flow south. The higher land that divides two different drainage basins and sends one river one way and the other in a different direction is known as the divide.

The Oak Ridges Moraine, just north of Toronto, divides two drainage basins. This **moraine** is the divide between rivers that drain north to Lake Simcoe and rivers that drain south to Lake Ontario. The Oak Ridges Moraine was created during the last Ice Age. The ridge of sandy hills acts as a giant rain barrel for the Greater Toronto Area. The sand and gravel of the moraine soak up rain and snow, and allow it to move down into large underground natural reservoirs called **aquifers**. Many communities dig wells into these aquifers for drinking water. Recent development has threatened to destroy this important physical feature and change the flow of the rivers that have their headwaters in the moraine.

Figure 8.3

The Oak Ridges Moraine is a long ridge of land stretching from the Niagara Escarpment in the west to Trenton in the east. Why is it important to protect the moraine and the rivers that begin in it?

The Great Divide

One of the most well-known heights of land in North America is the Great Divide. On one side of the divide, the water drains north to the Arctic Ocean, or east to the Atlantic Ocean. On the other side of the divide, water drains west to the Pacific Ocean.

Figure 8.4

Why do you suppose that geographers describe this drainage divide as the Great Divide? In which drainage system do you live?

North America and the Great Divide

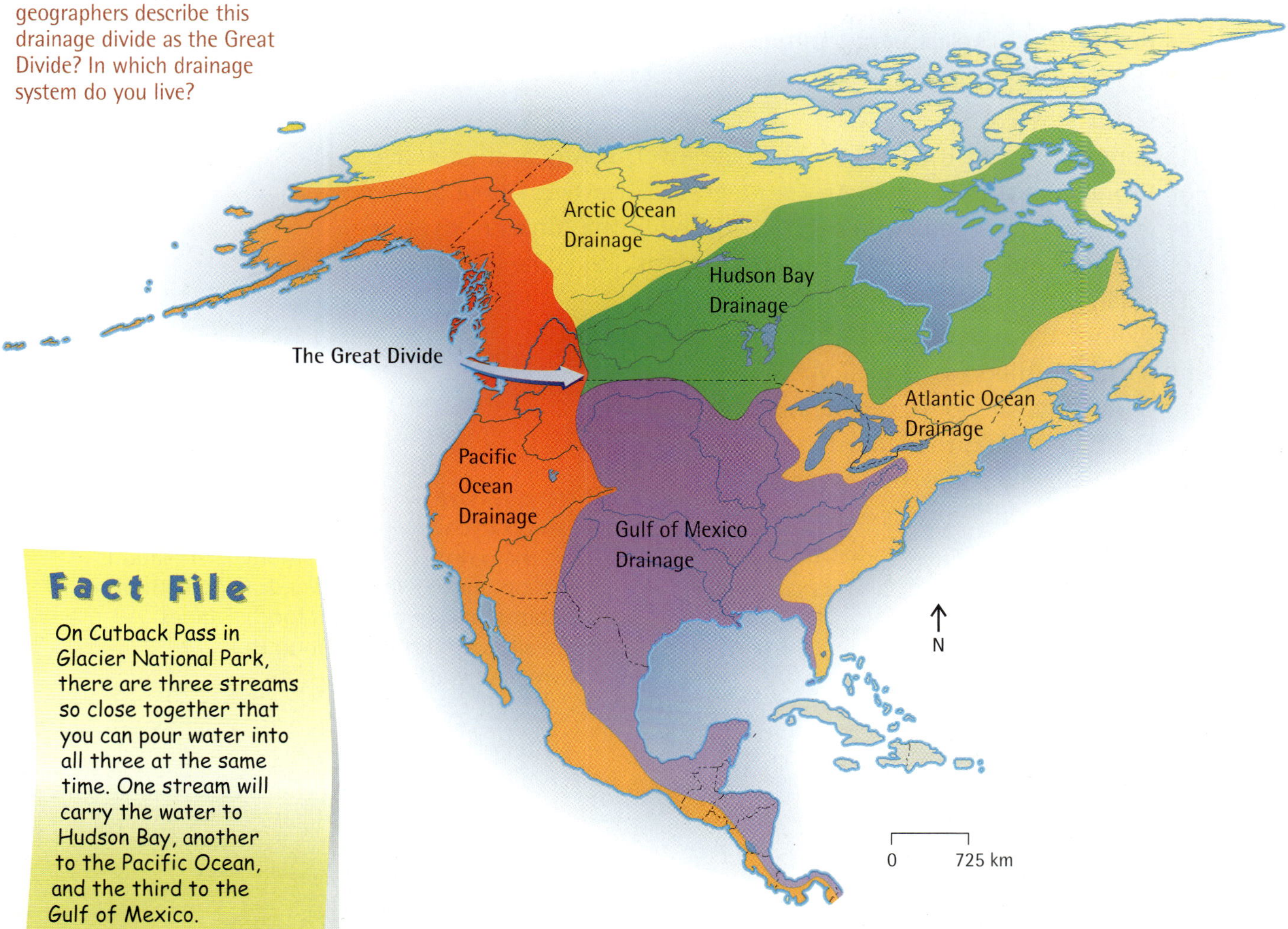

Fact File

On Cutback Pass in Glacier National Park, there are three streams so close together that you can pour water into all three at the same time. One stream will carry the water to Hudson Bay, another to the Pacific Ocean, and the third to the Gulf of Mexico.

Major River Systems of the World

Every continent has several major river systems (see Map Appendix). A river system is made up of the main channel of a river and all of the **tributaries** that flow into it. These rivers drain large areas of land, and they are often important features in many communities. Each of the major river systems takes runoff from a continent and drains into one of the oceans.

DURING READING

1. Consider this environmental saying: "We are always upstream of someone (water is flowing from you down to them) and downstream of someone else (water is flowing from them down to you)." Why should this encourage people to be careful with rivers and not pollute them?
2. List some rivers that are found in other parts of the world (see Map Appendix). Put a check mark beside any that you think are "superlative" rivers. (Hint: "superlative" means unmatched, without equal, or exceptional.) Explain why you think that they deserve this label.

Superlative Rivers

The longest river in the world is the Nile River in Africa. It stretches for an incredible 6670 kilometres through northeastern Africa before emptying into the Mediterranean Sea. Although the Amazon River in South America is not as long as the Nile River, it drains the largest area of land in the world. The Amazon River is 6570 kilometres in length, and it drains more than 6 million square kilometres of South America. Some geographers have estimated that there are 15 000 tributaries feeding into the Amazon. The Amazon contains one-fifth of the world's fresh water. It is so vast that large ships can travel two-thirds of its course.

CONNECTIONS TO History

The St. Lawrence River was an important route for humans long before it was "discovered" by Europeans. First Nations have lived along the St. Lawrence River for thousands of years. One First Nations name for this river means "the path that walks." Many First Nations travelled up and down the river, trading with other First Nations, and hunting for food. Canoes were ideally suited to navigating the St. Lawrence's waters.

Figure 8.5

This is the Nile River and Cairo, Egypt. The Nile Valley and the Nile Delta rank among the world's most fertile farming areas.

Figure 8.6

The Colorado River flows through the Grand Canyon, which is located in the U.S. state of Arizona. Estimate the shape of the river channel. For a hint, look at Figure 8.1.

North American Rivers

North America has many important river systems. The St. Lawrence River is a major Canadian commercial transportation route. In western Canada, the Fraser River is famous for its volume, power of water, and rugged scenery. The Mississippi is the longest river (3779 kilometres) in the United States. It drains almost all of the plains between the Rockies and the Appalachian Mountains. The Colorado River in Arizona is famous for the Grand Canyon and the Hoover Dam.

Literacy Tip

Creating Posters

Posters communicate a message using images and a small amount of written information. An effective poster delivers a clear message and leaves a lasting impression on the reader.

AFTER READING

1. Create a poster that illustrates the many ways we use rivers. Think about leisure activities, industry, food, transportation, and other uses. Give your poster a title that tells how important rivers are to us.
2. On an outline map of the world, draw and label the major rivers on each continent. Use an atlas or the Map Appendix to find this information.
3. Use an atlas or Internet map of North America to help you complete this chart. Find two large river systems from each of the five drainage systems in North America (refer to Figure 8.4). Locate the headwaters and mouths of the rivers, and describe the general direction in which they flow.

River	Location of the Source	Country/State/ Province Travelled Through	Location of the Mouth	General Direction in Which It Flows

River Patterns

Rivers never stay the same. They are constantly changing themselves and the land through which they flow. Any river is continually making its curves larger. On the **slip-off slope** of the river, material is deposited. On the **cut-off slope**, the current wears the bank away. This results in the curve increasing in size. Over time, if the river valley is wide enough, huge loops, or **meanders**, can form.

These meanders often become separated from the river. The river flows across the narrow strip of land at the base of the meander. Eventually, the meander is cut off from the new course of the river. This creates an enclosed piece of water called an **oxbow lake**.

BEFORE READING

1. Scan the headings and the illustrations in this section of the chapter. What are two questions that might be answered by reading this information? Write your questions in your notebook, and then read the section to see if you can find the answers.

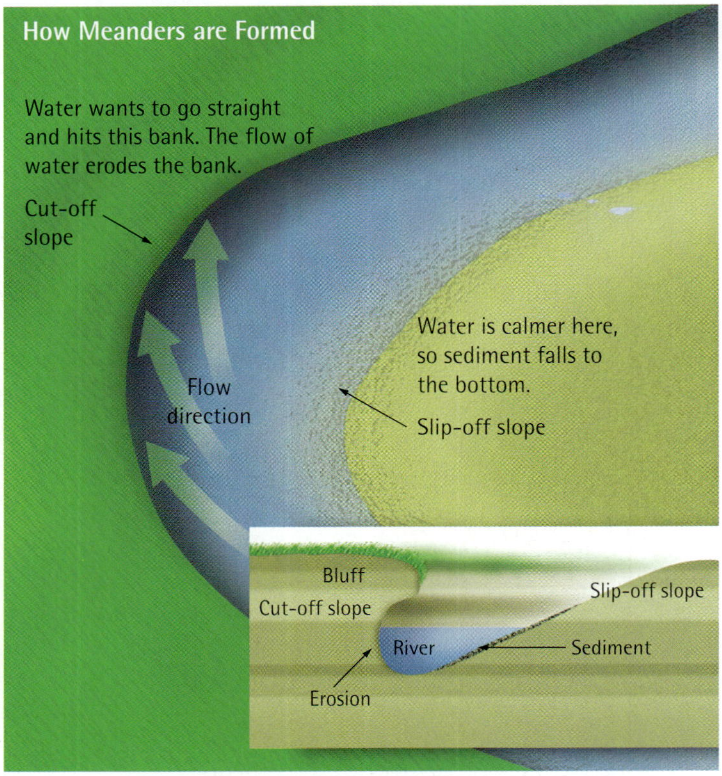

Figure 8.7

Curves may be found in most rivers. Meanders occur only where rivers have wide valleys and make great sweeps to and fro inside the valley.

Figure 8.8

Oxbow lakes are created by a combination of erosion and deposition.

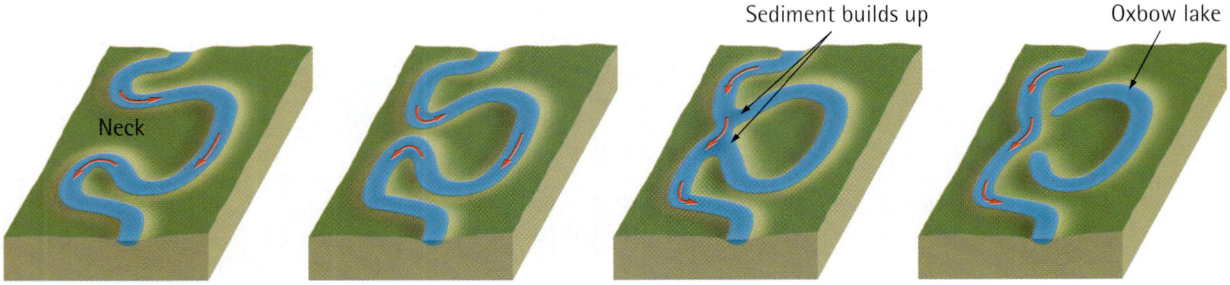

Rivers with pebbled bottoms and sides often form something called a braided pattern. Braided rivers have many small islands that split the flow of water into several streams. These streams or channels are joined and divided several times, forming a braided pattern.

The Liard River

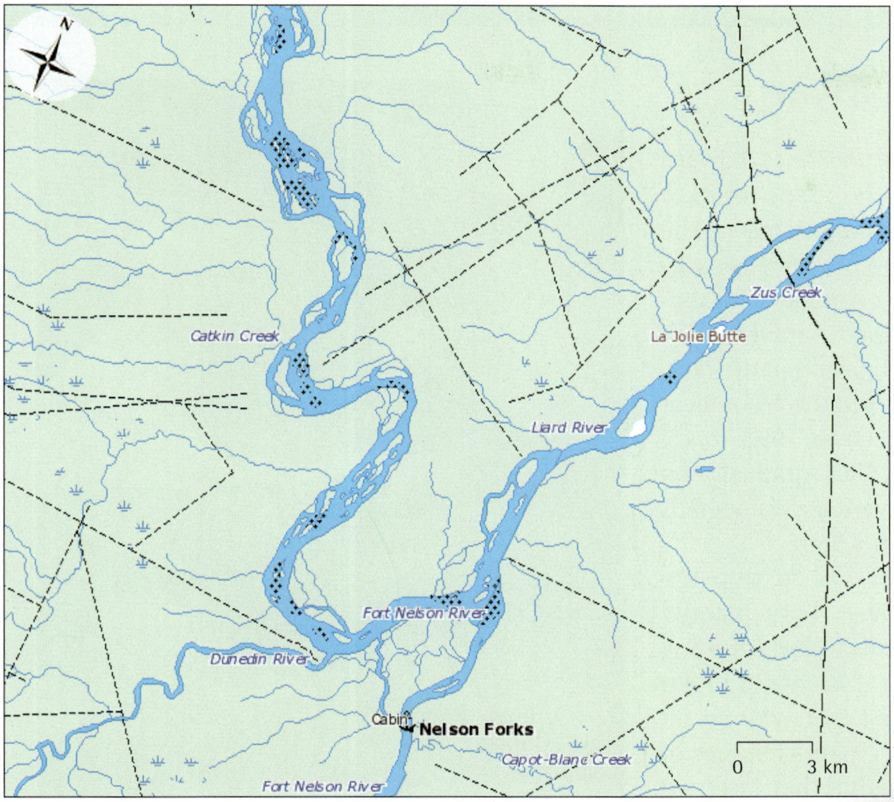

Figure 8.9

The Liard River in the Yukon is a very slow-moving river with lots of meanders. Predict where oxbow lakes are likely to form in the future.

Figure 8.10

This photograph of the Zaire River in western Africa was taken with an infrared camera from a satellite in space. In this image, the vegetation looks red because it is warmer than the water or the soil. Why do you think the Zaire is called a braided river?

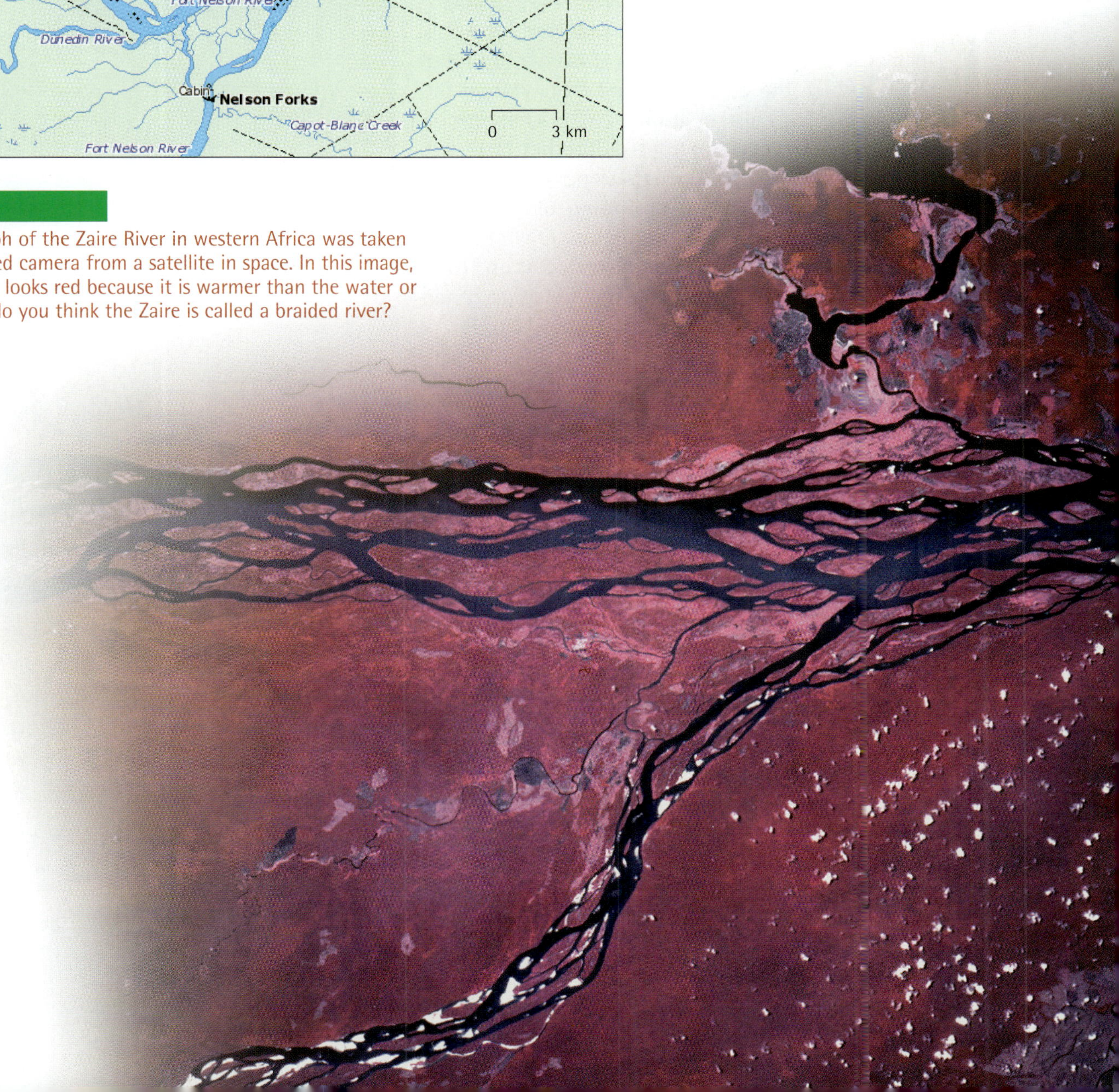

Go Geo-Green

Fixing a Damaged River

The Trout River is a small river on Prince Edward Island. It flows through an area of potato farms, a crop for which Prince Edward Island is famous. The red sandy soil of this part of the province is easily eroded. The Trout River used to be murky with sediment and polluted with pesticides that were used on the crops. Fish had trouble surviving in the dirty water. A group of volunteers started the Trout River Environmental Committee (TREC) in 1993 to try to save the river. Over the years, TREC gradually expanded its interests. It now covers six watersheds and over 150 kilometres of fresh water.

The committee's first action was to stop the soil from washing into the river. They planted trees and shrubs along the banks to hold the soil in place. They worked with local farmers to help them reduce the amount of soil that washed off their fields. They also built brush mats—clumps of evergreen trees tied together—that they fastened in the river. These brush mats trapped sediments so that the water ran clear. Adding bird and bat houses helped to restore the natural environment along the river's banks. After their success on Trout River, the committee has moved to clean up other rivers in the area.

Figure 8.11

Brush mats were installed on Trout River in Prince Edward Island to trap sediments. The water now flows through channels that are deep and clear, ideal for fish. Here, water samples are examined.

DURING READING

1. You can use diagrams as a visual outline to help you remember important information. Using the diagrams in Figure 8.8, work with a partner to explain how an oxbow lake is formed. Try to include the following words in your explanation: "meander," "sediment," "erosion," and "oxbow lake."
2. What is the closest river to where you live? What pattern has this river system formed: meandering, braided, oxbow lake? If this river does not look like any of these patterns, describe how it looks.
3. a) Farming disrupted some of the natural actions along the Trout River in Prince Edward Island. Think about the closest river to where you live. How do people's activities disrupt the natural actions of this river?

   b) The actions taken by the Trout River Environmental Committee restored some of the natural processes to the Trout River. What actions could be taken to help restore the natural actions to the river closest to where you live?

GeoSkills

Field Sketching

A field sketch is a quick, hand-drawn summary of a landform or landscape that is drawn while you are looking at it. These sketches should be simple, but they should highlight important features of the landscape. The features you include should be labelled. This is an excellent way to focus on how humans have had an impact on rivers and streams in your community.

Materials: pencil, paper, and a clipboard or other hard, portable surface.

Steps:

1. Look over the area that you are going to sketch, and decide on the important features that you want to include in your sketch. Stay in the same spot until you have completed the sketch.
2. Use your thumbs and pointer fingers to create a rectangle to frame your view.
3. On your paper, construct a rectangular frame that has been divided into thirds (refer to Figure 8.12).
4. Draw the skyline, and then add the main features of the landscape (for example, hills, river, roads, buildings, and so on).
5. Draw any details in the foreground, such as fences, trees, or buildings. Continue this step into the middle ground, and then into the background.
6. Add shading to your features.
7. Label and name important features of your sketch.
8. Title your sketch so that it represents your location and purpose.

Figure 8.12

Identify the foreground, middle ground, and background in the scene you are sketching.

Drainage Patterns

All the tributaries that feed into the main channel form different types of patterns called river drainage patterns. The drainage pattern is affected by the underlying rock—the rock that the river flows over. Different types of rock erode at different rates. Soft rock (for example, limestone) erodes more easily and faster than hard rock (for example, granite).

Dendritic Drainage Pattern

Most rivers have a **dendritic drainage pattern**. Imagine a leaf, with all the veins connecting to the main vein in the centre of the leaf. Think of the main vein as being the main channel of the river, and the small veins as being the tributaries. Tributaries join the main branch of the river in a V-shaped junction. The V points downstream, toward the mouth of the river. Dendritic drainage patterns usually occur in gently sloping areas where all the underlying rock is about the same hardness, so that it erodes or wears away in a uniform manner. Most of the rivers that drain into Lake Ontario have a dendritic drainage pattern.

Dendritic drainage pattern

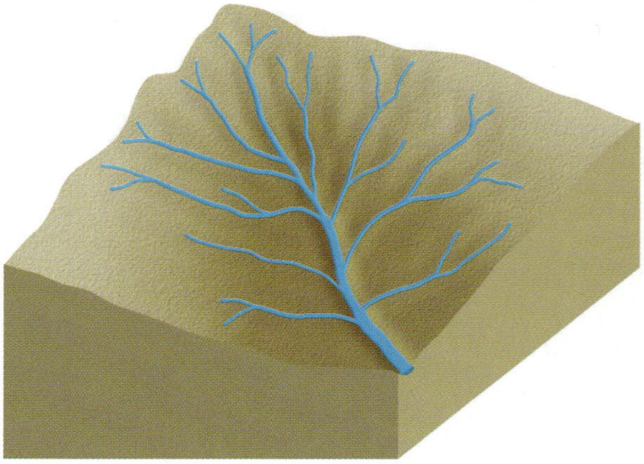

Trellis Drainage Pattern

Some rivers have a **trellis drainage pattern**—a rectangular pattern where the tributaries flow perpendicular to the main branch of the river. These tributaries are very often located where there are bands or rows of hard rock and soft rock. Tributaries travel along the areas that erode faster (softer rock) and break through the hard rock where they can.

Trellis drainage pattern

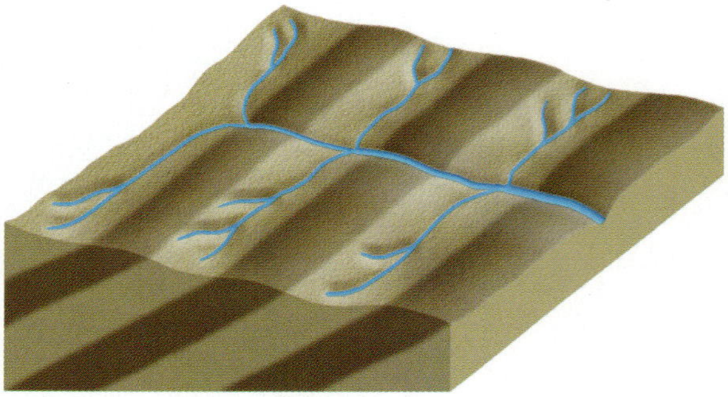

Figure 8.13

These are two common river patterns. Can you think of another pattern that rivers may have? Hint: think about the St. Lawrence River.

1. Find a map that shows the rivers in your own area. Do they have a dendritic form, a trellis form, or a completely different form? Describe the patterns that the rivers make in your area.
2. Look at a map of South America that shows rivers. Describe the drainage pattern of the Amazon River.

Knowledge and Understanding

1. In your own words, define these terms:
   a) source of a river
   b) main channel
   c) tributary
   d) mouth of a river
2. Explain how a meander is created. Include a labelled diagram as part of your answer.
3. Create a concept web for all the key words related to rivers. Start with the word RIVER in the centre. Make sure you include all the highlighted terms in this chapter.
4. In what ways do people affect rivers? In what ways do rivers affect people? Make a chart with these headings in your notebook:

Ways People Affect Rivers	Ways Rivers Affect People

Brainstorm points for each column. See if you can come up with seven points for each side of the chart.

Inquiry/Research and Communication Skills

5. Use an atlas, classroom or library resources, or the Internet to find a map of one of the major rivers of Canada. You might choose one of these rivers: Mackenzie, Athabasca, Fraser, Churchill, Saskatchewan, Ottawa, or St. Lawrence. Sketch this river, showing the headwaters and mouth of the river, and provinces and territories it passes through. Label your sketch using the correct terms. After sketching your chosen river, identify what type of drainage pattern it has.
6. Find one example of a river in Canada that has been helped by the actions of individuals or groups. You can use the Internet to find useful examples. Try key words such as the following for your search string: *Canada river environmental projects*.

Find answers to the following questions during your research:

- Where is the river located?
- What problems was the river having?
- What actions were taken to help the river?
- What are the signs of success that show the river has improved?

Communicate the answers to these questions in one of the following ways:

- PowerPoint presentation
- poster
- three-dimensional model
- written report
- oral presentation using before and after drawings or photographs

Map, Globe, and Graphic Skills

7. Use an atlas, reference book, or useful Internet site to find the 10 longest rivers in the world.
   a) List them in order of length.
   b) Give the direction in which each river flows.
   c) Name one major city each river passes through, or near.
8. **a)** Using an atlas, list 10 major rivers in Canada.
   b) Sort these rivers into two categories: high human use, and low human use. Explain how you decided which category to choose.

Figure 8.14
How is this river being used?

Application

9 Look at the sketch below.

a) Name each feature that is shown with an arrow and a letter.

b) What is the drainage pattern of the river that flows through South City? East City?

c) Name the source of South River, East River, and Moon River.

d) Name the location of the mouth of each river.

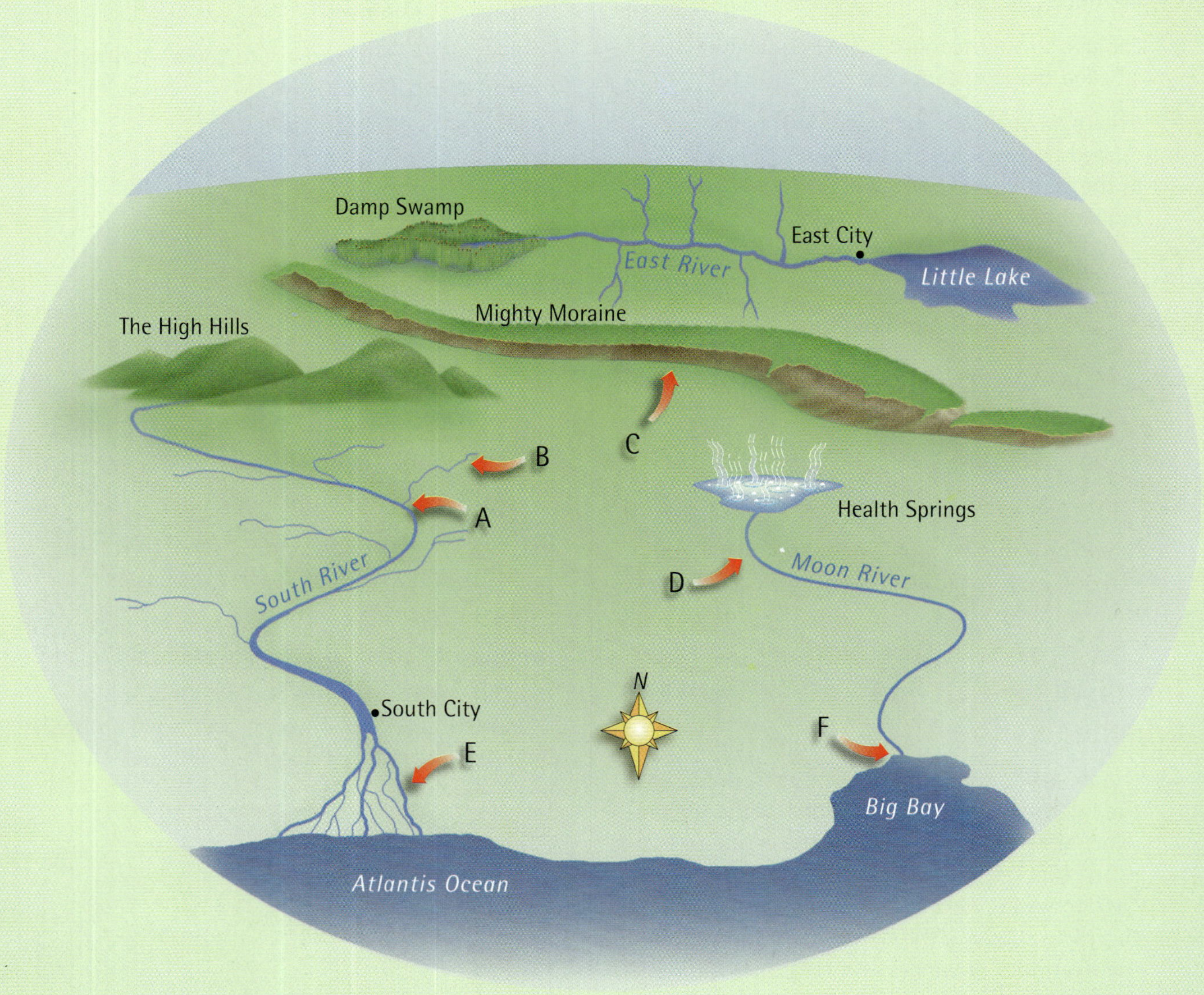

Figure 8.15

Use this diagram to answer question 9.

10 You have been hired by Global River Adventure Tours to design a brochure for their upcoming adventure tour. They want to use the brochure to attract potential customers, so it has to show the interesting aspects of their tour. You can choose the river. Remember that a brochure uses both written and visual text to communicate information in a detailed but concise way. Make the brochure inviting, exciting, and interesting. Include maps, places of interest, activities, dangers, and pleasures that will give the potential clients information and will make them want to sign up. Remember the following points to help you create an effective brochure:

- Plan the layout of your brochure before you start.
- Decide how many panels you will need and which panels you will use to present the various pieces of information that you want to give the reader. The front panel (the cover page) should be visually appealing with a short and simple written text (a word, a title, or a slogan) to catch the reader's attention.
- Use headings and subheadings to present your information. These headings should stand out, so use a bigger font, bold print, or different colour.
- Keep the written text short and simple. You can use points or very short sentences to present only the most important information or details.
- Use visuals like maps, graphs, photographs, diagrams, and charts to present or support your written text. Be sure these visuals communicate information to the reader about the adventure tour.

Figure 8.16

This is the Mosel River, which is located in Rhineland in western Germany. How would you promote this river tour?

9 Patterns from Interactions: Agriculture

IN THIS CHAPTER

- identify the characteristics of subsistence, commercial, and specialized agriculture, and describe the conditions that are needed for each type of agriculture
- show how factors like climate, raw materials, labour, and transportation influence commercial agriculture
- find out how landforms, climate, and vegetation help to shape specialized types of commercial agriculture
- use a variety of maps to identify patterns on the surface of Earth
- use the new terms in this chapter correctly as you investigate the topics
- locate and use helpful information from primary and secondary sources
- share the results of research for different reasons and audiences using options such as computer slide shows, videos, websites, oral presentations, written notes and reports, drawings, tables, charts, diagrams, maps, models, and graphs

KEY VOCABULARY

biotechnology
commercial agriculture
domesticate
Industrial Revolution
revolution
specialized agriculture
subsistence agriculture
topography

Food for Thought

BEFORE READING

1. Where does your food come from? Who produces your food? How does it get from where it is produced to your table? Record as many points to answer these questions as you can. Then, compare your list with a partner.

2. When people started travelling around the world, they began to see all the different foods available to them. What foods do you eat that originated in other parts of the world?

Some anthropologists and historians claim that our early human ancestors have been on this planet for about 8 million years. For all but the last 15 thousand of those years, our ancestors were hunters and gatherers. They hunted wild animals and gathered roots, berries, and seeds where they could. After the last Ice Age ended, nearly 15 thousand years ago, people started to explore new lands. They often followed the migration of animals.

Literacy Tip

Creating Flow Charts

A flow chart is a drawing that uses arrows to connect key events to their consequences. First, identify the main event in the text that you are reading. Then, identify the consequences. Summarize each consequence with a word or a short phrase. Use arrows to connect the consequences with the event. If there are many consequences, connect them in the order in which they occur. See examples of flow charts, or flow diagrams, on pages 183, 188, and 192.

Agricultural Revolution

About 10 thousand years ago, in some parts of the world, there was an important change in the way people got their food. They began to **domesticate** plants and animals. People began to gather and plant seeds to grow plants, and they began to tame animals. This meant that these people had a more reliable and handy food supply. It also meant that they could stay in one area and did not have to keep moving in search of new food sources. These groups of people could now spend their time learning how to build permanent structures such as houses and temples.

This improvement in food supplies was a dramatic change in the lives of these people. It was a drastic change in the way people thought and lived. In fact, it was a **revolution**. Once started, the revolution spread to different parts of the world. Perhaps, quite by accident, people had discovered the basics of what we now call agriculture—the planned planting and harvesting of crops or the raising of animals for food or clothing.

Origins of Food Worldwide

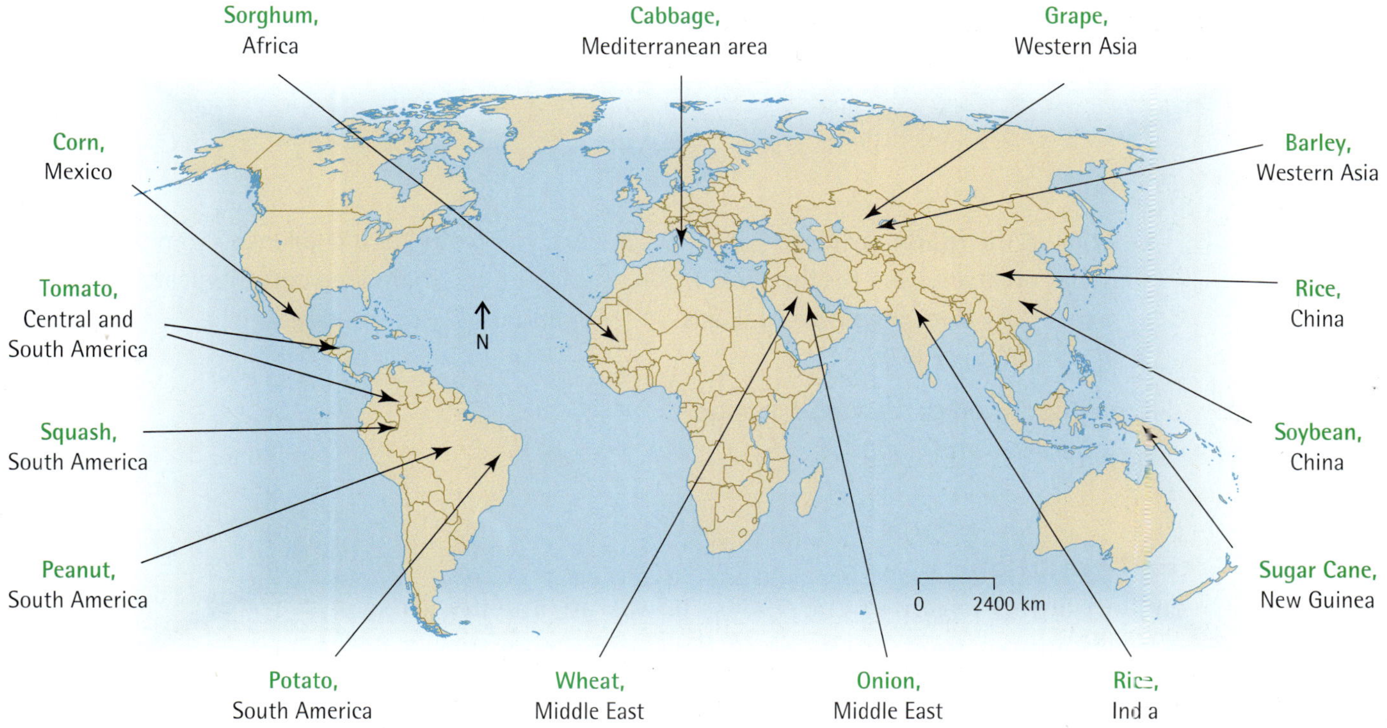

Figure 9.1

Note the places where these foods that we eat originated.

The Industrial Revolution

The **Industrial Revolution** began in the late 1700s. It marked the beginning of powered machines. Farmers gained new tools to help them plow their fields and plant their crops. The Industrial Revolution also brought improvements in transportation with new methods of road building, the development of rail lines, and the invention of the steam boat and steam locomotive. Agricultural products could be moved from the country to the city quickly and easily. Because of the new methods, farmers began to produce more food than they could use. They could sell some of their produce. That was the beginning of commercial farming.

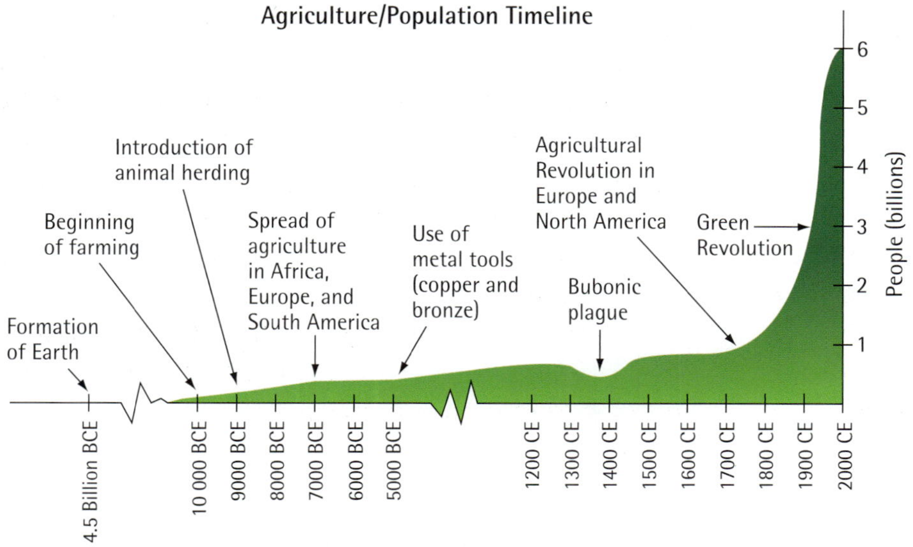

Figure 9.2

Agriculture has moved through periods of revolution. Important improvements were made in short periods of time. When change occurs slowly over a long period of time, we refer to that change as evolution.

1. Look at the graph in Figure 9.2. What units are used for the two axes? Why does the horizontal axis have squiggles in it?
2. How did the population of the world change between 10 000 BCE and 2000 CE?
3. Are you ready for a challenge? Can you capture the main idea communicated by this graph in two or three sentences?

The Green Revolution

The Green Revolution began in the 1960s. It was an attempt to increase the amount of food produced in developing countries—places that often had food shortages. The United Nations developed and shared new ideas about growing food. These ideas included better seeds and fertilizers. As a result, food production increased in many countries.

Fact File

An estimated 1 billion people suffer from hunger and malnutrition. If you counted one person per second, all day, every day, it would take you over 31 years to count all the people who suffer from hunger in the world today.

Literacy Tip

Using Word Parts

When you come across an unfamiliar word, remember to check if the word has a root. Then, check if a prefix or suffix has been added to the root word. Put the meanings of these two word parts together to create a definition of the word. You can use what you know about common root words, prefixes, and suffixes to help you figure out the meaning of unfamiliar words.

The Green Revolution has yet to solve the problem of world hunger, which remains one of our most serious problems. Today, global food production could feed the world's population. The problem is not how much food there is, but how to get the food to the people who need it. People in some parts of the world have so much food that obesity has become a problem, while people in other parts of the world face food shortages. Some of the barriers to fair food distribution are poverty, political unrest, poor transportation systems, and wars.

The Future of Agriculture

In the next decades, **biotechnology** will bring great changes to agriculture. The term *biotechnology* is used to describe the genetic engineering of plants and animals. Scientists are experimenting with changing the hereditary features that are passed on from parent to offspring. They are trying to improve the characteristics of the species. Genes are taken from one species and inserted into another. The goal is to produce a new type with more desirable characteristics. In some cases, the changes are designed to get more food from the same amount of land. In other cases, the goal is to develop plants and animals that are more resistant to diseases.

There are many people who are concerned about this "tinkering" with nature. They argue that we do not understand all the harmful effects that could result from biotechnology.

AFTER READING

1. In your own words, write a definition for the term "agriculture." Include examples in your definition.
2. The world has gone through several important changes that affect how we live, work, and get along with others. The sample flow chart below shows the first of these major changes. Name two other major changes. Create a flow chart like the one below for each major change that shows the resulting effects or developments. List two reasons why each change is considered so dramatic that it is called a "revolution."
3. Explain what the food distribution problem means for people going hungry, even though there is enough food being produced globally.

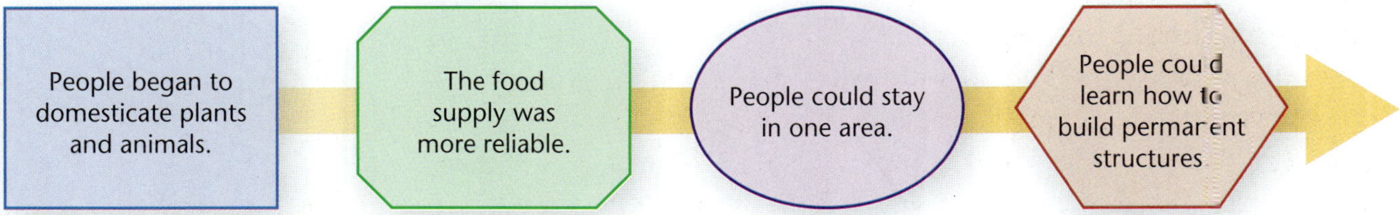

Three Types of Agriculture

BEFORE READING

1. When you think of the word "farm," what images come to mind? Compare and contrast your ideas with a partner. Brainstorm different products that are produced at farms. Can you think of some products produced at farms that are not food?

The type of agriculture that is practised depends on several factors including climate, soil, and surface features or **topography** (for example, hills, valleys, rivers, lakes, and so on). Some areas are fortunate enough to have sunny conditions, plenty of rain, rich soil, and flat or gently rolling topography. Others are faced with short growing seasons, lack of rainfall, and steep slopes. People have adapted their farming practices to suit their locations and climates. Different types of agriculture are practised in different parts of the world. Three main types of agriculture are subsistence, commercial, and specialized.

LITERACY TIP

Graphic Organizers

In the next section, you will read about the three types of agriculture. As you read, create a graphic organizer for the different types of agriculture. Complete the different sections of the organizer in point form. Use a similar organizer to help you summarize and remember important terms and information.

Subsistence Agriculture

In many parts of the world, farms can produce only enough food to support the farmers and their families. Everything the family produces goes toward feeding and providing for the household. Nothing is left over to sell. Farmers usually have to plant a variety of crops to meet their needs. This type of farming is called **subsistence agriculture.**

Subsistence farming exists in many developing countries. This is often because the soil conditions are poor. This type of farming also occurs in areas with harsh climates.

Figure 9.3

Muscle is the most common form of power in subsistence agriculture. What do you think that these Vietnamese farmers are doing?

Because of poor farming conditions, and the poverty that comes from this, subsistence farmers cannot afford to buy modern technology. They are forced to hold on to ancient practices. This makes producing abundant crops even less likely. Farming becomes a terrible trap for these people. They do not have enough to eat. There is no money to make their farms better, so they get less and less as time goes by.

Tsaatan Nomads

The Tsaatan nomads live in a remote part of northern Mongolia. This subarctic land of forests, lakes, and mountains is quite similar to some parts of Western Canada. The people are subsistence herders who depend on reindeer for their survival. The reindeer (called caribou in North America) provide most of the raw materials for shelter, food, and clothing. The Tsaatan live in teepees (similar to those of some of the early North American First Nations) made from reindeer skins.

Mongolia

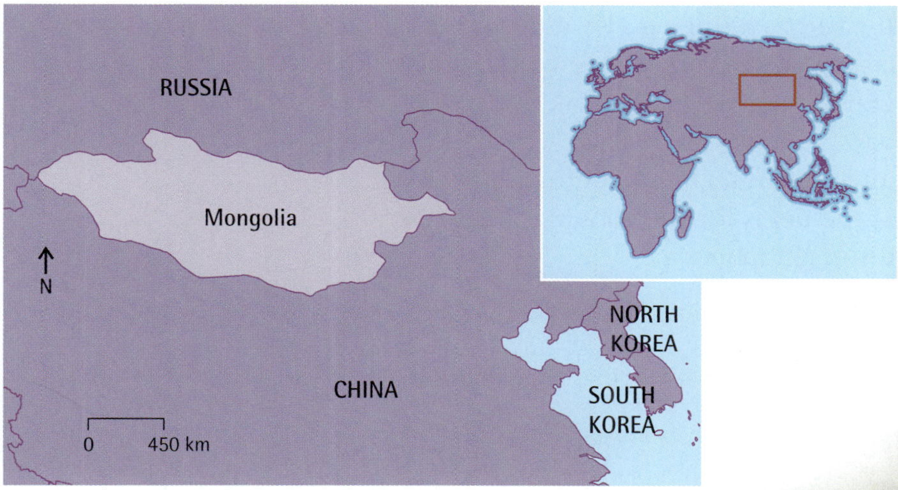

Figure 9.4

Describe the location of Mongolia in Asia. Why would it be difficult to point to a place on the map of Mongolia where the Tsaatan nomads live?

Figure 9.5

The Tsaatan nomads move often throughout the year looking for places for their reindeer to find pasture.

The People of Mustang

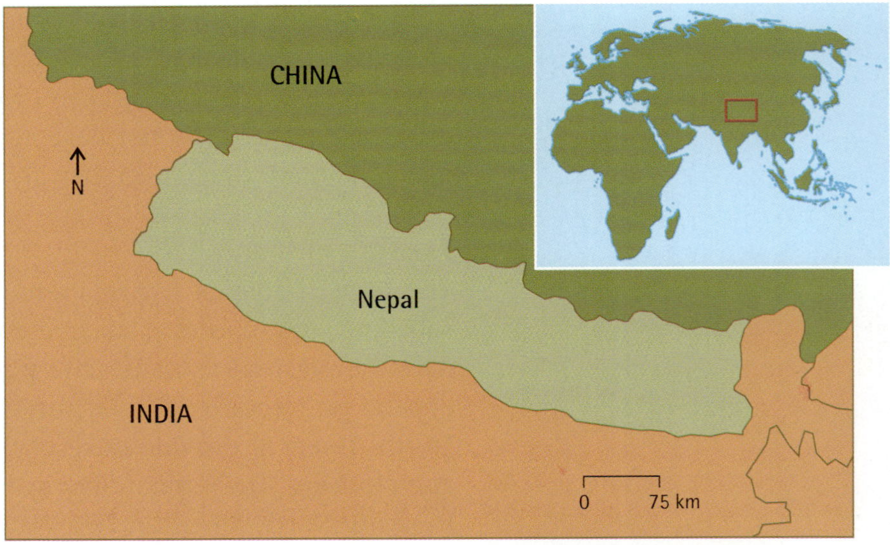

Figure 9.6

Describe Nepal's location in Asia. What are Nepal's closest neighbours?

Mustang (pronounced moo-stong) has been called "Nepal's forgotten corner." Much of this land is at a high altitude, and there are many barren areas of deep gorges and high cliffs. Other parts of the landscape are desert-like. Water is in short supply. Most of the people live in simple stone houses in small villages. The capital of Mustang, Lo Manthang, has a population of only 1000 people.

Traditionally, the people of Mustang have relied on their herds of goats and yaks. Every summer, the people leave their stone houses and follow their herds to pastures at higher elevations. There, they live in large tents. The yaks are used to carry the few household goods these farming families own. Farmers exchange yak butter and wool for household goods in markets.

Dried yak dung is the basic fuel in this region. Children have the task of collecting the dung from the fields for the cooking fires. The dung is also traded for grain with neighbours.

Figure 9.7

This is a photograph of small Mustang farm plots in Nepal. To help feed themselves and the goats and yaks over the winter, farmers have tiny fields of wheat. Every small farm plot seems to be carved from the side of a hill. Why do you suppose the Mustang people have come to rely on goats and yaks?

DURING READING

1. Compare and contrast the Tsaatan nomads and the Mustang. Use a graphic organizer like a Venn diagram to help you identify what they have in common and how they are different.
2. Where else in the world might subsistence agriculture take place? To find out, search for *subsistence agriculture* using a search engine on the Internet, or look in an atlas or the Map Appendix for world agriculture maps. For each place you identify, can you provide reasons that it is a likely place for subsistence agriculture?

Go Geo-Green

Farming Cities

In 1978, a group of young people became concerned about the amount of energy that is used to get food from where it is produced to the people who eat it in cities. They wanted to help the people of their city—Vancouver, British Columbia—to grow more of their own food. They pointed out that food can be grown in front and back yards (instead of grass), on balconies, on rooftops, in community gardens in city parks, under power lines, in school yards, and in many other places. In fact, surveys show that 44 percent of the people of Vancouver could grow at least some of the food that they eat. With some effort, city dwellers could produce up to 30 percent of their food within the city limits. This group of young people started an urban agriculture revolution. It has made Vancouver a model for how cities can be farmed.

The group wanted to help others become urban farmers. To encourage farming in cities, in 1994, the group went online. The World Wide Web was just starting to grow at that time. Now, the City Farmer website gets more than 4 million hits a year, from most countries of the world. Through the Internet, millions of people have become excited about urban farming.

Figure 9.8

There are over 1000 community garden plots like this in Vancouver, British Columbia. People who live in apartments use these plots to grow some of their own food.

DURING READING

1. If you wanted to become a city farmer, what type of food could you grow in your area? Where could you grow the food?

Commercial Agriculture

In the past, when farmers had more than they could use for their families, they took the surplus to the local market. These outdoor markets provided places for farmers to sell their produce. Today, **commercial agriculture** is the production of crops or livestock for sale. Large quantities of crops are grown, and farmers often specialize in one, or sometimes two, crops. Commercial agriculture produces crops such as rice in China and Japan, and corn in the United States. In Canada, the sale and export of wheat is a good example of commercial agriculture.

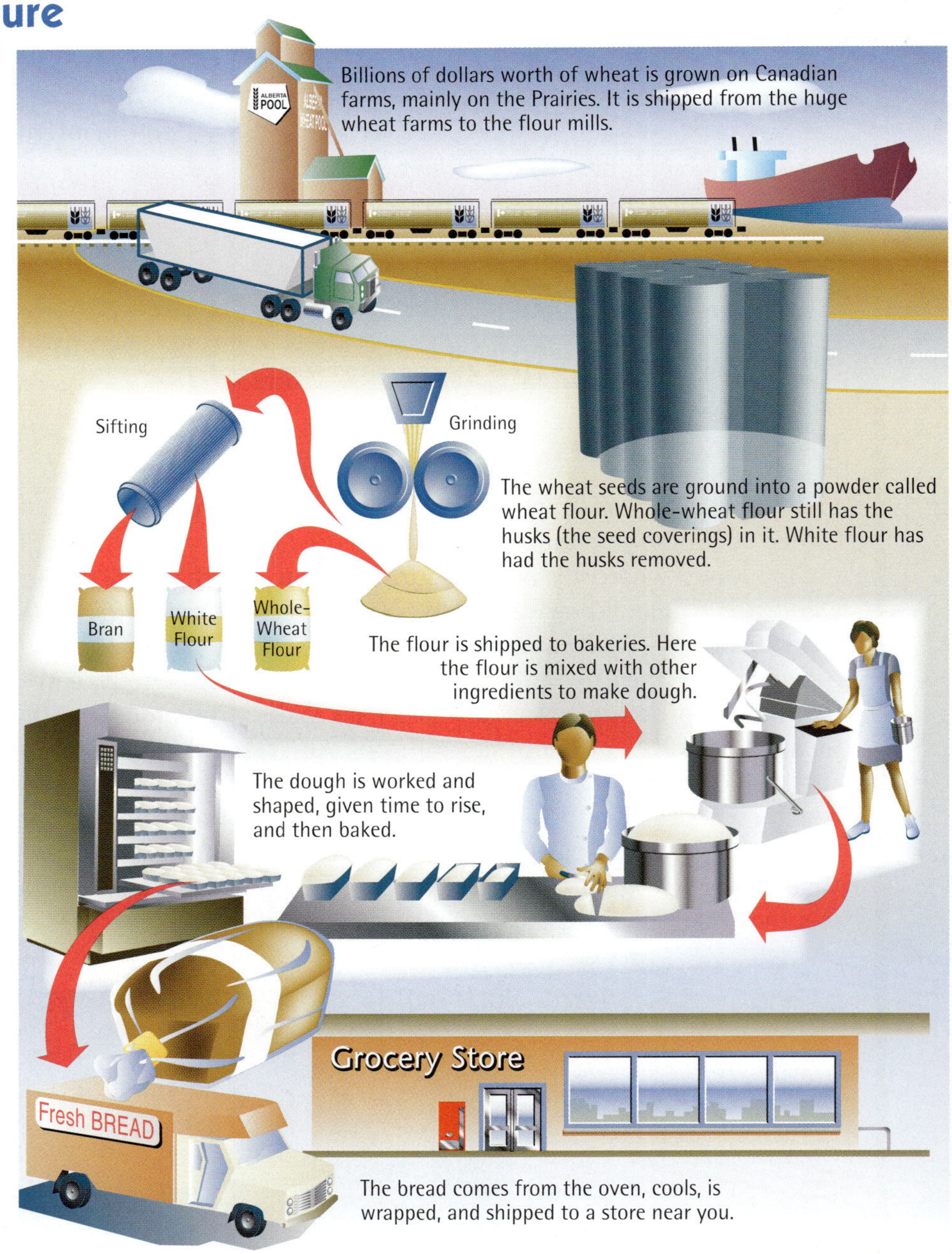

Figure 9.9

Wheat is used to make bread and many other products that we eat. Follow the steps in making bread that are shown in this flow diagram. How important is energy to this process?

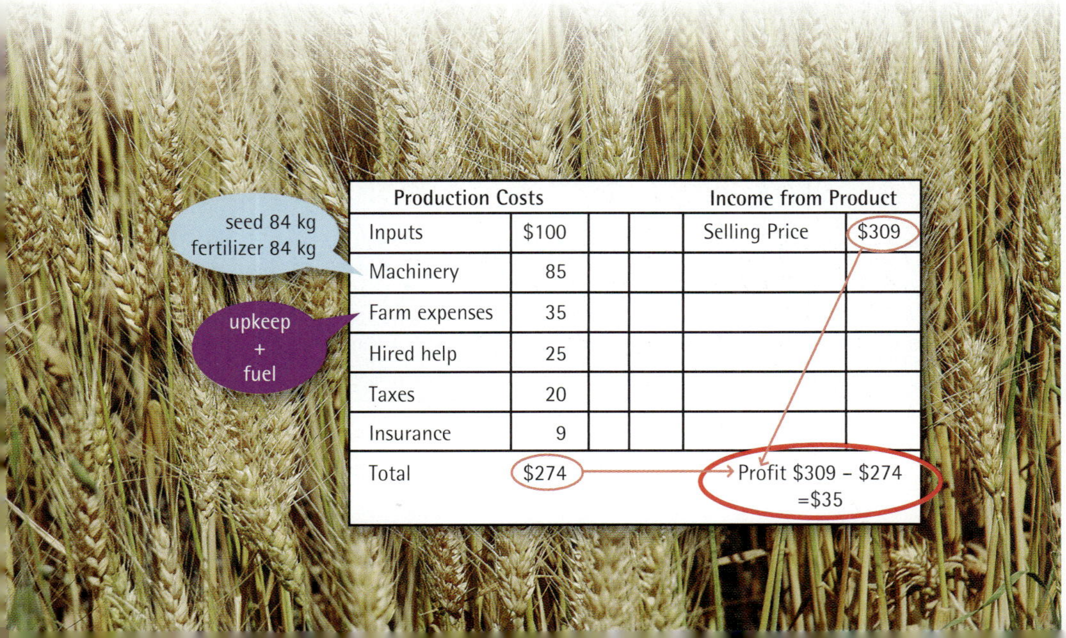

Production Costs		Income from Product	
Inputs	$100	Selling Price	$309
Machinery	85		
Farm expenses	35		
Hired help	25		
Taxes	20		
Insurance	9		
Total	$274	Profit $309 – $274 =$35	

Fact File

- In Canada, a hectare produces an average of 2000 kilograms of wheat.
- The wheat produced by one hectare can make 3400 loaves of bread.

Figure 9.10

What does it takes to grow a hectare of wheat? Sometimes prices fall, and growers do not earn enough to make a profit.

GEOSKILLS

Reading a Stacked Bar Graph

A stacked bar graph is a visual way to compare two sets of information at the same time. When reading these graphs, always remember TAPP (Title, Axes, Pattern, Purpose). Let us read the graph in Figure 9.11.

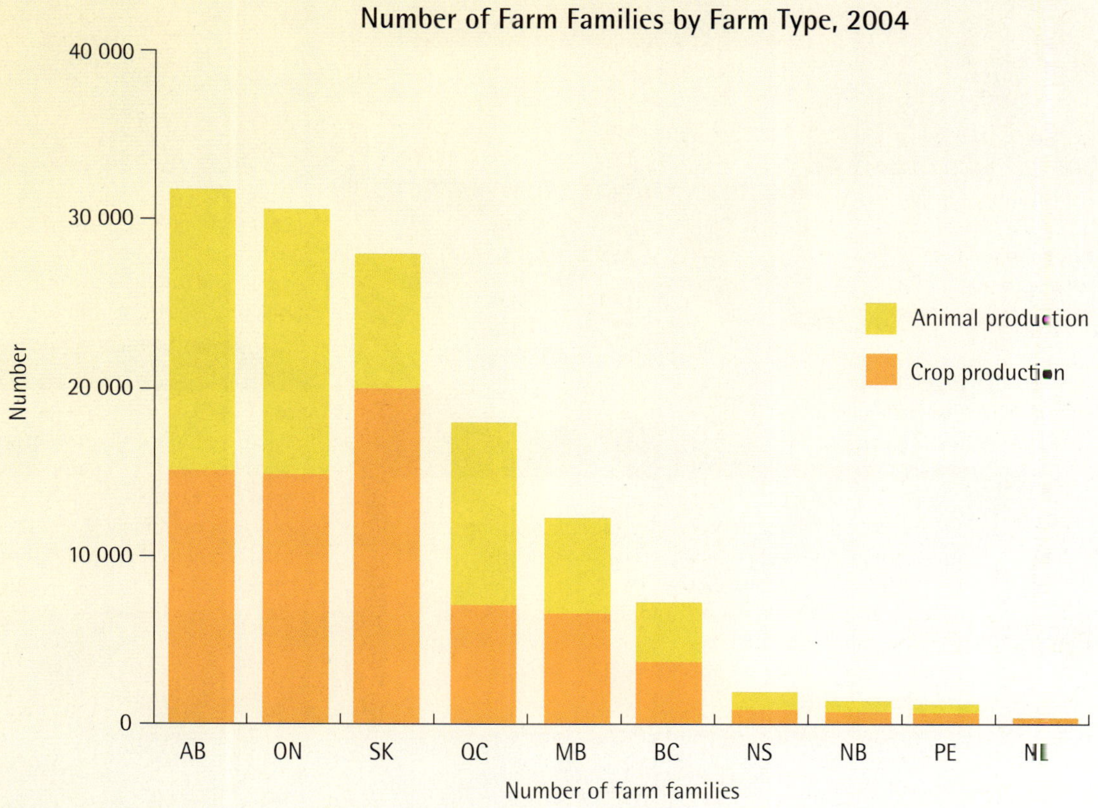

Figure 9.11

This graph shows the number of farm families by farm type and by province for 2004.

Guide Questions for Reading a Graph

Title: What does the title tell you about the graph?

Axes: What are the two axes telling you? What is the unit of measurement? Is there a legend? If so, what does it tell you?

Pattern: Is there a pattern (trend) in the graph? Explain what you see. What do you think the pattern means? Look at the legend. What comparison is being made?

Purpose: Who do you think would use this information? How does the information on this graph relate to this chapter?

Factors Influencing Commercial Agriculture

Commercial agriculture is influenced by six major factors: location, climate, raw materials, market, labour, and transportation. A single factor, or a combination of factors, can affect the type and quantity of agricultural products that can be produced in a given area.

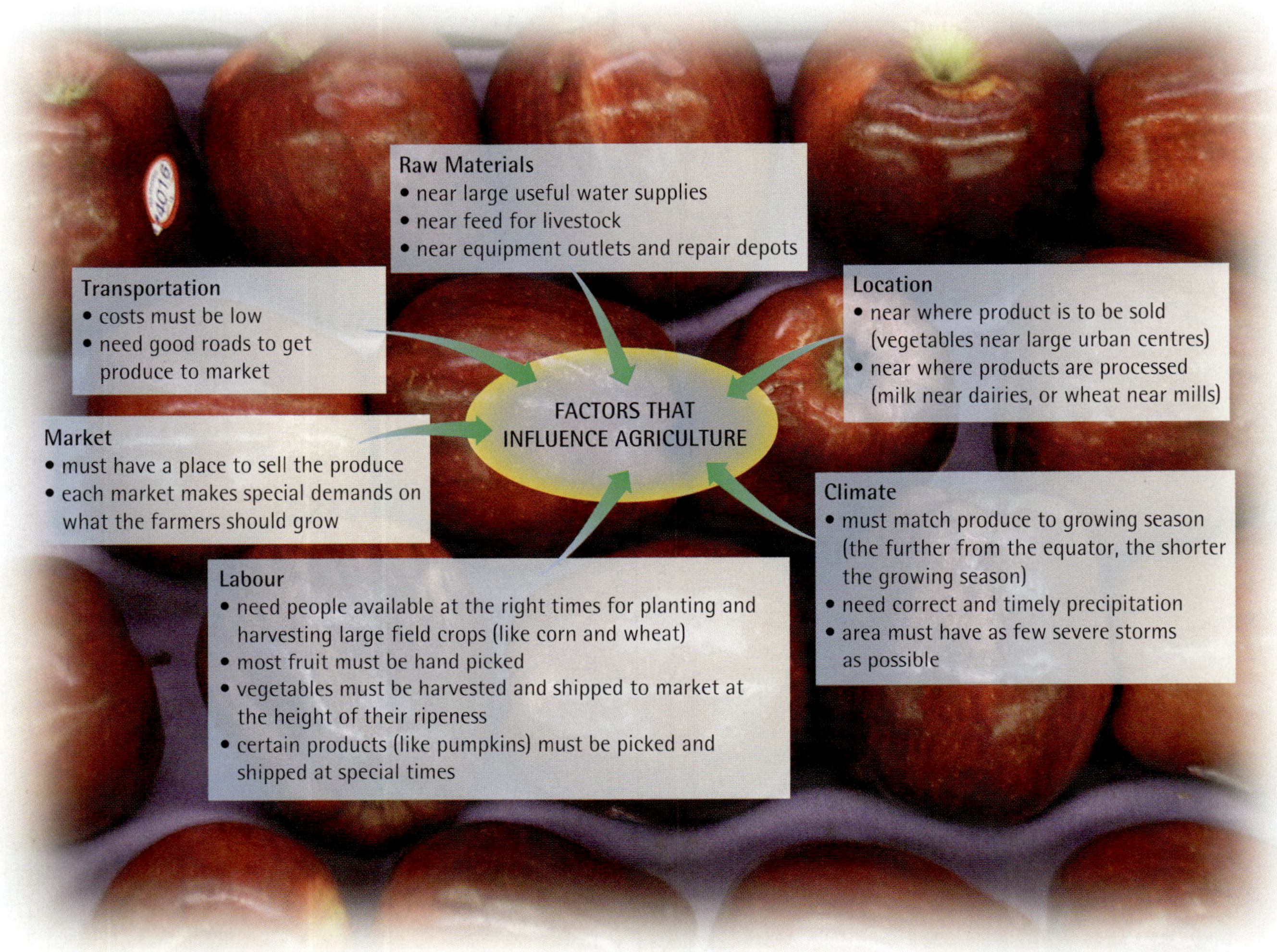

Figure 9.12

This mind map shows the factors that influence agriculture both in Canada and around the world.

DURING READING

1. Wheat is an important crop for Canada's prairie provinces. Can you use the six location factors shown in Figure 9.12 to explain why wheat is grown in the Prairie region?
2. Think about the agriculture that goes on in your area. Of all the factors shown in Figure 9.12, which two are most important in shaping the agriculture that goes on in your area? If there is no agriculture in your area, can you use the factors to explain why it is not found there?

Figure 9.13

A sheltered river valley is an ideal environment for growing rice.

Figure 9.14

Why is this land in Australia used to graze sheep instead of growing crops?

Rice in South China

Rice is farmed commercially in China. Much of it is harvested along the Yangtze River in southern China. Because this area is sheltered by the Ch'in Ling mountain range, the climate is more moist and more stable than in northern China.

Sheep Farming in Australia

Two-thirds of Australia is capable of supporting livestock. Sheep farming is a major industry in the country. The huge surplus of meat and wool is exported to other countries.

Commercial Agriculture—Plantations

Plantations are farms where large areas are planted in one type of product, such as bananas or tea. Coffee is another plantation crop that is in high demand in most countries of the world.

DURING READING

1. Where did the bananas come from that are currently being sold in your community? Gather a few banana stickers and bring them to class. Record the names of the banana companies and producing countries. Locate and name the countries on a map of the world.

2. Imagine that you are an exporter of bananas. What actions would you take to make sure that your bananas arrive in Canada in good condition? Record your ideas, and then compare them with the actions that are shown in Figure 9.16.

Let's Go Bananas

Bananas are a plantation crop grown in the coastal lowlands of Central America, Colombia, Ecuador, Philippines, and throughout many parts of tropical Africa. Banana plants need hot weather, at least 120 millimetres of rain per month, and deep rich soil.

Figure 9.15

Why do you think that bananas are shipped on the stalk, instead of in some other form, such as in cans or frozen?

WEB LINK

For more information about the growing of bananas, go to **www.nelson.com/phygeo7**.

Figure 9.16

This flow diagram shows the journey of bananas from the plantation to you. What environmental problems might be caused by the transportation of bananas to you?

Figure 9.17

Why are tea plantations in places such as India considered commercial agriculture?

Tea Plantations in India

India is famous for its tea plantations. These large farms have been planted with bushes that produce tea leaves. Most of these plantations are set on the Himalayan slopes and the fertile plains of northeast India. Tea plantations in India are successful because of the rich soil and high rainfall.

Specialized Agriculture

Specialized agriculture is a term used to refer to crops that are produced only in certain places. Specialized agriculture is successful because these crops or livestock require unique conditions that are found in these locations. Pineapples, for example, require hot temperatures and can be grown only in tropical countries. Citrus fruits are also specialized crops requiring hot temperatures.

DURING READING

1. As you read about different specialized crops, identify what conditions are required for these crops. Suggest other crops that require special growing conditions and where these crops are grown.

Figure 9.18

Oranges and grapefruit are very successful in Southern California and in Florida. Why are oranges not grown as a specialized form of agriculture in Canada?

Figure 9.19

Vineyards such as these in Napa Valley, California, are a specialized form of agriculture. Grapes for eating and winemaking need fertile soils. They also need a long growing season without the danger of frost. Where are grape-growing areas in Canada?

CONNECTIONS TO History

Sometimes being too specialized is not a good thing. After potatoes were introduced into Ireland, they became the single most important food crop. Potatoes grew well in the cool, moist climate. However, between 1845 and 1850, a fungus, often called a blight, destroyed potato crops. This event was called the Great Potato Famine or the Great Starvation. It is estimated that over a million people died of hunger. Over two million people left Ireland, and many of them came to live in Canada.

Rice-Fish Farming

Rice-fish farming has been practised for centuries in China and other southeast Asian countries. Most varieties of rice are grown in flooded fields called paddies. The paddies are kept filled with water for most of the growing season. Small fish are released into the water and they live there until harvest time. These fish feed on the weeds and other plants in the paddies that would otherwise compete with the rice for sunshine, fertilizer, and nutrients. The fish droppings add to the fertility of the soil and increase crop production. When the rice crop is harvested, so are the fish.

Figure 9.20

This is a rice-fish farm in northern Philippines. In what ways does this method help farmers get maximum returns from their land?

Specialized Agriculture in Canada

Canada's size means that there are many different types of growing conditions. Because of this, Canada has many types of specialized agriculture.

Cranberries in the Fraser Valley

British Columbia's Fraser Valley is Canada's cranberry capital. This region produces 80 percent of the country's cranberries. The peat bogs that are used for cranberry fields are swampy and highly acidic.

Fact File

Cranberries are British Columbia's largest berry crop. The province produces about 17 million kilograms per year, worth about $25 million.

Figure 9.21

What growing conditions are necessary for the production of cranberries? Where else in Canada might these conditions be found?

Blueberries in Cumberland County

Cumberland County produces 75 percent of Nova Scotia's blueberry crop. The blueberries are grown in a very acidic soil that is not good for crops like corn, peas, or beans. The farmers discovered what would grow successfully, and which crops would help them earn a profit. Blueberries are very hardy plants that can survive in harsh conditions, including poor soil and cold winters.

Cumberland County, Nova Scotia

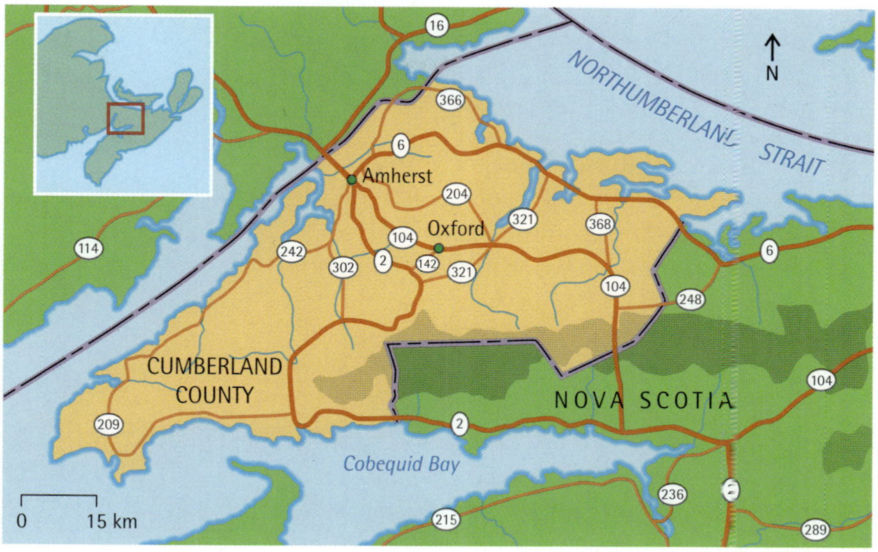

Figure 9.22

Blueberries are common in many parts of Canada. However, they are grown on a large scale in only a few places, such as Cumberland County in Nova Scotia.

Fact File

North American ginseng is used to make some popular over-the-counter cold and flu medications.

Ginseng from the Okanagan Valley

Ginseng has traditionally been regarded as a "miracle cure" in Asia. Today, ginseng has become one of British Columbia's most profitable specialized crops. The hot, arid region in and around the Okanagan Valley provides desert-like conditions. The ginseng root thrives in this rain shadow because the hot and dry conditions reduce the spread of fungus and root rot. Ginseng requires a good deal of labour to grow and harvest. Roof-like covers must be constructed and maintained, and the ripe berries must be picked by hand. However, its high market value makes it a profitable crop.

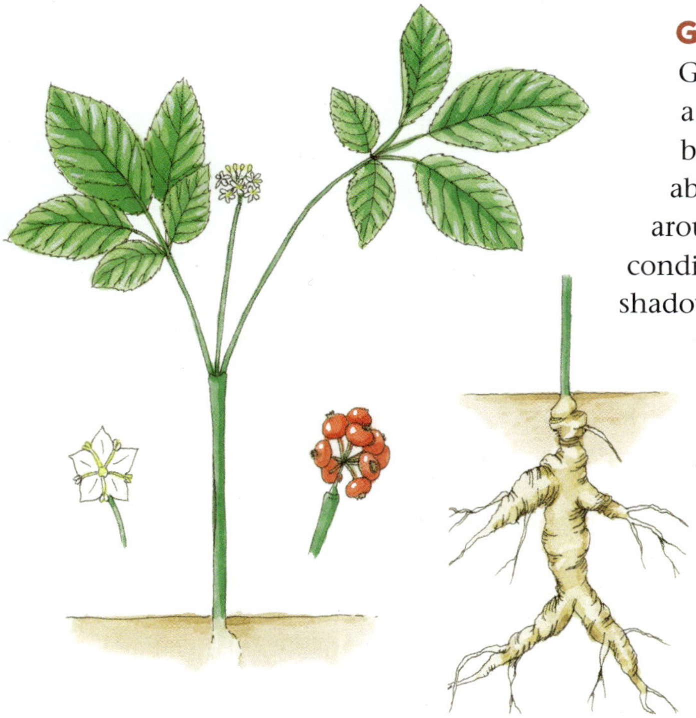

Figure 9.23

Ginseng is not a traditional crop in the area, but it grows well in the unique growing conditions of the interior of British Columbia.

AFTER READING

1. Why do you suppose people continue to be subsistence farmers if they are not making money from their farms?
2. Which of the three types of agriculture do you think produces the most food in Canada? Explain the reasons for your answer.
3. Make up a bumper sticker that advertises one specialized crop grown in Canada, and persuades people to try the crop. Bumper stickers are often slogans. Refer to Chapter 4 to review how to create an effective slogan.
4. Choose one of the following specialized forms of agriculture— potatoes, cotton, sugar cane, or dairy farming. Describe the landforms, climate, and vegetation patterns that are favourable to this form of farming. If necessary, research using the Internet or library resources.

Knowledge and Understanding

1. Identify two ways that subsistence, commercial, and specialized forms of agriculture are alike and two ways that they are different.

2. Use ideas from this chapter to write a paragraph with the following topic sentence: "Developing more commercial agriculture is the best way for the world to feed its hungry people." When you write a paragraph, it is a good idea to "see" the points that you will be making to prove your topic sentence. Each point or reason you give should have an explanation supported with proof. Connect your points with transition words, and conclude your paragraph with a closing sentence that ties all your points together.

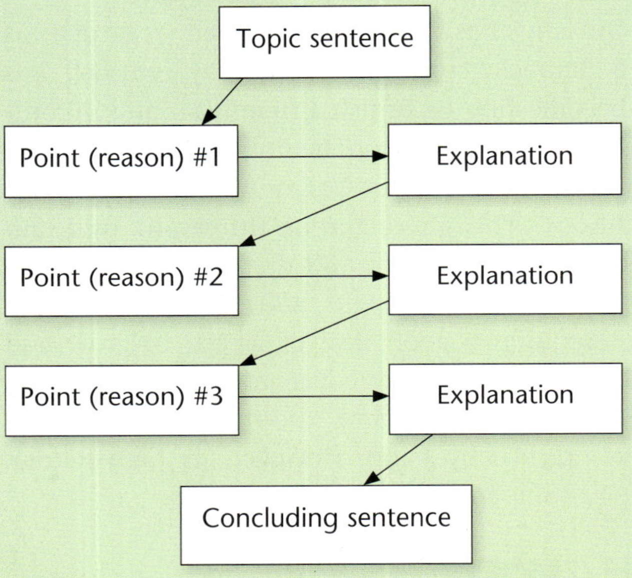

3. Make up a chart to compare the three specialized crops in Canada that are identified on pages 194 to 195. In your chart, comment on growing location, product uses, and growing conditions for each of these crops.

Specialty Crops	Growing Location	Product Uses	Growing Conditions

4. **a)** Put the six factors that influence agriculture in order based on how easily farmers can change and improve the conditions. The first one on your list should be the factor that farmers can change most easily. Explain why you placed each of the six factors in this order.

   b) When you are finished, compare your list with another person in the class. How are your lists the same? How are they different? What reasons might there be for differences in the order you placed the six factors?

Inquiry/Research and Communication Skills

5. Research and compare the ideal growing conditions for wheat and for rice. Record your findings in a comparison chart with these headings:

Topics to Compare	Wheat Growing	Rice Growing
Amount of precipitation needed		
Average temperature needed		
Soil conditions best suited to growing		
Topography best suited to growing		
(Add one other topic of your choice)		

6. Design a magazine advertisement to promote an agricultural product that is produced in Canada. On the back of your advertisement, identify the images or symbols used in your advertisement, and explain why you chose them.

Map, Globe, and Graphic Skills

7 **a)** Find a map that shows global precipitation patterns, and one that gives information about global agriculture (see Map Appendix). Compare the maps. Make two observations about the patterns that you see.

b) Compare a map showing global temperature patterns to the agriculture map (see Map Appendix), and note the patterns.

8 **a)** On an outline map of the world, shade the countries that are the top banana-producing countries in the world. (See chart below.)

Top Banana-Producing Countries of the World, 2005

Country	Annual Production (thousands of tonnes)
India	16 800
Brazil	6 700
China	6 400
Ecuador	5 900
Philippines	5 800
Indonesia	4 500
Costa Rica	2 200
Mexico	2 000
Thailand	2 000
Colombia	1 600
Burundi	1 600

b) On your map, use arrows to join Canada to each of the countries that are the likely sources of most bananas eaten in your community. Draw the arrows to show the routes that the bananas would probably take.

Application

9 Six major factors influence commercial agriculture. Describe the two factors that you think are most important for these parts of Canada:

a) southern British Columbia, near Vancouver

b) southern Ontario, near Toronto

c) Prince Edward Island, near Charlottetown

In each case, give reasons for your choices.

10 Make a flow diagram to show the process involved in growing, harvesting, and processing a plantation crop such as pineapples, or a Canadian crop such as wheat. (Refer to Figure 9.9 and Figure 9.16.)

Figure 9.24

Canada is one of the world's leading producers of wheat.

UNIT 3

Natural Resources

IN THIS UNIT

- describe how humans get, manage, and use natural resources, and point out conditions that affect the importance we give those resources
- use a variety of resources and tools to find, organize, and share geographic information about natural resources
- show how human activities affect the resources that we have available to us and the health of the environment

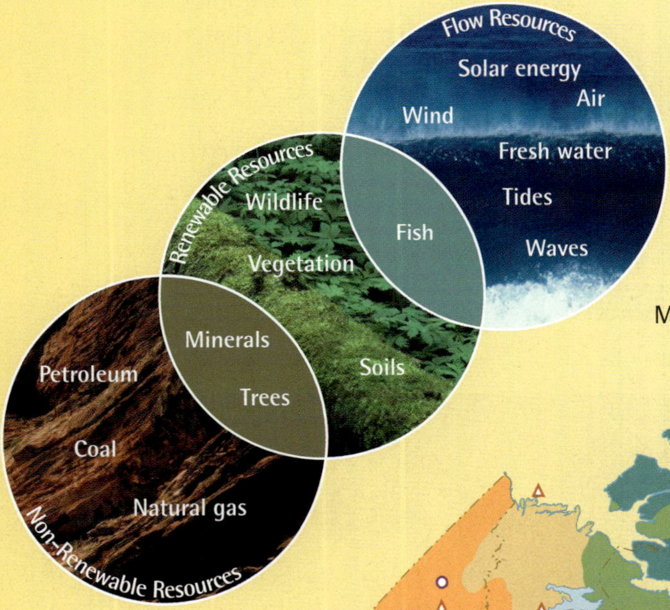

1 We talk about natural resources using three categories: non-renewable, flow, and renewable. Give one example of a natural resource for each category.

Mining Activity and Landform Regions

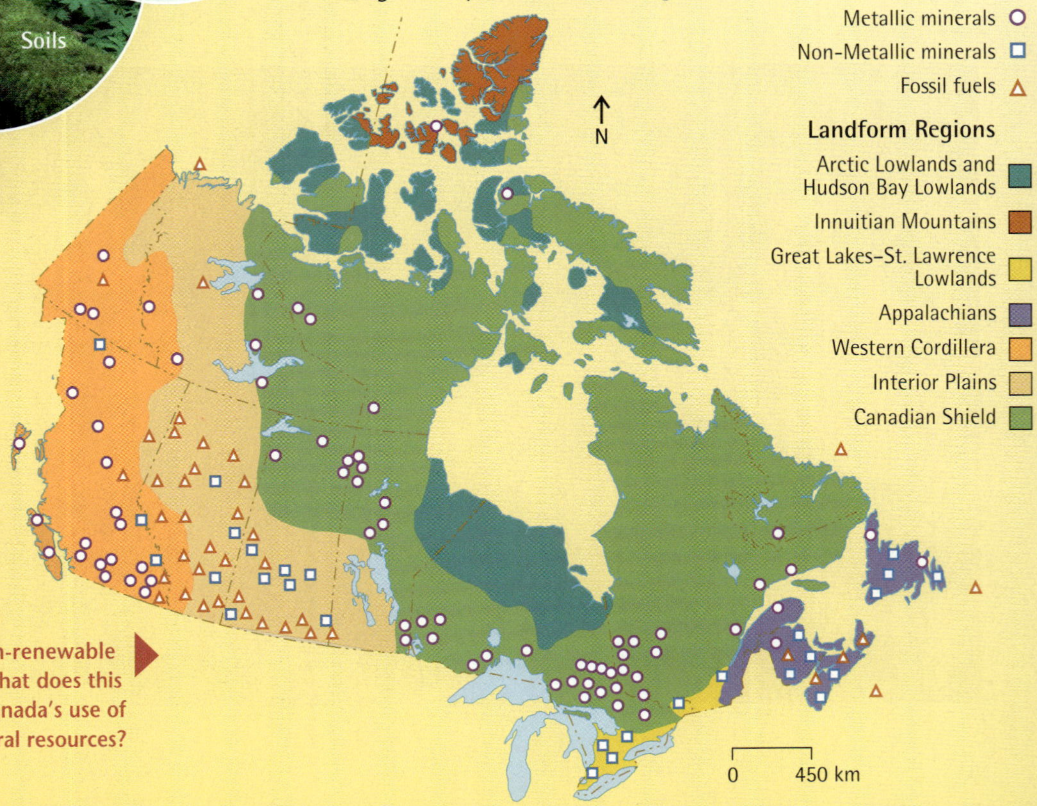

2 Minerals are non-renewable natural resources. What does this map tell us about Canada's use of non-renewable natural resources?

3 How does our use of natural resources affect the physical environment? How does the use of new technology affect the way we use up our natural resources?

4 What patterns does the graph show? How does the graph relate to the information in the diagram?

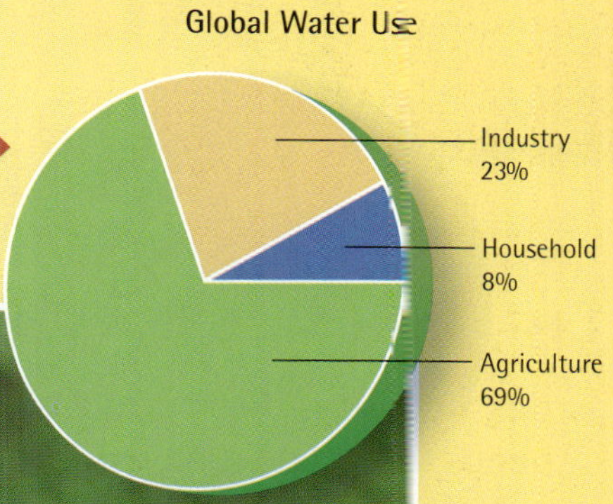

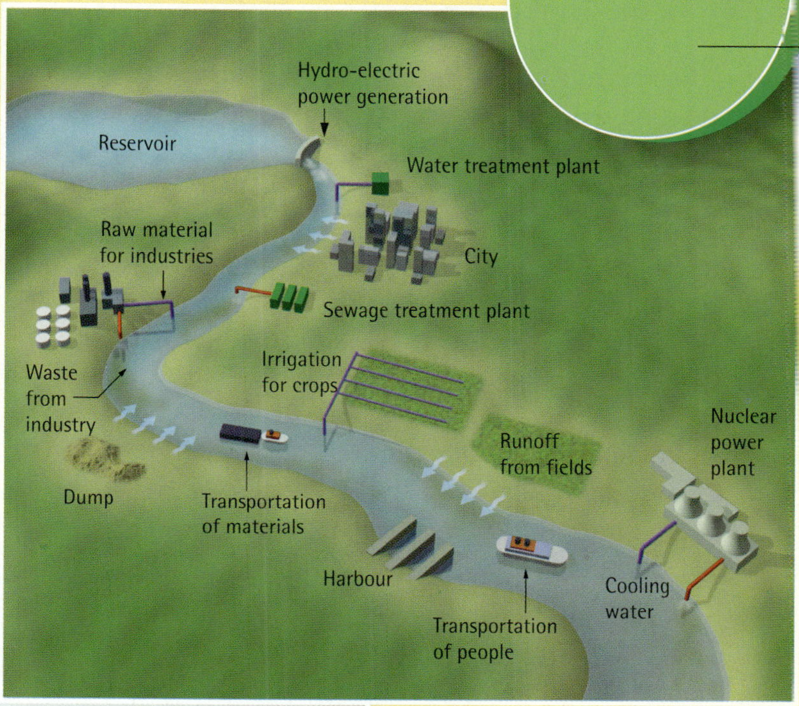

5 Why are many people against the hunting of whales? Why might Inuit want to hunt whales?

6 Who should lead the change to a sustainable use of our natural resources? What is one way you can help move us faster toward sustainable use of our resources?

10 Types of Natural Resources

IN THIS CHAPTER

- describe ways that people use natural resources to meet their needs, including renewable, non-renewable, and flow resources
- point out patterns in where resources are located and how they are used
- show how technology has affected our use of natural resources
- support a point of view about how a resource should be used
- use the new terms in this chapter correctly as you investigate the topics
- locate and use helpful information from primary and secondary sources
- share the results of research for different reasons and audiences using options such as computer slide shows, videos, websites, oral presentations, written notes and reports, drawings, tables, charts, diagrams, maps, models, and graphs

KEY VOCABULARY

demand
non-renewable
process
raw material
renewable
resource
shifting cultivation
supply
sustain
technology
traditional technology

Resources Are Life

Without materials like air, water, and soil, none of us could exist. Each of us needs these **resources** to live. We must breathe, eat, and have shelter. To meet our needs and wants, we use a wide variety of resources in many different ways. This is especially true in a resource-rich country like Canada.

All the things that we use are made from **raw materials** that originally come from our natural environment. These raw materials are our natural resources. These natural resources help us to meet our needs. In economic terms, our needs and wants are called the **demand**, and the natural resources are called the **supply**. In this chapter, we will see what humans demand, and how supplies, or natural resources, are taken from the environment.

Not all materials found in the natural environment are resources. We cannot call something a resource if we have not figured out how to use it to meet our needs. For example, mosquitoes are plentiful in northern Ontario. However, we do not think of them as a resource because they do not directly supply any human demand.

BEFORE READING

1. a) Think of something that you might like to have, such as a new game system, a new item of clothing, or something to decorate your bedroom. List all the materials that would be used to make that object—metals, plastics, fabrics, wood, and so on. Does your object need power? If so, list "energy" as a material that you will need.

b) Compare your list of materials to the lists of others in the class. How are your lists similar? How are they different?

Types of Natural Resources

Organizing natural resources into categories helps us understand the similarities and differences between them.

Figure 10.1

This chart explains the three different categories of natural resources.

Resource Category	Definition	Examples	Explanation
Renewable resources	• resources that can replace themselves even if they have been used, as long as they are not overused	• trees in forests • crops that are produced by agriculture • natural fish stocks	These resources are capable of regrowing or renewing themselves over a period of time.
Non-renewable resources	• resources that are gone once they are used	• minerals such as gold, iron, and nickel • fossil fuels such as coal and petroleum	These resources can be created only under quite specific conditions.
Flow resources	• resources that are replaced by natural actions whether humans use them or not	• fresh water flowing through streams and rivers because of precipitation • ocean currents • wind	These resources exist because of natural systems and natural processes.

Figure 10.2

These pictures show the three types of natural resources that we use to meet our needs and wants. Which type of natural resource is most important in your life?

Resource Overlap

There is some overlap among categories of resources. For example, trees that cannot grow back because of farming activities can be seen as **non-renewable** resources. On the other hand, minerals can be considered **renewable** if they are recycled.

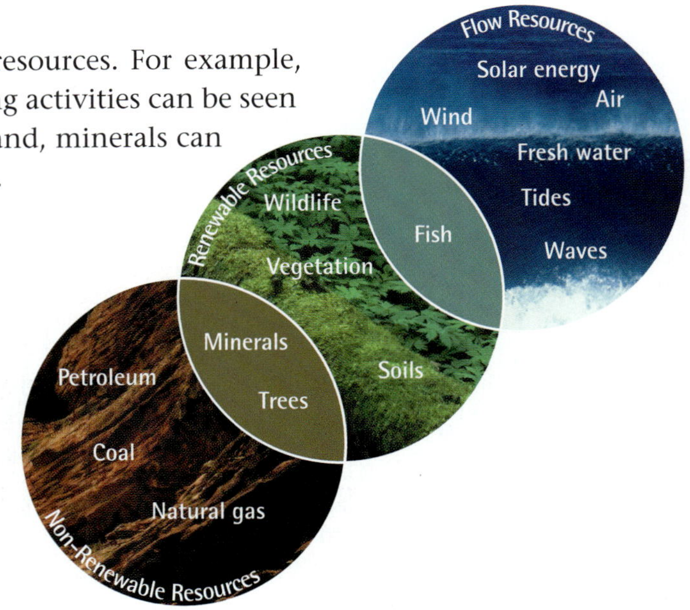

Figure 10.3

This diagram shows examples of natural resources arranged by categories. Notice that the categories overlap. Why are fish both flow resources and renewable resources? How can minerals and trees be renewable *and* non-renewable resources?

Fact File

People in the richer countries of the world use the most resources. In Canada, each one of us uses up to 85 tonnes of natural resources per year. This is equal to more than 300 large shopping bags of natural resources per week!

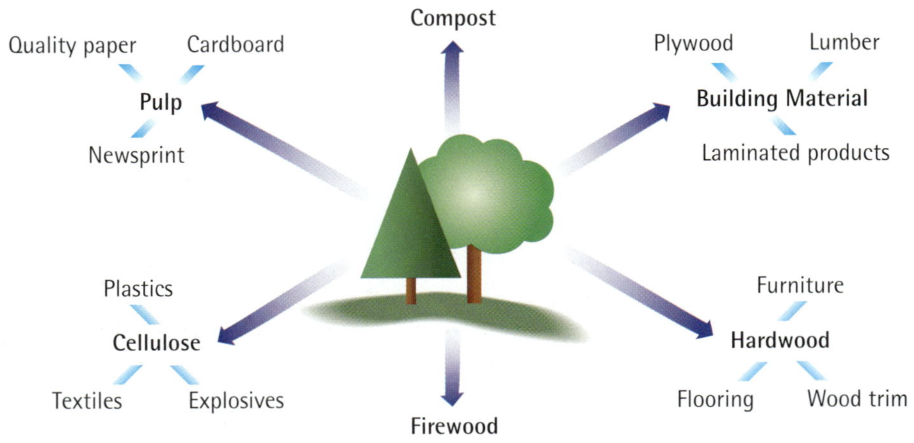

Figure 10.4

Trees provide important materials for meeting our needs. How can they be considered both renewable and non-renewable resources?

DURING READING

1. Use a graphic organizer to define renewable resources, non-renewable resources, and flow resources. Then, use your completed organizer to help you explain to someone in the classroom the differences between these types of resources.
2. Create a flow chart to illustrate the life cycle of a renewable, non-renewable, or flow resource. You can use pictures from magazines or the Internet, your own drawings, articles from newspapers, and your thoughts and ideas to illustrate and prepare your flow chart. You should include the following in your flow chart:
   - your chosen resource in its natural state
   - the products we make from the resource you chose
   - how we use the products we make from your chosen resource
   - what happens to these products when we are done with them

LITERACY TIP

Defining Key Vocabulary

Write the term to be defined (for example, "renewable resources") in the middle of a box that is divided into four equal sections (see the example on page 289). Then, list the characteristics of the word in the top left-hand corner. List examples in the top right-hand corner and non-examples in the bottom left-hand corner. Finally, write a definition in your own words in the bottom right-hand corner.

Supplying Our Demands

Natural resources come from our environment. Almost all natural resources must be changed before we can use them. These changes are called **processes**. One exception to this is some foods. We can eat berries and nuts just as they grow in nature. No changes have to be made before they can be eaten.

Figure 10.5

This chart shows some common processes that change natural resources into items we use.

Resource	Process	Product
Trees	**Sawing**—reducing the logs to usable, manageable lengths and widths	Boards and lumber for building
Iron ore	**Purifying**—removing the valuable iron from the waste rock in which it is found	Iron and steel made into a wide variety of products
Fish	**Cleaning**—removing the unwanted parts of fish so only the flesh is sold	Fish fillets or other cleaned fish products
Crude petroleum	**Refining**—removing impurities and chemically changing the raw material to make it cleaner and more suitable for a variety of different products	Gasoline, plastics, drugs, and many other products

Processing Resources

To understand how resources have to be processed, trace the steps in making a pair of jeans. The natural resource—the cotton—must first be grown and picked. The cotton bolls are then trucked to a mill where the fibres of the boll are wound together into cotton thread. Large machines weave the individual threads together into a cotton fabric. The cloth is dyed blue or black, or whatever colour is popular, and shipped to a clothing manufacturer. There, the fabric is cut into shapes and sewn together into a pair of jeans. Labels are put on the jeans, and they are shipped out to stores.

Figure 10.6

These four pictures tell the story of how a pair of jeans is made. What does each picture show about the process?

Advancing Technology

Humans have learned how to process natural resources to better meet our needs. We use **technology** as a tool to modify resources. Technology is the practical use of scientific knowledge to solve problems.

Technology has changed over time. As technology changed, our use of natural resources also changed. Early humans used only plants and animals to meet their clothing needs. Modern humans still use plants and animals, but now we also use other natural resources that require much processing, such as minerals and chemicals made from petroleum. The use and processing of resources can affect the natural environment, as you will learn in this unit.

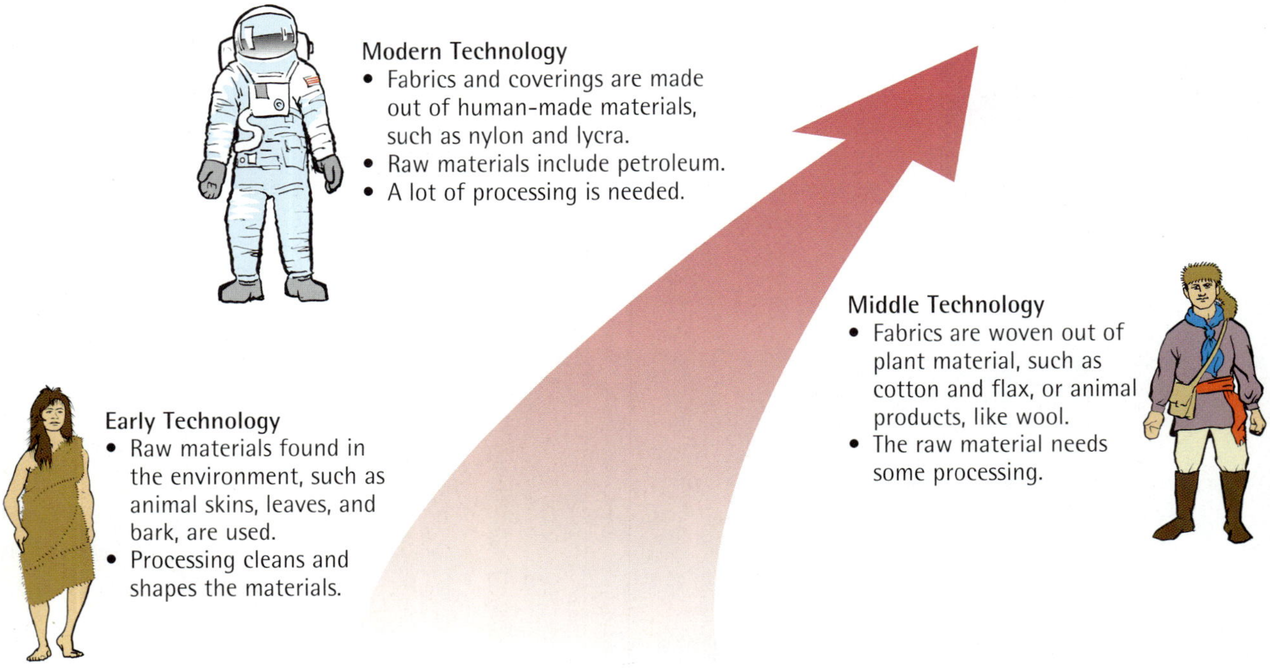

Figure 10.7

The technology to make clothing has changed over time. How are changes in clothing technology likely to affect your life?

AFTER READING

1. a) Name three products that you use that have undergone a great deal of processing.

   b) In your opinion, will the products that you use in the future be more processed or less processed than the ones that you use now? Explain why you think so.

2. Figure 10.7 illustrates how clothing technology has changed. Draw and label a similar diagram to show how our technology for one of the following has changed: writing, cooking, or transportation on land.

Taking Care of Our Resources

BEFORE READING

1. Suppose you want to reduce the amount of resources that you use in your daily activities. What three actions might you take to reduce your use of resources?

Resources are used to meet our needs, and this creates jobs and wealth. Our economy is made stronger because we harvest natural resources. However, harvesting and processing our natural resources often harms the natural environment. For example, to make hydro-electric energy, rivers are dammed up, which may cause large areas of land to be flooded. Societies are forced to make some tough decisions. Do they encourage more wealth by using resources, but harm the environment in doing so? Or, do they protect the environment, but use fewer natural resources? Finding a balance between gaining wealth and preserving the environment is a hard thing to do.

Figure 10.8

Large-scale hydro-electric dams such as the Aswan Dam in Egypt have created environmental problems, both upstream and downstream. What do you think these problems are?

Fact File

In Canada, about 676 000 jobs are directly tied to getting and processing natural resources (for example, miners and jewellers).

Factors Affecting the Use of Resources

When societies try to find a balance between using natural resources and protecting the environment, they must consider important factors. These factors affect the way we look at natural resources.

Growing Consumption

An important fact in our world is that most people want more things. They want nice cars, trendy clothes, larger homes, more food, a lot of electronic goods, and so on. The demand is growing for just about every natural resource. Some experts think that between 2005 and 2055, the total amount of the world's natural resources that people consume, or use, will grow by at least 100 percent, and perhaps by up to 500 percent. Energy consumption will be an important part of this growth. Experts warn that non-renewable supplies like oil and natural gas will eventually run out.

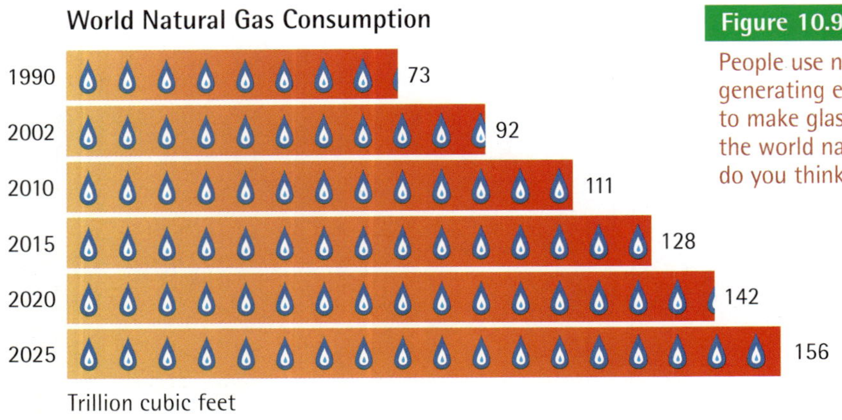

Figure 10.9

People use natural gas for cooking, heating their homes, generating electricity, and fuelling their vehicles, as well as to make glass, steel, plastics, and paint. This graph shows the world natural gas consumption predicted to 2025. Why do you think that the consumption of energy is growing?

Making Consumption More Fair

Twenty percent of the world's population lives in rich countries like Canada. Most people in these countries already have many things. In fact, the people that make up this 20 percent use 86 percent of all the world's goods. Now, people in poorer countries want to enjoy them as well. As people's incomes in poorer countries rise, there will be tremendous pressure to use more of the planet's resources to supply them with products.

Figure 10.10

This table shows the consumption of global resources by the richest and poorest parts of the world's population.

Consumption of Global Resources

Resources	The Richest 20% of the World's Population	The Poorest 20% of the World's Population
Fish and meat	45%	5%
Energy	58%	4%
Telephone lines	74%	1.5%
Paper	84%	1.1%
Vehicles	87%	1.0%

Literacy Tip

Reading Tables

Follow these five steps when reading a table with statistics:

1. Read the title to learn the purpose of the table.
2. Read the headings to find out what the statistics will tell you.
3 Read the data under the headings.
4. Read the data again. Look for patterns or differences.
5. Use the information from the table and what you already know about the topic to make concluding statements.

1. Is it OK to consume more resources if we only use renewable natural resources? Use the organizer below to help you make your decision.

Evidence that Supports Consuming More Resources if We Use Only Renewable Natural Resources	Is it OK to Consume More Resources if We Use Only Renewable Natural Resources?	Evidence that Opposes Consuming More Resources if We Use Only Renewable Natural Resources
•		•
•		•
•		•
Decision:		
Reasons:		

2. a) What is the purpose of the table in Figure 10.10?
b) What do the headings tell you?
c) What do the percentages tell you about the consumption of resources?
d) What pattern do you notice in the data presented?
e) Why should people be concerned about this information?

Figure 10.11

Why do you think that it is important to limit the use of natural resources? What can you do to help?

Concerns about Natural Resources

Many people are recognizing that their use of natural resources is harming the physical environment. They are encouraging other citizens and their governments to take actions that will help reduce the use of resources and protect the environment. One action that more and more Canadians are taking is buying hybrid cars that are powered by both gasoline and electricity. This is one way that they can reduce their consumption of energy.

Making Resources Last

How do we make our natural resources last for generations to come? People must work to **sustain** them. The best way to do this is to learn about how resources are used to provide you with the things you need and want. We have to make sure that our way of life does not use up non-renewable resources and does not waste renewable resources. We all can make sure that we practise the 3 Rs—reduce, reuse, and recycle—to the fullest extent possible.

You Are Important

As a consumer, you have a big role to play in helping to reduce, reuse, and recycle. Think about the pop cans that you use. A large part of the aluminum that is produced in the world is used for beverage and food containers. Aluminum is made from bauxite, a mineral dug from the ground. Not recycling aluminum pop cans means that the bauxite is rapidly being used up. When it is gone, it will be gone forever. It also means that more energy must be used to process the aluminum needed to replace the pop cans. Making pop cans from recycled aluminum takes only 5 percent of the energy that it takes to make pop cans from bauxite. Recycling metals saves valuable non-renewable minerals, and, therefore, energy. It helps to sustain our natural resources.

Figure 10.12

This table shows the proportion of energy saved by recycling materials. Why do you suppose the amount of energy saved varies from one material to another?

Proportion of Energy Saved by Recycling

Material	Percent of Energy Saved
Steel	74%
Aluminum	95%
Copper	85%
Lead	65%
Paper	64%
Plastics	80%

GO GEO-GREEN

Recycling and Reducing Waste

Did you know that your school lunch creates 30 kilograms of waste per year? Did you realize that it is now the law that all schools in Ontario with more than 350 students must complete a waste audit for their school? Canadians generate a lot of waste. In fact, we produce about 410 kilograms of waste per person per year. Fortunately, this amount of waste is balanced by efforts to increase our recycling. In 2004, the average Canadian recycled 112 kilograms of material. That is up from 71 kilograms in 2000. Schools and students have an important role to play in making recycling programs work.

Many school-based recycling initiatives exist across Canada:

- The Ontario Waste-Free Lunch Program was introduced in 2007 by the Ministry of the Environment, The Recycling Council of Ontario, and Ontario Eco-Schools. The waste-free or litterless lunch is built on reusable food and drink containers and reusable lunch bags or boxes. Schools were challenged to hold at least one waste-free lunch in April.
- In British Columbia, Encorp Pacific (Canada) has developed an elementary school incentive program for the recycling of beverage containers. Students bring beverage containers to school every day. Encorp supplies the containers and the depots for recycling, and the schools earn the money. Refunded money can be used for school fundraising. On average, participating schools raise between $50 and $100 a month.
- Northwestel, in Yellowknife, Northwest Territories, will contribute $3700 to elementary schools to reward them for participating in their Directory Recycling Program. Schools are invited to collect old Northwestel phone books to qualify for cash awards.

Both Encorp and Northwestel guarantee that the items they collect are recycled and not burned or sent to landfills. Programs such as these encourage students to recycle. As a class, you could look for sponsorship programs in your community to help with recycling and waste reduction.

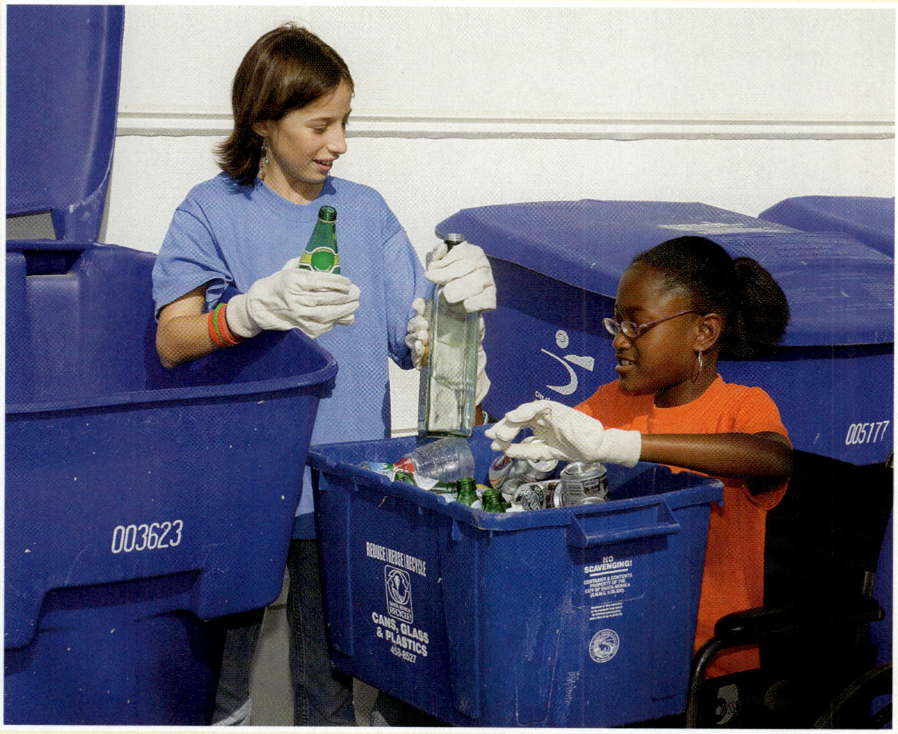

Figure 10.13

How can you help to reduce, reuse, and recycle, both at school and in your community?

AFTER READING

1. a) Think about the advantages of harvesting all the natural resources that we need. Then, think about the advantages of working to protect and conserve natural resources. Record your ideas in a chart similar to the one below.

Advantages of Harvesting All the Natural Resources that We Need	Advantages of Conserving Natural Resources and Using Them Carefully
•	•
•	•
•	•

b) Write one conclusion that you can make using your completed chart.

2. Suppose you decide to take action to use natural resources wisely and to protect the environment. List five actions that you could take. For each action, explain how it would help to conserve natural resources.

3. Supply five different endings for the sentence beginning "We should recycle because …" or "We should reuse because …."

GeoSkills

Reading a Photograph

By now, you have seen well over 100 pictures in this textbook. Photographs are useful because they help show physical and human patterns. How much time have you actually spent looking at these pictures? Reading photographs takes specific skills, just like reading a graph or map. When you read a picture, you are making conclusions based on inferences, or educated guesses. On the next page is a method that you can use to develop your photograph-reading skills.

Figure 10.14

Look carefully at the photograph below and the chart at the top of page 211. How does the "I See, I Know, So" method help to develop skills in reading photographs?

GeoSkills

Reading a Photograph *(continued)*

I SEE What is in the picture	I KNOW Information based on what you already know or have experienced	SO Conclusions about where the photo is taken and why it is included
• yellow field	• This is a crop that is all one colour.	• probably taken in Manitoba or Saskatchewan
• building(s)	• A farm: the buildings are by themselves and are right beside the field.	• showing the size of prairie farms and the flatness of the land
• big sky that takes up much of the picture; thick clouds	• Clouds are cumulus and look like they are getting heavy with rain; they are grey in colour.	• maybe looking at prairie cloud formations
• flat land	• This is in an area with plains or lowlands.	

Look at the picture below. Draw an "I See, I Know, So" chart in your notebook. Fill out the chart, and then share your ideas with a partner or a small group. This is a great way to see how other people formed their conclusions about the same photograph. You can adapt this chart for graphs and other visuals as well.

Figure 10.15

Complete an "I See, I Know, So" chart using this photograph.

Traditional Technology

Humans have learned how to use new technology to improve living conditions. As technology changed, so did the use of natural resources. However, some groups of people did not change their ways of life. They kept their **traditional technology** and continued to do things much as their ancestors had done.

BEFORE READING

1. This section is about people who live in a tropical rainforest. List five things that you already know about what it is like to live in a tropical rainforest.
2. The people being discussed in this section have lived just as their ancestors did for thousands of years. How might they use the environment to get food and build homes?

The Yanomami People

An example of a traditional society—one that existed almost undisturbed until the 1950s—is the Yanomami people. Today, there are an estimated 27 000 of them. They live in the rainforest between the Amazon and Orinoco rivers in northern Brazil and southern Venezuela. The Yanomami have occupied this forest for thousands of years. The dense underbrush has kept them isolated from the outside world.

Northern South America

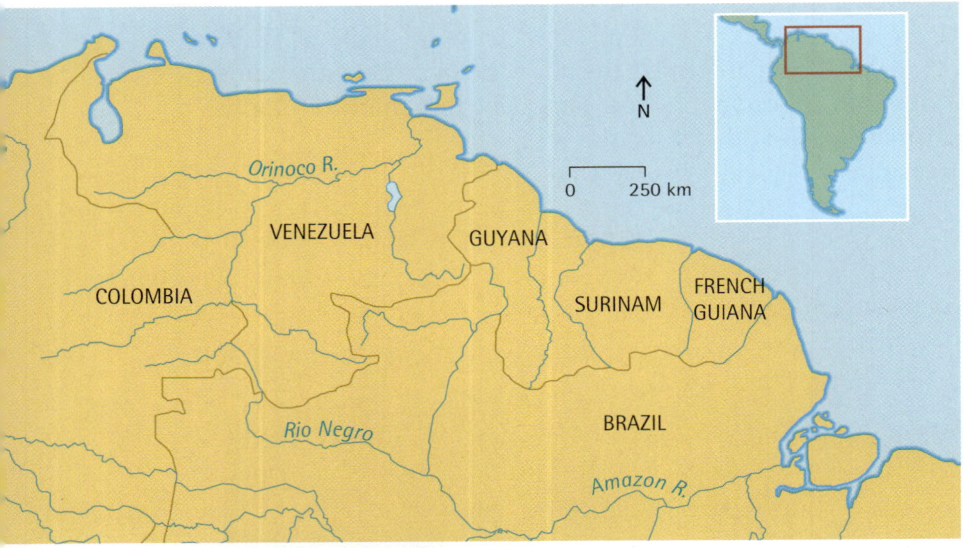

Figure 10.16

The Yanomami people are located near the border between Brazil and Venezuela.

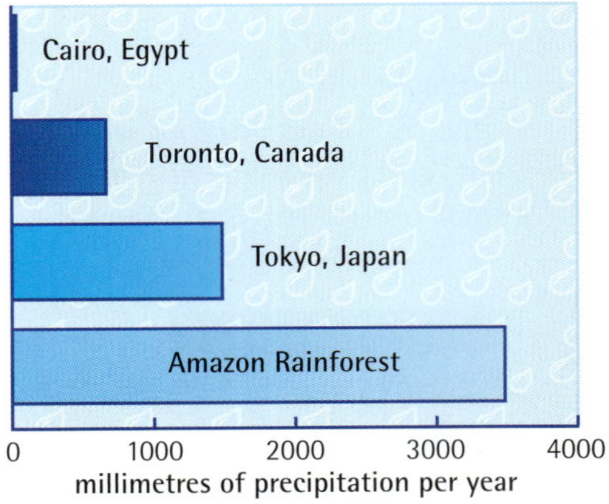

Figure 10.17

Precipitation levels are given here for four places. How might the amount of precipitation affect the ways in which people live their lives?

The Environment of the Yanomami

The rainforest environment is lush and rich. Over 3500 millimetres of rain falls each year, and temperatures average 27 °C. Daytime temperatures are often higher than 35 °C. Trees grow quickly in this climate. Growth is so lush that the canopy of upper tree branches intertwines to almost block out the Sun from the lower layers of the forest.

Figure 10.18

Note the layers of natural vegetation found in this typical example of a rainforest.

DURING READING

1. As you read the next section, make a flow diagram or series of sketches to show how the Yanomami make a garden in the middle of a tropical rainforest.
2. In what ways does the traditional technology of the Yanomami help to sustain the resources of the people?

Figure 10.19

This sketch shows how a Yanomami garden would be organized. What are some advantages of shifting cultivation over permanent gardens?

Fact File

Burning the vegetation in the rainforest helps kill insect pests and weed seeds. The wood ash makes good fertilizer.

Growing Food in a Forest

The Yanomami plant gardens to grow their food. Their system of planting is known as **shifting cultivation**. Each family has its own garden patch where they grow plantains (similar to bananas) bananas, yams, manioc (a root vegetable), and sugar cane. They also grow non-food crops—cane for arrow shafts, reeds whose sharp leaves are used for cutting, and tobacco. After several years, weeds invade the gardens, and the soil becomes exhausted. The Yanomami simply shift to a new location and make a new garden.

To make a garden, the Yanomami must clear the dense forest, which is a difficult task. They begin by choosing a site with good drainage and soil. Small trees and underbrush are cut and piled to dry out and be burned. Large trees are girdled—a strip of bark is cut off the trunk all the way around the tree—so that the tree dies. Brush is piled against dead trees and set on fire. Even if large trees do not fall down, their branches are burned off. Then, the sunlight can reach the ground below.

Figure 10.20

The Yanomami coat the tips of their arrows with curare. This poison is made from a vine that grows in the forest. The curare causes animals' muscles to relax, so that they fall out of the trees to the hunters below. What other natural resources do you think this Yanomami hunter uses to make his arrows? Are these resources renewable or non-renewable?

Other Food Sources

The gardens do not provide the Yanomami with all their food. The great variety of wildlife in the forest—mammals, reptiles, birds, and insects—add protein to their diet. The Yanomami particularly like to hunt tapir and peccary. These pig-like mammals forage on the forest floor. Termites, caterpillars, and locusts are also a source of high-protein food.

Living in the Forest

The Yanomami live in large communal dwellings called *shabonos*. The people use poles cut from the forest to build a circular structure. Then, they thatch the roof with leaves. Each family sleeps and eats in its own section of the *shabono*. Communal activities like cooking and socializing take place in the central area.

WEB LINK

For more information about the Yanomami, go to www.nelson.com/phygeo7.

Intruders in the Forest

The years since the 1950s have not been good for the Yanomami. Outsiders searching for minerals and forest products brought diseases such as tuberculosis with them. Many Yanomami, especially babies, died. The infant death rate for the Yanomami is 13 percent, compared to 1.5 percent for all of Brazil. Most frighteningly, the outsiders are killing the Yanomami in order to get control of their land. The area in which the Yanomami live is rich in minerals, especially gold. During the 1970s and 1980s, over 20 percent of the Yanomami were killed by outsiders. Other threats to their existence come from ranchers and rubber plantation owners who want the land.

Figure 10.21

Food is stored on a shelf above the family's hammocks. How does the roof of the dwelling appear to be constructed?

Figure 10.22

These people were travelling to a local feast when it began to rain. How have they used the environment to solve a problem?

Literacy Tip

Reading Cartoons

Cartoons are humorous drawings that present an issue or event and make a comment about it. They are visual tools used to express an opinion and present a message. They are meant to get readers thinking about the topic presented. When you are reading a cartoon (for example, Figure 10.23), remember that the cartoonist is trying to present a message. You will need to interpret the information presented in order to understand that message.

The Future for the Yanomami

There are some good signs for the Yanomami. In 1992, Brazil set up a 9.4-million-hectare reserve for the Yanomami people. This has slowed down the rate at which outsiders enter the area. However, patrolling it is very difficult, and prospectors still get through. The way of life of the Yanomami is changing as outside influences come into this remote area. Their use of resources will change as well. In the future, they may find that the forest will not satisfy all their needs.

Figure 10.23

What techniques has the cartoonist used to create a message?

Wicks/Rothco. Reprinted by permission.

CONNECTIONS TO **Cartoons**

This cartoon criticizes the attitudes of many outsiders toward the Amazon forest. How do these attitudes compare to those of the Yanomami?

AFTER READING

1. a) You live a very different life than the Yanomami. Compare the Yanomami way of life to your own. Make a chart in your notebook like the one below.

b) What would happen to your way of life if all the electricity in the world failed? What would happen to the life of the Yanomami?

2. Identify five natural resources that the Yanomami people use. Give at least one purpose for each resource.

3. Suppose you were to visit a Yanomami *shabono*. What would you find appealing about the way of life of the Yanomami? What aspects do you think you would find unappealing?

Item	Yanomami Way of Life	My Way of Life
• where our food comes from		
• daily activities		
• our houses		
• our two biggest problems		

Knowledge and Understanding

1. Complete these sentences:
   a) The most important reason that people use natural resources is ....
   b) Trees are a renewable resource because ....
   c) Technology is ....
   d) Consumption of resources will grow because ....
   e) The hardest part about shifting cultivation is ....

2. Below are three pairs of terms. How do the meanings of the terms in each pair differ?
   a) renewable resources and non-renewable resources
   b) supply and demand
   c) bauxite and aluminum

3. a) Identify three factors that will likely cause more natural resources to be consumed in the future.
   b) Suggest two actions that could be taken to change the factors that are leading to more consumption.

Inquiry/Research and Communication Skills

4. Suppose you want to learn more about how people use technology to process natural resources. Make up three research questions that you might use to focus your research. Start each of your research questions with one of these beginnings: How ...? How much ...? Why ...? How did ...? How might ...? How will ...?

5. The Yanomami practise a form of technology called shifting agriculture. What technology did the First Nations in your part of the province use before Europeans arrived in North America? Use the Internet and other research sources to answer this question. Make a poster to show your research findings (refer to the Literacy Tip on page 171 of Chapter 8). Be sure to include sketches of the foods and the tools that were important, and an explanation or illustration of the traditional methods used.

6. Choose one country anywhere in the world. Using the Internet, an encyclopedia, or other sources of information, decide which natural resources seem to be important to that country. In order to decide this, look at the industries in the country and the types of products that they make and export. Organize the resources into renewable, non-renewable, and flow categories.

Map, Globe, and Graphic Skills

7. Figure 10.3 uses circles to show the relationships between renewable, non-renewable, and flow natural resources. Use your own ideas to come up with another way of illustrating the same relationships. Think about the following methods to help get you started:
   - Use three-dimensional objects, such as blocks.
   - Use objects that move, perhaps suspended from the ceiling.
   - Use "found" objects, such as those you might find in the recycling box or trash.

8. Make a collage of products that we all use every day. Split the collage into two parts. On one part, show products that are highly processed, like DVDs, TVs, and cars. On the other, show products that require very little processing before we can use them, like eggs, fruit, and flowers.

Application

9. You are making a movie about Canadians working with the Yanomami people. The Canadians' job is to help the Yanomami acquire modern technology without destroying their environment, the tropical rainforest. Your movie will illustrate what the Canadians are doing to help the Yanomami. Outline your movie as a set of pictures (storyboard) that shows your plan for your video. A storyboard shows what will happen in your video in the order you plan to record the actions or events. Each major action or event is shown with a sketch and a written summary.

10 **a)** There are always some Canadians who are out of work or living in difficult circumstances. Some Canadians argue that because of this, we must continue to create wealth by harvesting our natural resources as fast as we can. However, other Canadians want us to work harder to conserve our resources and protect the environment. What is your opinion, or point of view, on the topic? Use an organizer like the one below to help you decide on your point of view.

b) Present an argument for one side of this problem. Try to convince people on the other side that you are right. Present at least three reasons for your side. (You may refer to Writing an Opinion Paragraph on page 233.) Then, share your written argument with other people in the class, and discuss the differences you have in your arguments.

11 Read the following newspaper article. Write a letter to the editor of the paper expressing your feelings about the situation.

Yanomami tribe attacked, flee

Reports are coming out of a remote part of Brazil that a small Yanomami tribe was attacked by outsiders on Tuesday. The Yanomami people escaped unharmed. However, their village was burned and crops were destroyed.

The attackers have yet to be identified, but officials think they might be renegade miners trying to move onto reserve lands. Officials have pledged to put a stop to any more violence in the area.

Evidence to Support Harvesting Our Natural Resources as Fast as We Can	**Should We Create Wealth by Harvesting Our Resources as Fast as We Can?**	**Evidence that Supports Working Harder to Conserve Our Resources and Protect the Environment**
•		•
•		•
•		•
Decision:		
Reasons:		

11 Non-Renewable Natural Resources

IN THIS CHAPTER

- describe ways that people use natural resources to meet their needs, including renewable, non-renewable, and flow resources
- point out patterns in where resources are located and how they are used
- show how technology has affected our use of natural resources
- describe ways that natural resources are important to a country
- use maps to find patterns in natural resources
- use the new terms in this chapter correctly as you investigate the topics
- locate and use helpful information from primary and secondary sources
- share the results of research for different reasons and audiences using options such as computer slide shows, videos, websites, oral presentations, written notes and reports, drawings, tables, charts, diagrams, maps, models, and graphs

KEY VOCABULARY

aggregate
beneficiation
carat
environmental assessment
mineral
open-pit mining
ore deposit
right
tailing
underground mining

Spaceship Earth

BEFORE READING

1. Brainstorm a list of non-renewable resources that you use in your life. Identify ways in which these non-renewable resources help you to live a better and more comfortable life.
2. Explain why we should be careful about how we use non-renewable resources.

You are part of the crew of a space laboratory orbiting the Sun. Your mission will keep you and the rest of the crew in space for at least 10 years. Everything you need for life support is on board: food, water, oxygen, heat, and light. There is not a lot of room on board, so there are no areas for growing anything or for replenishing your supplies. When your supplies are gone, they are gone for good. When you run out of something, it cannot be replaced. Your whole mission could be lost. If you were really up in space, would you not want to be careful about using your supplies—your non-renewable resources? Your life could depend on it!

Metallic minerals

DURING READING

1. Information about minerals is given on pages 219 and 220 as text, as pictures, in a chart, and in a mind map (or ideas web). Which way makes it easiest for you to understand the different types of minerals? What does this say about the way you learn best?
2. Suppose you had to explain the different types of minerals to a friend. Which method would you use? Why?

In fact, you are in that situation, in real life. The spaceship is the planet Earth, which is orbiting the Sun. The crew is all of us living on Earth. Everything we need for life is on spaceship Earth. However, many of the resources are limited and non-renewable. When they are used up, they cannot be replaced. Should we not be very careful about how we use and take care of our resources? Our lives do depend on them!

Non-Renewable Resources

Non-renewable resources are those that are gone forever once we have taken them from the natural environment. **Minerals** are some of our most important non-renewable resources. We put minerals into the following four categories: metallic minerals, non-metallic minerals, structural minerals, and fossil fuels.

Figure 11.1

Minerals are very important to us. Can you name the minerals in the pictures below?

Structural minerals

Non-metallic minerals

Fossil fuels

Figure 11.2

These four types of minerals are non-renewable resources.

	Metallic Minerals	Non-Metallic Minerals	Structural Minerals	Fossil Fuels
Description	• have a metallic shine • good conductors of heat and electricity	• have a dull appearance • break apart easily	• a subgroup of non-metallic minerals • used in construction	• raw materials for a wide variety of products, including energy
Examples	Iron, gold, copper, nickel, aluminum, zinc	Salt, potash, asbestos	Limestone, sand and gravel, gypsum	Petroleum, coal, natural gas
Formation	Usually found in rocks that have cooled from magma	Usually found with sedimentary rocks	Associated with sedimentary rocks	Formed from the ancient remains of plants and animals buried underground

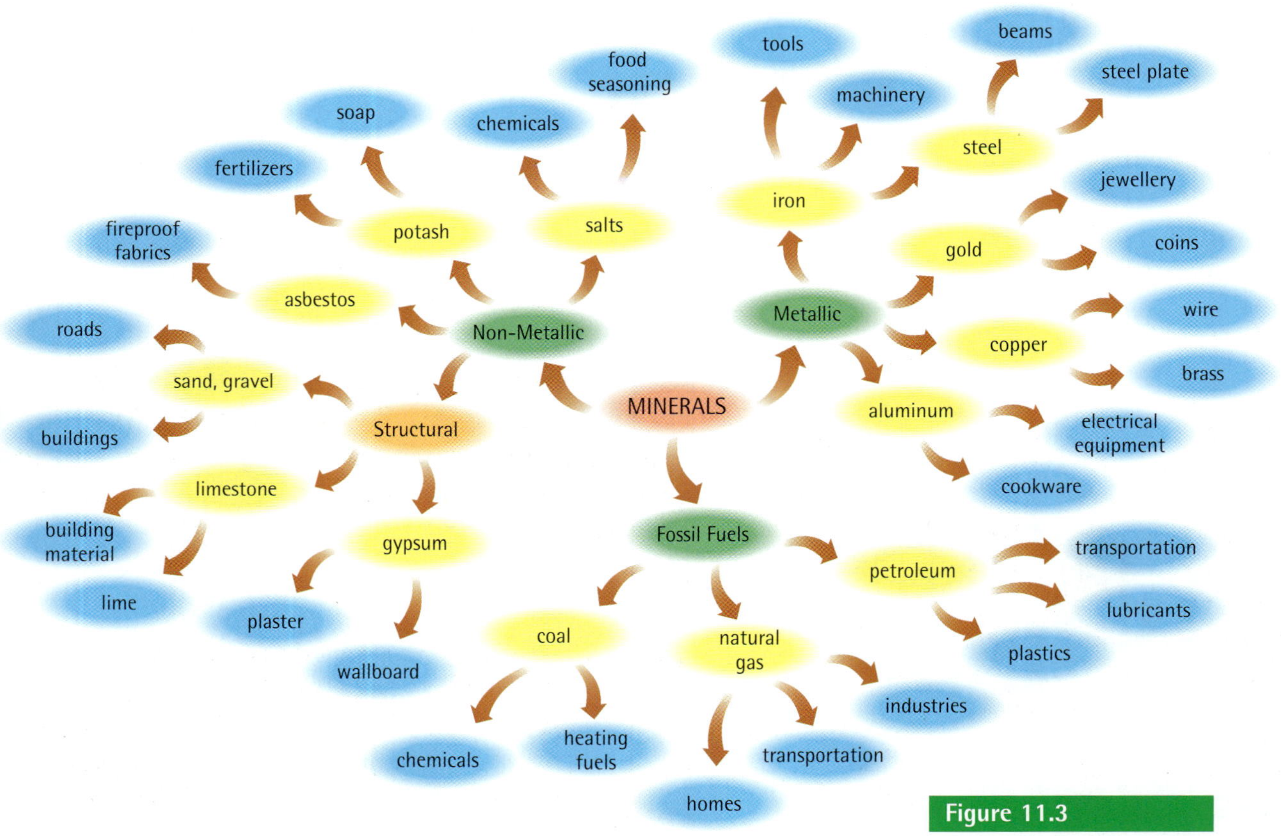

Figure 11.3

Trace the arrows from the centre bubble, MINERALS, to the four types of minerals. From each mineral type, follow the arrows outward to the mineral examples and the products made from each mineral.

Using Minerals to Meet Our Needs

Think about what your home would be like without minerals. Start by taking away all the appliances. They are made using a number of metals. Now, remove all the electrical wiring. Wires are made of copper or aluminum. The plumbing goes, too. Pipes are made of copper. Throw out your heating system, since furnaces and electric heaters need metal. Knock down the walls, too, since they are made using gypsum, another mineral. Can you keep the concrete blocks in the walls? Sorry, they are made with sand, gravel, and lime. Even roofing is made using fine gravel. Not much of your home is left without minerals, is it? Now, think about all the other things in your life that would be gone without minerals.

AFTER READING

1. Make up a bumper sticker promoting the wise use of our non-renewable resources. The best bumper stickers are short, interesting, and funny. A bumper sticker is like a slogan. (Refer to the Literacy Tip on creating slogans on page 85 of Chapter 4.)
2. The following nine terms are connected to non-renewable natural resources: "fertilizer," "copper," "fossil fuels," "metallic," "plastics," "non-metallic," "wiring," "potash," and "petroleum." Show how these words are related by arranging them in a mind map (or ideas web), with "non-renewable resources" in the centre.
3. Design a room for yourself that contains no metal at all. Describe the materials you choose to use in place of metals.
4. List five non-renewable resources. Then, list two products we get from each.

Literacy Tip

Asking Questions

Asking questions gives a focus to your reading and helps you understand what you read. There are two types of questions:

- Closed questions help you find specific facts in the text you are reading.
- Open-ended questions may require you to read between the lines or look beyond the text for an answer.

When forming either closed or open-ended questions, remember the 5 Ws and 1 H questions.

Minerals of the World

BEFORE READING

1. Look at the lists and maps on pages 221 and 222. Make up three closed questions that you think can be answered using this information, and three open-ended questions that will require looking beyond the information given on these two pages.

Top World Producers of Selected Minerals
(percent of world production, 2003)

Aluminum		Copper		Diamonds		Gold	
China	19.5%	Chile	36.1%	Australia	20.7%	South Africa	14.8%
Russia	12.4%	U.S.A.	8.3%	Botswana	20.3%	Australia	11.2%
Canada	10.0%	Indonesia	7.4%	Congo (D.R.)	19.3%	U.S.A.	11.0%
U.S.A.	9.6%	Peru	6.2%	Russia	16.0%	China	8.3%
Australia	6.7%	Australia	6.1%	South Africa	8.4%	Peru	6.9%

Gypsum		Nickel		Potash		Zinc	
U.S.A.	16.5%	Russia	22.2%	Canada	32.3%	China	19.6%
Spain	12.4%	Australia	14.2%	Russia	16.9%	Australia	16.1%
Canada	9.3%	Canada	12.1%	Belarus	14.9%	Peru	14.9%
Iran	8.7%	Indonesia	10.6%	Germany	12.6%	Canada	8.9%
Mexico	7.2%	New Caledonia	8.3%	Israel	6.9%	U.S.A.	8.0%

Figure 11.4

Which three countries seem to be important sources of minerals worldwide?

World Mineral Locations

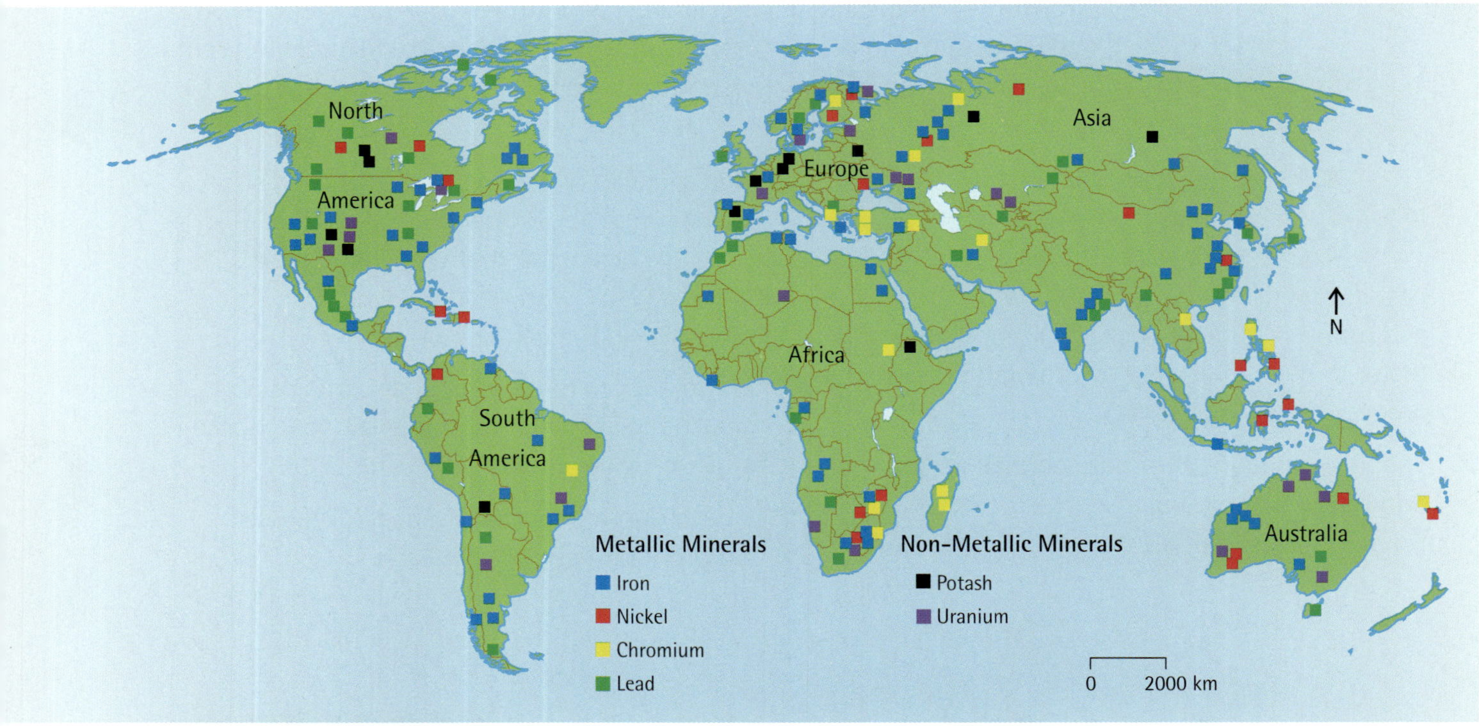

Figure 11.5

Which continent seems to have the most minerals?

World Fossil Fuel Locations

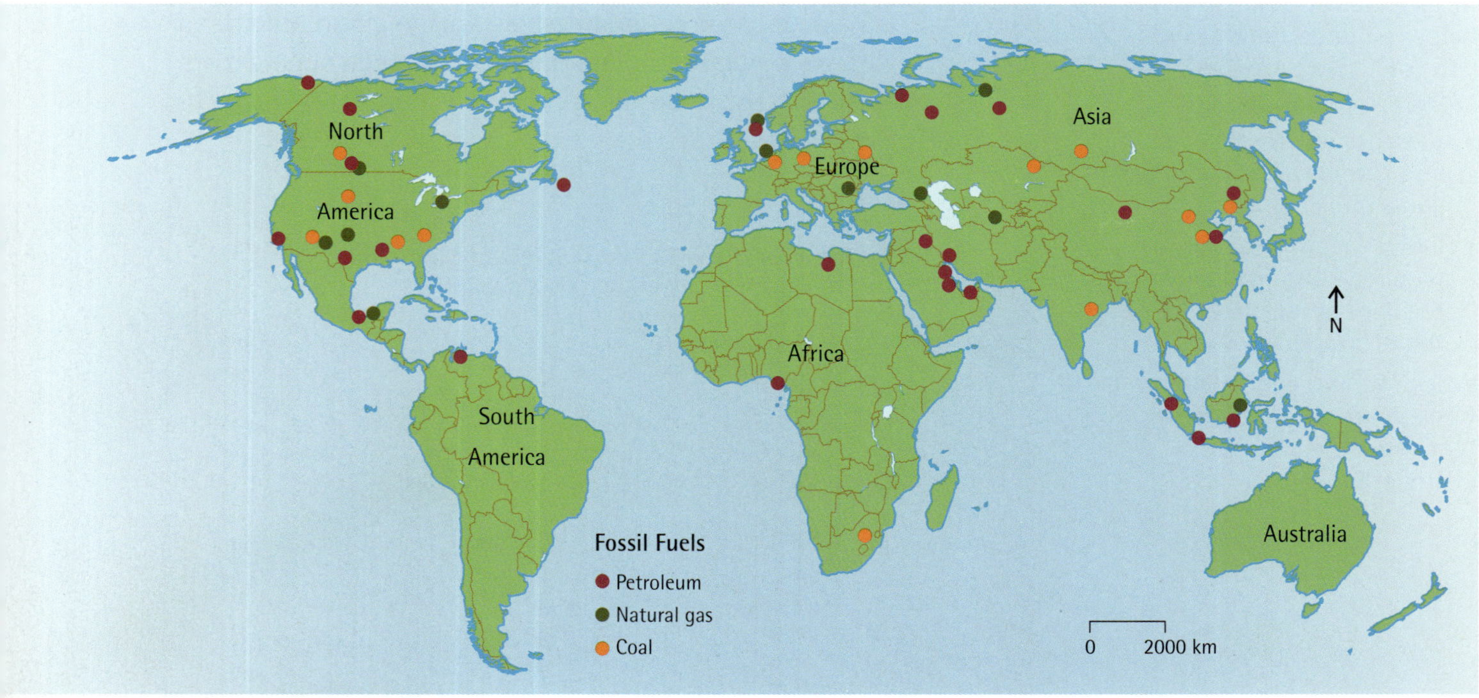

Figure 11.6

Name a part of the world that has very few fossil fuel resources. Consider the type of rock in which fossil fuels are found. Can you suggest a reason why some of the areas have fewer fossil fuels?

AFTER READING

Use the maps and lists in Figures 11.4, 11.5, and 11.6 to help you answer the following questions. Identify which of the questions are closed and which are open-ended.

1. Name two parts of the world where there are very few minerals mined or fuels extracted. Name two parts of the world that seem to have a variety of minerals and fuels.
2. In what parts of Canada is mining an important economic activity? Where are fossil fuels important? Which parts do not seem to have much mining or fuel extraction? Explain why you think this is so.
3. Using the lists of countries in Figure 11.4, count and record how many times each country is named in the lists. Which countries seem to be the most important mining countries? Why do you think that is?

Mining Minerals

BEFORE READING

1. How do you think geologists know where to find minerals?
2. With a partner, brainstorm the different ways that minerals are extracted (removed) from rocks.

DURING READING

1. List the people or groups that might be affected by the discovery of minerals and the decision to develop a mine. Put a check mark beside those who you think will be happy about having a mine and an X beside those who may be unhappy about a mine. Beside each person or group, write down a point that summarizes why they would be happy or unhappy about a mine.

Minerals are important for our way of life, but they are not easy to get. To start with, just finding them is often very difficult. Then, we have to be able to harvest them. Even if we find a concentration of the mineral—an **ore deposit**—and we can extract the ore from the ground or the ocean, we have to separate it from all the rock it is usually mixed with. After that, many processes are needed to make the mineral into a form we can use. There are many steps between wanting the minerals, finding them, processing them, and using them.

Figure 11.7

This photograph shows ore being excavated from a mine in Sept-Îles, Québec. Extracting ore from the ground can be very difficult. Why do you think that is?

Prospecting for Minerals

How do prospectors find ore that is buried deep underground? To start, prospectors study samples of rock that they find at the surface. They have learned that certain ore deposits are usually found with certain types of rocks. Prospectors also use indirect methods. One technique is to fly over an area towing an instrument that measures the magnetic field of the rocks below. When a site looks promising, small drilling rigs are brought in to get samples from below the surface. This is very expensive and takes a lot of time. In the end, only one test in a thousand leads to the development of a mine.

Developing a Mine

When a site has a large deposit of ore, it may be chosen for development into a mine. The process of developing a mine takes many years. Many difficult jobs have to be done before the first minerals can be sold.

Figure 11.8

This airplane is towing a magnetometer that measures the magnetic field of the minerals in the ground below. Mining companies use this data to help figure out what minerals are in the ground.

CONNECTIONS TO History

Minerals have been important to people for a very long time. People began using metals about 5000 years ago. Copper was the first, and later came tin. Then, a mixture of copper and tin, called bronze, was used. All sorts of tools and weapons were made from bronze because it is a very hard metal. Historians call the time when bronze was so important "The Bronze Age"—from about 3000 BCE to 1000 BCE.

Obtaining the Rights to Mine Minerals

The land that the ore is on usually does not belong to the mining company. The company must get permission from the owners before it can take the ore out. This is called getting the **rights**, which means buying the legal rights to the ore from whoever owns those rights. In some cases in Canada, First Nations people of the area have those rights.

Figure 11.9

Demonstrators protest against uranium mining in the Sharbot Lake area, which is located north of Kingston, Ontario. Getting the rights to extract minerals often means negotiating with First Nations people who live in the area. If these negotiations break down, protests may follow.

Protecting the Environment

Many countries, including Canada, require mining companies to be sure that they will not cause severe, long-lasting damage to the environment or hurt people before they are allowed to build a mine. This **environmental assessment** involves a study of what the mine will do to the land, the air, the wildlife, and the people of the area. The mining company must show the effects of the mine on the ecosystem. The study must show that the mine's impact on the environment will be at an acceptable level.

Building the Mine

The mining company must determine the best way to extract the ore from the ground. One method is **underground mining**. The mining company digs a vertical shaft down into or near the ore body. Horizontal stopes, or tunnels, are built out to the ore face. At the ore face, the ore is blasted into rubble. Load-haul-dump machines pick up the broken ore and carry it to an elevator. This method is best when the ore is found far below the surface.

When the ore is found near the surface, mining companies use **open-pit mining**. First, the overburden is removed; this is the rock, soil, vegetation, and sometimes even a water body such as a creek or a beaver pond that covers the ore. Then, heavy equipment is used to dig a deep hole into the ore body. Whole mountains have been completely removed using this mining method.

DURING READING

1. Think about what it might be like to work in an underground mine. Describe what you might hear, see, smell, and taste in an underground mine.

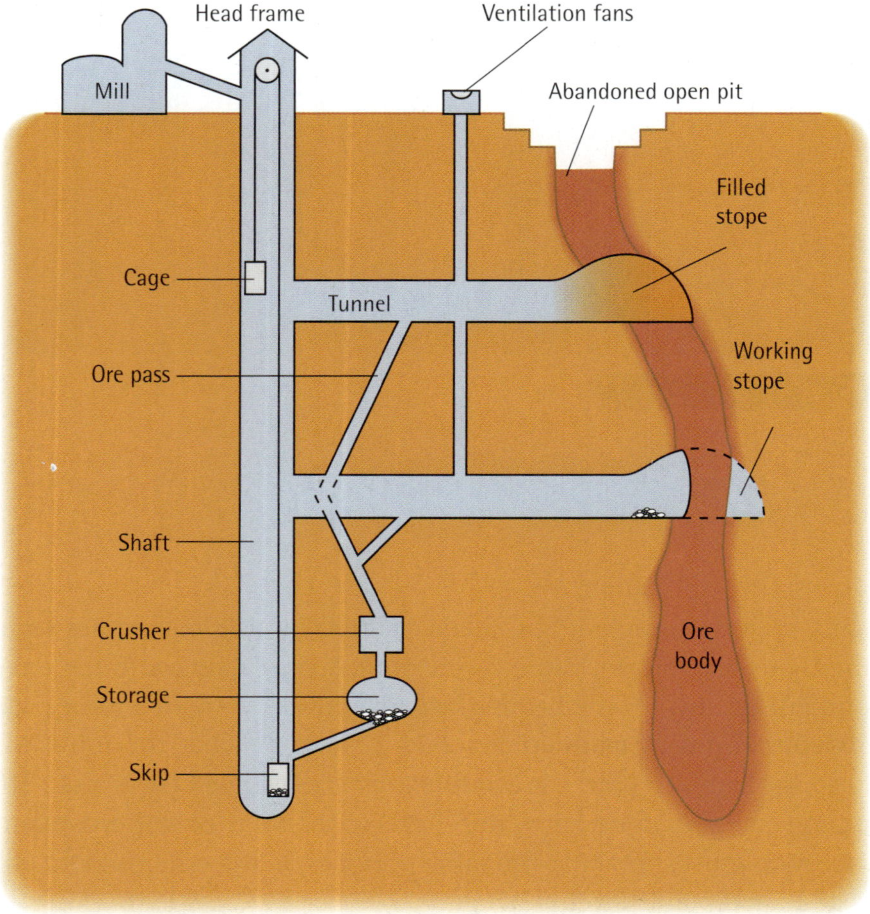

Figure 11.10

Underground mining requires a good attitude toward safety. Fresh air must be pumped down into the mine, and stale air and fumes must be drawn out by a ventilator system.

Figure 11.11

This is a photograph of the Diavik Diamond Mine, which is located in the Northwest Territories, north of Yellowknife. Notice how the ground in this open-pit mine has been cut into ramps that snake up the sides of the pit. The heavy trucks drive on these ramps. In what ways do open-pit mines disrupt the natural environment?

Fact File

A typical open-pit copper mine will report these statistics before it is closed:

- 900 million tonnes of overburden will be removed from on top of the ore body.
- Over 450 million tonnes of ore will be dug out and sent to the refinery.
- 4.5 million tonnes of copper metal will be shipped to buyers.
- Almost 450 million tonnes of tailings, or leftover materials, will be created.
- The mine will leave a hole almost 4 cubic kilometres in size. That is big enough to hold three of Toronto's Rogers Centre.

Refining the Ore

Useful minerals must be separated from the waste rock. This process is called **beneficiation**. Some minerals are separated by melting the ore in a smelter. Other minerals are best separated by chemical action in a refinery mill. Beneficiation is done as close to the mine as possible to reduce transportation costs because there is so much heavy waste rock to transport. Only a small percentage of mineral is found in the ore. Figure 11.12 shows how the cost of chromium—a mineral that is combined with steel to prevent it from rusting—rises through each stage of refining and manufacturing.

DURING READING

1. As you read through this section, list some ways that mining, and all the activities that go with it, have an impact on the environment.
2. What are two things that are done to try to reduce the harmful impacts of mining on the physical environment?

Figure 11.12

This chart shows the cost of chromium at different stages of processing.

Stage of Processing	Cost
Chromite ore (30% chromium) 	$200/tonne
Ferrochromium (52% chromium) 	$860/tonne
Stainless steel (18% chromium) 	$15 166/tonne
Manufactured products (such as stainless steel pots and pans) 	$32 000/tonne

Dealing with Waste

After the valuable minerals are extracted from the ore, the mining companies face a big problem. What should be done with the leftover material, called **tailings**? Very often, the valuable minerals make up only about 2 percent of the ore. This means that mining companies must dispose of tailings equal to about 98 percent of the original material from the mine. In open-pit mines, the tailings are sometimes dumped in parts of the pit where the ore has been exhausted. In other cases, the waste is simply put into pits or piles nearby.

One problem with tailing piles is that they often contain dangerous chemicals and minerals that can be washed out of them. These poisons make their way into the groundwater and streams of the area. Careful planning and design of tailing storage facilities are needed to stop tailings from becoming sources of pollution.

Reclamation

Mining scars Earth's surface. Many countries require mining companies to make the area safe and productive once mining has stopped. It is impossible to return the area to a completely natural state. However, trees or grasses can be planted on mined areas and over tailing piles to hide some of the scars. Eventually, the land may be used for grazing animals or for recreation.

Figure 11.13

This photograph shows an area in Sudbury, Ontario, that has been reclaimed after mining. What appears to have been done to make the area safe and attractive?

Go Geo-Green

Reclamation of Gravel Pits and Quarries

If you look out of your classroom window, you will probably see a number of items that are made using **aggregates**. Aggregates are structural minerals that include gravel and sand. These aggregates are used to build roads, buildings, and sidewalks. They are used to filter water and do landscaping. They are also used to make toothpaste, cosmetics, paint, vinyl flooring, and bubble gum. The places where they are dug from the ground are called pits and quarries.

For many years, when a gravel pit was no longer needed, companies would leave it and move on to another area. The old pits would sit idle. They had little use for anything else. Now, with the help of public campaigns and government programs, the aggregate companies are beginning to return these old gravel pits to somewhat natural environments. The following examples show what is being done.

- In British Columbia, one company has worked with local towns to establish plant growth on its old gravel pits. It used the nutrient-rich organic material from waste-water treatment to fertilize the ground. Through community meetings, the towns decided on the type of vegetation to be planted. School kits were developed to allow students to explore the requirements for good plant growth. This joint project has been a successful way to create environmentally healthy ecosystems in places that were once damaged.
- Another company has worked with the Greater Vancouver Regional District to develop the "Pit to Park" plan. This plan will create a large recreational space in an old gravel pit. The recreational space will have a lake for canoeing, marshland, a concert bowl, and open green space.
- In Ontario, one large company hired a planner to help it convert its abandoned gravel pits and quarries to wilderness and parkland. Recently, the company gave 1000 acres of rehabilitated land to the local conservation authority.

You can get involved in rehabilitation projects by working with community groups and conservation authorities. Look for groups that need help with planting trees or spring flowers. By helping with and learning about local rehabilitation projects, you are helping today's environment, and making a cleaner and greener Earth for years to come.

Figure 11.14

This is an old, abandoned quarry near Guelph, Ontario.

continues...

GO GEO-GREEN

Reclamation of Gravel Pits and Quarries *(continued)*

Figure 11.15

This is a rehabilitated quarry in Elora, Ontario. What improvements appear to have been made to the ecosystem as a result of the rehabilitation?

1. Explain how each of the following situations might stop a rich ore body from being mined:
   - There are very few customers for the mineral in the world.
   - The refined mineral would have to be transported a long distance.
   - The price the mineral is selling for is low.
   - A new form of plastic can do the same things as the mineral.
   - First Nations claim the mining area as their land.
   - The environmental assessment required by law has to be completed.

2. Select one of the roles listed below. Write for the audience listed, in the format suggested, and on the topic provided.

Role	Audience	Format	Topic
Mining executive	Shareholders	Letter	The discovery of a new rich mineral body
First Nations leader	First Nations community	Speech	Proposal to mine on First Nations lands
Experienced miner	New miner	Dialogue	Working in an underground mine
Environmentalist	A group of protesters	Speech	How mining causes environmental damage

3. Brainstorm possible ways to solve the problem of tailings. Consider the following:

- Tailings often contain low concentrations of the ore that is mined.
- There might be other uses for the tailings.

4. Mining can have a harmful impact. The effects of mining can include the following:

- disrupting First Nations peoples' use of the land
- harming the environment
- disturbing wilderness areas

Is getting the minerals worth these costs? Write down your opinion (yes or no), and give three facts that convince you that your opinion is right. To help you make a decision, use a "Both Sides Now" organizer, such as the one shown below. The organizer will help you visualize the arguments for and against mining minerals and help you arrive at an opinion that you can support with facts.

<table>
<tr><th>Evidence that Supports the Opinion that Mining the Minerals Is Worth the Cost</th><td rowspan="5">Is Mining Minerals Worth the Cost?</td><th>Evidence that Supports the Opinion that Mining the Minerals Is Not Worth the Cost</th></tr>
<tr><td>•</td><td>•</td></tr>
<tr><td>•</td><td>•</td></tr>
<tr><td>•</td><td>•</td></tr>
<tr><td>•</td><td>•</td></tr>
<tr><td colspan="3">Decision:</td></tr>
<tr><td colspan="3">Reasons:</td></tr>
</table>

GeoSkills

Writing an Opinion Paragraph

The purpose of an opinion paragraph is to express your ideas about an issue. A clear opinion paragraph will persuade readers to accept your point of view. In order to make a clear and concise opinion paragraph, you must remember the 4 Cs: Catch, Commit, Convince, and Close.

Catch

Commit

Convince

Close

Bringing the Cost of Oil Sands Production Home

What would it be like to live in your house if it had no reliable source of running water or a working furnace? If Alberta's oil sands development is allowed to increase, depleting water and gas resources could become reality for many people in Canada. Recovering usable oil from the oil sands is a process that needs a lot of water and natural gas, which are used when the sticky oil is separated from the sand. For every barrel of oil that is produced, two barrels of water are used. By 2025, the high volume of water usage in oil sands production will threaten the Athabasca River. Also, the refining process will use up 20 percent of Canada's annual natural gas production. This is the same natural gas that 80 percent of Canadians use to heat their homes and water. If expansion of production in the oil sands is not stopped, Canadians will not have enough water for their homes or gas to heat them.

Figure 11.16

Read the paragraph above, and note the 4 Cs.

Catch: This is the first sentence in your paragraph. It is the most important sentence because it is the one that will grab the reader's attention. You must find a way to introduce your topic so that the reader will want to keep reading. You might try starting with a question, a quote, or an information bite.

Commit: This is the second sentence in your paragraph. Its job is to state the topic and your opinion clearly.

Convince: This is where you prove your point and support your opinion. You can use information from research and from your own knowledge and experience to write this section. Make sure that your points are clear and concise.

Close: This is your conclusion, and it may be one or two sentences long. You must restate your opinion, and you may want to summarize the most important point in your paragraph. This is where you can leave the reader wanting to find out more about the topic or to get involved with the issue.

Mining in Canada

BEFORE READING

1. Brainstorm with a partner the names of towns or cities in Canada where mining is an important industry. Use an atlas, and note which minerals are important to the economy of these towns or cities.
2. Which parts of Canada have the greatest amount of mining activity?

Mining and mineral processing create many jobs in Canada. In 2005, about 388 000 Canadians were working for mining and mineral-processing companies. Mining added $40 billion to the country's economy in 2006. It is a very important part of Canada's economy.

Metallic Minerals

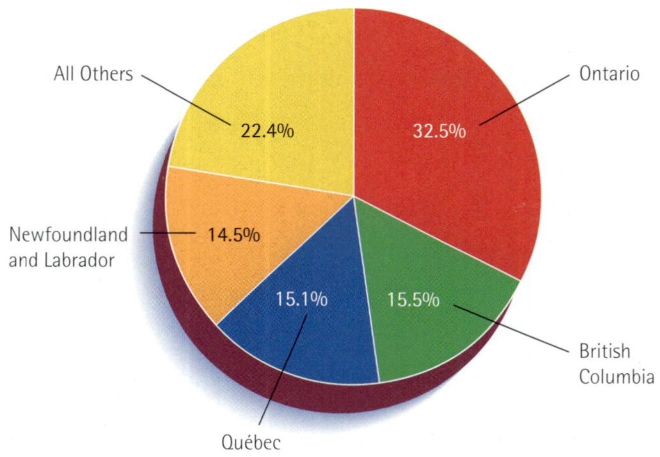

Non-Metallic Minerals

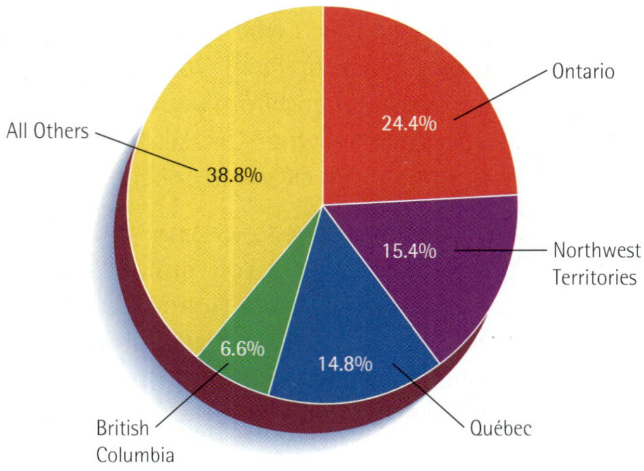

Figure 11.17

These graphs show the leading provinces and territories for metallic and non-metallic mineral production for 2006.

Fact File

- Canada produces more than 60 minerals and metals.
- There is mining activity in every province and territory.
- In 2006, nickel was the top metallic mineral produced in Canada, when $6.2 billion of nickel was shipped. Potash was the top non-metallic mineral, at $2.2 billion.
- Weekly wages in the mining industry are about 1.5 times the national average.

Literacy Tip

Creating Timelines

A timeline plots events in a graphical way.

- Choose the most important events.
- List these events in chronological order (earliest to latest).
- Decide what unit of time you want to use for your timeline (for example, years).
- Calculate how many segments you will need on your timeline.
- Draw a horizontal or vertical line and divide it equally into the number of segments that you need.
- Label the dates from left to right on a horizontal timeline, and from bottom to top on a vertical timeline.

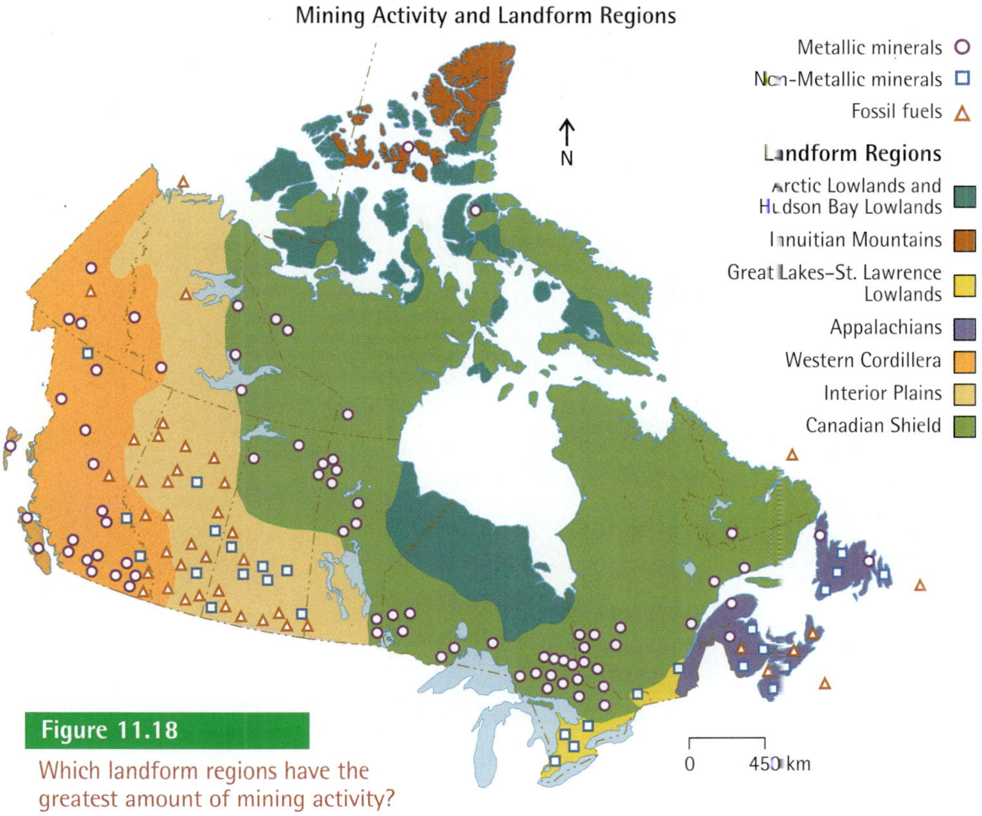

Figure 11.18

Which landform regions have the greatest amount of mining activity?

DURING READING

1. As you read the next section, draw a timeline to show the development of the diamond industry in Canada. Start your timeline at 1991, and label the events that occurred.

Diamond Mining in the Northwest Territories

The first diamonds were discovered in Canada in 1991 at Lac de Gras, which is about 300 kilometres northeast of Yellowknife, Northwest Territories. The Ekati mine opened in 1998, and it produced one million **carats** of diamonds the first year. A second mine in the Northwest Territories, the Diavik Diamond Mine, began production in 2003. In 2004, these two mines produced 12.6 million carats of diamonds, worth more than $2 billion. This is equal to about 1.5 kilograms of diamonds a day for the year.

Fact File

Diamonds and other precious stones are measured in carats. A carat is a unit of weight equal to 100 milligrams.

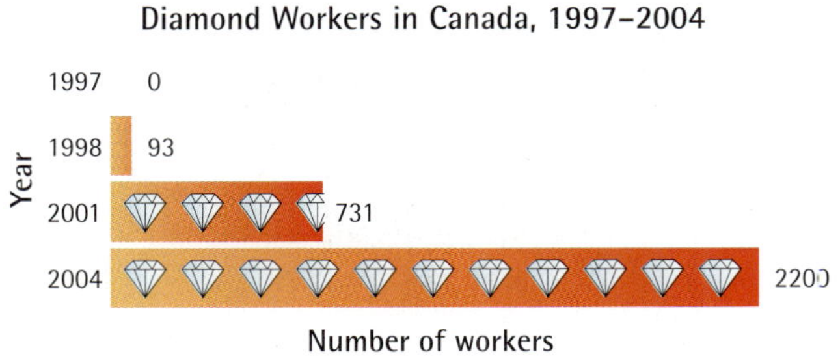

Figure 11.19

This graph shows the number of workers in Canada in the diamond industry from 1997 to 2004. About 40 percent of the workers are Aboriginal peoples, and about 60 percent are non-Aboriginal peoples.

Figure 11.20

Aurora College, in Yellowknife, Northwest Territories, trains students to cut and polish diamonds through its Diamond Cutting and Polishing program. Here, a student is polishing a diamond.

WEB LINK

For more information about the Canadian diamond industry, go to **www.nelson.com/phygeo7**.

Between 2005 and 2007, three more mines started producing diamonds—one each in Nunavut, Ontario, and the Northwest Territories. This added production makes Canada the third-largest producer of diamonds by value in the world, after Botswana and Russia. The diamonds mined in Canada are of good quality. They are etched with an image of a polar bear to mark them as Canadian diamonds.

Many jobs have been created because of diamond mining. The stones have to be cut and polished. A number of businesses that do this have started in the Northwest Territories. At first, highly trained diamond cutters were brought in from places such as Armenia, Israel, and China. Now, a college program in Yellowknife is turning out trained workers. Other jobs have been created in areas such as house construction and road building.

The existing mines are expected to keep producing some of the world's best diamonds for at least 20 years. Mining companies are continuing to search for new deposits of diamonds. The Aboriginal peoples in the North are partners in this development.

Fact File

Canadian diamonds are etched with a tiny polar bear symbol to distinguish them from "blood diamonds" mined in Africa, where the profits help fund civil wars that have child soldiers fighting in them.

1. Look at Figure 11.18. Why do you think the landform regions were marked on this map of mineral and mining locations?
2. Figure 11.18 shows that there is little mining in northern Québec and Nunavut. Give three reasons to explain why you think this is.
3. Work with a partner to brainstorm some ways that diamonds are used.
4. Why are some people in Canada very excited about this country's diamond industry?

Knowledge and Understanding

1. Column A in the chart below is a list of products made from non-renewable resources. Column B is a list of the non-renewable resources. In your workbook, match the products with their correct non-renewable resource.

Column A (products)	Column B (non-renewable resources)
Bricks	Talc
Concrete sidewalks	Iron
Aluminum pop cans	Lead
Car body parts	Clay
Batteries	Bauxite
Talcum powder	Limestone

2. In your workbook, make a chart with the following headings: Stage of Development (left column), and Problems to Overcome (right column). In the left column, write down each of the headings used in the section Mining Minerals, on pages 223 to 229. In the right column, record any problems that the mining company has to solve in each stage of development.

3. Identify the advantages and disadvantages of mining non-renewable natural resources. Consider the following topics as you think about the advantages and disadvantages:
   - the environment
   - economic effects
   - impacts on Aboriginal peoples
   - jobs
   - other topics that you think are important

Inquiry/Research and Communication Skills

4. These are some mining towns in Canada: Chibougamau, Kimberley, Labrador City, Marathon, Port Hardy, Sudbury, Thompson, and Trail. Choose three of these, and conduct research to find out which minerals are extracted in each location. The Internet and Canadian encyclopedias and atlases will be good sources for your research. Show the locations of the three towns on a map of Canada.

Figure 11.21

How is this non-renewable resource being processed?

5 Make up three possible research questions on the topic of Canada's energy supply. One question should be a closed question, such as a comparison question (for example, "Which is larger …?"). Another question should be an open-ended question, such as a cause-and-effect question (for example, "Why did *x* happen?"). The third question should also be an open-ended question, such as a question in which you wonder (for example, "What would happen if …?"). Use classroom and library resources to answer one of your questions.

6 **a)** Conduct research on the Alberta Tar Sands, a rich deposit of oil-soaked sands in northern Alberta. Find information on the following topics:

- size of the resource
- ways of extracting the oil
- reclamation efforts
- issues/problems
- opportunities

Organize your findings in a display, such as a poster or a PowerPoint presentation.

b) Compare the amount of oil found in the Alberta Tar Sands to the deposits in another country. Research to find out about the oil resources in Mexico, Venezuela, or Saudi Arabia. Make a comparison chart to show your data.

Map, Globe, and Graphic Skills

7 Make a flow diagram to show the stages in mining, from prospecting through to reclaiming the land. Make small sketches to illustrate what is going on at each step in your diagram (see sample flow diagrams on pages 188 and 192 of Chapter 9).

8 In Canada, wages paid to workers in the mining industry are high compared to other jobs. Review "Creating a Bar Graph" in the GeoSkills on page 107 of Chapter 5 before you construct a bar graph to show this information.

Sector	Weekly Wage (2006)
Mining	$1346
Forestry	$967
Manufacturing	$906
Construction	$895
Retail trade	$485

Figure 11.22

The scale of the Alberta Tar Sands is huge, from the amount of oil in the ground to the massive trucks used to move the sands. These trucks are three stories high and cost $5 million each.

9 **a)** A good way to see the economic importance of mining to a province is to look at its share of mining employment. Construct a bar graph to show mining employment by province/territory. (Refer to "Creating a Bar Graph" in the GeoSkills on page 107.)

Province/Territory	Employment
Newfoundland and Labrador	4.3%
Nova Scotia	2.3%
New Brunswick	4.4%
Québec	21.0%
Ontario	28.2%
Manitoba	5.2%
Saskatchewan	11.9%
Alberta	5.6%
British Columbia	13.3%
Nunavut	3.4%

b) Make up two questions about the data in this chart and shown on your graph for a partner to answer.

Application

10 Mining has had a long history in Canada. Locate some photographs or diagrams that show something of the working conditions and technology of earlier times. A museum or library with a big collection of books on the history of Canada would be a good place to begin your search. You could also search on the Internet for historical images of mining in Canada. Try a search string such as *mining history Canada* and click "images." Display copies of the pictures you find on a poster, in a PowerPoint presentation, or in some other interesting arrangement.

11 Should mining companies be forced to pay the cost of reclaiming a mine site? Before you decide on your answer, make up two lists. On one list, write points in favour of making companies pay. On the other list, write points against it. Based on your lists, decide on your answer. Write a paragraph giving your opinion on the topic. For help in writing opinion paragraphs, review the GeoSkills on page 233.

12 Who has a role to play in making sure that non-renewable resources are recycled? With a partner, brainstorm a list of people or groups (for example, concerned citizens or politicians) who you think should lead Canada's efforts to recycle. For each group, identify some actions that they could take, or have taken, to improve recycling. When you have finished, write a paragraph in which you identify the group that you think has the greatest potential to improve the country's recycling efforts.

12 Renewable Natural Resources

IN THIS CHAPTER

- describe ways that people use natural resources to meet their needs, including renewable, non-renewable, and flow resources
- point out patterns in where resources are located and how they are used
- show how technology has affected our use of natural resources
- describe some ways that natural resources are important to a country
- make maps to show where natural resources are located in Canada
- use maps to find patterns in natural resources
- use the new terms in this chapter correctly as you investigate the topics
- locate and use helpful information from primary and secondary sources
- share the results of research for different reasons and audiences using options such as computer slide shows, videos, websites, oral presentations, written notes and reports, drawings, tables, charts, diagrams, maps, models, and graphs
- make a report on conditions that will affect the natural resources that are available in the future

KEY VOCABULARY

cartographer
cash crop
clear-cut logging
coniferous forest
deciduous forest
domestication
hardwood
logging
natural regeneration
pulp and paper
replanting
selective logging
softwood
strip logging
temperate forest
tropical forest

Nothing Is Forever

BEFORE READING

1. Make up two lists with the headings "Products from Animals" and "Products from Plants." Think of the products that you use. How many products can you list under each heading that come from plants and animals?
2. How can plants and animals be classified as renewable natural resources?

Renewable resources are those that will grow back again or reproduce themselves. They will be available for our use later, even if we use some of them now. While renewable natural resources are able to grow back, sometimes our actions make that difficult. These resources may be lost if we overuse them or change the conditions in which they live. For example, some animals have been hunted to extinction. Also, we are destroying tropical rainforests, which contain half of Earth's plant species. All renewable resources will be available to us only if we treat them with respect and care.

Animals as Resources

Humans have always hunted wild animals for food. **Domestication**, or the taming of wild animals, started as early as 12 000 years ago. Then, animals could be used for many more purposes. Dogs protected people and their animals (for example, sheepherding), while sheep, goats, and cattle served as easily available food sources. Over time, other animals were tamed for use as pets and beasts of burden (or work animals). People used the skins of domestic animals to make clothing and shelter. Many domestic animals had dual purposes. Cattle provided milk, and they were also used as draft animals to help people do their work.

Distribution of Domesticated Animals Worldwide

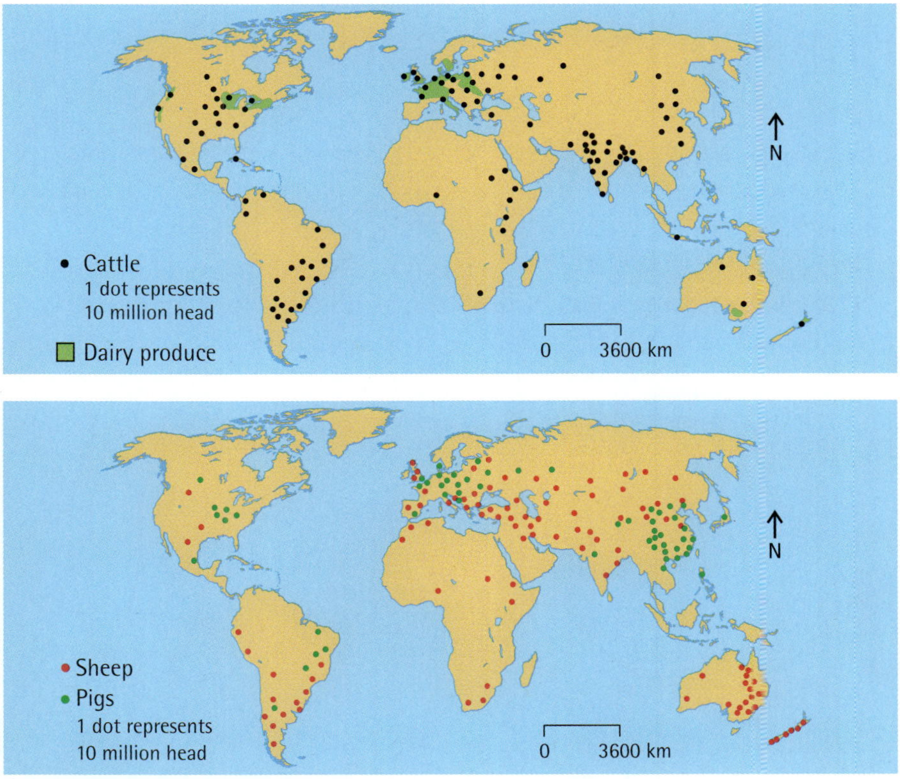

Figure 12.2
These maps show the distribution of domesticated animals worldwide.

Figure 12.1
Humans often use animals for labour, as here in Ethiopia in eastern Africa. What are some other ways animals are used by people?

DURING READING

1. Examine the maps in Figure 12.2. Which areas of the world seem to have few domesticated animals? Why do you suppose that is the case?

GeoSkills

Understanding Map Projections

Earth is a sphere. When we draw a map, we flatten this sphere to make it fit on a sheet of paper. Because of this flattening, all maps are distorted in some way.

Figure 12.3

Map makers can stretch the surface of Earth so that the parts are less curved.

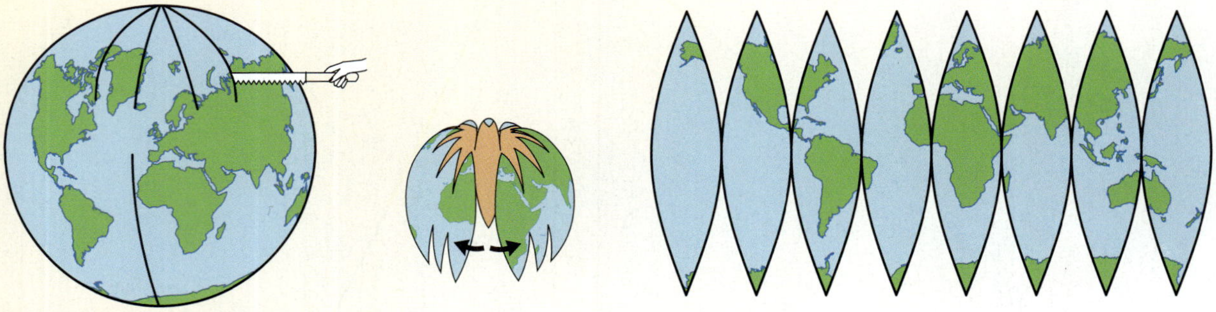

Figure 12.4

Map makers can also cut the surface of Earth to flatten it.

Map makers, called **cartographers**, use projections to draw their maps. If you were to build a clear glass globe with black cardboard continents and place a light in the centre, it would project, or cast, shadows all around it. The cartographer traces those shadows to create a reasonably accurate picture of our planet. There are different types of projections.

continues...

GeoSkills

Understanding Map Projections *(continued)*

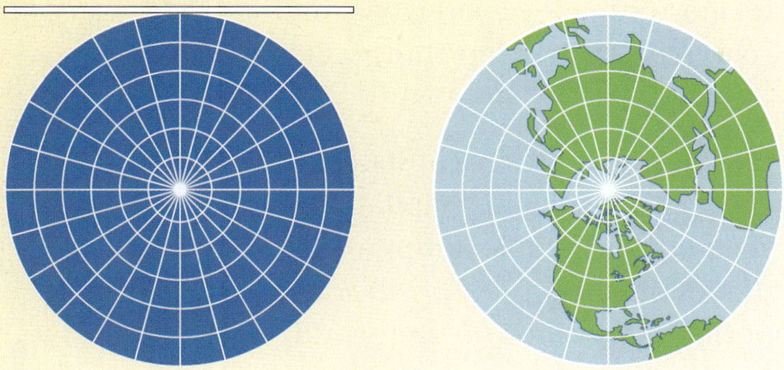

Planar Projection
Earth is projected onto a flat surface that touches the globe only at a single point. A map of this type is most accurate at the centre and becomes more distorted as you go out to the edges.

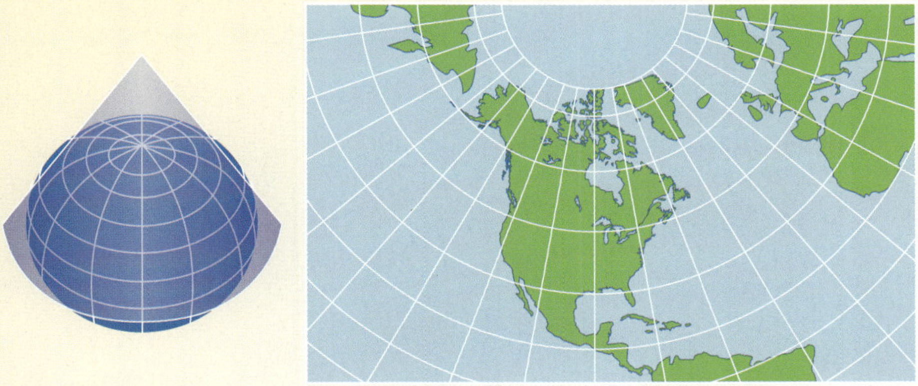

Conic Projection
Earth is projected onto a paper cone placed on top of the globe. The map will be the least distorted on the line where the cone touches the globe. This is a common projection used for portraying Canada.

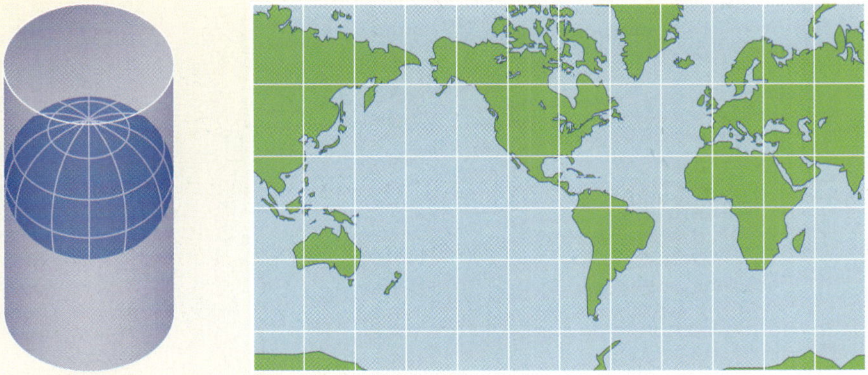

Cylindrical Projection
Earth is projected onto a paper cylinder wrapped around the globe. This projection is most accurate near the equator, but it is distorted near the poles. The Mercator projection is a famous cylindrical projection.

Figure 12.5

Three types of projections are planar, conic, and cylindrical.

Just as mechanics need to choose which tool is best suited for a job, geographers need to choose which map projection best suits their needs. Geographers must make sure that the map they choose is appropriate for the task.

Plants as Resources

Plants are healthy, nourishing food sources. Starch provides energy. Minerals, together with proteins and vitamins, promote good health. Some people get the starch and minerals they need from potatoes, corn, and beans. However, grasses like rice and wheat are the most important plants for starch globally. The top three grain crops are described below:

- Over half the world's people rely on rice as a source of starch. It grows best in tropical areas where there is high precipitation.
- Wheat is vital to the diet of many of the people of the world. There are over a thousand varieties of wheat.
- Maize is the third most important grain crop in the world, after rice and wheat. In North America, maize is called corn. It is native to the drier upland areas of Mexico. Maize was taken from there and introduced into other parts of the world.

Fact File

Maize is the raw material for many products, such as the following:

- bread and porridge when ground into a flour
- cooking oil when pressed
- a baking ingredient when prepared as a starch
- cosmetics
- glue
- feed for livestock
- fuel

Figure 12.6

This table shows some non-food uses for plants. Can you think of other examples?

Purpose	Examples of Plants Used
For fabrics	• cotton woven from the hair fibres that cover the seeds of cotton plants • linen woven from the stem fibres of flax, and rope woven from the stem fibres of jute plants
For ceremonies	• incense made from aromatic plant resins, including frankincense and myrrh • alcohol, a common religious symbol, made from many fruits and grains
For healing	• quinine taken from the bark of the tropical chinchona tree and used to prevent malaria • aspirin made from salicin found in the bark of willow trees • the periwinkle of Madagascar used in the treatment of childhood leukemia
For pleasure	• gardens made with flowering plants and attractive foliage • modern gardens using mixtures of native, introduced, and hybrid plants
For building	• wood from trees used as a construction material because of its strength and durability
For fuel	• for most of human history, wood from trees as a source of fuel

Two important human activities based on renewable natural resources are agriculture and forest industries. This chapter focuses on forests as renewable natural resources.

AFTER READING

1. The following terms are related to renewable resources: "wheat," "wool," "dual-purpose animal," "grasses," "oats," "animals," "horses," "plants," "beast of burden," "sheep," and "meat." Show how these words are related by categorizing them in a mind map (or ideas web) with "Renewable Resources" at the centre of the web.
2. Name three non-food uses for plants and for animals.
3. a) Explain why forests usually fit the category of renewable natural resources.

   b) In what situation would it *not* be correct to label forests as renewable natural resources?

Literacy Tip

Categorizing Words

Categorizing words means arranging them into groups that show the connections between words.

- First, look at the words to see how they are similar or different.
- Group words that are related.
- Name each group to show how the words are connected.

Using Forest Resources

BEFORE READING

1. This section begins by noting that about one-third of the world's land surface is covered by forests. What covers the other two-thirds of Earth's surface? (Hint: See Figure 7.23 on pages 160 to 161.)
2. Brainstorm the different ways that we use forests or that forests are important to the quality of life of Canadians. Share your list with two other people and add any new ideas to your list.
3. The remainder of this chapter focuses on forests as a renewable resource. In your notebook, draw a KWHL organizer (refer to question 9 on page 91 of Chapter 4). In the first column, record what you know about forests as a renewable resource. In the second column, record questions to show what you want to know about this topic. Remember that you can create two types of questions: closed questions and open-ended questions. Think of the 5 Ws and 1 H as you record your questions. In the third column, record how you can find this information. As you read this chapter, record what you learn to answer your questions in the fourth column.

Types of Forests

About one-third of the world's land surface is forested. Since growing conditions are different around the world, forests are different, too. Forests belong to two big categories:

- tropical forests
- temperate forests

Temperate and Tropical Forests

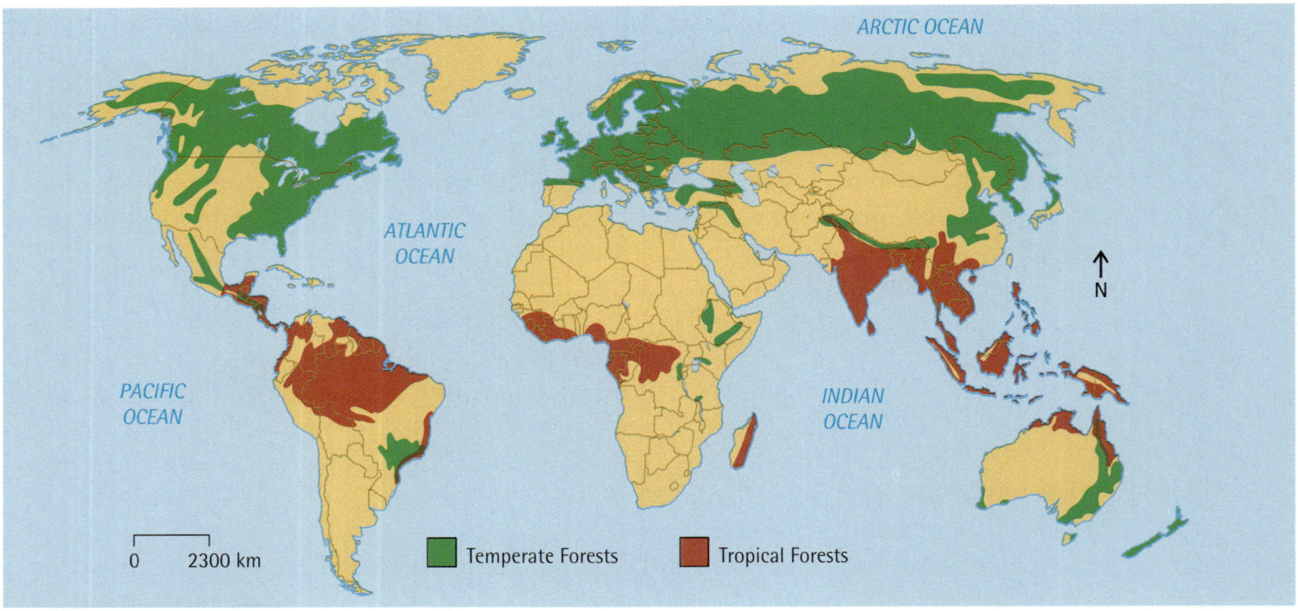

Figure 12.7

What type of forest is found in Canada?

Total World Forested Areas

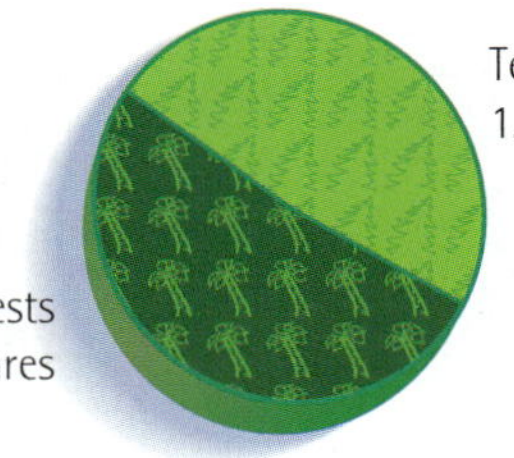

Figure 12.8

What do you think is happening to the total amount of forests in the world?

Tropical Forests

Tropical forests are located between the tropics of Cancer and Capricorn, on both sides of the equator. These forests have the following characteristics:

- get 2000 millimetres or more of rainfall each year, about three times the amount that southern Ontario gets
- have temperatures usually above 27 °C
- grow thick and lush trees reaching 45 metres above the ground
- contain 40 to 50 percent of Earth's plant and animal species

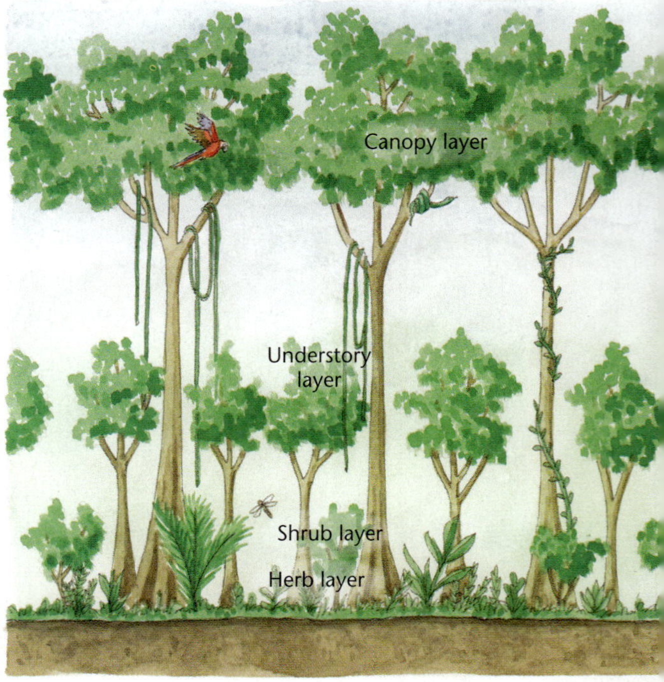

Figure 12.9

This diagram shows a tropical forest. How is this different from the forests found in Canada?

Temperate Forests

Temperate forests are located north of the tropic of Cancer and south of the Tropic of Capricorn. These forests grow in climates that are cooler and less moist than in the tropical regions. They have growing conditions that vary considerably. These growing conditions produce the following different types of forests:

- **Deciduous forests** have trees with broad leaves that fall in the autumn (including oak, maple, beech, and hickory). Deciduous forests occur where it is warmer.
- **Coniferous forests** have trees that keep their needle-shaped leaves all year round and bear their seeds in cones. These forests grow where it is cooler. Tree species include pine, spruce, and fir.
- Mixed forests grow between coniferous and deciduous forests. These forests have trees from both kinds of forests.

Figure 12.10

Deciduous trees lose their leaves when the weather gets cold in the fall.

Figure 12.11

In what ways is this coniferous forest in the U.S. state of Montana similar to and different from the forests found in your area?

1. Compare tropical and temperate forests using a table with the same headings as the one below:

Characteristics	Tropical Forests	Temperate Forests
Location		
Temperature		
Rainfall		
Types of trees		

2. Use sketches with labels to show the differences between deciduous, coniferous, and mixed forests.

The Disappearing Tropical Forest

Tropical forests are being cut down at a rate of about 20 million hectares per year. This is more than three times the area of Nova Scotia. In Central America, only 40 percent of the original forests remain. Other places have lost even more. In the Philippines, up to 80 percent of the forests are gone. Tropical forests are being cut down for the following main reasons:

- Loggers want the wood.
- Farmers are clearing land to make homes and livelihoods for themselves and their families.
- Land is being cleared or burned to grow **cash crops** that can be sold to earn an income, like strawberries, cotton, sugar cane, and pineapples.

Figure 12.12

Rainforests are often burned to make way for cash crops.

Figure 12.13

In what ways do you personally benefit from forests?

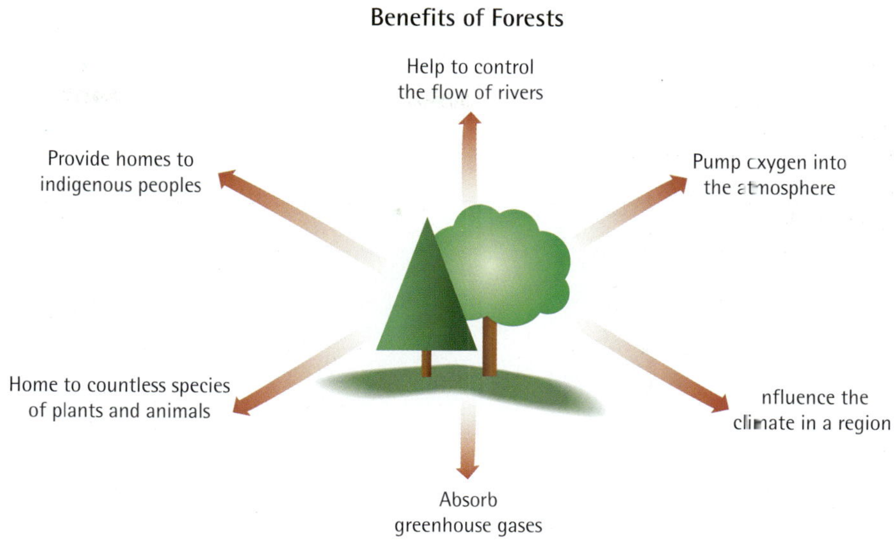

The Forest Industries

Since there is so much variety in the forests of the world, there is also variety in the industries that use them, but the main ones are **logging** (using the trunks of the trees), and **pulp and paper** (using the wood fibres).

Figure 12.14

This chart compares logging and pulp and paper, the two largest forest industries.

	Logging	Pulp and Paper
Use of trees	• The trunks of trees are cut into smaller pieces. • Large trees are preferred. • Hardwoods and softwoods are used.	• The wood fibres of the trees are used. • Smaller trees and limbs are useful. • Softwoods are used.
Products	• lumber, plywood, beams, furniture, utility poles	• paper, cardboard, cellulose (to make plastics)
Harvest methods	• Trees are cut down, and the trunks are sawn into smaller pieces.	• Trees are cut down, and the wood from most parts of the tree is used. Fibres are separated.

Figure 12.15

This British Columbian tree is being cut down with a chain saw. How do you think modern technology has affected the forest industry?

Figure 12.16

This machine is being used to harvest smaller trees in Chile in South America. These trees will be used in making pulp and paper.

AFTER READING

1. Provide an example of a use of the forest in Canada that does not fit either of the two categories of logging or pulp and paper.
2. Refer to Figures 12.15 and 12.16 and predict what might be some environmental impacts of the forest industries.
3. People are alarmed that tropical forests are being cut down at a rapid rate. Should we be concerned about the cutting of temperate forests in Canada? To help you make a decision, use a "Both Sides Now" organizer, such as the one below.

Evidence that Supports the Opinion that We Should Be Concerned about the Cutting of Temperate Forests in Canada	Should We Be Concerned about the Cutting of Temperate Forests in Canada?	Evidence that Supports the Opinion that We Should Not Be Concerned about the Cutting of Temperate Forests in Canada
•		•
•		•
•		•
•		•
Decision:		
Reasons:		

Explain your decision by writing an opinion paragraph (refer to GeoSkills, Writing an Opinion Paragraph, on page 233 in Chapter 11).

LITERACY TIP

Making Predictions

Predictions are "educated guesses" based on clues or evidence found in a text. Take the information in the text. Combine it with what you already know about the topic to come up with a convincing answer about what you think will happen.

BEFORE READING

1. Discuss ways that forests are important to people, animals, and the environment.

Logging in Canada

The logging industry cuts down trees to make products that use wood's natural strength and durability. The trunks are the only part of the trees that are used for logs. The larger the trunk, the more valuable the tree. The rest of the trees may be used to make various other wood products.

The types of wood products made from logs depend on the types of trees that are being cut. Deciduous trees found in warmer temperate locations are **hardwoods**. This wood is dense and hard. It is useful for making furniture and flooring. Needle-leafed coniferous trees that grow in cooler climates are **softwoods**. Their wood is not as strong as hardwoods, but the trees grow faster. Canada produces 20 percent of the world's total softwood. Most of it comes from British Columbia.

Figure 12.17

Which of these products that result from logging do you have in your home?

	Trees	Products
Hardwoods	Maple, oak, hickory, ash	Furniture, wood trim, panelling, flooring, veneers, handrails, cabinets
Softwoods	Pine, spruce, fir, cedar	Lumber, plywood, panelling, roofing, siding, hardboard, paper

Figure 12.18

This truck is hauling logs to lumber and pulp and paper mills in Alberta. What environmental problems might this method of transportation cause?

The Logging Process

The following process is used to harvest trees for logs:

- The best trees are marked.
- Loggers come in and cut down the marked trees.
- Branches are cut off the fallen trees.
- The trunks are "bucked"—cut into smaller lengths.
- The logs are hauled to a loading area using heavy equipment like bulldozers or winches.
- The logs are hauled to a lumber and pulp and paper mill by trucks, or are floated there down the river.

Connections to Music

Many early Canadian folk songs tell stories of loggers in the woods of this land. The loggers spent the winter in the bush cutting trees and dragging them to rivers. In the spring, the flooding waters carried the logs to mills farther downstream. Trouble occurred when logs jammed up. Loggers would have to go out onto the jam and attempt to free enough logs so that the jam would break up. Look up some songs in the music library or order some music videos (for example, "Log Driver's Waltz") from the National Film Board.

Selective Logging

Strip Logging

Clear-Cut Logging

Figure 12.19

Why is clear-cut logging considered the most environmentally harmful?

Saving Forests by Cutting Responsibly

Selective logging means cutting down only the mature trees in a forest. Younger trees are left uncut. With this approach, only about 20 trees of the 400 in a hectare of forest would be taken down. However, the cutting and transporting of logs can damage almost half of the trees in the forest.

Most companies do not use selective logging because they say it is too expensive. They argue that it takes too much time to locate and reach each mature tree.

Other Logging Methods

Most logging companies want to use one of the following types of logging:

- **strip logging** (which takes down all the trees in a 20-metre-wide path)
- **clear-cut logging** (which cuts down every tree in a huge area). Clear-cut logging completely destroys the ecosystem of the forest. The habitat of the plants and animals that lived there is gone.

Web Link

For more information about clear-cut logging and the Canadian forest industry, go to **www.nelson.com/phygeo7**.

Literacy Tip

Persuading Your Audience

When you want to convince a reader of your point of view, use the following tips to deliver your arguments:

- Start by presenting a scenario or facts to grab the audience's attention.
- Use emotional words or phrases ("It is vital that …" or "It is in your best interest that …") to appeal to the audience.
- Use descriptive words, superlatives (*most* profitable, *best* method), and strong verbs to strengthen your arguments.
- Leave the audience with a lasting impression.

DURING READING

1. If forests are a renewable natural resource, why is it important to reduce waste and protect the forests?
2. Why do you suppose many logging companies prefer to use clear-cut logging instead of selective logging?
3. Imagine that you are an executive of a logging company or an environmentalist speaking to an audience about the best method to log wood. Write a short persuasive speech aimed at convincing your audience that your preferred method of logging is the best.

Milling the Logs

Logs are sorted by type and quality. Most logs are cut into lumber for a variety of uses. Straight, knot-free logs are used for special veneers. Some softwood is used to make plywood.

Figure 12.20

This forestry technician in Mexico measures the diameter of a tree trunk with calipers. This allows loggers to estimate the amount of usable wood in the tree.

Figure 12.21

This diagram shows how planks and large timbers are cut from a log.

Saving Resources by Reducing Wastes

The logging industry has become concerned about the amount of wood they are wasting. Most of the waste occurs in wood debris left in the forest. Some steps have been taken to reduce waste created by logging. For example, edges and ends of logs that were thrown away in the past are now being used to make new products, like chipboard and particleboard. Even the sawdust shavings and bark that were once thought of as garbage are now burned to run the logging mills, or processed into useful items like pet bedding.

Helping the Environment by Replanting

In the past, many logging companies relied on **natural regeneration** to fill in cut forests. Seeds from nearby trees would blow into the area where trees used to be. However, it takes several years before new trees take hold. Soil is washed away during this time because trees are not there to hold it in place. **Replanting** is a better method. Seedlings are planted right after the forest has been cut. The seedlings have been raised in nurseries and are already growing quickly. Before long, their roots are deep into the soil, helping to prevent erosion.

Fact File

- There are roughly 400 million hectares of forests in Canada.
- About 1 million hectares of forests are harvested each year in Canada.
- Approximately 470 000 hectares are replanted or reseeded each year.
- Twenty species of trees are used for replanting.

Figure 12.22

This student is planting a tree as part of a reforestation project following a fire in Boise National Forest in the U.S. state of Idaho. Many students go tree planting for summer jobs. They stay in the bush, often for weeks at a time. What are some of the problems and dangers these young people may face?

BE A GLOBAL CITIZEN

Urban Logging

Cities often have large trees along streets or in parks. When these trees die or have to be removed, it is very costly for the municipality. Some private companies and local governments are beginning to realize that these trees do not have to become firewood, be left to rot, or chipped into mulch. These trees can be turned into usable lumber, which will save trees in natural forests from being cut down.

In California, the California Department of Forestry (CDF) has been promoting the idea of urban logging. By selling their old trees, cities could earn money for other urban forestry projects, including the planting of new trees. The CDF began a pilot program to help communities. They loan "micro-mills" to communities and organizations that are interested in harvesting wood from cities. One non-profit organization is using one of these mills to create urban wood furniture. Another organization uses municipal trees to make hardwood flooring and panelling.

In Ontario, Urban Tree Salvage takes logs doomed for landfills, fireplaces, or compost piles and processes them into lumber for furniture makers and general woodworkers. The company is certified by the SmartWood's Rediscovered Wood program, and it produces only eco-friendly products. Urban Tree Salvage's goal is to get rid of urban forestry waste and help preserve our natural forests. The company is a true eco-friendly wood source. Harvest House Furniture, Humber College in Toronto, and a number of small furniture shops across Ontario use Urban Tree Salvage's wood.

Just as consumers are looking at where their clothes and toys are made, people also need to become more aware of how their wood products were harvested and manufactured. How can you become more aware as a consumer and help reduce the deforestation of natural forests?

- Find out which local or regional products or companies have been certified for the Rediscovered Wood program. With this certification, the Rainforest Alliance confirms that the company is reclaiming or using reclaimed, recycled, and/or salvaged wood materials. The Rediscovered Wood program has been around since 1989 and has 2051 certified operations in 61 countries around the world.
- Contact the Rainforest Alliance to find out how you can become involved with its programs.

Figure 12.23

The owner of Urban Tree Salvage holds a piece of elm wood that will be built into a table. How do you think getting rid of urban forestry waste can help to preserve forests?

AFTER READING

1. Find or draw at least five pictures of products that come from the logging industry. You can find pictures on the Internet, in magazines, catalogues, or advertisements that come in your newspaper. Group your pictures into two categories: hardwoods and softwoods.
2. a) Explain why large trunk logs are the most valuable to the logging industry.

   b) How might the value of large trunk logs affect decisions about where a logging company would choose to cut trees?
3. Suppose you were standing on a hill watching a logging company at work in the valley below you. Write a diary entry describing your feelings and thoughts about seeing the trees being cut down.

Pulp and Paper in Canada

BEFORE READING

1. Some people have predicted that the use of technology like the Internet and cellphones will lead to a paperless society. Is it possible to run our society without using paper? Explain your ideas.

Imagine what your life would be like without paper products. There would be no newspapers, magazines, or even textbooks. There would be no wrapping paper, greeting cards, or writing paper. We would not have many personal hygiene products, such as toilet paper, facial tissue, and paper towels. Paper has become an indispensable part of our day-to-day life.

Figure 12.24

Can you name all the paper products shown here? What are some other paper products that are not shown here?

Fact File

- Over 56 000 Canadians work in pulp and paper mills.
- About $6 billion of pulp and $11 billion of paper are exported every year from Canada, mostly to the United States.
- Each direct job in pulp and paper creates four more indirect jobs.

Paper can be made out of many raw materials: different types of grasses and reeds, rice, or bark. It just happened that trees were abundant near the major cities of North America and Europe when the demand for paper was growing. That is why the industry developed using trees as the raw material.

DURING READING

1. Choose five of the items shown in Figure 12.24. Name a product that could be substituted for each product if paper was not available. List the natural resources that would be used for your substitute product.

The Paper-Making Process

In the paper-making process, the wood is separated into fibres and mixed with chemicals and water to form pulp. The pulp is pressed and dried to make paper in machines that are nearly two football fields in length. The paper machine operates at over 90 kilometres per hour.

Figure 12.25

Follow the steps in making paper in this flow diagram.

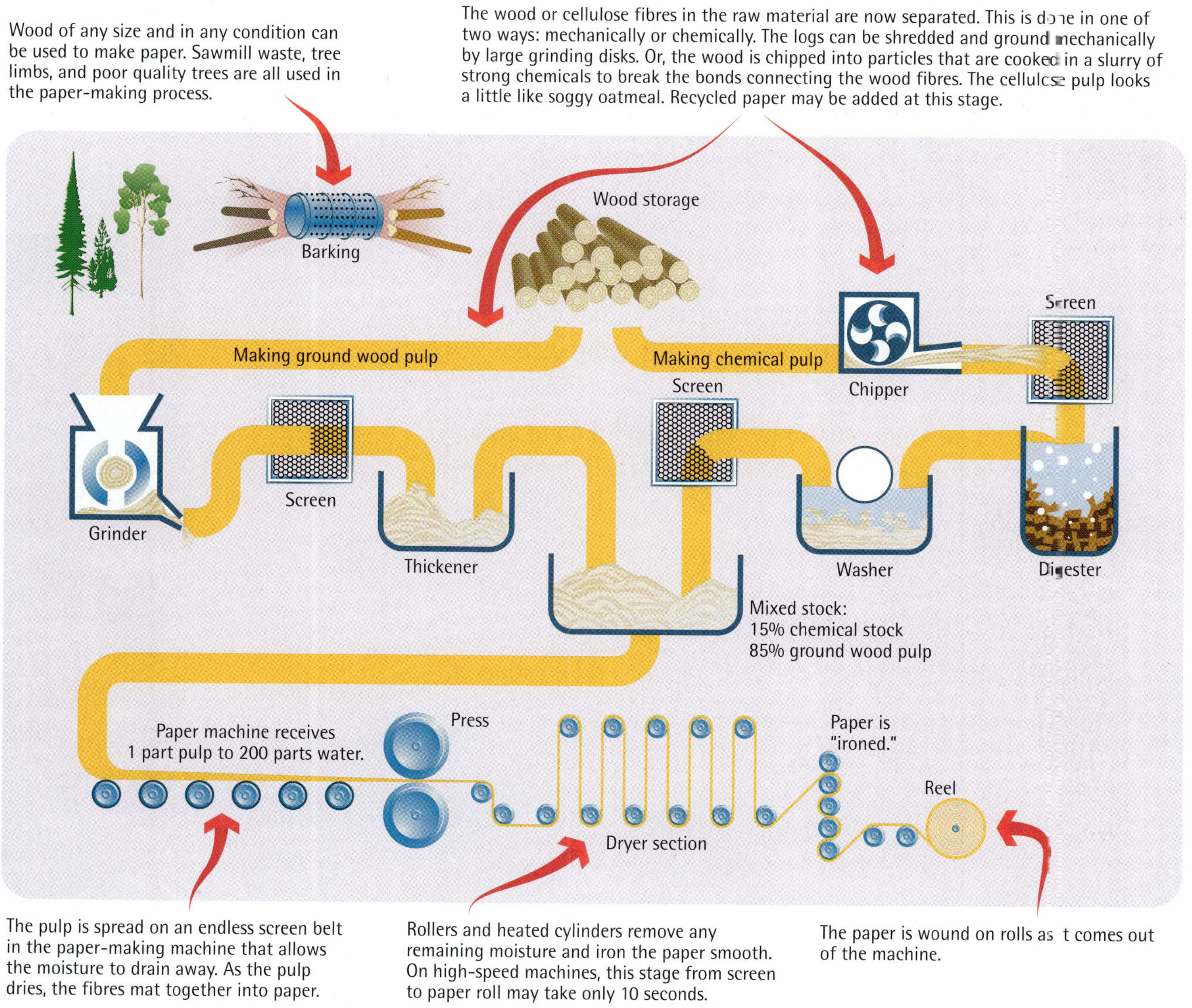

Making Forests Last through Technological Change

New technologies have changed paper making in the following ways:

- Researchers have discovered new ways to make paper that use fewer chemicals and bleaches. (Bleach is used to make the paper white.) This means that fewer chemicals are released into the environment.
- The harmful substances that the industry does use are being treated more carefully. The industry has reduced its waste output by 34 percent over a 15-year period.
- Less water is used to make pulp. In fact, water usage is down by over 50 percent over the past 20 years. This reduces the risk of overusing waterways that are important wildlife habitats.
- Recycled paper now makes up 26 percent of the fibre in paper making. Leftover materials from sawmills make up 56 percent of the fibre.
- Mills have reduced energy consumption by 10 percent in the past decade.

1. You have probably noticed that there are different kinds of paper—from high-quality paper for cards and letters to inexpensive paper for newspapers. Use Figure 12.25 to explain what might be done to get the different kinds of paper when making it.
2. The Fact File on page 257 in this chapter says that direct jobs in pulp and paper create four times as many indirect jobs. Explain how this works.
3. All the citizens in your community have been asked to vote to approve building a new pulp and paper factory in your area. Give three reasons why you might vote "yes," and three reasons why you might vote "no."
4. Explain how each of the following technological changes in the pulp and paper industry is an improvement:
   - The amount of bleach needed in paper making is reduced.
   - The amount of water that is used is reduced.

Knowledge and Understanding

1. a) Organize the following terms into two lists under the headings "Logging," and "Pulp and Paper": "chippers," "recycling," "hardwood," "bleach," "logs," "fibre," "clear-cut," and "selective cutting."

   b) Add two more terms to each list.

2. Imagine that you are a reporter investigating an environmental story. You are interviewing the plant manager of a pulp and paper mill. Make up five questions that you would want her to answer. (Refer to the Literacy Tip on page 221 in Chapter 11.) Remember, reports use the common set of questions known as the 5 Ws and the 1 H.

3. Suppose that a logging company wants to cut trees in a forest near your town. A town meeting is called. Many people give their opinions about the plan. Write five points that might show up in a short speech that each of the following people might give:

   a) a logger

   b) a campground operator

   c) the owner of a grocery store

Inquiry/Research and Communication Skills

4. Will there always be forests in Canada to support the forest industries? Use Internet and library resources to identify factors that will affect the availability of trees. Some questions that you might want to consider are as follows:

   a) Who determines how many trees are cut down each year?

   b) What natural threats are hurting the forests?

   c) How are forests replanted or replaced?

   d) How will climate change affect forests?

   Use your research findings to prepare a brief oral presentation on the future availability of forests in Canada.

5. Look at other industries in Canada that use renewable natural resources. Choose one of these industries:

   - fur trapping
   - maple–syrup producing
   - herb farming
   - hunting as a recreational activity

   Research to find information to answer the following questions:

   a) Where does the industry take place?

   b) What activities take place in this industry?

   c) Who is involved in this industry?

   d) How much is produced in this industry?

   e) What is this industry worth to Canada's economy?

   f) When do the activities in this industry take place each year?

   g) What technology is used in this industry?

   Make a poster with your research findings. Be sure to put a map on your poster to show where this industry takes place.

Figure 12.26

How would you feel if a logging company wanted to cut trees in a forest near your community? Explain your answer.

Map, Globe, and Graphic Skills

6 a) Figure 12.7 shows the location of temperate and tropical forests around the world. Find climate information (either climate graphs or climate statistics) for two places with tropical forests and two places with temperate forests. You can locate this information on the Internet, in an atlas, or in other resources. Make a chart in your notebook like the one below, and record details about the climates.

	Tropical Forests		Temperate Forests	
	Location 1	Location 2	Location 3	Location 4
Hottest month and temperature				
Coldest month and temperature				
Wettest month and rainfall				
Driest month and rainfall				
Total rainfall				

b) Make up two questions that ask a partner to compare the data on this chart.

7 Examine the data in the table below. This table shows the percent of Canada's forest harvested in each province.

Percentage of Wood Harvested by Province, 2004

Province/Territory	Percentage
Newfoundland and Labrador	1.1%
Prince Edward Island	0.3%
Nova Scotia	3.3%
New Brunswick	5.3%
Québec	20.8%
Ontario	12.1%
Manitoba	1.0%
Saskatchewan	2.9%
Alberta	11.3%
British Columbia	41.8%
The North	0.0%

8 Use the information in the table to construct a bar graph. (Refer to Creating a Bar Graph on page 107 of Chapter 5.) Draw bars to show the four largest producers of wood in order of size. Then, add up the figures for all the other provinces, and draw a bar labelled "Other Provinces." What pattern do you seein your graph?

a) Find a map of the world showing areas that are losing tropical forests. List the names of 10 countries where loss of forests is occurring.

b) Use the Internet to access sites of environmental groups such as Greenpeace and the World Wildlife Fund. Find out what is being done to improve the situation in one of these 10 countries. Share what you find out with the class.

Figure 12.27
What type of forest is this? How can you tell?

9 **a)** Ask your teacher for an outline map of Canada. Use Figure 12.7 to mark on your map the parts of Canada that are covered by forests.

b) Use the Internet, library, or classroom resources to find the names and locations of seven towns in Canada that have mills to cut lumber. Mark these locations on your map using a symbol that shows they are lumber mills.

c) Find seven towns that have pulp and paper mills, and mark these on your map using an appropriate symbol.

d) Describe the pattern that you see on your map. Identify one way that this pattern might affect the attitude that Canadians have toward their forests.

Application

10 The loss of forests around the world has become a serious problem. Many people think that the cutting of forests is harmful to the environment. What is your personal opinion about the cutting of forests? Write an opinion paragraph to present your point of view (refer to GeoSkills, Writing an Opinion Paragraph, on page 233 in Chapter 11).

11 Design an advertisement that will encourage other people to do a better job of recycling paper. Most people already know about paper recycling. However, if you look in most garbage containers, there are still some paper products that could be recycled. Think of a message that would encourage all Canadians to recycle all paper. Use this message to create an advertisement that will inspire Canadians to do a better job.

12 You are captain of your debating team. The topic for debate is: "The government should force logging companies to practise selective cutting of trees." Choose the side of the debate you want your team to take. Prepare five points that you want your team to give in the debate.

13 You have been asked to give a speech to business leaders. The title of your speech is "The Environment and the Forest Industries." List five points that you will make in your speech that will appeal to business people and get them to participate more in saving our forests. (Refer to the Literacy Tip on persuasive writing on page 253 in this chapter.)

13 Flow Natural Resources

IN THIS CHAPTER

- describe ways that people use natural resources to meet their needs, including renewable, non-renewable, and flow resources
- point out patterns in where resources are located and how they are used
- show how technology has affected our use of natural resources
- describe some ways that natural resources are important to a country
- use maps to find patterns in natural resources
- use the new terms in this chapter correctly as you investigate the topics
- make up questions to help you research problems and different points of view about managing and using natural resources
- locate and use helpful information from primary and secondary sources
- share the results of research for different reasons and audiences using options such as computer slide shows, videos, websites, oral presentations, written notes and reports, drawings, tables, charts, diagrams, maps, models, and graphs

KEY VOCABULARY

continental shelf
deficit
drip irrigation
flow resource
global commons
hydrologic cycle
penstock
river diversion
sprinkler irrigation
surface irrigation
surplus
terracing

Figure 13.1

Imagine that you are sitting here on the shore of George Lake in Killarney, Ontario. What resources would you be using?

Sun, Wind, and Water

1. How are flow resources and non-renewable resources different? (If you need to review these types of resources, refer to Chapter 10.)
2. Can you identify five ways you can use the Sun, wind, and water in your daily life?

Imagine yourself in the picture shown in Figure 13.1. The Sun is warm. Gentle breezes catch your hair. The water makes soft lapping sounds. What a relaxing place to spend an afternoon!

The breezes that cool you, the Sun that warms you, and the moving water that refreshes you are all natural resources. These are called **flow resources** because they do not remain in one location. Flow resources move about because of natural actions in the physical environment.

Humans use flow resources in a variety of ways. In fact, we refer to flow resources as the **global commons**. These are resources that are available to everyone. This chapter looks at how we use just one flow resource—water.

Figure 13.2

We use these flow resources in our lives.

Flow Resources	Reasons for Movement
Solar energy	The Sun gives off vast amounts of solar energy. Only a tiny amount of the total energy produced by the Sun reaches Earth's surface.
Winds	Earth's surface is hotter near the equator and colder near the poles. This creates areas of high air pressure at the poles and low air pressure at the equator. Winds blow from areas of high pressure to areas of low pressure.
Moving water	Winds carry moisture from the oceans over land where it falls back to Earth. This water flows down to the oceans. The **hydrologic cycle** is the natural "machine" that moves water about.

AFTER READING

1. Create a diagram to show how solar energy, winds, and moving water are all connected. Add labels to your diagram.
2. Why can some flow resources also be considered renewable natural resources?
3. Explain why it is difficult for people or businesses to own flow natural resources.

Running Water as a Resource

BEFORE READING

1. a) List different ways that people use water under these categories: "Industrial Use," "Agricultural Use," "Transportation," and "Personal Use." Try to list at least 10 ways in total.

   b) What is the most important way that you use water?
2. Give an example of how water can be polluted in each of the categories listed in the previous question.

Water flows from higher places to lower places. This moving water is an important resource for humans. However, not all parts of the world have enough—or any—running water. It only occurs in places where there is a water **surplus**. A region gets a surplus when more precipitation falls than can sink into the ground or be used by plants and animals. The extra runoff water becomes streams and rivers—running water. Figure 13.3 shows that most regions of Canada have a water surplus. On the other hand, most regions of Africa have a water **deficit**, the opposite of surplus.

Figure 13.3

This map shows that some parts of the world have a surplus of water, which is more than they need. Other parts of the world have a deficit. They need more water to meet their needs.

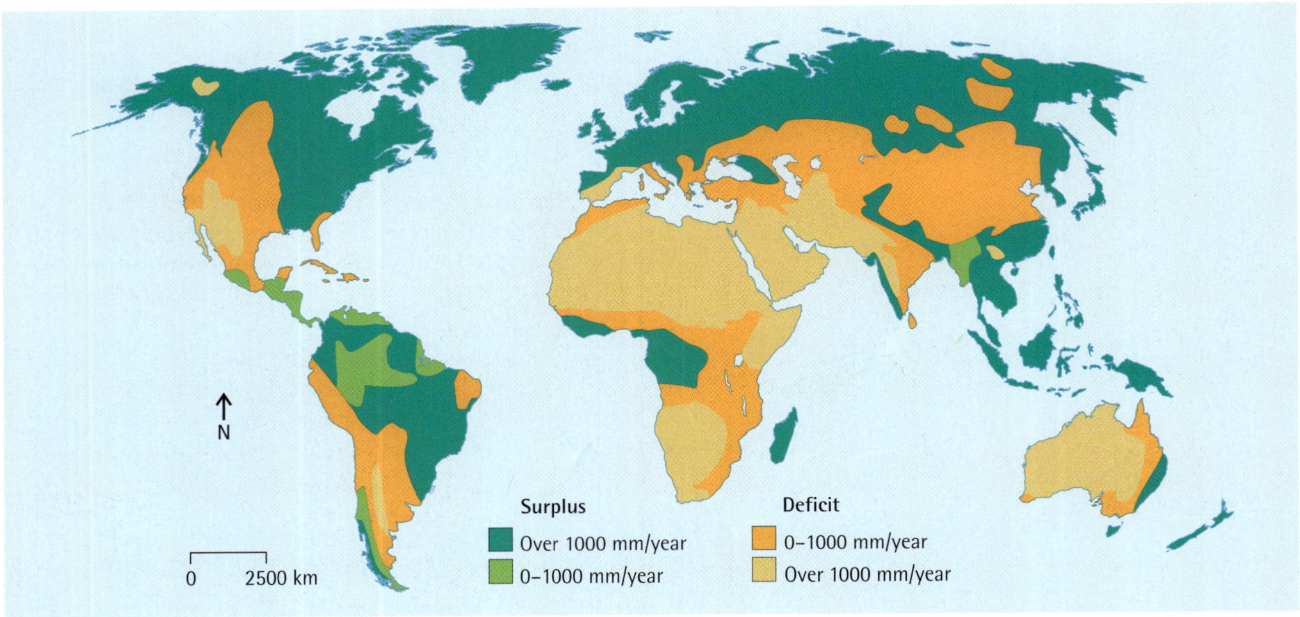

1. a) Look at Figure 13.3 above. Name three areas of the world that have a water surplus. Which areas have a water deficit?

b) Describe a pattern that you see in the map. For example, can you see irregular bands across the map from west to east? Why do you suppose this pattern happens? Remember to use the TLC method you learned about in Chapter 1.

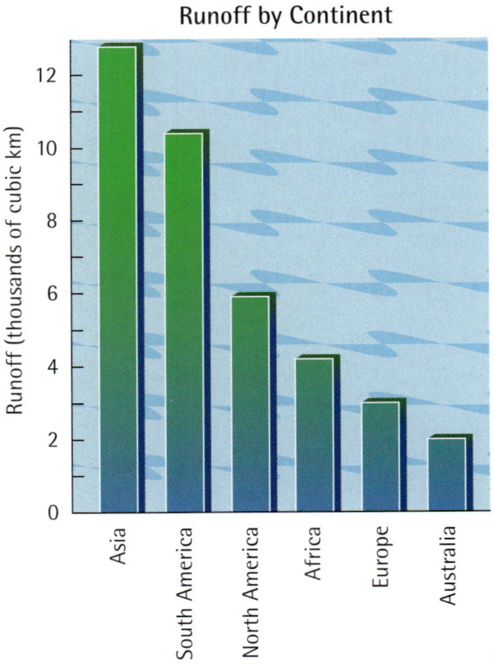

Figure 13.4

Can you name one major river from each continent? Use the Map Appendix or an atlas as a reference.

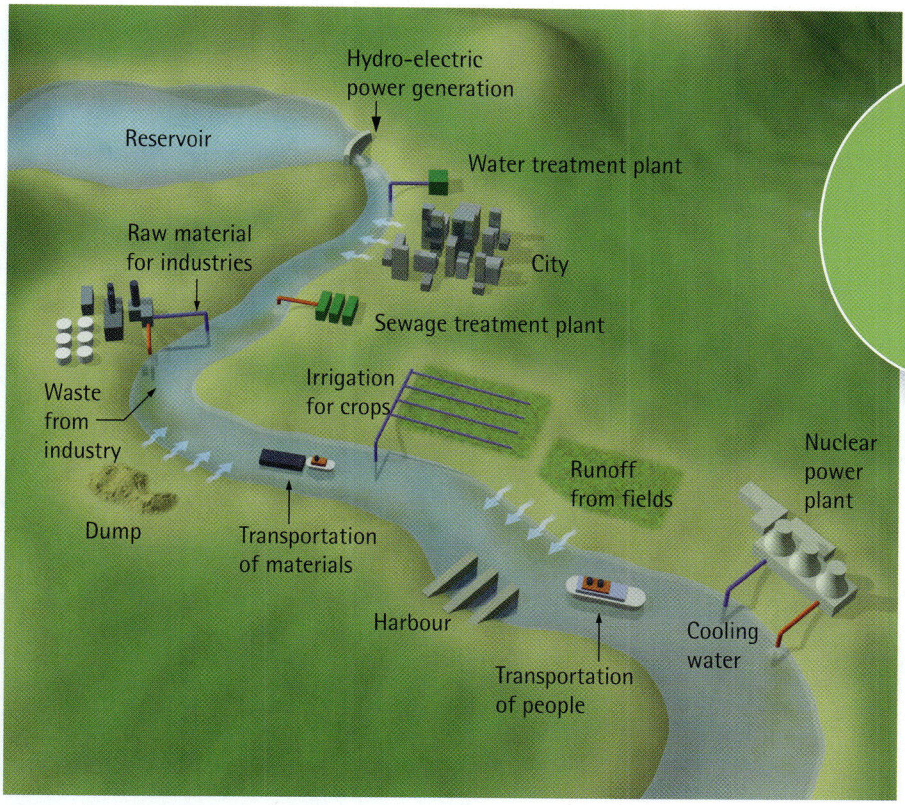

Global Water Use

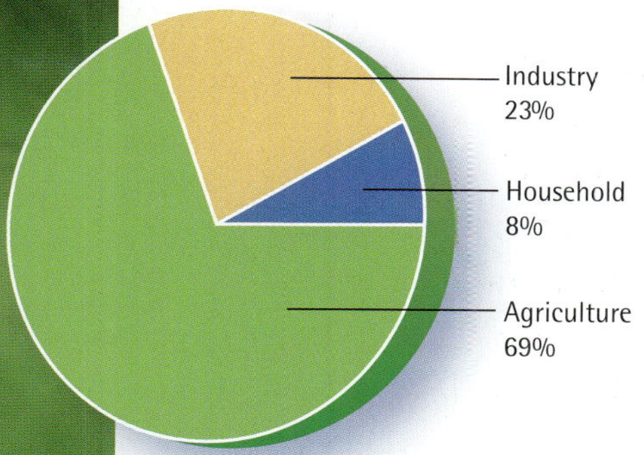

Figure 13.5

Can you name one use for water in each of the three categories shown in this circle graph?

Figure 13.6

Look at the possible sources of pollution along this river. How could we stop rivers from becoming polluted?

Literacy Tip

Using an Atlas

An atlas is a book of maps and other geographical information. There are two common ways of using an atlas.

- You can use the table of contents to look up the map(s) you want to use.
- You can also use the index or gazetteer found in the back of the atlas. Names are listed alphabetically. Beside the name, you will find the page number of the map. You will also find the grid coordinates or latitude and longitude coordinates.

Fact File

Each Canadian uses an average of 390 litres of water per day. This is equal to about four bathtubs full of water. We use this water in the following ways:

- toilet flushing — 40 percent
- showers, baths, and personal grooming — 35 percent
- dishes and laundry — 20 percent
- drinking and food preparation — 5 percent

Amount of Water Needed for Food Production

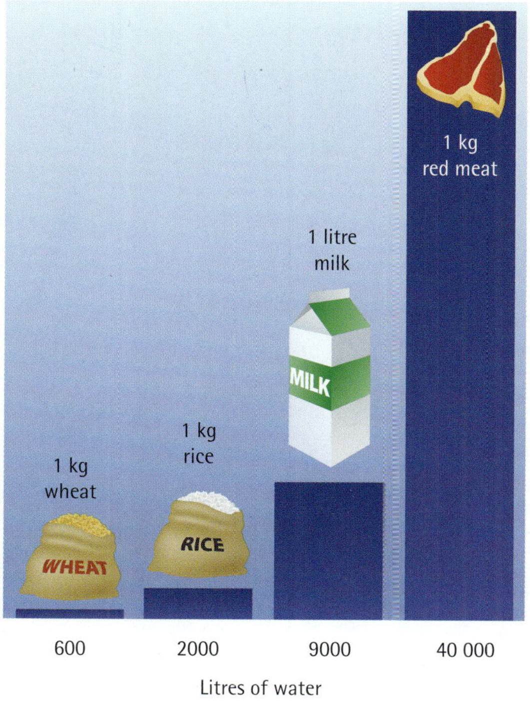

Figure 13.7

Various quantities of water are needed to produce these food items. Why do you suppose it takes so much water to produce meat?

Using Water Resources to Irrigate Crops

Figure 13.5 shows that agriculture is by far the largest user of running water in the world. Globally, about 215 million hectares of land are irrigated. This is 16 percent of all the farmland in the world. Yet, this 16 percent—the irrigated land—produces about 40 percent of all the world's crops. There are three main types of irrigation: surface, sprinkler, and drip.

Figure 13.8

These photographs show the different types of irrigation systems. Can you identify each type? What environmental problems might be caused by irrigation?

Surface Irrigation

Most places where irrigation is practised use **surface irrigation**. In fact, about 96 percent of all irrigation is surface irrigation. Pipes, canals, and ditches carry water to the fields. Farmers make small openings in the walls of the pipes to let the water flow into the canals and ditches and onto the fields. When the soil is wet, the openings are closed. Some of the water evaporates when this method is used.

Surface irrigation

Sprinkler Irrigation

With **sprinkler irrigation**, the water is carried by pipes to the field. Then, the water is sprayed onto the crops using a sprinkler head, much like how lawns are watered. This system is used mainly by North American farmers.

Drip Irrigation

In **drip irrigation**, water pipes run to each plant. Water drips directly onto the roots. Very little water is wasted with drip irrigation. Because of the high costs involved—the cost of labour, the pipes used, and the high level of technology needed—this system is used only in rich countries.

Sprinkler irrigation

Drip irrigation

Using Technology for Better Use of Water

One productive form of surface irrigation is **terracing**. This ancient technology is used where the land is mountainous and farmers must grow crops on steep slopes. In these areas, farmers face two problems. First, they must stop rainwater from running off their fields too quickly. Second, they have to prevent their soil from washing away. Terracing solves both of these problems. Farmers turn the mountainsides into giant "stair steps," or terraces. Walls are built of stone to hold the soil in place. Terracing allows farmers to control the water. The farmers decide when to allow water to pass to the next lower terrace. Terracing is common for growing rice in East Asia and Southeast Asia.

Figure 13.9

Why is it very difficult to use large machines to farm on terraces?

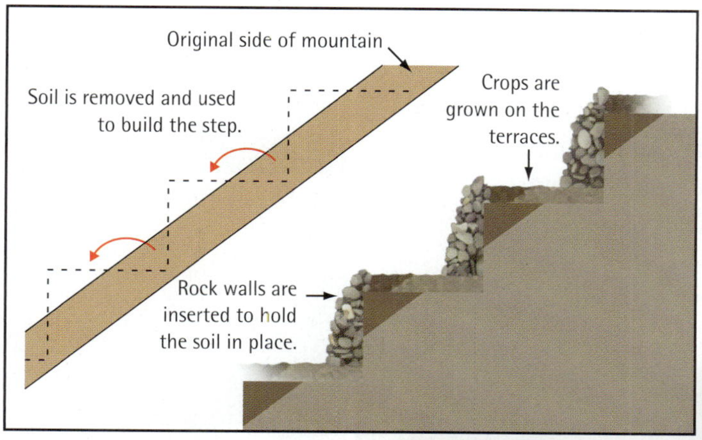

Figure 13.10

These rice terraces in northern Philippines resemble stair steps built into the side of the mountain.

1. a) Identify two ways that technology has been used to improve the supply of water to croplands.

   b) What problems might be caused by changing the flow of water to improve croplands?

2. a) Look carefully at the photograph in Figure 13.10. In what ways is terracing different from the types of farming done in Canada?

   b) What might be some challenges in farming in this way? Consider the following: using machinery, transporting crops, and ownership of land.

River Diversions

Often, farmers in a region want a lot more water than what they have to set up irrigation processes. To get the extra water for these farmers, governments will actually move rivers. The direction and course of a river are changed. These changes are called **river diversions**.

Positive Results of River Diversions

Irrigated crops need a great deal of water. Dams and canals are built to move water to irrigated fields. Today, about 38 000 dams divert rivers into thousands of kilometres of canals. The central valleys of California are productive agricultural lands because of canals and ditches filled by water from river diversions. Hundreds of thousands of hectares of new or improved farmland have been created this way.

Problems Caused by River Diversions

River diversions have many serious harmful effects on the physical environment. Diversions cause huge areas to lose their water. These areas face water shortages. The number of plants and animals in the region will decrease and some species may die off. People's livelihoods are destroyed.

Those places that receive the water face a new challenge—salt. The water carries minerals that soak into the irrigated soil. When the water evaporates, the minerals are left behind. Over time, these minerals form large deposits of salt. These deposits are harmful to plants and ruin the soil over time.

Figure 13.11

This open canal stretches across the arid land in central Arizona. Why do you think this canal was necessary?

The Aral Sea Disaster

The Aral Sea was once the third largest lake in the world. Only the Caspian Sea and Lake Superior were larger. However, this lake has shrunk in area by 50 percent in the past 30 years. Its surface is now 20 metres below what it was in 1960. Why did this happen? Much of the water from the two rivers that feed the lake was diverted to irrigate cotton crops.

The result was an environmental disaster. The little water that continued to flow into the lake quickly began to evaporate. Minerals were left behind.

Aral Sea on World Map

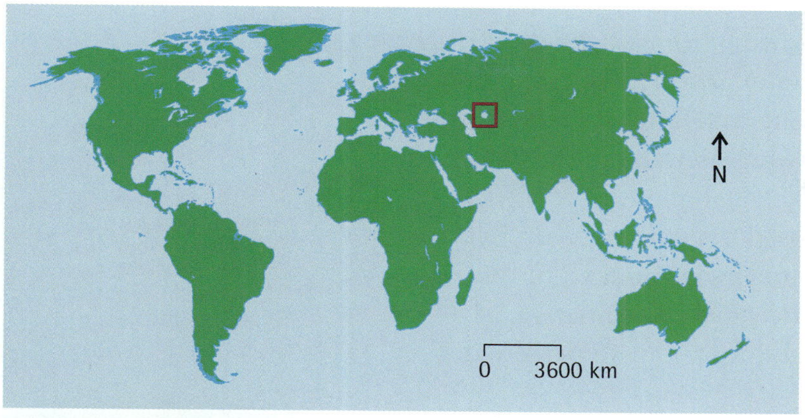

Figure 13.12

The Aral Sea is located in Asia.

The water became more and more salty. It is now three times saltier than before the diversions were built in the 1960s. The fish in the Aral Sea died because of the salt. With them died the lake's fishing industry. Rusting fishing boats have been left high and dry many kilometres from the water's edge.

The cost of the diversions has been very high, and the costs may grow higher. If no action is taken to undo the river diversions and to give back its waters, the Aral Sea will be gone by 2020.

Aral Sea, 1960–2006

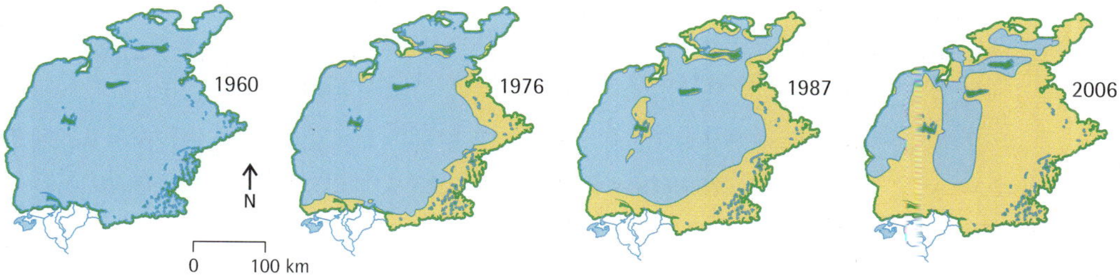

Figure 13.13

The Aral Sea is now less than half of its original size. How might this change have affected the communities around the Aral Sea?

Fact File

The land left by the shrinking of the Aral Sea is a salty desert. By 2000, this desert was 42 000 square kilometres in size. Every year, an estimated 100 million tonnes of salty dust blow off the desert onto neighbouring lands.

DURING READING

1. Create a t-chart to compare the positive and negative impacts of river diversions.

Figure 13.14

This is a photograph of an abandoned fishing boat near the shores of the diminishing Aral Sea. If you had worked on this fishing boat, what would you think about the changes in the Aral Sea?

Using Water for Hydro-Electric Power

Electrical power is generated by water flowing from a reservoir—often created by a dam—down a **penstock** (a chute). The rushing, falling water pushes on the blades of a turbine and causes them to spin. A generator connected to the turbine spins as well and produces an electrical current.

Many rivers around the world are used to generate hydro-electric power. Globally, about 2 percent of all energy is obtained in this way. Canada has developed its hydro-electric power because we have so many powerful rivers. In Canada, we produce about 15 percent of the world's hydro-electricity.

Positive Effects of Hydro-Electric Power

Producing hydro-electricity has the following advantages:

- It does not use up any non-renewable fossil fuels.
- It is produced from a flow resource—running water.
- It does not produce greenhouse gases as burning fossil fuels does.

Used wisely, hydro-electric power is a source of energy that could continue indefinitely. It is a clean, sustainable energy source.

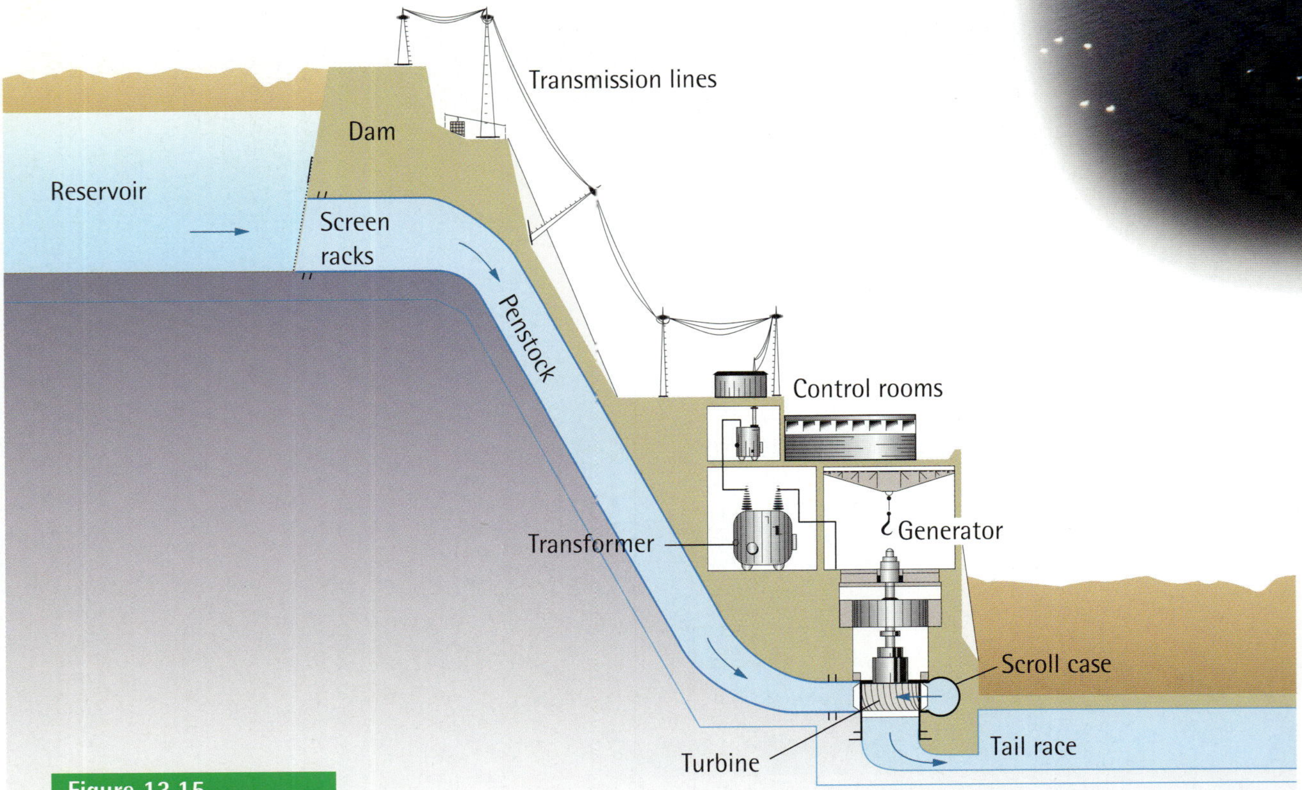

Figure 13.15

Why is it necessary to build a dam to get hydro-electric power?

Connections to History

Hydro-electric projects are usually planned for places that are far from cities. These remote areas are often lands belonging to First Nations. Near the end of the 1990s, in northern Québec, the Innu tried to stop an expansion of the Churchill Falls power project. They argued that the construction would destroy their way of life. The reservoir would flood their hunting areas and destroy ancestral lands. The Innu had the following to say about the project:

"Go home! Go home! Let the Innu live!"
"I feel as if it's my own heart that's going to be flooded."
"We demand respect for our territory, our way of life, and our rights."

The Innu protests, along with other problems, stopped the expansion project. There still are many who would like to see the Churchill Falls power project create more wealth for Canadians.

Figure 13.16

This is a photograph of the Caribou Falls Generating Station, located near Kenora, Ontario. A hydro-electric dam has a huge impact on a river.

Negative Effects of Hydro-Electric Power

The creation of hydro-electric power has the following negative effects:

- The flow of the river that is used must be diverted.
- The habitat for the fish and wildlife in the area is changed for the worse.
- Migration routes for animals may be disrupted. This happened to large herds of Canadian caribou.
- In some cases, unique ecological areas are flooded to create the reservoirs. These special and often beautiful places are lost forever.
- Many First Nations people of the area rely on the natural environment for their way of life. The hydro-electric power plants significantly disrupt their lives.

GeoSkills

Reading a Graphic Story: Water Heroes

Do you read graphic novels or stories? Do you see other students reading graphic novels or stories in school? Reading a graphic story is not the same as reading a written story. You need to make a lot of inferences to understand what is happening in a graphic story.

When reading a graphic story, you do not look at just what is being said. You also observe what is being shown through facial expressions and body language. By looking at these things, you can make inferences about how that person is behaving or how he or she may have said the words. Look at the second frame. How is the boy feeling? How do you know that? In order to answer that question, you need to make inferences based on how he is drawn.

The dialogue in graphic stories generally follows the same patterns as in written stories. Read dialogue boxes from left to right and top to bottom.

There is a code used in dialogue boxes to show how words are to be read. Go back to the second frame and look at the one word there. You may read only "Ack!", but by looking at how it is written (the font and the size of the letters), you are able to determine the sound and the emotion behind that word. How would you describe how Tek Powermaker said that one word? How do you know that?

The setting is shown by the artist. Look at the main frame on this page. Where is this part of the story taking place?

Figure 13.17

When reading graphic novels, use the tips in the green boxes.

The frames give us only a snapshot of the story. Readers must understand what is being implied between two frames or two pages. You need to be aware of what happened but was not shown. Viva is above Tek in frame two and is beside him in frame three. Obviously, she has moved.

Literacy Tip

Supporting Your Opinion

When you want to convince someone of your opinion, you must present convincing arguments that are logical and based on facts. A simple way to organize your argument is to use the "point, proof, and comment" strategy. Introduce a point (the idea), give proof (facts, statistics, examples, or experience), and wrap up the point with a comment.

During Reading

1. Look carefully at the diagram of a hydro-electric power plant in Figure 13.15. Use the diagram to explain how running water is used to generate electricity. Include all the labels in the diagram in your explanation.
2. Would you be in favour of a plan to dam up a local river to generate hydro-electric power? Why or why not? Can you provide at least three points to support your opinion?

Threats to Running Water

Many people see hydro-electric projects and diversions as threats to rivers. The diversions change the amount of water in rivers and affect natural environments. The Aral Sea illustrates the damage that can be done. Other threats are shown in Figure 13.18.

Figure 13.18

Humans create a number of threats to running water.

Pollution	Introduced Species
• Human waste is emptied into rivers and lakes. • Industrial waste (chemicals and toxins) is dumped into rivers and lakes. • Fertilizers and pesticides run off farmlands into water bodies.	• Introduced species have no natural enemies and over-reproduce. • Introduced species destroy natural species. • Introduced species eat up the food supply.
Overuse	**Overfishing**
• Over-populated areas need so much water that the rivers and lakes are often used up. • Too many people using too little water creates dirty, unhealthy, low-quality water.	• Too many fish are taken from lakes and rivers. • Fish cannot reproduce as fast as we catch them, so fish species disappear.

After Reading

1. Four types of threats to running water are identified in Figure 13.18. For each type of threat, suggest two actions that could be taken to reduce the threats and protect water. Explain why you think that your suggestions would make a difference.
2. You are working in a restaurant. Your manager asks you for advice on cutting down on water consumption. What are three actions that the restaurant could take?
3. Do research to identify the biggest threats to the rivers around your community. Interview five family members or friends to find out what people in your community think about this topic. Start by making up survey questions to ask. Survey questions are usually written as closed questions. (Refer to the Literacy Tip on creating closed and open-ended questions on page 221 of Chapter 11.) Think about the kinds of answers you might get and ways that you can easily write down answers. Often, surveys use rating scales ("On a scale of 1 to 10…") or checklists. When you are finished your interviews, make a poster to show your results. (Refer to the Literacy Tip on creating posters on page 171 of Chapter 8.)

BE A GLOBAL CITIZEN

Development of Wind Energy

The use of non-renewable energy resources like coal and petroleum is damaging the environment and our health. Many countries are looking for energy sources that are clean and plentiful. One flow energy source that governments and individuals are turning to is wind power. Wind turbines are a very clean form of energy. They cause few environmental problems. Wind farms allow people to continue to use the surrounding land for agriculture or recreation.

The cost of wind energy is declining, and it is now seen as a low-cost energy source. Many governments around the world are looking at wind power as a key element in their energy generation for the future. Electricity generation from wind power is growing by 25 to 30 percent per year.

European countries are leading the way in wind power generation. On June 15, 2007, the European Wind Energy Association (EWEA) held its first European Wind Day. Twenty-two countries participated. This signalled the first mainstream support for wind energy. Officials from EWEA estimate that by 2020, 16 percent of Europe's electricity needs can be met by wind energy alone. Denmark, Spain, and Germany continue to be the leaders in wind power generation. By the end of 2005, Germany had 18 428 megawatts generated by wind turbines. In comparison, Canada had only 943 megawatts, with Ontario contributing only 122 megawatts.

Canada must work harder to establish alternate sources of energy. If Canada follows the example set by Europe, we may be able to slow down our use of non-renewable energy sources and see alternate energy sources as our future. How could your class or environment club become part of this wind power movement? You could look for funds and community sponsorships to help you install a small wind turbine at your school. This would lessen your school's use of non-renewable energy resources.

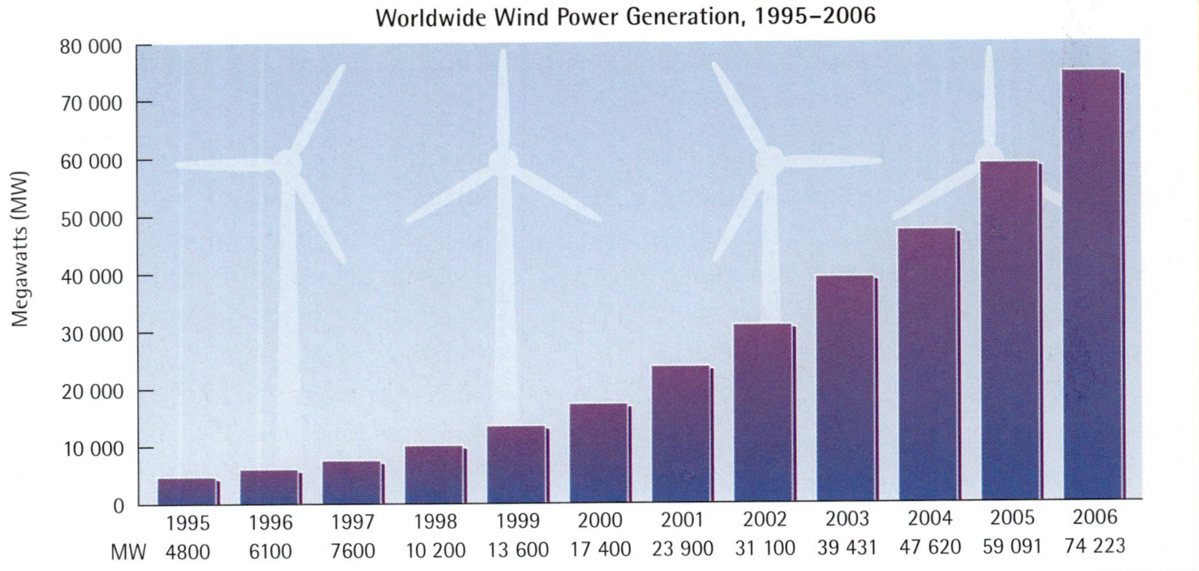

Figure 13.19

Wind power generation increased dramatically worldwide between 1995 and 2006, and it will continue to do so.

continues...

BE A GLOBAL CITIZEN

Development of Wind Energy *(continued)*

Figure 13.20

This is a photograph of the Cowley Ridge Wind Electric Generating Station, located near the town of Pincher Creek in Alberta. Wind turbines are becoming increasingly common in Canada. However, we have a long way to go before we catch up with leading wind generation countries such as Denmark, Spain, and Germany.

LITERACY TIP

Researching Effectively

You have many choices of where to find information when you are doing research. To become an effective researcher, it is important to choose the best way to find the information you need in the shortest amount of time. You can go to the library and use hard-copy or online resources such as an encyclopedia, or use a search engine to locate information on the Internet.

The Oceans as a Resource

BEFORE READING

1. Identify ways that oceans are important to the following:
   - Canada's history
   - Canada's physical environment
   - Canada's economy
   - Canada's transportation
2. Why can the oceans be considered a flow natural resource and part of the global commons?

About 97 percent of all Earth's water is in the oceans. Perhaps we should call our planet Ocean instead of Earth! In fact, there is just one ocean—one continuous body of water. We give names to different parts of the ocean for convenience. The smaller parts of the world ocean, near the continents, are also given names. These names begin or end with "gulf," "sea," "strait," or "bay." In total, the world ocean covers 71 percent of Earth's surface. If used wisely, it is a vast sustainable resource.

Figure 13.21

The world's oceans cover huge areas and plunge to amazing depths.

Ocean	Area (sq. km)	Deepest Point	Depth (m)
Pacific	166 241 000	Mariana Trench	10 924
Atlantic	86 557 000	Puerto Rico Trench	8 605
Indian	73 427 000	Java Trench	7 258
Arctic	9 485 000	Eurasia Basin	5 122

Figure 13.22

What is the difference in height between the lowest point in the oceans and the highest point on land?

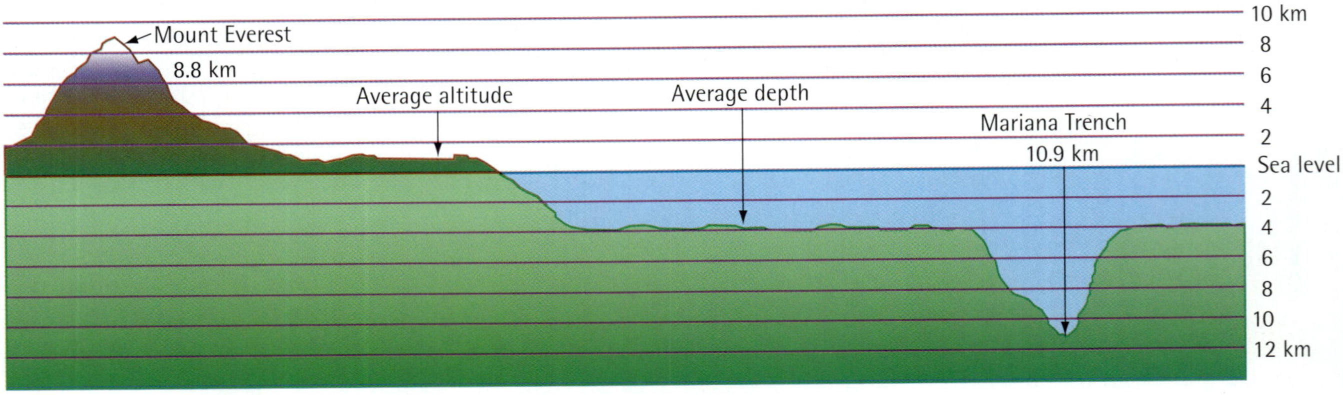

CONNECTIONS TO Science

Why are the oceans salty? Rivers carry minerals such as calcium and sodium from the land into the oceans. Some of these minerals are used by sea creatures to make their shells. Other minerals are taken up by plant life. Still other minerals simply sink into the mud at the bottom of the ocean. The two minerals that together make salt—sodium and chlorine—are not used up in these ways. They remain in the ocean water. When the Sun evaporates water, the salt is left behind. Gradually, the oceans have become salty from these minerals.

WEB LINK

For more information about ocean currents, go to www.nelson.com/phygeo7.

Ocean Currents

Oceans can be considered flow resources because the water moves around Earth. Ocean currents are flows of water in the oceans. They are pushed by winds and by the spinning of Earth on its axis. A current that moves from a warm area to a colder one is called a warm current. A current that moves from cold to warm water is a cold current.

Ocean Currents of the World

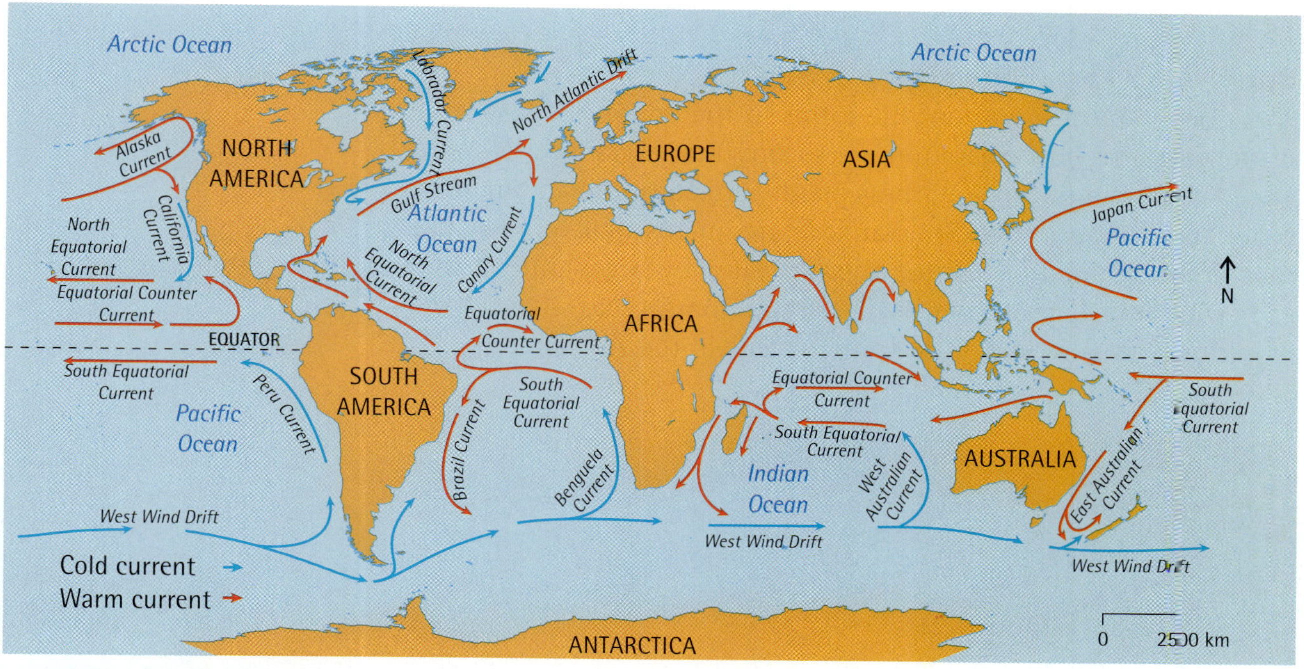

Figure 13.23

Identify the oceans, and follow the warm and cold ocean currents of the world. Many scientists are concerned that warming of the oceans due to climate change may cause the Gulf Stream to change course or stop altogether. How might this affect the climate of northern Europe?

Fact File

The cold Labrador Current flows southward along Canada's Atlantic Coast. It often carries icebergs out of the frigid waters of Baffin Bay. In April 1912, the *Titanic*—the largest passenger ship in the world at that time—collided with an iceberg 640 kilometres south of Newfoundland and sank. About 1500 people died in the disaster.

The Distribution of Life in the Oceans

The life that exists in the oceans is very important to people. Most of the life forms live in the top 80 metres of water. Sunlight can reach down this far, so plants are able to grow. These plants are food for fish.

Below 80 metres, there is little light, little plant growth, and few species of fish. Only in recent years have scientists learned a little about the types of species that are able to thrive in such low light conditions. We have much to learn about ocean ecosystems.

Underwater Food Pyramid

Some of the most important life forms in the oceans are also some of the smallest. Phytoplankton are so tiny that a glass of sea water would contain millions. Yet, these plants can take minerals out of the water and grow and live. Zooplankton are microscopic animals that eat the phytoplankton. In turn, they are eaten by larger animals such as herring and blue whales. Flesh-eating animals like sharks, tuna, dolphins, and salmon eat the animals that eat the zooplankton.

Figure 13.24

Dolphins are high on the food pyramid. They eat fish and squid.

The Continental Shelves

The shallow areas of the oceans near the coasts of the continents—the **continental shelves**—provide about 84 percent of the world's catch of fish. New technologies, such as fish finders and larger nets, have produced greater catches. In some developing countries, the fish catch is so important that the people get 40 percent of their animal protein from fish.

However, these areas are vulnerable to threats. Global warming will have a serious impact on the species of phytoplankton that grow on the continental shelves. A small change in this basic food source for marine life will cause enormous changes in all other species.

Fishing Areas of the World

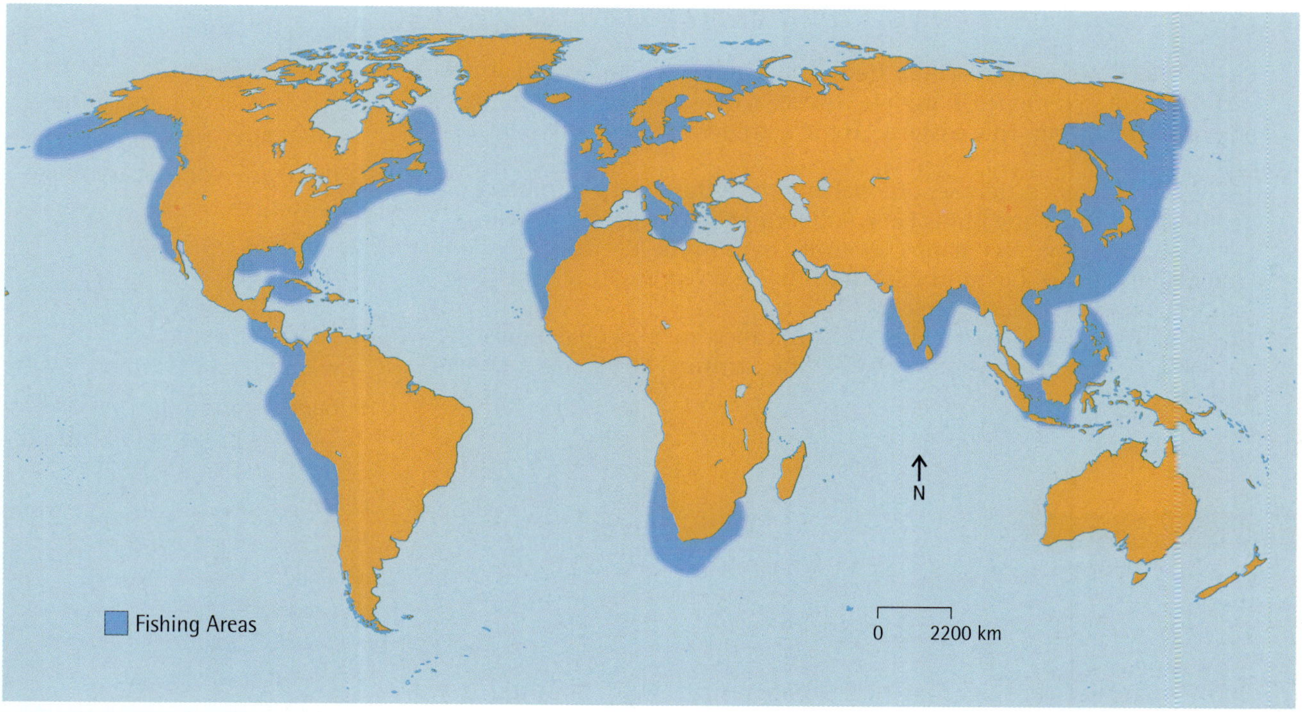

Figure 13.25

Note how the major fishing grounds of the world are found on continental shelves.

DURING READING

1. When you look at a map of the world, you can see the names of several major oceans (refer to Figure 13.23). How can the statement "there is just one ocean" be true?
2. Examine the map in Figure 13.25. Along which coastal areas are there no fishing areas? Why do you think this is so? What impacts might this have on the peoples in those parts of the world?

Inuit and Whale Hunting

Whales were a traditional source of food for Inuit of Canada's Arctic. However, over-hunting of whales put them on the endangered species list. Most countries of the world banned whaling. In July 1998, Inuit hunters decided to celebrate the creation of the new territory of Nunavut by hunting a bowhead whale.

Wednesday, July 22, 1998

Bowhead whale harpooned

Baffin Island Inuit on first hunt in 50 years

PANGNIRTUNG, N.W.T.—Inuit hunters, travelling in canoes and armed with an explosive-tipped harpoon, ended a five-day hunt by killing a bowhead whale in the eastern Arctic's frigid waters early Tuesday morning.

The killing immediately set off celebrations in the small community on Baffin Island, where the hunts have not been held for the past 50 years.

"People are very, very happy about it," said Annie Keenainak, whose father Simeonie led the hunting parties. "It was a very exciting experience for our people. We are overjoyed."

The hunt held a large cultural significance to a people preparing for self-government next April, when the territory of Nunavut comes into existence.

Figure 13.26
This newspaper article reports on an Inuit whale hunt.

Many people were against this whale hunt. They claimed it was a needless killing of a threatened species. Inuit argued that it was important for their culture. Eric Joamie pointed out, "Our ancestors were involved in harvesting any kind of animals they were able to come across for their survival." Annie Keenainak said that the hunt was "an opportunity to celebrate our culture."

DURING READING

1. Should Inuit be hunting whales? Write down ideas for and against the whale hunt in a chart with the following headings: "Ideas in Favour of Inuit Whale Hunt" and "Ideas Against Inuit Whale Hunt."

Literacy Tip

Newspaper Reports

A newspaper report of an event is supposed to be factual and objective, and has the following parts:

- a headline—tells what the article is about and attracts the reader's attention
- the lead—one or two sentences briefly answer all the 5 Ws and 1 H questions, tell the reader what happened, and "hook" the reader into wanting to read more
- background information—gives more details about the 5 Ws and 1 H
- quotations—from someone who was involved in or affected by the event, present a person's view or opinion about the event
- conclusion—a sentence or two about what might happen because of the event or what might happen next

Figure 13.27

Why did Inuit want to hunt bowhead whales? Why did some people criticize them for it?

Threats to Ocean Resources

We know little about the oceans' ecosystems because they are so complicated. The oceans provide a huge variety of species and conditions. The world's oceans are so vast that most people believed we could never affect them. They were very wrong!

Overfishing

With our modern technology, we have become so efficient at catching fish that we are overfishing the oceans. Some fish species are disappearing. The United Nations has estimated that the most that can be fished from the oceans is 80 million tonnes of fish per year. If more than this is harvested, the fish cannot reproduce quickly enough. They will disappear. We are currently harvesting about 101 million tonnes of fish a year, which is well over the limit. If this overfishing continues, fish catches will drop in the future. More people around the world will go hungry as a direct result.

Canada is already suffering the effects of overfishing. In the 1990s, the amount of cod being fished on the East Coast of Canada dropped. The government of Canada banned fishing for cod in 1992 because so few fish were left. It was hoped that the ban would allow the fish to become plentiful again, but that has not happened. Only a very few cod can now be caught each year. A similar situation is developing with the salmon stocks on the West Coast.

Figure 13.28

This commercial fishing boat is fishing for salmon off Vancouver Island in British Columbia. Using high-tech efficiency, the net is hauled over the back of the boat and emptied into the hold.

Figure 13.29

Note the changes in the amount of cod caught on Canada's East Coast from 1989 to 2005.

Year	Amount (tonnes)	Year	Amount (tonnes)
1989	426 090	1999	55 478
1991	309 031	2001	40 440
1993	76 522	2003	22 768
1995	12 438	2005	26 156
1997	29 605		

Pollution

Pollution is another threat to the oceans. Pollution reaches the ocean waters in the following ways:

- through rivers
- from the atmosphere
- from factories and cities along the coasts
- directly from ships

Oil spills from damaged ships pollute the water. Ships often just dump their sewage and waste oil directly into the ocean. Those parts of the world with large populations, such as the coasts of Europe and Asia, are heavily polluted. People and pollution seem to go hand in hand.

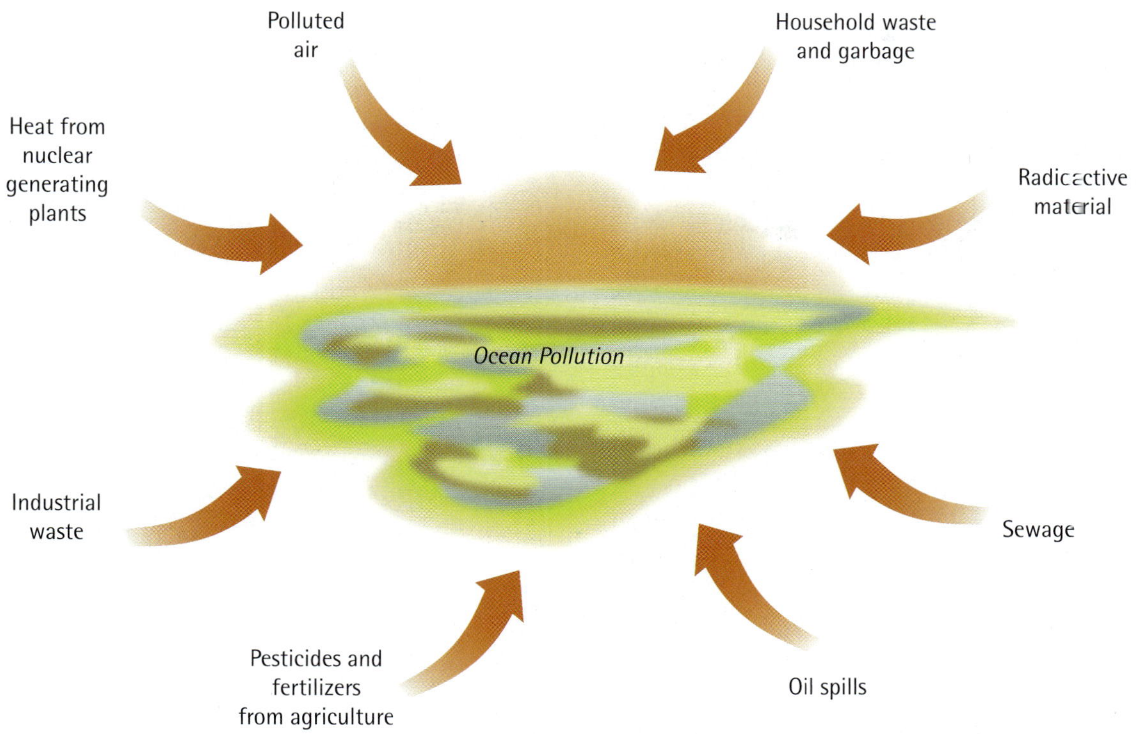

Figure 13.30

As big as the oceans are, they cannot handle all the pollution that humans dump into them.

Literacy Tip

Drawing Line Graphs

Follow these steps to draw a line graph:

- Identify the variables (for example, time and quantity).
- Place the independent variable (time) on the *x*-axis (along the bottom of the page).
- Place the dependent variable (amount) on the *y*-axis (along the left side of the page).
- Draw the axes big enough to fit all the data.
- Label the axes and the units clearly and neatly.
- Plot the data by drawing a line between the points you have plotted.
- Give the graph an appropriate title.

1. Write five endings to the sentence beginning: "The oceans are important because ..."

2. Standing on the shores of the Great Lakes, many people think that they resemble oceans. Why do you suppose the Great Lakes are not salty?

3. Draw a food pyramid to show the connections between forms of life in the top 80 metres of the oceans' water.

4. a) Make a line graph to show cod catches on the East Coast of Canada. Use the data from Figure 13.29. Make sure that you put the years across the bottom of your graph, and the fish catches (amount in tonnes) up the side. Give your graph a title. (Refer to the GeoSkills and the line graphs on page 79 of Chapter 4 to help you visualize what a good line graph looks like.)

b) In two sentences, describe what your graph tells you.

Knowledge and Understanding

1. Rivers have just a hundredth of one percent (0.01 percent) of Earth's water. Think about it this way: If you have 100 litres in your bathtub to represent all the water in the world, and you take out one litre, you have 1 percent of the water. If you take 10 millilitres out of that one litre, the amount you take represents all the water in all the rivers of the world. Explain why rivers are so important when they hold such a small amount of water.

2. Imagine that you are a newspaper reporter watching the opening of a new irrigation project. Many kilometres of canals and dams had to be built to get enough water for the crops.

   a) Identify three good points about the project that you might write about in your article.

   b) What are three problems that you might point out to your readers?

   Remember to review the Literacy Tip about newspaper articles on page 280 before you answer this question.

Inquiry/Research and Communication Skills

3. You are in the advertising business. Make up a magazine or newspaper advertisement to encourage people to conserve water. If you want, you could write a script for a 30-second television advertisement. Make sure that you give reasons to convince people that conservation of water is important.

4. What is the water supply for your community? Contact the department in your municipality that is responsible for the water supply to find answers to the following questions:

   - What is the source of the water (river, wells, and so on)?
   - How is the water treated before it is used?
   - How is the water treated after it is used?
   - Where does the water go after your community is finished with it?

   Create a poster with a flow diagram to show stages in the collection, use, and discharge of water in your community. (See sample flow diagrams on pages 188 and 192 of Chapter 9.)

5. One suggested river diversion plan for Canada is to turn James Bay into a lake. The water would then flow to the thirsty cities of the United States. Conduct research to find information about this plan. Find answers to the following questions:

   - Why is the project considered necessary?
   - What rivers would be diverted?
   - How would James Bay be made into a lake?
   - How would the water get to the United States?

   Answer these questions through research using encyclopedias, the Internet, or other resources that you have available. If you search for information using a search engine on the Internet, remember to use keywords from the questions as your search terms.

   Share what you learn from your research by writing a letter to the editor of your local newspaper, either supporting the plan or arguing against it.

6. **a)** The fishing industry around the world and in Canada is in trouble. Make up three open-ended research questions about the problems in the fishing industry. Your questions should consider different points of view about the problems and solutions in the fishing industry. Your questions should include words like "problems," "overfishing," and "management," plus other words about fishing. Look back over this chapter to find suitable words.

   b) Answer one of your questions through research using encyclopedias, the Internet, or other resources that you have available. In your answer, you should try to point out different points of view about problems and solutions in the fishing industry. Report your answer as a newspaper article investigating troubles in the fishing industry.

7. **a)** Look at the newspaper article in Figure 13.26 and identify the following:

   - the headline
   - the lead
   - the background
   - answers to the 5 Ws and 1 H questions

   b) Facts are statements that can be shown to be true. Opinions are what someone thinks is true. In your notes, identify one fact and one opinion from the article.

Map, Globe, and Graphic Skills

8 Choose one of the oceans that touches Canada. Name it. Then, use an atlas to list all of the bays, gulfs, straits, and seas that touch our shore.

9 Use the information below to compare the sizes of the oceans.

a) Get a piece of graph paper. Colour in one square for each 1 million square kilometres of ocean. For example, you will need nine full squares plus a half of a square for the Arctic Ocean. Shade in the right number of squares in a rectangle shape on the graph paper.

b) Label the areas you have shaded in with the names of the oceans. Give the page a title, and write the scale that you have used.

Ocean	Area (sq. km)
Pacific	166 241 000
Atlantic	86 557 000
Indian	73 427 000
Arctic	9 485 000

c) Make up two questions using this data for a partner to answer.

Application

10 Most of the world's water is salty. Humans and animals cannot drink salt water. Research to find out some ways that salt can be removed from ocean water. Use the information that you find to make a model or a demonstration.

11 **a)** What should be done to stop pollution from getting into rivers and oceans? Brainstorm with one or two other people possible answers to this question. List as many ideas as you can. When you are brainstorming, remember not to worry about how good or bad the ideas seem. Just try to get as many ideas as possible. Unusual ideas will trigger different, perhaps better, ideas. When you run out of new thoughts, look carefully at your ideas, and try to decide which ones are the best ideas for stopping pollution.

b) Think up an appropriate way to communicate your best ideas to the rest of the class. You might use a poster, a short play, a poem, a newspaper article, or some other method.

Figure 13.31

Pacific chinook salmon make their way back to their spawning grounds. This photograph captures part of the ecosystem that exists within a river.

14 Sustainable Development

IN THIS CHAPTER

- describe ways that people use natural resources to meet their needs, including renewable, non-renewable, and flow resources
- explain what is meant by sustainable development, and describe how it affects the environment
- use the new terms in this chapter correctly as you investigate the topics
- make up questions to help you research problems and different points of view about managing and using natural resources
- locate and use helpful information from primary and secondary sources
- share the results of research for different reasons and audiences using options such as computer slide shows, videos, websites, oral presentations, written notes and reports, drawings, tables, charts, diagrams, maps, models, and graphs
- make a report on conditions that will affect the natural resources that are available in the future

KEY VOCABULARY

alternative energy source
compost
co-operative
fair trade
organic waste
sustainable development

Disaster Strikes

BEFORE READING

1. What might happen if natural resources like water, minerals, and forest products become in short supply? Draw and label a picture to show your ideas. Show it to another person and explain your ideas to him or her.
2. Suppose you were cast away on a deserted island. Make a list of five things that you would like to have with you. For each item in your list, explain how it would help you to survive on the island.

Disaster! Your plane has crashed. You and two friends are stranded on a small island. There is no hope of being rescued. However, you can survive. There is food—nuts, berries, and fish in the sea. A small stream provides drinking water.

You survive for a few months, but then you begin to think of ways to use the island's resources to improve your life. You discuss your plans with your friends. "Why don't we cut down more trees and build a really nice hut? Why not eat more fish? They're there just for the taking."

Figure 14.1

You can survive on the island for a long time if you take only those resources that you need each day.

Your friends point out some problems. If you cut down the trees to build a hut, you will destroy the plants that provide your nuts and berries. Also, catching too many fish today means that there will be fewer fish to catch tomorrow. The improvements that you want to make are going to use up your resources now so you will not have them in the future.

This is the same dilemma facing the people of the world. How can we use our resources wisely without using up or polluting our resources? We need to use resources today in such a way that they are still available for our grandchildren and their grandchildren. That is what **sustainable development** is—looking after our resources without using them up.

Attitudes toward Resources

We must use natural resources to satisfy our needs for food, shelter, and clothing. However, we usually want more than we really need. We also seek comfort, entertainment, luxury, and other non-essential things. Resources for these non-essential wants must be taken from the environment, too. Unfortunately, we often want more than the environment can provide in a sustainable way.

Figure 14.2

People have different attitudes toward resources. Which of these attitudes have been expressed by people who you know?

	Use What We Want	Manage What We Have	Sustain Our Resources	Preserve Our Resources
Attitudes toward the environment	Take what we want. There will always be plenty for everyone!	Waste not, want not!	Development today, development tomorrow!	We must not harm our environment!
Actions that take place	Resources are unending. Humans can take whatever they want without worrying about the environment.	People use the resources that they find, but they try not to waste them foolishly.	People use natural resources, but they make sure they will be available for future generations.	Our job is to keep the natural environment from suffering any harm because of human action.
Example actions	• clear-cutting forests • throwing metal waste into the garbage	• planting trees in areas that have been cut • recycling metals in a blue box program	• selectively cut trees in a forest • reduce, reuse, and recycle metal products	• set up forest preserves where no trees can be harvested • ban all mining of mineral resources
Thoughts about the future	When these resources are used up, we will simply move to a new location. Technology will come up with a solution.	There are plenty of resources, but we know that eventually they will run out.	The next generations will need at least as many resources as we have. We must make sure that every natural resource is used fully. That way, nothing is wasted.	Future generations will have completely natural environments. Nature is just too valuable to play around with. Once an ecosystem is gone, it can never be replaced.

DURING READING

1. Look at the ideas in Figure 14.2. Which of the attitudes best describes your view about resources? Provide personal examples to support your choice.
2. Why will the "Use What We Want" and "Preserve Our Resources" attitudes not work very well over a long period of time?

Use — Do Not Abuse

Some people want to use resources now and not worry about the future. Other people try to preserve the environment, making it hard to meet our needs and wants now. Sustainable development means that our needs can be met, and the environment can be protected at the same time. To accomplish sustainable development, we must change the way we use resources. We cannot keep doing the same old thing.

CONNECTIONS TO History

The First Nations of North America had a way of life that was sustainable. They used many resources—buffalo, deer, beaver, grasses, trees, and so on—but they took only what they needed to survive. They lived for thousands of years on this continent without damaging it. Everything changed after the Europeans arrived. The Europeans were not satisfied with just surviving. They took a lot more from the environment. Our modern society has much to learn from traditional First Nations' ways of life. Discover one practice that First Nations have that all people should consider having.

KANE, Paul: Indian Encampment on Lake Huron, 1845

Figure 14.3

The artist and explorer Paul Kane (1810–1871) painted this encampment of First Nations people on Lake Huron. What natural resources can you identify in the picture?

The population of the world is increasing at an ever-faster rate. This makes sustainable development extremely hard to achieve. A lot more people will be using Earth's natural resources in the future. Many people are hoping that technology will help us make better use of our natural resources. Technology has helped in some ways. It has allowed more use of **alternative energy sources**, including solar energy and wind power. However, technologies are not enough. People have to change the way they use natural resources.

AFTER READING

1. In your notebook, complete the following organizer to define "sustainable development."

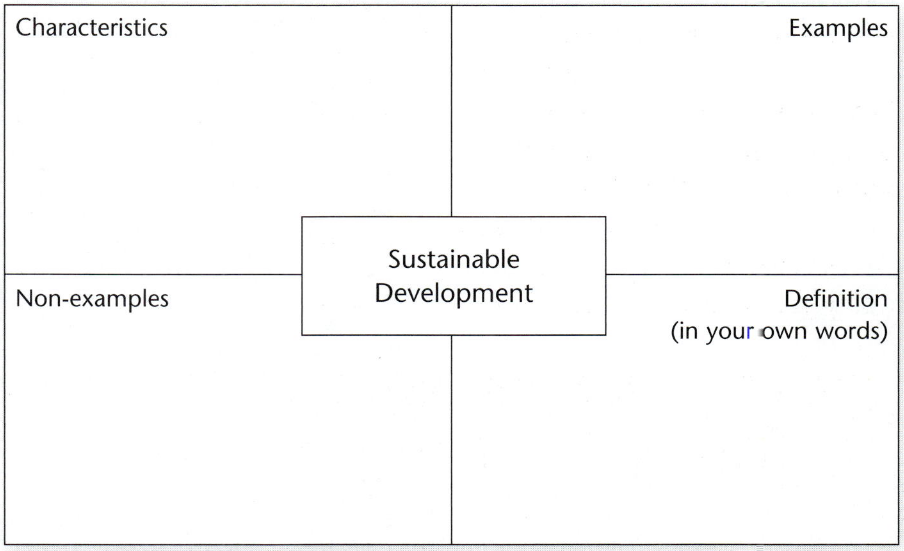

2. Explain why clear-cutting a forest is *not* sustainable development, while selective cutting is.

3. Imagine that you were one of the three people who survived the plane crash described at the beginning of this chapter. What three things might you have done to improve your life on the island without using up your resources?

4. In Figure 14.2, two sets of example actions are given to show how resources (forests and metals) would be used differently with each of the attitudes. Write example actions to show each of the different attitudes for our freshwater resource.

GeoSkills

Making an Informed Decision

September 13, 2007

Maskinonge River near "the point of no return"

Drought, irrigation drying up river

A river doesn't run through it any more.

Leaning on his cane, Roland Peacock surveys the dry riverbed that, on maps at least, should be the Maskinonge River. This is where fish normally would be swimming, but raccoon paw prints crisscross the cracked dry mud, indications of nocturnal prowling in a vain attempt to get a drink of water. It is the worst he has seen in 50 years.

With increasing alarms being sounded about the health of the Maskinonge and the amount of water being pumped out to irrigate sod and vegetable farm fields, the Ministry of the Environment has begun an investigation into water users in the watershed.

"Save the Maskinonge" was actually formed several years ago by citizens concerned about the abandoned aluminum smelter plant, with deadly chemicals only a few hundred metres from the river. The Ministry of the Environment has since ordered a cleanup of the property. Having dodged that particular environmental bullet, the river now struggles to survive a combination of human-made and natural threats to its existence.

The river meanders along an area where extensive farming has taken place for generations. Part of that land is slated for development as a business and industrial park, ironically a development that could actually help the Maskinonge.

But in the meantime, the business park's designated area remains the site of row upon row, acre upon acre of vegetables, soaked every day by long arcs of water spitting from massive sprinklers —water being sucked from the dying river.

Mr. Peacock warned, "The Maskinonge River has almost reached the point of no return."

Figure 14.4

This newspaper article tells the story of the Maskinonge River, which is located in the Lake Simcoe region in Ontario.

Read the article above. Use this information to come up with a solution that will help protect this river.

When you need to decide on the best solution, you must identify the criteria you will use to make your final decision. Criteria are the standards that you will use to judge the situation and the options. In this case, you must find a way to use the Maskinonge River in a sustainable way so that both the environment and the economic needs of the people are considered. Use your understanding of what sustainable development is to develop criteria for your final decision.

In order to make an informed decision, you need to look at all sides of the problem. In this case, there are several groups of people who are interested in the Maskinonge River. An organizational chart is a great way to see all people's perspectives.

1. Complete a chart like the one below:

Who	Wants/Needs	Effects on River
Farmers		
Concerned local citizens		
Urban planners		
Aluminum smelter owners		

continues...

GeoSkills

Making an Informed Decision *(continued)*

2. Think about the points you put in your chart, and then come up with an idea about how to save the Maskinonge River. Remember that you cannot please everybody, but your plan should have some benefits for all the groups involved. Most importantly, try to make sure your solution works to protect the river.
3. Write a paragraph explaining your plan for saving the river and how you arrived at that decision. Be prepared to discuss your ideas in a group.

We Must Do Better

BEFORE READING

1. Who are the people in our society who could help Canadians work harder to protect the environment? Work with two other students to brainstorm a list of people who could be part of changing people's attitudes and actions toward the environment. Then, explain why each of these people could have an influence on changing attitudes.

We humans have not done a very good job of taking care of the environment. Mostly, we just have not thought much about it. Fortunately, attitudes are changing.

Figure 14.5

Which of these reasons is most common for people who you know?

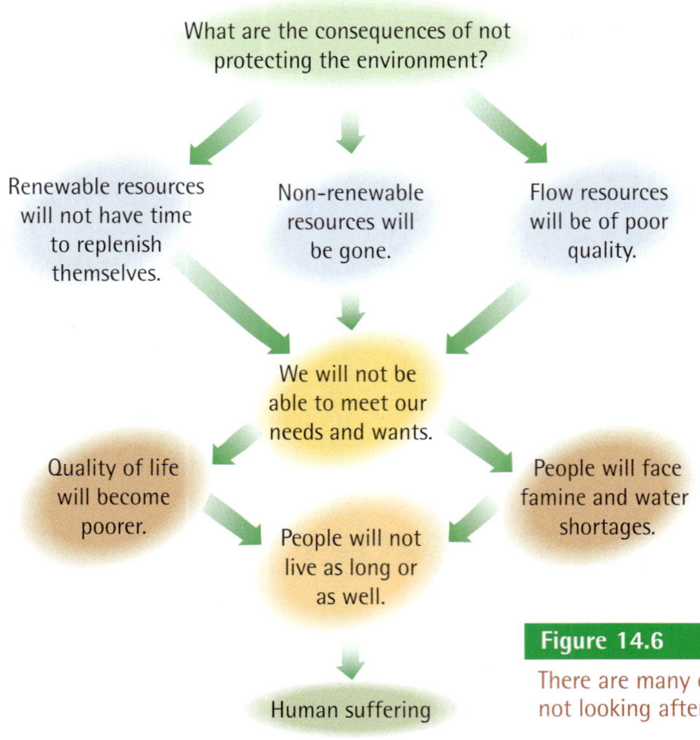

Figure 14.6

There are many consequences of not looking after our resources.

Literacy Tip

Reading a Complex Web

Figure 14.6 is an example of a complex web. Note how the arrows that connect the idea bubbles are all pointing downward. This idea web illustrates how one set of consequences (inaction, in this case) creates a chain reaction of consequences.

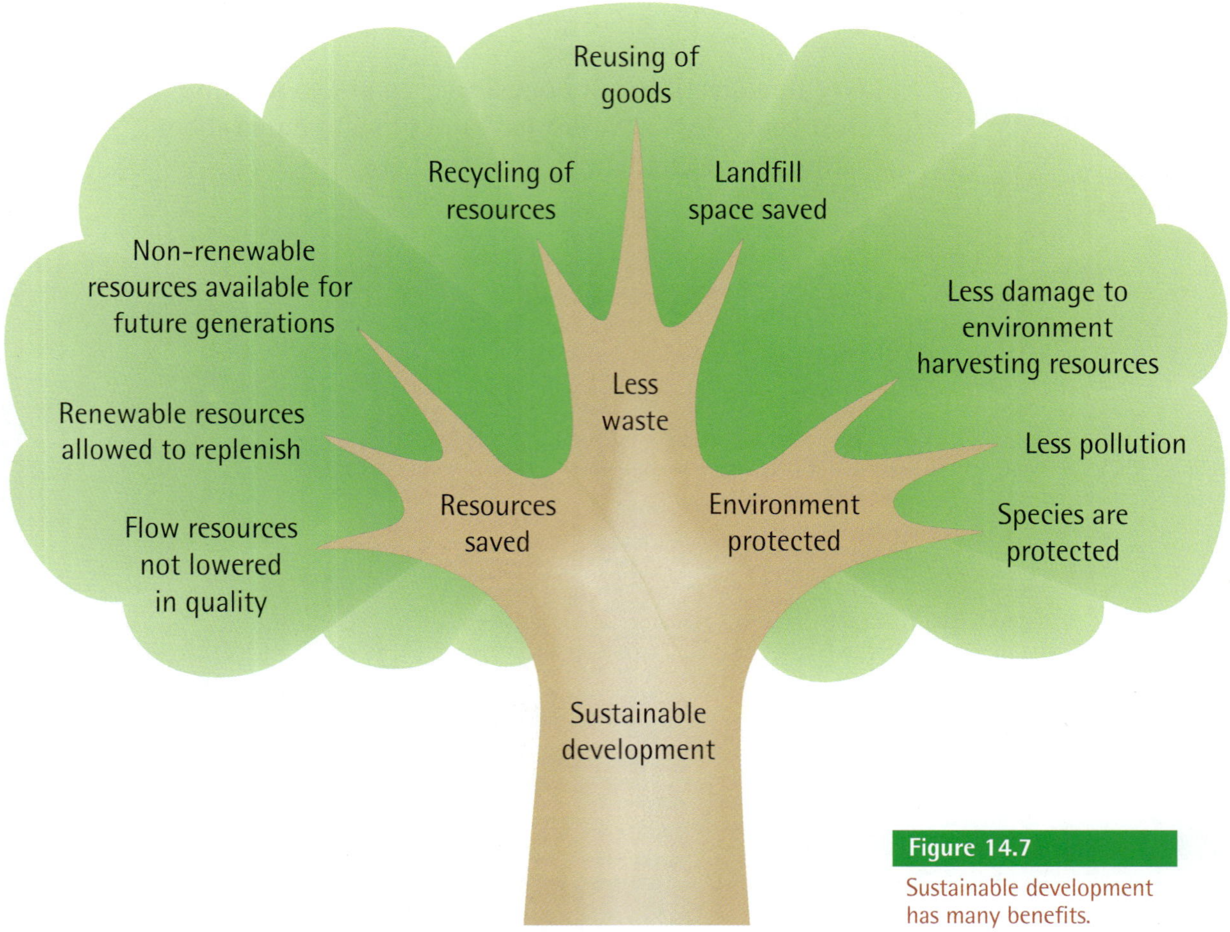

Figure 14.7

Sustainable development has many benefits.

A Sustainable Future

Let us look at some ways that sustainable development will change the way we do things.

Figure 14.8

Sustainable development will mean learning new ways of living.

The Old Way	The Sustainable Way
Fossil fuels make up most of our energy sources because they are cheap and convenient.	We use many different alternative energy sources, such as the following: • clean-burning fossil fuels like natural gas • fuels made out of plants • wind power • solar power We also develop other energy sources including the hydrogen fuel cell.
Cars are the most common way of getting from place to place.	Mass transit (buses, subways) has become more convenient. These "people movers" use less fuel. Energy sources last longer, and there is less air pollution. Transit vehicles are made from fewer natural resources than all the cars that they replaced.
Waste is buried or dumped in large storage places. This is the cheapest method of getting rid of unwanted material.	Very few natural resources are labelled waste because we reuse and recycle most materials. Household materials are recycled or composted. Any materials that cannot be reclaimed are used to create energy.
Farmland is lost because cities grow out into farming areas. Population densities are low—that is, there are fewer people per hectare.	Cities grow up instead of out. High-rise and low-rise apartment buildings are common. Parks and natural areas are important parts of cities. Cities are designed for people instead of cars. People walk and ride bikes to many places in their community.

Web Link

For more information about what young people can do to help the environment, go to **www.nelson.com/phygeo7**.

Fact File

As a typical North American, you will probably use all of the following resources over your lifetime:

- 486 tonnes of construction materials (gravel, cement, stone)
- 16 tonnes of paper (newsprint, photocopy paper)
- 21 tonnes of wood (furniture, housing)
- 29 tonnes of chemicals (detergents, cleaners)

BE A GLOBAL CITIZEN

Sustainable Development and Poverty

Poverty and environmental destruction go hand in hand. In many countries, much of the best agricultural land is used to grow crops such as cotton, tea, tobacco, sugar, and cocoa. Local farmers grow these crops for big corporations rather than producing the food they need to eat. These farmers are paid very poorly.

In some poor countries, farmers who grow cocoa beans live in absolute poverty. Cocoa beans are used to make the chocolate that we all enjoy. In 2002, the average wage for cocoa growers in West Africa was US$30 to $110 per year. The people who produce the crop that makes our chocolate bars will probably never taste a bar themselves!

In order to earn more money, some farmers overwork their lands. In time, the soil becomes exhausted from overuse. The environment suffers. Some aid groups believe that the only way to protect people and the environment is to ensure that farmers are paid well enough that they can take care of their lands.

One way for farmers to earn more money is to work together to sell their crops through community **co-operatives**. Farmers work as a team, not as individuals.

Another way farmers can earn more money is called **fair trade**. Organizations have been set up to make sure the producers of the crops get a fair price. Fair trade requires producers to reduce their use of chemical fertilizers and pesticides and to take other actions that are more sustainable. By buying products labelled as fair trade, you are helping farmers in poor countries overcome poverty and to farm in a sustainable manner.

Figure 14.9

Buying fair-trade products such as these chocolate and coffee products found in Kensington Market in Toronto, Ontario, helps farmers in poor countries. It also helps to protect our environment. Does your community have stores that sell fair-trade products? Conduct research to find out.

LITERACY TIP

Finding the Main Idea

When you read a long section of text, begin by identifying the main idea. The main idea

- usually occurs at the beginning of the text
- usually captures the whole point of the text
- often appears in the title

The main idea is always followed by supporting ideas, which strengthen the main idea and can include facts, examples, and interesting points.

Who Should Lead the Change?

Using our resources in a sustainable way is the only hope humans have for a good future. Who should be leading this change in the way we do things?

Figure 14.10

There can be many leaders of change in our society. What other groups might you add?

Governments

People who are in the government can make laws and rules. Laws force people to use resources and the environment properly. An example is the law that stopped lead from being added to gasoline. This reduced air pollution.

Industries and Businesses

The people who run industries and businesses can change the way they do things. By using resources properly, not wasting, and not polluting, these people can accomplish a great deal.

Consumers

The people who buy products and services can insist that the environment be protected. They can refuse to buy from businesses that do not use resources well. They can boycott businesses that use too much packaging for their goods. Consumers can also pressure governments to pass laws.

You

You are the best person to protect the environment. Your actions every day can make a big difference. You can lead the change by showing others how important it is to practise sustainable development. Individual actions make an enormous difference when added together.

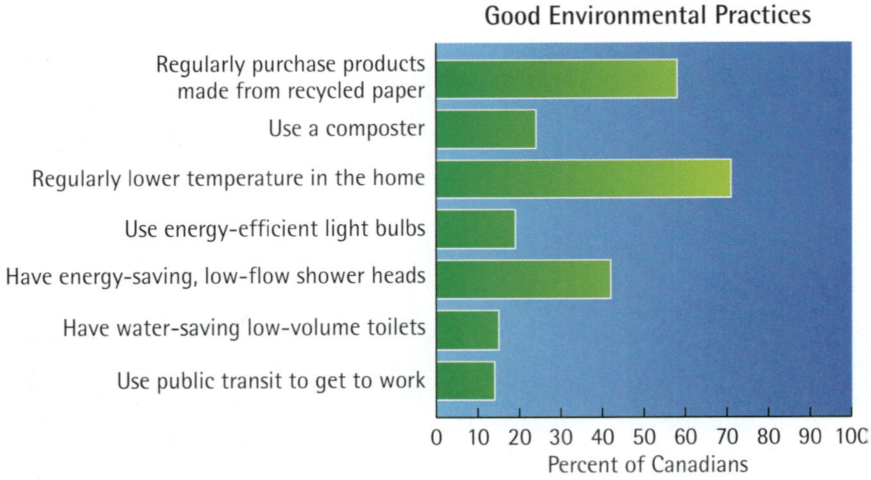

Figure 14.11

Note the percentage of Canadians who engage in good environmental practices.

DURING READING

1. In your opinion, what are the three most important reasons why humans have not done a very good job in looking after the environment?

2. The chart in Figure 14.8 compares the old and the sustainable ways of dealing with the environment. Compare these two ways using "water" as the environmental topic.

What Can You Do?

You are a leader in the fight to save natural resources and the environment. You are a consumer. You are important. Let us look at some actions you can take.

Practise the 3 Rs

Reduce, reuse, recycle. The most important of the 3 Rs is "reduce." This will save resources that are used to make products and the packaging that goes with them. For example, you might share books and magazines with a friend rather than each buying the same ones.

Figure 14.12

Reducing consumption is the first step to a sustainable society. What other products could you buy used instead of new? Can you think of another way to reduce unnecessary consumption?

Travel Wisely

Use a bicycle or public transit whenever possible. By not using automobiles, you are saving energy and reducing pollution. At the very least, commuters should use a car pool so only one vehicle is being used instead of several.

Figure 14.13

Using public transit like streetcars in Toronto, Ontario, saves energy and money, too. How often do you take the bus or subway? How often do you and your family bike or carpool?

Figure 14.14

Composting turns waste food into good soil. Does your household compost?

Do Not Throw It Out

Compost your **organic waste**. Putting vegetable peelings, apple cores, banana skins, and other waste in a composter is not a big job. The wastes turn into valuable soil, and the landfill sites are not filled up. People who live in apartments can compost by using red wriggler worms. They are safe, clean, and fun to watch.

Turn It Off

Help to save energy at home. We waste energy at home in the following ways:

- setting the heating thermostat too high and the air conditioner too low
- leaving lights on
- keeping windows and doors open during the heating or air-conditioning seasons
- letting hot-water taps drip

Saving energy helps to save non-renewable fossil fuels.

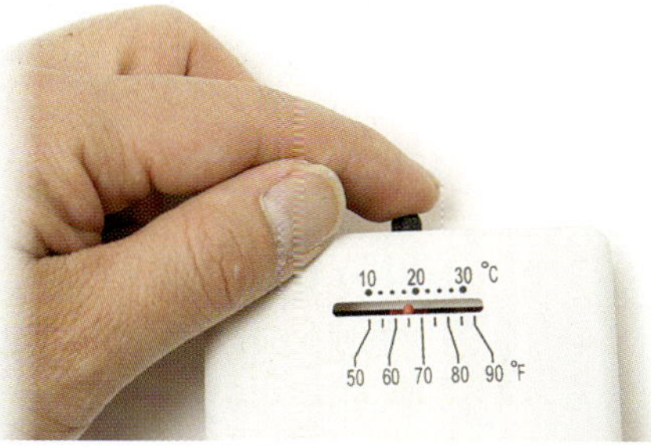

Figure 14.15

Home heating uses up energy. Why not wear a sweater instead of heating the whole house?

Be a Leader

Encourage others to act in a sustainable manner. Often, other people are just not aware that their actions are environmentally harmful. Help them understand and change their habits. You will help improve the environment.

Figure 14.16

Onondaga Nation children participate in their community's annual roadside cleanup program in Syracuse, New York. You can help, too. Remember, think globally, and act locally!

AFTER READING

1. Four groups are identified as leaders in the change to sustainable development in Figure 14.10. What other group of people might be leaders in the change? Hint: Think about people whose livelihoods are tied to the environment.
2. The section What Can You Do? on pages 296 to 298 describes five actions that you can take to protect the environment. With a partner, brainstorm at least three more things that you can do.
3. Figure 14.11 gives the results of a survey about what people are doing to protect the environment. Conduct a survey of people in your school or community. Find out about the number of people who participate in the same environmental practices as in Figure 14.11. Calculate percentages based on the total number of people you survey. Compare the results of your community with the results for all of Canada.

Knowledge and Understanding

1. **a)** Think about all the people you know. Who would you name as the person who
   - is most concerned about the environment?
   - is most careful to recycle?
   - does the best job of composting food waste?
   - is best at conserving natural resources?

   b) Why is it important that individual people act to protect the environment?

2. **a)** Define the words "sustainable" and "development" based on what you have learned in this chapter.

   b) Pick one resource and describe how it is used now. How can it be used in a sustainable manner?

3. Decide whether each of the following statements is true or false. Write each of the true statements in your notebook. Change each of the false statements to a true statement, and write the true one in your notebook.

   a) The First Nations harmed their environment by killing too many animals.

   b) Consumers have a role to play in protecting the environment because they make decisions about what to buy.

   c) People who want to protect the environment do not allow any trees to be cut down.

   d) The most important of the 3 Rs is "reduce."

4. Think about what you use at home. Make a list of five things that you could reduce as a way to help the environment. Identify the two items in your list that you think should be made a top priority by you and your family. Write an action plan for how you can bring about these reductions.

Inquiry/Research and Communication Skills

5. New technologies will help us to become a sustainable society. Research new technologies in transportation to find out ideas for the future. As you are doing your research, make sure that you record all the sources that you use, especially Internet sites. Present your research findings as a poster or some other visual display. Be sure to include pictures and diagrams in your report.

6. **a)** People have different attitudes toward the environment. Using the Internet and other library resources, collect three articles that show different points of view on one environmental topic. A good topic might be the expansion of the Churchill Falls power project, or the use of Ontario's or British Columbia's forests. Your teacher will help you select a topic.

   b) For each article that you collect, note if the writer is in favour of development or opposed to it, and the reasons the writer gives. You may wish to use a comparison chart (for example, a t-chart like the one below) to help you identify the reasons the writer gives for or against the proposed development.

Reasons in Favour of Development	Reasons Opposed to Development
•	•
•	•
•	•
•	•
•	•

7 Suppose you had a chance to interview the Canadian environmentalist David Suzuki on the topic of sustainable development. What questions would you ask him? To help plan for your interview, make up a list of seven questions that you could ask. Be sure to include some of these types of questions in your list:

- cause and effect (Why did ...?)
- speculation (What do you think would happen if ...?)
- comparison (Which is better ...?)

When you are finished your list of questions, share them with someone else in the class and together make up a new list of your five best questions. Consider creating a master list of the best questions from your class and including them in a class letter to the David Suzuki Foundation.

Figure 14.17

David Suzuki has worked very hard to protect Earth. He is the co-founder of the David Suzuki Foundation. Its mission is to "find ways for society to live in balance with the natural world that sustains us."

Map, Globe, and Graphic Skills

8. Carbon dioxide is a gas given off when fossil fuels are burned. It adds to the problem of global warming. The graph below identifies the sources of Canada's carbon dioxide emissions. For each source, suggest one way that emissions could be cut back.

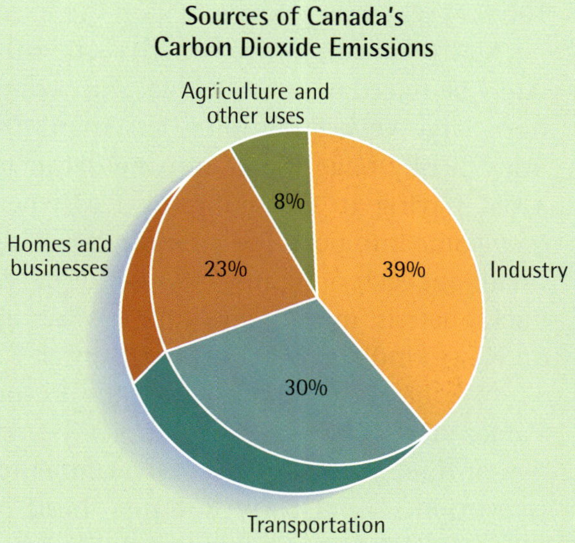

Figure 14.18

The graph shows the sources of Canada's carbon dioxide emissions.

9. One of the good signs for the environment is shown in the graph below (Figure 14.19). Look at it, and then answer the following questions:

a) In what year was the highest number of spills? About how many spills occurred?

b) In what year was the lowest number of spills? About how many spills took place?

c) Describe the general trend or pattern shown by the graph.

d) Give two reasons that might explain the pattern.

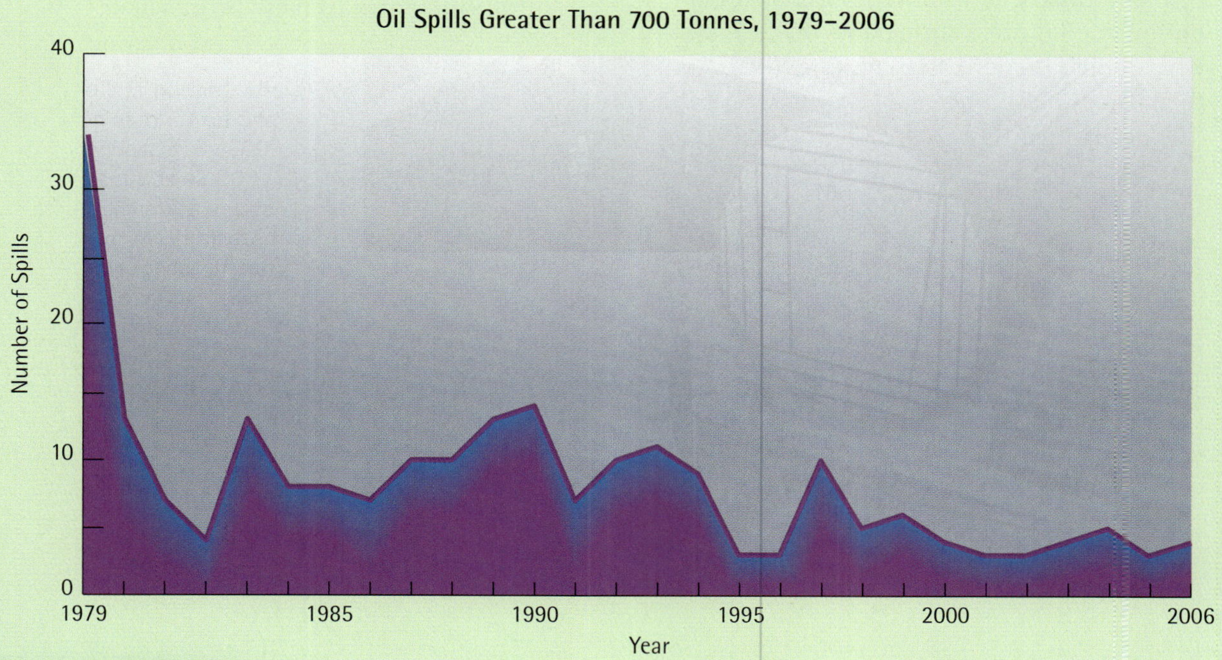

Figure 14.19

This graph shows the number of oil spills greater than 700 tonnes from 1979 to 2006.

Application

10 **a)** Discover some actions that your local government has taken to help your community's environment. You might look for actions that have been taken to reduce waste, improve water supplies, or fight pollution.

b) With a partner, brainstorm the factors that will affect the availability of natural resources, like water, air, and land, in your community. Remember, factors are those things that will affect or influence conditions. Then, group the items in your list into "Natural Factors" and "Human Factors."

c) Write a newspaper article or prepare a television news item to share your research findings and the results of your brainstorming session.

11 Draw a cartoon or make a pamphlet that encourages people to use less energy in their lives.

12 Suppose you are reading a newspaper and see the following article. Write a letter to the editor expressing your feelings about the problem being discussed. In your letter, explain how dumping oil is not a sustainable practice and what should be done in the future. (Refer to the Literacy Tip on persuasive writing on page 253 of Chapter 12.)

Oil spills killing birds by thousands

Newfoundland death toll "catastrophic"

Clandestine oil spills off the coast of Newfoundland are spelling death to as many as 100 000 sea birds a year.

Many of the spills, which can only rarely be traced to an individual ship, come from large vessels dumping less than 100 litres of oily bilge water into the ocean to avoid having to pay pumping fees when they come into port. The amounts of oil are small, but each one causes thousands of sea ducks, petrels, murres, and gulls to wash up on Newfoundland beaches every winter.

"We have the equivalent of the Exxon Valdez taking place off Newfoundland every two or three years .... It's an environmental catastrophe," said Barry Rothfuss, head of Maritime Atlantic Wildlife, a wildlife rehabilitation centre in New Brunswick.

Figure 14.20
Use this article to practise your persuasive writing skills.

Map Appendix

Global Landforms

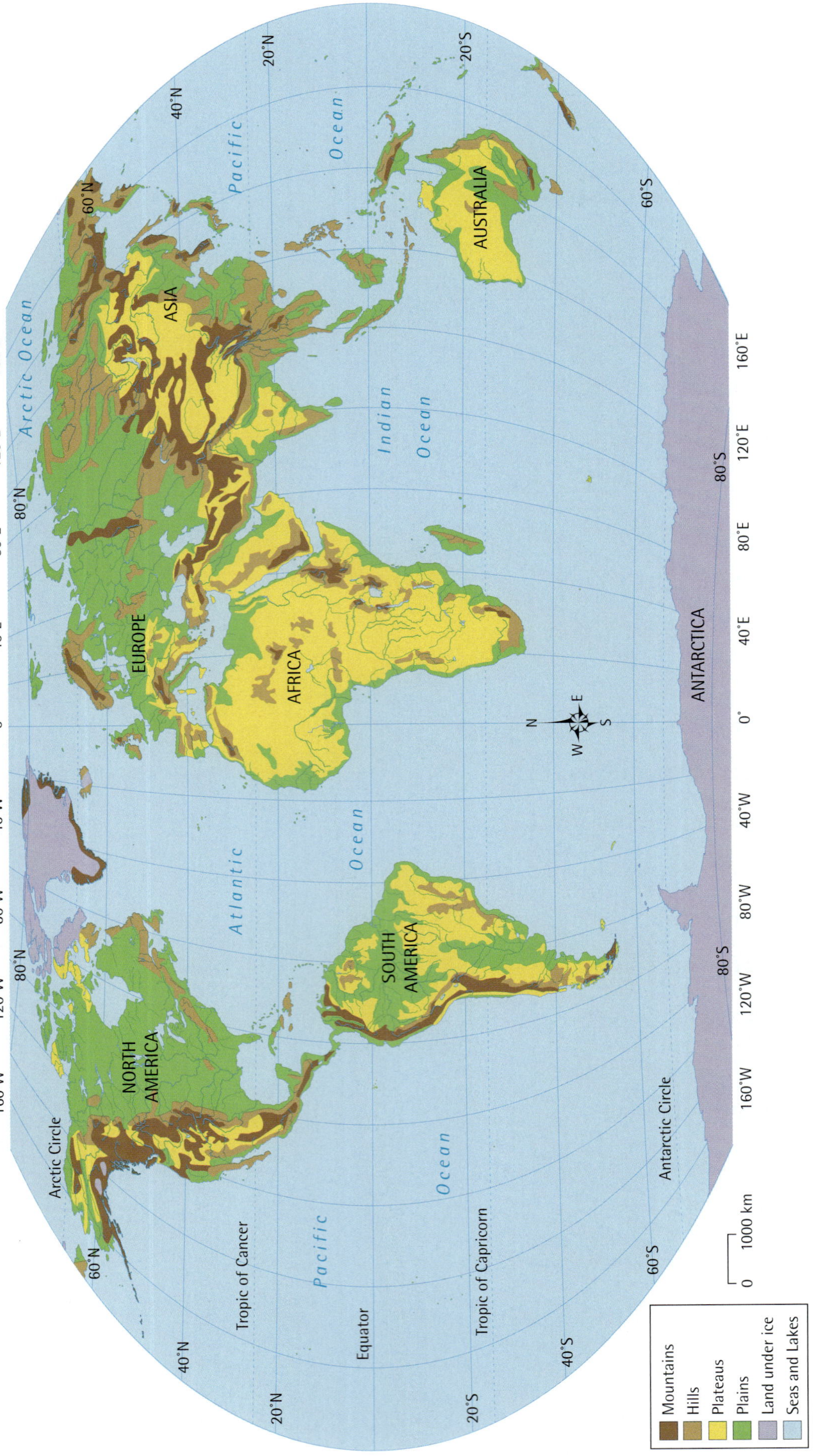

Plate Boundaries

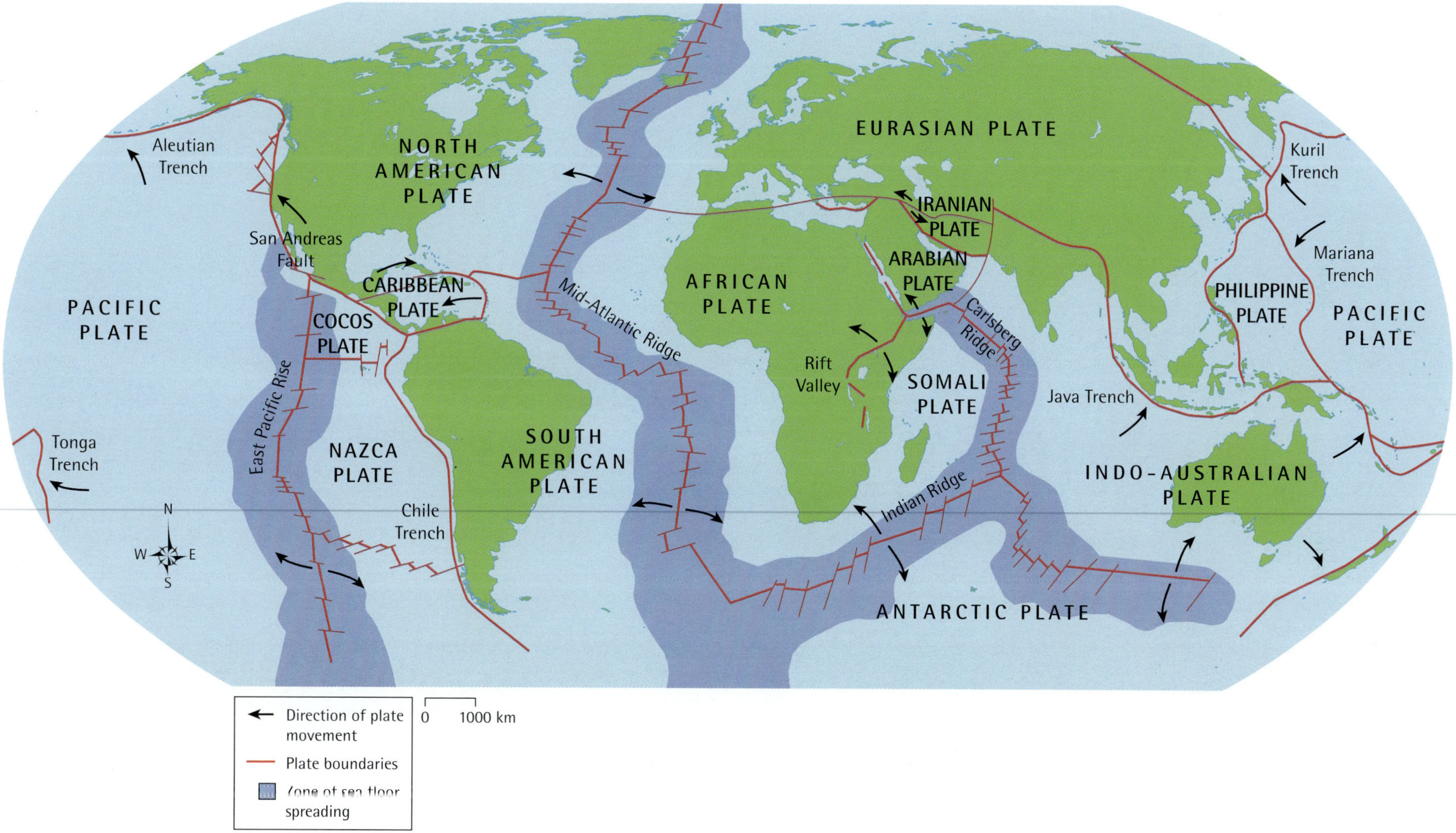

Volcanoes and Earthquakes

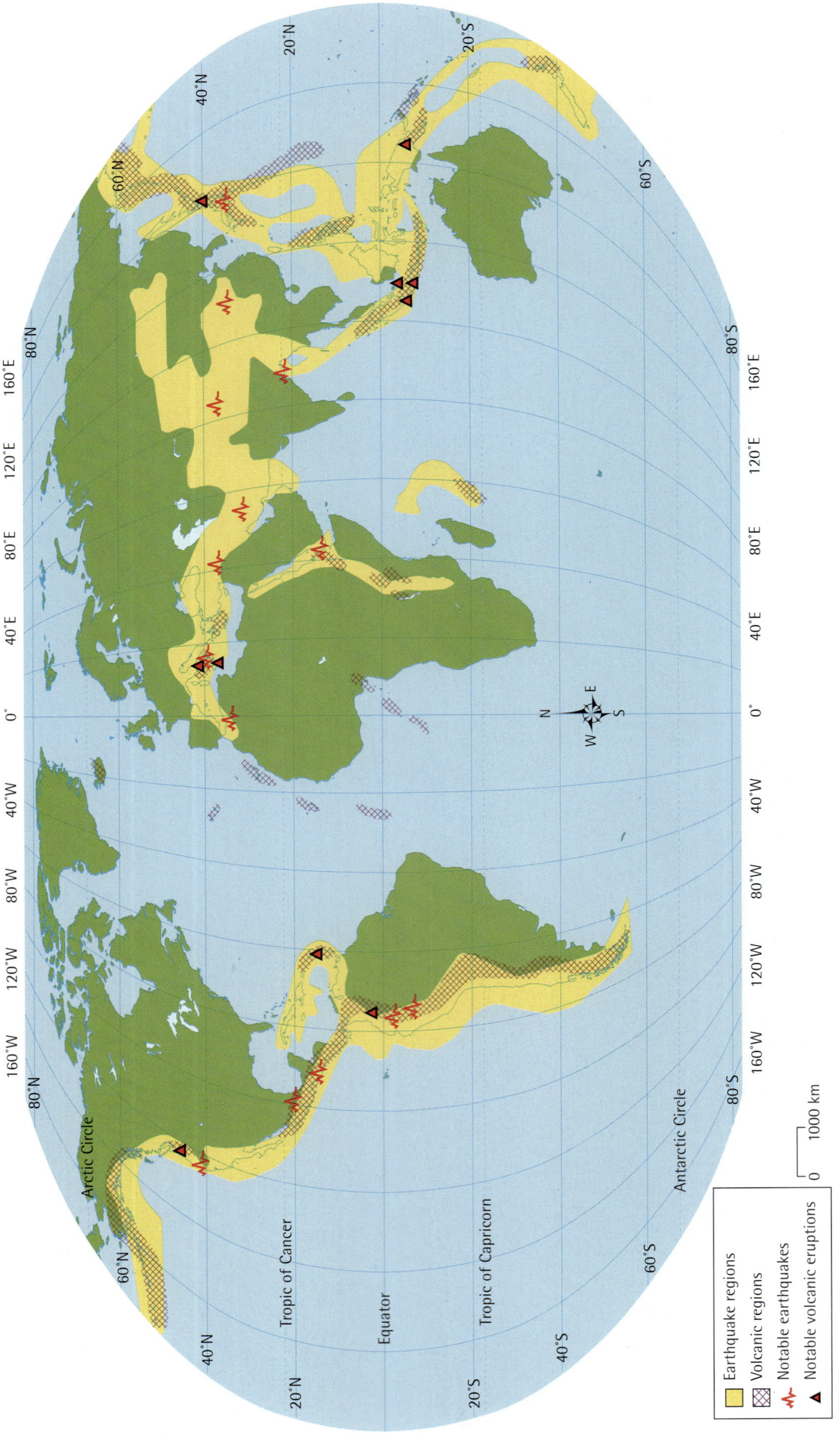

Global Climate Regions

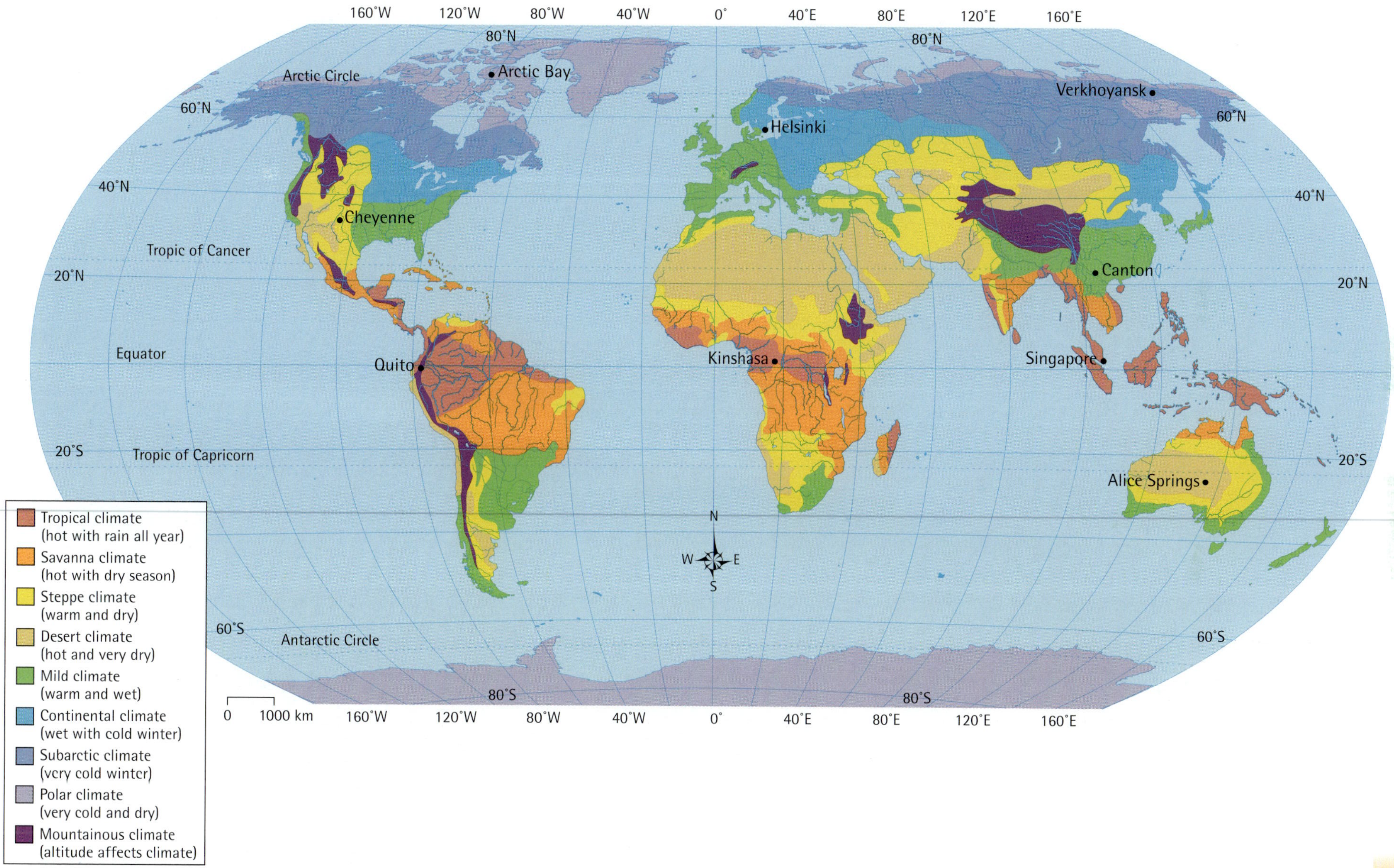

Annual Precipitation

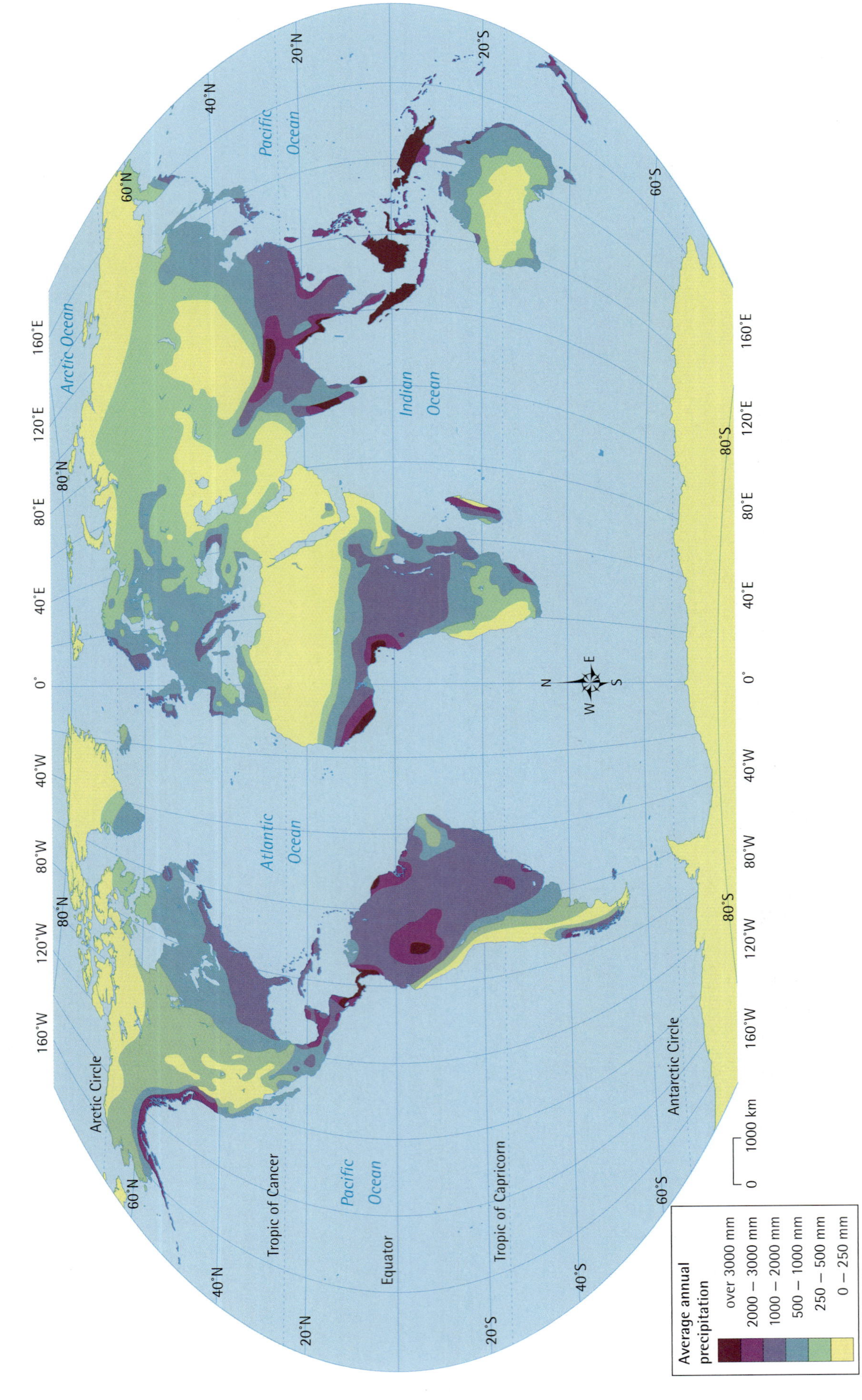

Global Temperatures

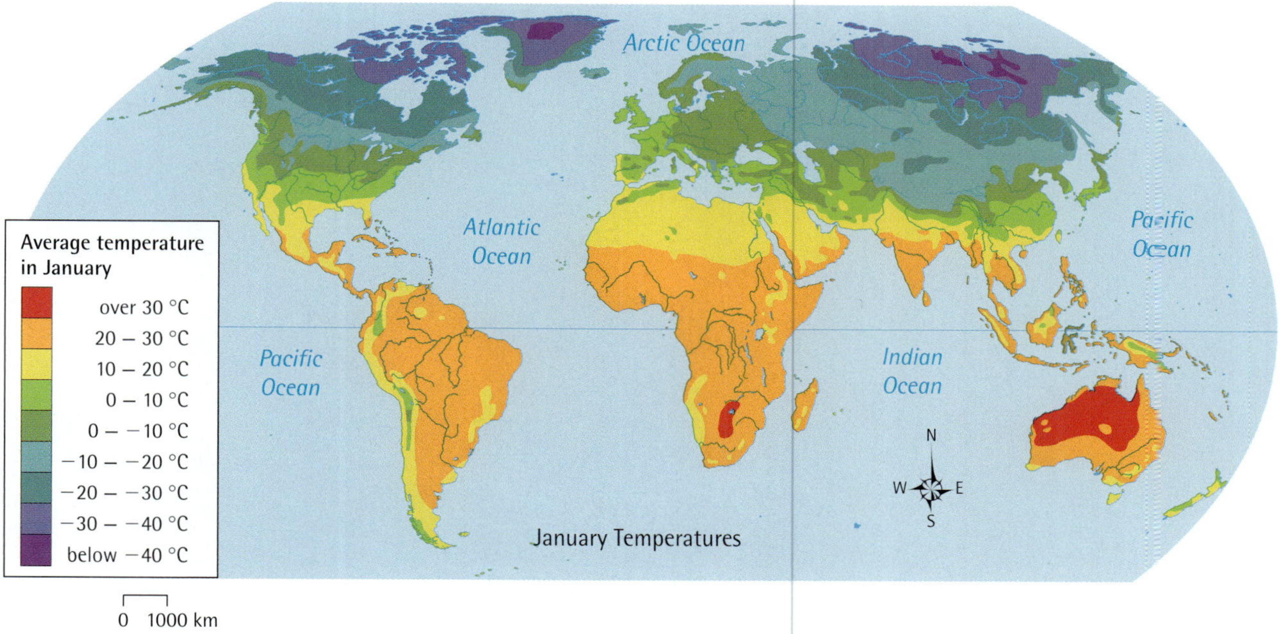

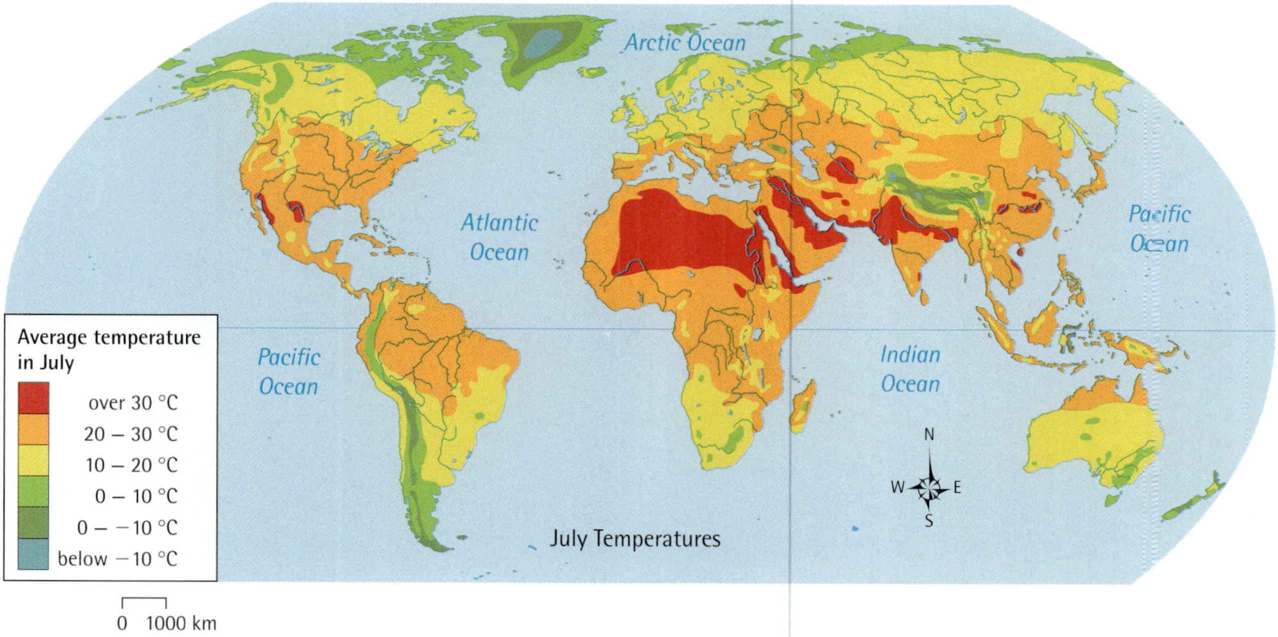

Global Wind Patterns

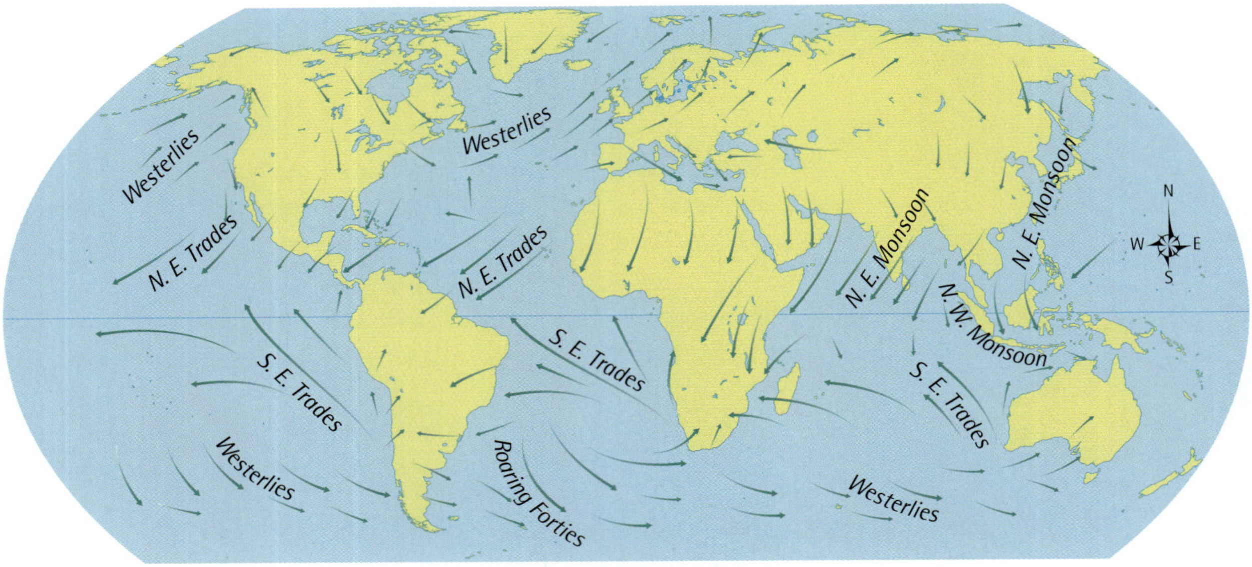

0 1000 km

January Prevailing Winds

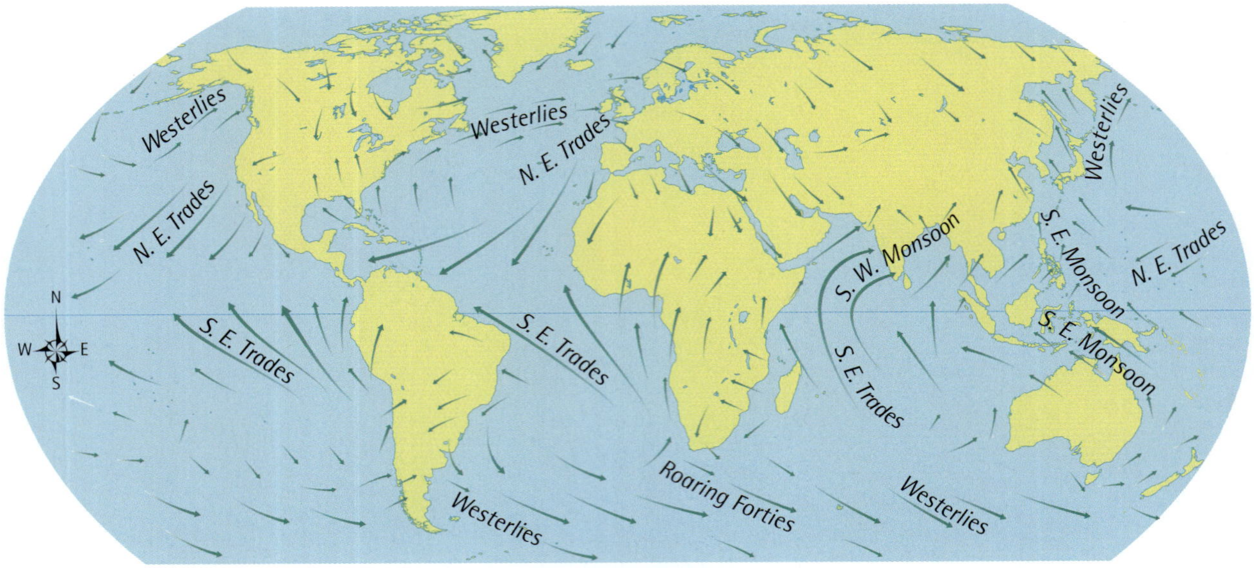

0 1000 km

July Prevailing Winds

Global Ocean Currents

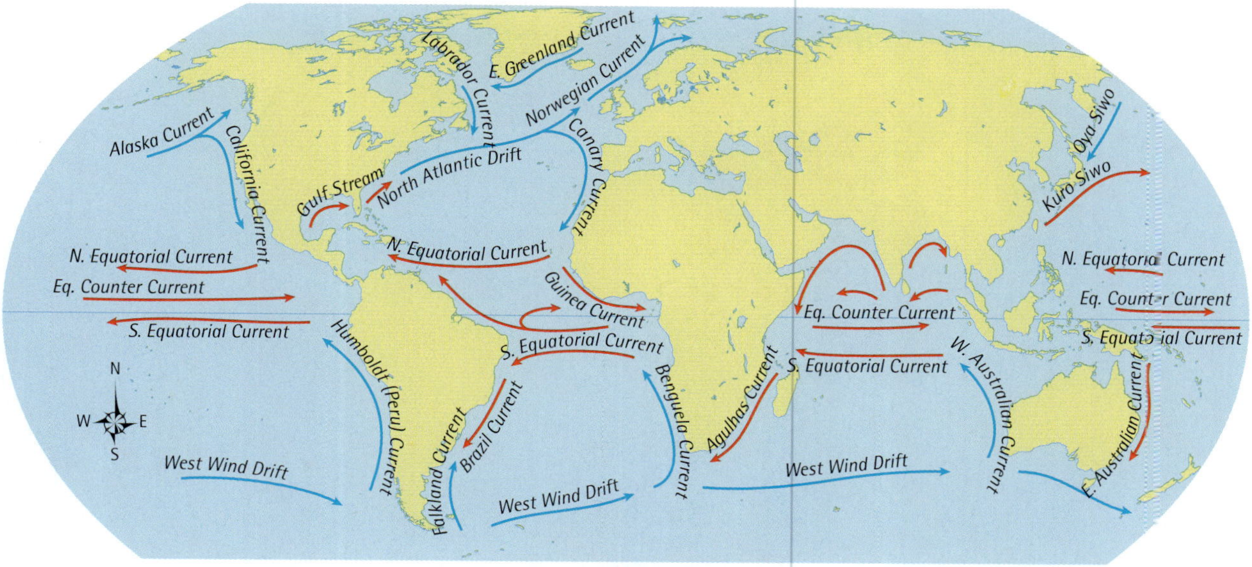

0 1000 km

January Prevailing Currents

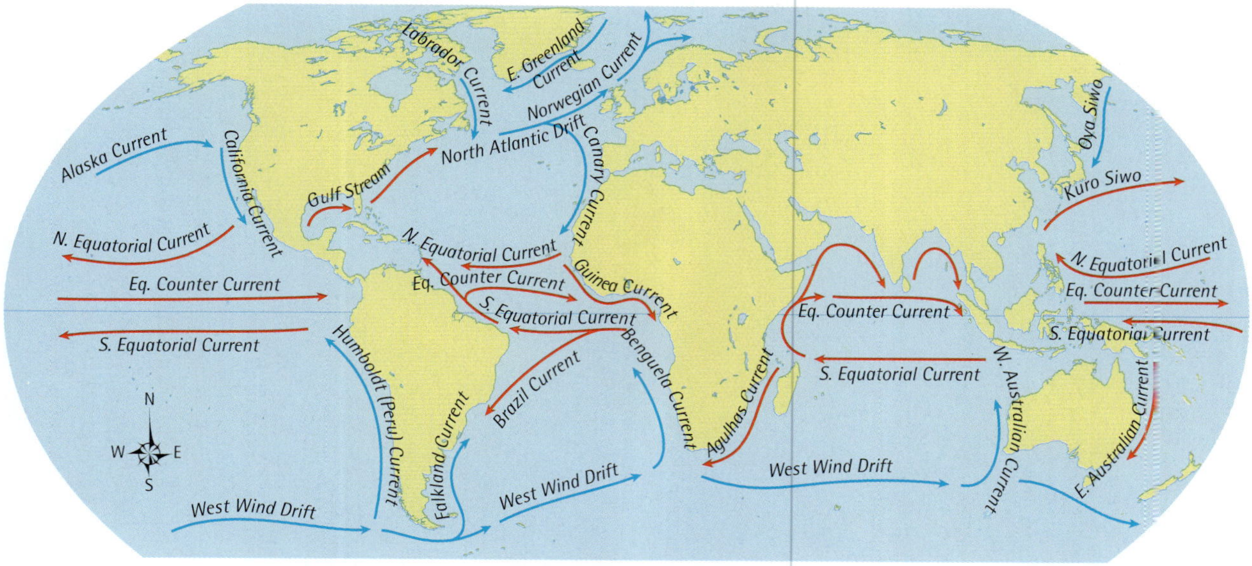

0 1000 km

July Prevailing Currents

- Cold current
- Warm current

Global Ecosystems

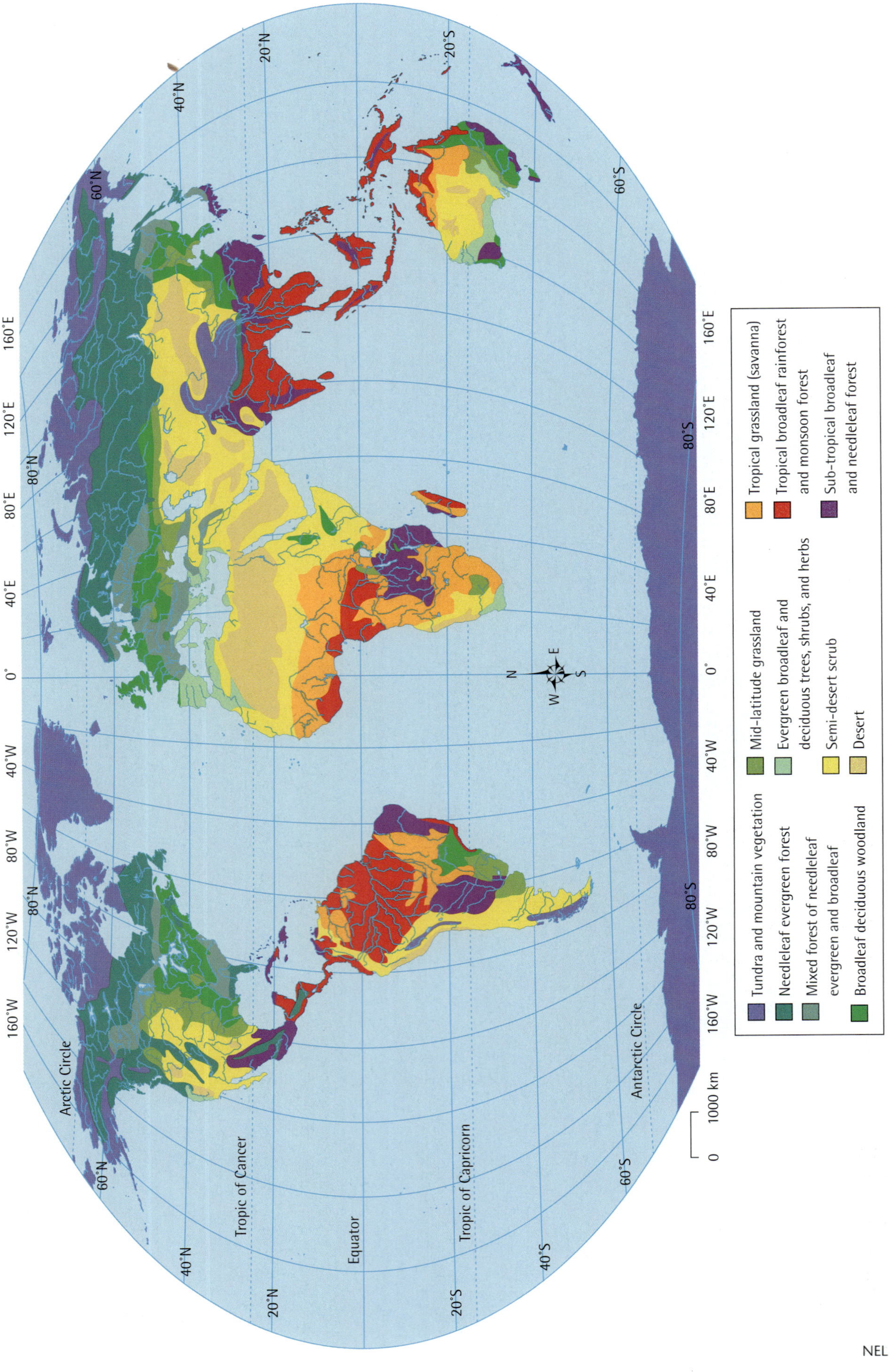

Rivers of the World

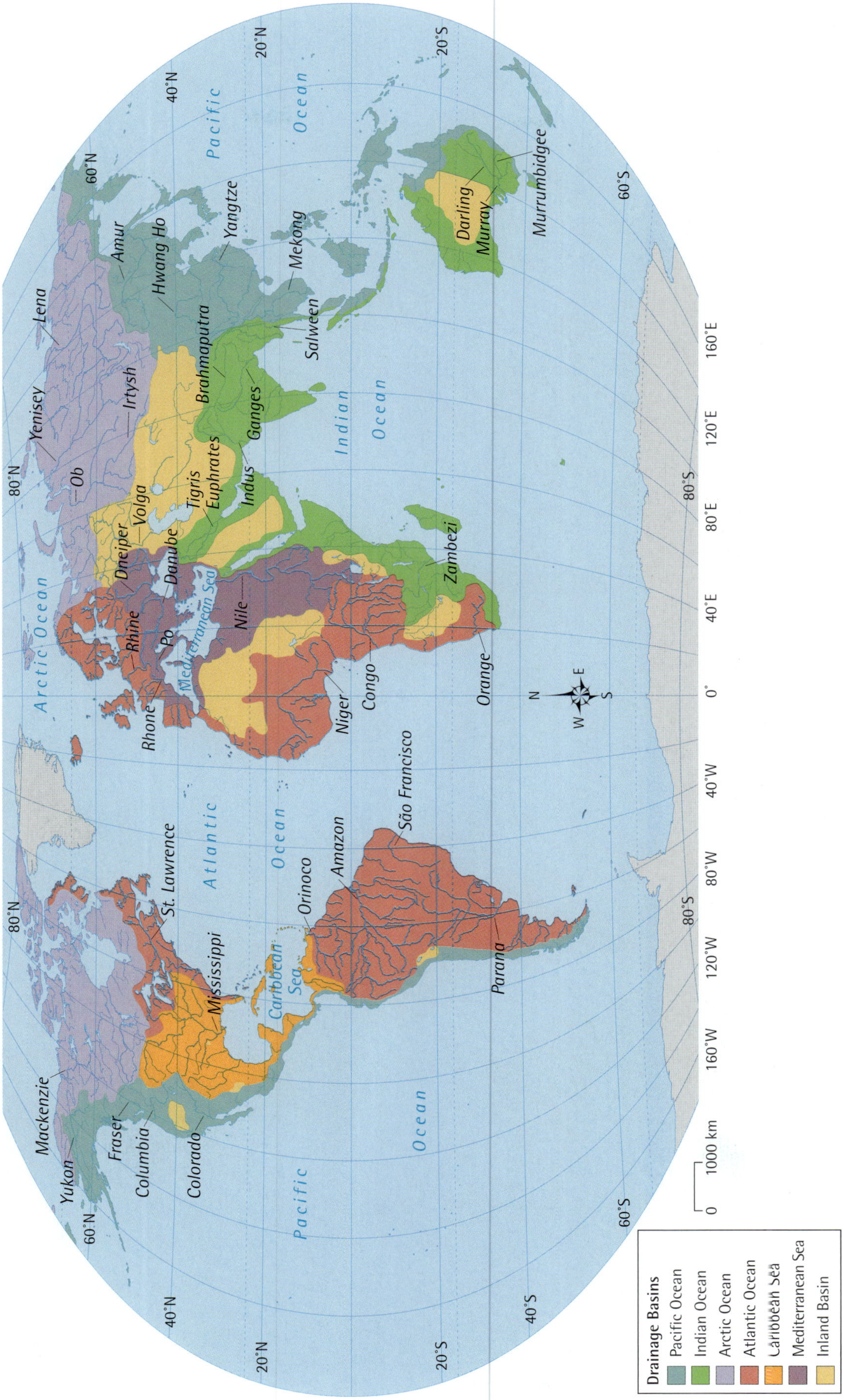

Land Use

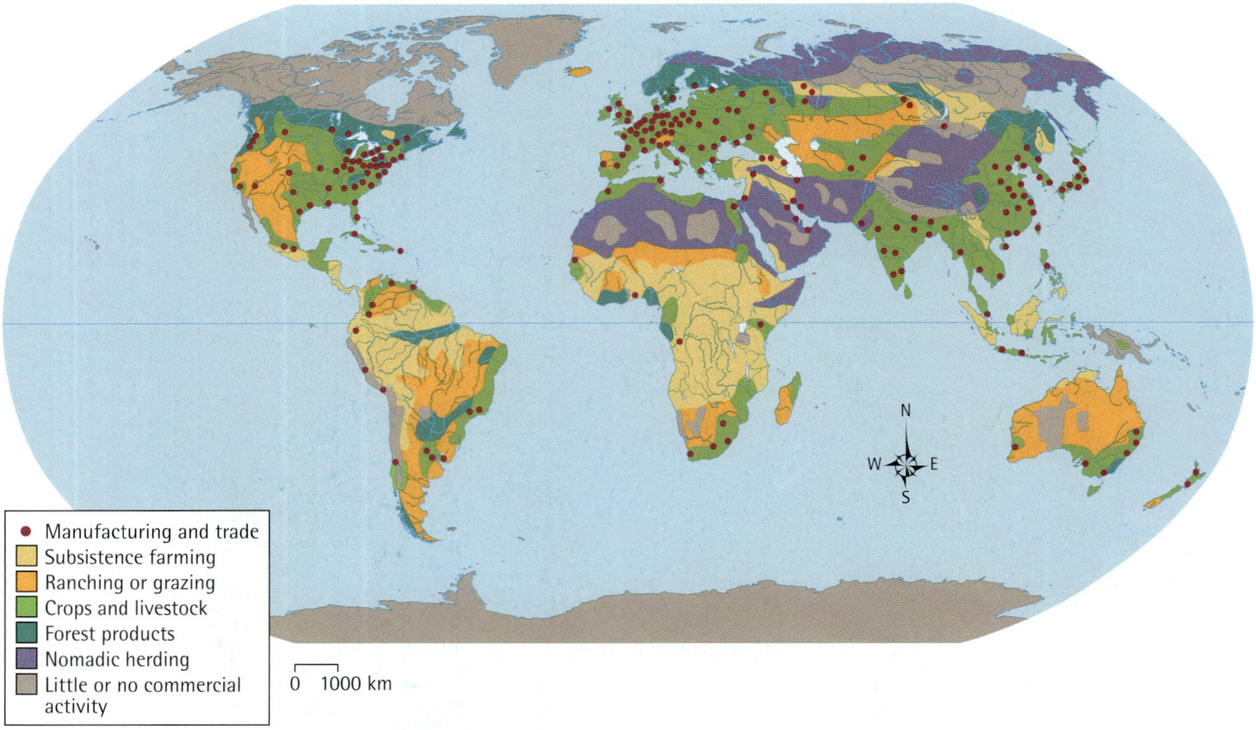

Agriculture and Fishing

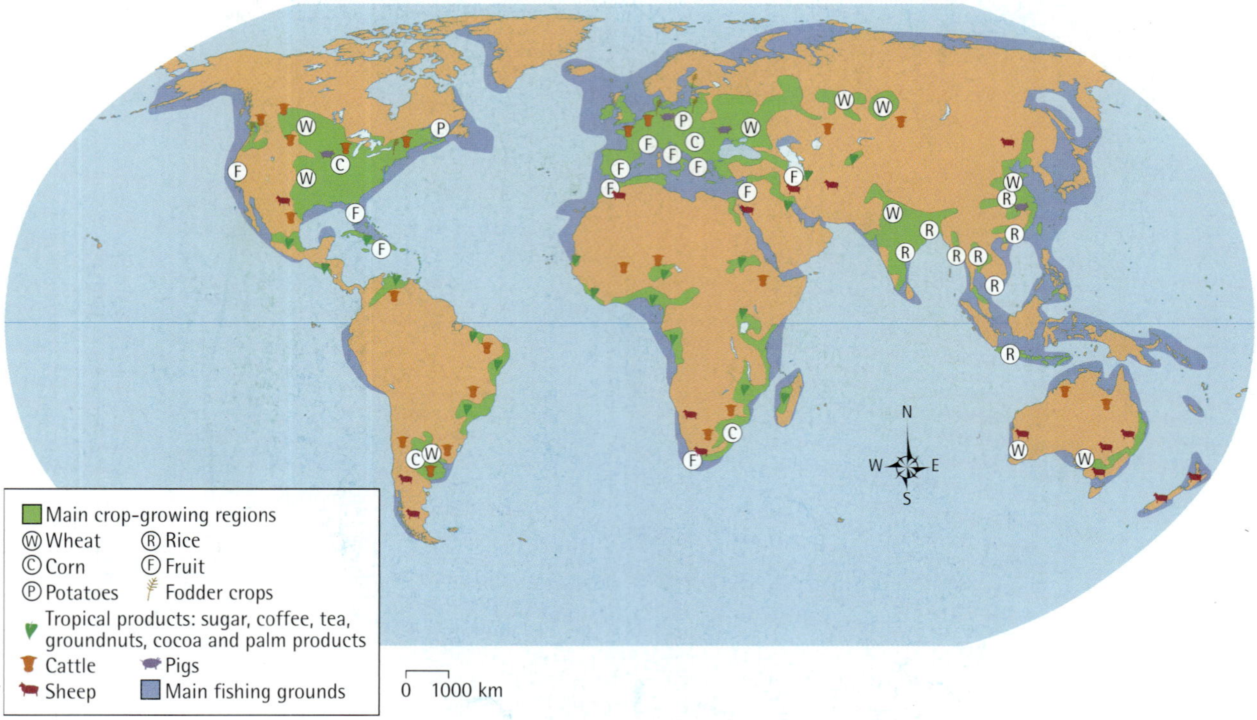

Oceans of the World

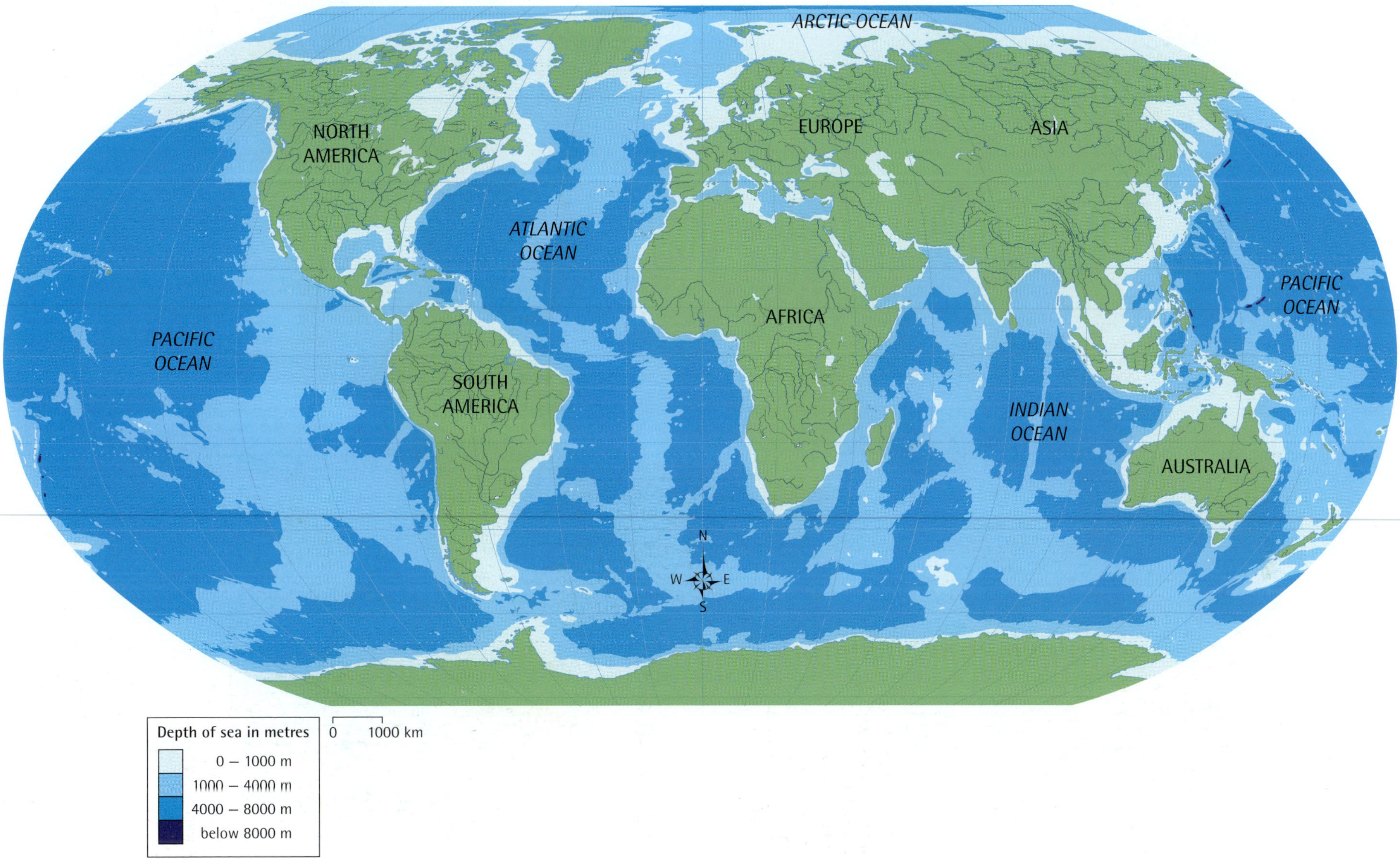

Countries of the World

30°E
60°E
90°E
120°E
150°E
ARCTIC
OCEAN
RUSSIA
60°N
NORWAY
SWEDEN
FINLAND
ESTONIA
LATVIA
LITHUANIA
RUS.
POLAND
BELARUS
GERM.
LUX.
CZECH REP.
UKRAINE
AUS.
SLOVAK REP.
HUN.
MOLDOVA
ROM.
ITALY
BULGARIA
MAC.
ALB.
GREECE
TURKEY
GEORGIA
ARMENIA
AZERBAIJAN
KAZAKHSTAN
UZBEKISTAN
TURKMENISTAN
KYRGYZSTAN
TAJIKISTAN
MONGOLIA
NORTH KOREA
SOUTH KOREA
JAPAN
Tokyo
CHINA
TUNISIA
CYPRUS
LEBANON
SYRIA
ISRAEL
JORDAN
IRAQ
Tehran
IRAN
AFGHANISTAN
PAKISTAN
NEPAL
BHUTAN
Cairo
LIBYA
EGYPT
KUWAIT
SAUDI ARABIA
QATAR
U. A. E.
OMAN
BANGLADESH
INDIA
BURMA (MYANMAR)
LAOS
VIETNAM
THAILAND
CAMBODIA
Taipei
TAIWAN
Manila
PHILIPPINES
International Date Line
30°N
PACIFIC
Tropic of Cancer
NIGER
CHAD
SUDAN
ERITREA
YEMEN
DJIBOUTI
ETHIOPIA
SOMALIA
NIGERIA
CAMEROON
CENTRAL AFRICAN REPUBLIC
GABON
CONGO
DEMOCRATIC REPUBLIC OF THE CONGO
UGANDA
KENYA
RWANDA
BURUNDI
TANZANIA
SRI LANKA
BRUNEI
MALAYSIA
Singapore
INDONESIA
Jakarta
EAST TIMOR
PAPUA NEW GUINEA
Equator
0°
OCEAN
INDIAN
ANGOLA
ZAMBIA
MALAWI
MOZAMBIQUE
MADAGASCAR
NAMIBIA
ZIMBABWE
BOTSWANA
Tropic of Capricorn
AUSTRALIA
FIJI
NEW CALEDONIA
SWAZILAND
SOUTH AFRICA
LESOTHO
Cape Town
30°S
OCEAN
NEW ZEALAND
60°S
ANTARCTICA

World Population Density

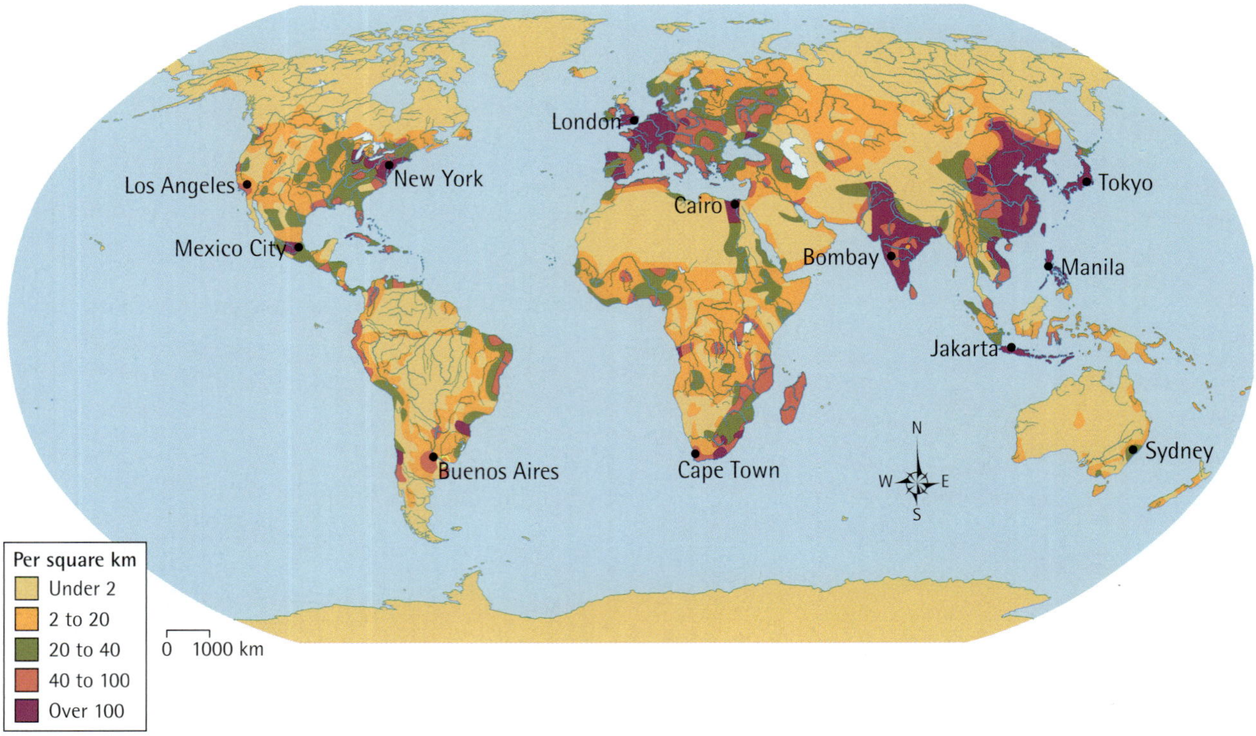

Time Zones

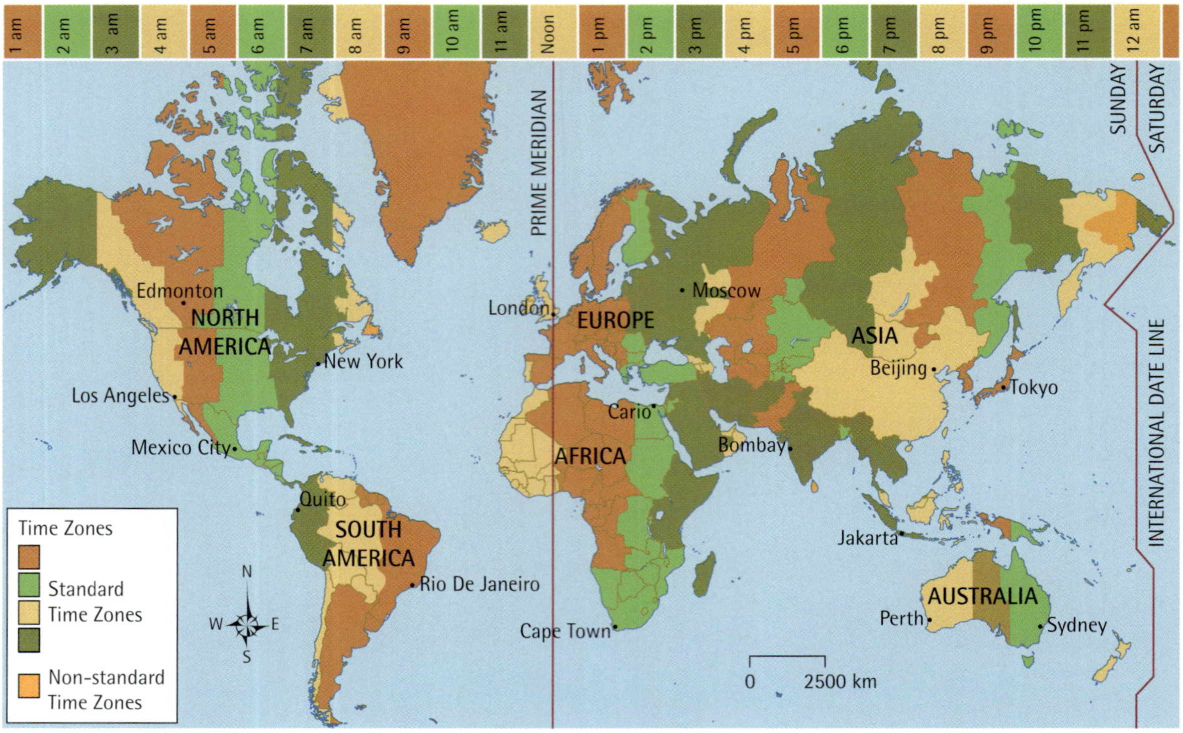

North America

Canada Physical

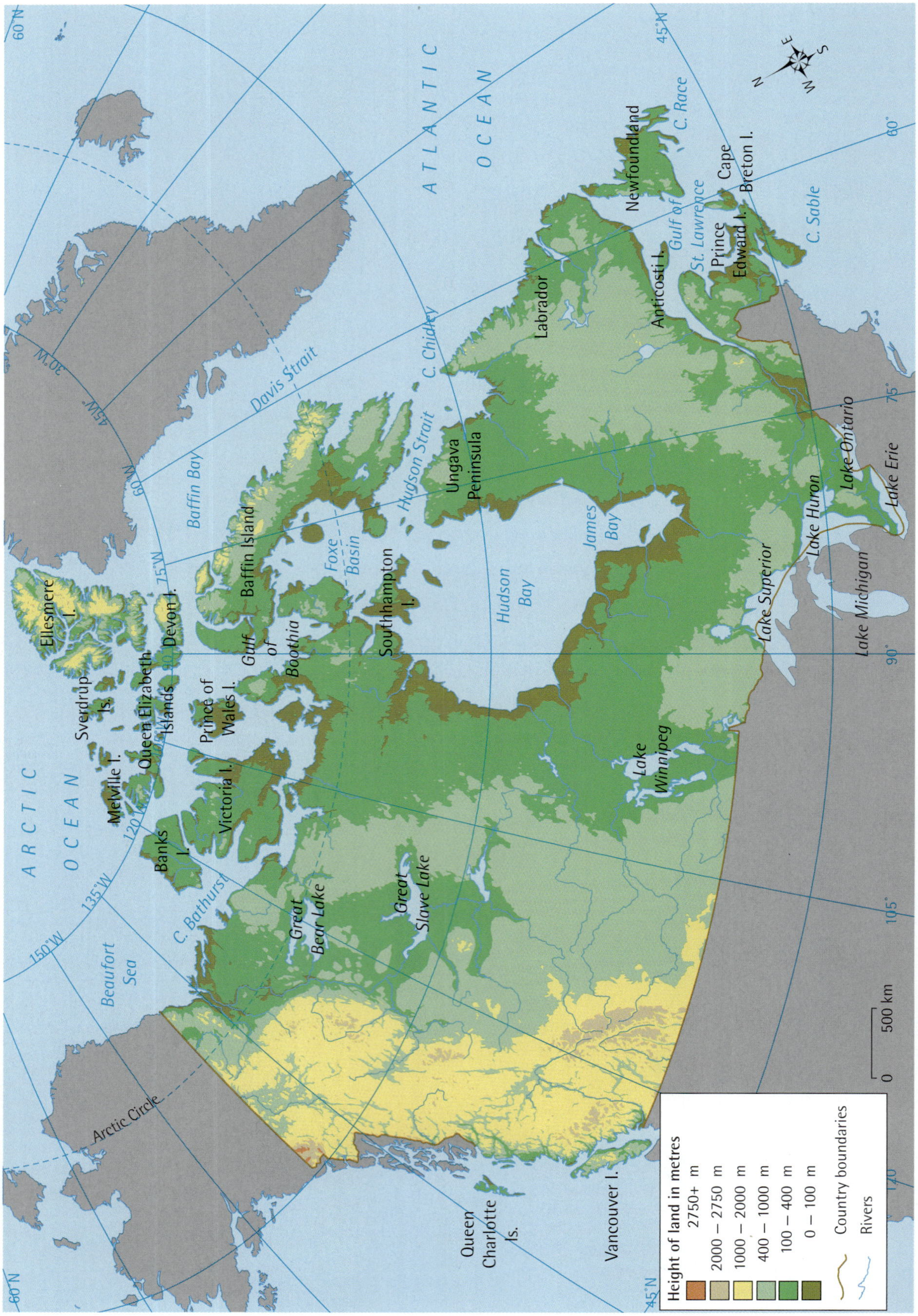

Canada Political

South America

Europe

Greenland Sea
ARCTIC OCEAN
Denmark Strait
ICELAND
Norwegian Sea
ATLANTIC OCEAN
White Sea
Arctic Circle
SWEDEN
FINLAND
NORWAY
ESTONIA
LATVIA
North Sea
DENMARK
Baltic Sea
LITHUANIA
RUSS.
RUSSIA
IRELAND
UNITED KINGDOM
NETH.
BELARUS
POLAND
English Channel
BELGIUM
GERMANY
UKRAINE
LUX.
CZECH REP.
SLOVAK REP.
FRANCE
MOLDOVA
AUSTRIA
SWITZERLAND
HUNGARY
Bay of Biscay
SLOV.
CROATIA
ROMANIA
GEORGIA
Black Sea
BOS./HER.
ANDORRA
SERBIA & MONTENEGRO
BULGARIA
ITALY
Adriatic Sea
PORTUGAL
SPAIN
MACEDONIA
ALBANIA
TURKEY
GREECE
Aegean Sea
Strait of Gibraltar
Mediterranean Sea
SYRIA
CYPRUS
MALTA
IRAQ
LEBANON
MOROCCO
TUNISIA
Mediterranean Sea
ISRAEL
JORDAN
ALGERIA
SAUDI ARABIA
LIBYA
EGYPT
20°W
10°W
0°
10°E
20°E
30°E
40°E
50°E
60°N
50°N
40°N
30°N
N
W
E
S
Height of land in metres
2750+ m
2000 – 2750 m
1000 – 2000 m
400 – 1000 m
100 – 400 m
0 – 100 m
Country boundaries
Rivers
0
500 km

Africa

PORTUGAL
SPAIN
ITALY
GREECE
TURKEY
MALTA
Strait of Gibraltar
Tangier
Algiers
Tunis
Oran
TUNISIA
CYPRUS
SYRIA
Casablanca
Rabat
Tripoli
Mediterranean Sea
LEBANON
ISRAEL
IRAN
IRAQ
Marrakesh
Benghazi
Alexandria
JORDAN
MOROCCO
ALGERIA
Cairo
KUWAIT
El Aaiún
In Salah
LIBYA
EGYPT
WESTERN SAHARA
Al Jawf
Aswan
QATAR
SAUDI ARABIA
Tropic of Cancer
MAURITANIA
Wadi Halfa
MALI
Port Sudan
Red Sea
Nouakchott
SUDAN
Timbuktu
NIGER
CHAD
ERITREA
Dakar
Asmara
YEMEN
SENEGAL
BURKINA FASO
Niamey
Khartoum
GAMBIA
Banjul
Bamako
N'Djamena
El Obeid
DJIBOUTI
Gulf of Aden
Djibouti
GUINEA-BISSAU
Bissau
Ouagadougou
Kano
GUINEA
BENIN
NIGERIA
Hargeisa
Conakry
Freetown
COTE D'IVOIRE
GHANA
TOGO
Abuja
Wau
Addis Ababa
SIERRA LEONE
CENTRAL AFRICAN REPUBLIC
ETHIOPIA
Lomé
Lagos
Monrovia
Abidjan
Porto Novo
CAMEROON
LIBERIA
Accra
Douala
Bangui
Juba
SOMALIA
Gulf of Guinea
Yaoundé
UGANDA
KENYA
EQUATORIAL GUINEA
Kisagani
Kampala
Mogadishu
Equator
Libreville
CONGO
RWANDA
GABON
DEM. REP. OF THE CONGO
Kigali
Nairobi
Franceville
BURUNDI
Brazzaville
Bujumbura
Mombasa
Pointe-Noire
Kinshasa
Kananga
TANZANIA
Mbuji-Mayi
Dodoma
Dar es Salaam
ATLANTIC OCEAN
Luanda
Lubumbashi
Benguela
ANGOLA
MALAWI
Ndola
Lilongwe
Nacala
ZAMBIA
Blantyre
MOZAMBIQUE
Lusaka
Harare
Mozambique Channel
ZIMBABWE
Antananarivo
NAMIBIA
BOTSWANA
Beira
Bulawayo
Tropic of Capricorn
Walvis Bay (S. Africa)
Windhoek
MADAGASCAR
Gaborone
Pretoria
Maputo
Johannesburg
SWAZILAND
INDIAN OCEAN
LESOTHO
SOUTH AFRICA
Durban
Cape Town
East London
Port Elizabeth
35°N
30°N
25°N
20°N
15°N
10°N
5°N
0°
5°S
10°S
15°S
20°S
25°S
30°S
35°S
15°W
10°W
5°W
0°
5°E
10°E
15°E
20°E
25°E
30°E
35°E
40°E
45°E
50°E
N
S
E
W
Height of land in metres
2750+ m
2000 – 2750 m
1000 – 2000 m
400 – 1000 m
100 – 400 m
0 – 100 m
Country boundaries
Cities and towns
Rivers
0
500 km

Middle East and Asia

Australia

INDIAN OCEAN
PACIFIC OCEAN
Timor Sea
Arafura Sea
Gulf of Carpentaria
Torres Str.
Coral Sea
Solomon Sea
Great Barrier Reef
Great Australian Bight
Tasman Sea
Tropic of Capricorn
JAVA
BALI
SUMBAWA
SUMBA
FLORES
INDONESIA
WEST TIMOR
EAST TIMOR
TANIMBAR
ARU
WEST PAPUA
PAPUA NEW GUINEA
Port Moresby
NEW BRITAIN
SOLOMON ISLANDS
VANUATU
FIJI
NEW CALEDONIA (France)
AUSTRALIA
WESTERN AUSTRALIA
NORTHERN TERRITORY
SOUTH AUSTRALIA
QUEENSLAND
NEW SOUTH WALES
VICTORIA
TASMANIA
Port Hedland
Broome
Newman
Geraldton
Perth
Bunbury
Albany
Esperance
Kalgoorlie-Boulder
Darwin
Alice Springs
Whyalla
Adelaide
Mount Isa
Cairns
Townsville
Winton
Mackay
Rockhampton
Bundaberg
Charleville
Brisbane
Gold Coast
Broken Hill
Mildura
Tamworth
Dubbo
Newcastle
Sydney
Wollongong
Canberra
Melbourne
Geelong
Launceston
Hobart
NEW ZEALAND
NORTH ISLAND
SOUTH ISLAND
Auckland
Hamilton
Wellington
Christchurch
Dunedin
Invercargill
N
E
S
W
115°E
120°E
125°E
130°E
135°E
140°E
145°E
150°E
155°E
160°E
165°E
170°E
175°E
10°S
15°S
20°S
25°S
30°S
35°S
40°S
45°S
Height of land in metres
2750+ m
2000 – 2750 m
1000 – 2000 m
400 – 1000 m
100 – 400 m
0 – 100 m
Country boundaries
Cities and towns
Rivers
0
500 km

Pacific Rim

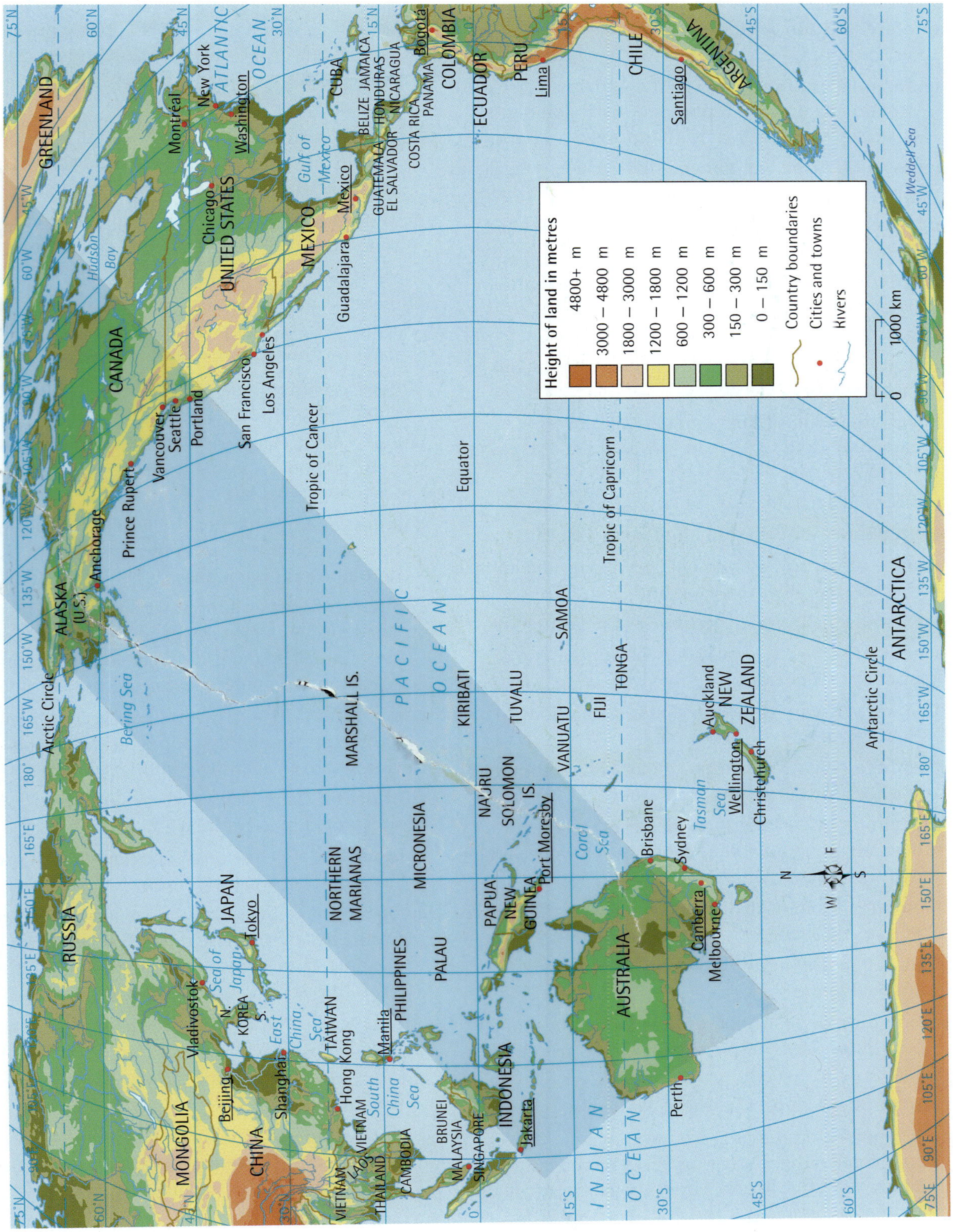

Height of land in metres
4800+ m
3000 – 4800 m
1800 – 3000 m
1200 – 1800 m
600 – 1200 m
300 – 600 m
150 – 300 m
0 – 150 m
Country boundaries
Cities and towns
Rivers
0 1000 km
N S E W
Arctic Circle
Tropic of Cancer
Equator
Tropic of Capricorn
Antarctic Circle
PACIFIC OCEAN
ATLANTIC OCEAN
INDIAN OCEAN
Bering Sea
Hudson Bay
Gulf of Mexico
Sea of Japan
East China Sea
South China Sea
Coral Sea
Tasman Sea
Weddell Sea
GREENLAND
CANADA
ALASKA (U.S.)
UNITED STATES
MEXICO
CUBA
BELIZE
JAMAICA
HONDURAS
GUATEMALA
EL SALVADOR
NICARAGUA
COSTA RICA
PANAMA
COLOMBIA
ECUADOR
PERU
CHILE
ARGENTINA
RUSSIA
MONGOLIA
CHINA
N. KOREA
S. KOREA
JAPAN
TAIWAN
PHILIPPINES
VIETNAM
LAOS
THAILAND
CAMBODIA
MALAYSIA
BRUNEI
SINGAPORE
INDONESIA
PAPUA NEW GUINEA
AUSTRALIA
NEW ZEALAND
NORTHERN MARIANAS
MICRONESIA
PALAU
MARSHALL IS.
NAURU
SOLOMON IS.
KIRIBATI
TUVALU
VANUATU
FIJI
TONGA
SAMOA
ANTARCTICA
Anchorage
Prince Rupert
Vancouver
Seattle
Portland
San Francisco
Los Angeles
Chicago
Montréal
New York
Washington
Guadalajara
Mexico
Bogotá
Lima
Santiago
Vladivostok
Beijing
Shanghai
Hong Kong
Tokyo
Manila
Jakarta
Port Moresby
Perth
Brisbane
Sydney
Canberra
Melbourne
Auckland
Wellington
Christchurch

Glossary

absolute location — the precise position of any point on Earth

acidic precipitation — rain or snow that is contaminated by acids from industrial pollutants, especially sulphur dioxide and nitrogen

aggregate — structural mineral that includes gravel and sand; used to build roads, buildings, and sidewalks

air mass — a large body of air with nearly the same conditions of temperature and humidity throughout

alternative energy source — energy source that is based on renewable energy, such as wind or solar power, rather than fossil fuels

altitude — the vertical height of land; measured in metres above sea level

Appalachian Mountains — mountain ranges extending from Georgia to Newfoundland in eastern North America

aquifer — large underground natural reservoir

atmosphere — the mass of air surrounding Earth

balance of nature — the number of plants and animals that an ecosystem can support

barrier — something that makes it difficult to move

beneficiation — the process of separating useful ores from waste materials

biome — a large region with similar vegetation throughout

biosphere — living organisms and their environments; the life zone of air, land, and water

biotechnology — scientific changes to the genetic engineering of plants and animals to produce more useful characteristics

boundary — a limit that is put on a region that defines its size and shape

carat — a unit of mass for precious stones equal to 200 milligrams

carbon dioxide — a colourless gas formed by animals' breathing, plants' respiration, decay of matter, and combustion

cartographer — a person who makes maps

cash crop — a crop that is produced to be sold to earn an income rather than to be eaten by the farmer's family, like strawberries, cotton, sugar cane, coffee, and pineapples

chinook — a warm, dry wind that blows down the eastern side of the Rocky Mountains and can raise the temperature as much as 24 °C in as little as 15 minutes

chlorofluorocarbon (CFC) — chemical compound used in air conditioners and aerosol sprays that thins Earth's atmosphere

clear-cut logging — a type of logging that cuts down every tree in a huge rectangular area; completely destroys the ecosystem of the forest

climate — seasonal weather patterns observed over many years; yearly patterns that emerge when all the daily weather patterns are combined

climate region — an area defined by having similar climate conditions

commercial agriculture — a farming method where farmers produce a small variety of crops, livestock, or products for sale

compost — a helpful, healthy fertilizer, made from household waste broken down by natural decomposers like worms

coniferous forest — a forest with trees that keep their small needle-shaped leaves all year round; bear their seeds in cones; and grow where it is cooler; tree species include pine, spruce, and fir

continental drift — a theory that the continents were at one time united in a super-continent and have slowly moved apart over millions of years

continental shelf — the shallow submerged zone of an ocean next to a continent

contour line — a line on a topographic map used to join points of equal elevation

co-operative — an association owned by and operated for the benefit of those using its services; for example, farmers can work together to sell their crops through community co-operatives

criteria — a feature that is considered in defining a region

cut-off slope — the river bank that is eroded by the flow of water

deciduous forest— a forest of trees with broad leaves that fall in the autumn (including oak, maple, beech, and hickory); occurs where it is warmer

deficit — moisture shortage

demand — pressures that we put on resources to meet our needs and wants, such as our demand for materials to build houses

dendritic drainage pattern — river drainage pattern formed when tributaries join the main branch of the river in a V-shaped junction; the V points downstream, toward the mouth of the river

desalination — the process of turning salt/sea water into fresh water using distillation

desert — a region of extreme dryness, generally under 250 millimetres of precipitation annually

domesticate — to change animals or plants from a wild to a tame or cultivated condition; for example, the domestication of wild dogs to make them pets or working dogs

domestication — taming of wild animals or the cultivating of wild plants

drainage area or **drainage basin** — the area drained by a river system

drainage divide — the line of high ground that separates water flowing in one direction from another

drip irrigation — one of the main types of irrigation; water pipes run to each plant so that water drips directly onto the roots; little water is wasted; involves high costs (for example, labour, pipes, technology)

eastings — locational coordinates moving from west to east on a topographic map

ecology — the branch of science involved in the study of organisms and their relationships to the environment

ecosystem — a specific environment where certain plants and animals live together; it includes the soil, the climate, and the physical location

ecozone — an area created by combining natural features and human activities

El Niño — a huge mass of unusually warm surface water that is part of major ocean current circulation in the central Pacific Ocean

endangered — a species that is threatened with extinction and needs protection to survive

environmental assessment — a scientific study of what effects a project will have on the natural and human systems of an area

extinct — a species that has died out or has been eliminated

fair trade — organizations have been set up to make sure the producers of the crops get a fair price; producers are required to reduce their use of chemical fertilizers and pesticides, and to take other actions that are more sustainable; when consumers buy products labelled as fair trade, they are helping farmers in poor countries overcome poverty and to farm in a sustainable manner

fault zone — an area of weakness in Earth's crust, often along plate boundaries

finite — a limited supply, such as having only so much of a mineral on Earth

flow resource — a resource that does not stay in one location (for example, solar energy, winds, and moving water); moves about because of natural actions in the physical environment; also referred to as the global commons

fold mountain — mountain formed when plates collide and the resulting pressure forces the rock to bend and rise up

functional characteristic — a way to define a region by the way it is used (for example, for farming or for industry)

functional region — an area defined by how the region is used

geologic region — an area defined by common features related to rock structure and rock type

geothermal spring — heated water produced deep inside Earth that rises to the surface

global commons — elements of the environment shared by all people, such as water, solar energy, and air; also referred to as flow resources

Global Positioning System (GPS) — an electronic unit that receives signals from a satellite to pinpoint a location precisely

greenhouse effect — more and more heat is trapped in the atmosphere due to the increase of gases like carbon dioxide caused by our activities

greenhouse gas — results from the burning of fossil fuels, such as coal, gasoline, and natural gas; traps and holds heat in the atmosphere, and stops it from escaping back out to space; produces a similar effect to the glass in a greenhouse that you might see in a garden centre or on a farm

grid coordinate system — a system for locating points using numbered line patterns on a map; the numbered line patterns help you find absolute, or exact, locations

groundwater — water that is held or flowing beneath Earth's surface

habitat — the place or region where each living thing survives

hardwood — broadleaf trees found in warmer temperate locations (for example, maple and oak trees) whose wood is hard and dense; used for furniture and flooring

headwater — the source or beginning of a river

human characteristic — one of the ways to define a region, which includes religion, language, or culture

human region — an area defined by features that are people-based (for example, population density, language, religion, or culture)

humus — decaying plant and animal life found in topsoil

hydrologic cycle — the natural cycle that moves water from the oceans to the land and back to the oceans; winds carry moisture from the oceans over land where it falls back to Earth; this water flows down to the ocean

hydrosphere — all of the water vapour and bodies of water that cover much of Earth's surface

Industrial Revolution — the period that saw the changeover from a mainly farm-oriented society to a mainly industrial society, beginning in England in the mid-1700s

Innuitian Mountains — the mountain ranges of the Arctic Islands

Interior Plain — the vast plain that includes the Great Plains of the United States, the Prairie grasslands, and the Mackenzie Valley from the Gulf of Mexico to the Arctic Ocean

introduced species — a new species in an ecosystem often brought in by people's activities

island arc — volcanic islands that form an arc shape in the Pacific Ocean

land-based ecozone — area created by combining natural features and human activities on our continents

landform — a natural physical feature of Earth's surface, such as a plateau, a mountain, or a plain

landform region — an area defined by having the same surface features; area comprised mainly of one major landform, like a mountain region

latitude — imaginary lines on Earth drawn east and west; latitude measures are given north and south of the equator

light year — the distance light travels in one year, about 9 460 500 000 000 kilometres

lithosphere — the outer, solid part of Earth, including the crust and upper mantle

logging — one of the main forest industries; the activity of cutting down trees and using the trunks of the trees for building materials

longitude — imaginary lines on Earth drawn north and south; longitude measures are given east and west of the Prime Meridian

low-pressure area — an area where the atmospheric pressure is lower than the surrounding area

magma — molten rock found below Earth's crust that can often make its way to the surface through crustal weaknesses

mantle — the middle layer of Earth, lying between the crust and the core

marine-based ecozone — area created by combining natural features and human activities in our lakes and oceans

meander — an S-shaped curve in a river

mental map — a sketch of a map from memory, using images that we carry in our minds, usually of familiar places

Mid-Atlantic Ridge — a zone down the central Atlantic Ocean where two plates are moving apart and forming volcanic mountains and islands, like Iceland

migration — the movement of people from one place to another; an immigrant moves into a country while an emigrant leaves

mineral — naturally occurring substance found in Earth's rocks that can be used to meet human needs

monsoon — rainy season, most pronounced in southern Asia

moraine — a long ridge that consists of material (usually clay, sand, and pebbles) deposited by a glacier

mountain chain — ranges of mountains in a line or group

mountain range — several mountains clustered together as a group

movement — the act or process of moving

natural force — an influence that promotes physical regions like heat, slope, precipitation, and wind

natural regeneration — the regrowth of forests after they have been cut down by allowing nearby trees to seed the area; takes several years before new trees take hold

natural vegetation — plants that are native to an area; plants that grow without human interference

nitrogen — a colourless gas that makes up about 78 percent of the atmosphere and is part of all living things

nitrogen cycle — the continuous series of natural processes by which nitrogen gases pass through land, air, and water

non-point pollution — environmental damage caused by sources spread over a wide area, like all the airplanes flying through the atmosphere

non-renewable — relating to something that is finite and cannot be replaced once it is used up

northings — locational coordinates moving from south to north on a topographic map

ocean current — a flow of water that moves in one direction within an ocean; pushed by winds and by the spinning of Earth on its axis; a cold current has a temperature lower than the surrounding water; a warm current has a temperature higher than the surrounding water

open-pit mining — a method of mining where the ore is close to the surface and can be reached by digging large holes

ore deposit — a concentration of a particular mineral large enough to be economically mined

organic waste — waste materials that come mainly from plant or animal sources (for example, vegetable peelings, apple cores, banana skins, egg shells, coffee grounds)

orographic precipitation — when moisture-bearing winds meet mountains, they move up the sides of these barriers; as the air rises, it cools and the moisture condenses, which produces clouds and then rain; by the time the air reaches the tops of the mountains, it has released most of its moisture

oxbow lake — an enclosed piece of water caused when a river flows across the narrow strip of land at the base of a meander and cuts off the meander from the new course of the river

oxygen — a colourless, tasteless gas that forms about 21 percent of the atmosphere and is essential for life

ozone layer — a region of ozone gases high in the atmosphere that protects us from ultraviolet light

pattern — a distinctive arrangement or distribution

penstock — the chute down which water flows from a reservoir in a hydro-electric dam; at the bottom of the penstock, the water pushes on the blades of a turbine, causing it to spin and produce an electrical current in a generator that is connected to the turbine

permafrost — permanently frozen ground where only a thin surface layer thaws in summer

photosynthesis — the process by which plants convert sunlight into energy for growth

physical characteristic — natural condition of an area or region, such as plains, mountains, or shield

physical region — an area defined by features such as landforms, climate, soil, and vegetation

place — an area with unique physical or human characteristics; the space occupied by someone or something and used for a particular purpose

plain — large flat to gently rolling region that was formed under a large water body and became exposed after the water disappeared

plate — one of the large divisions of Earth's crust that floats or moves on the molten layer of material below it

plateau — a fairly flat area in mountain regions that has been uplifted by plate movement

point pollution — environmental damage caused by a single source, like a waste leak into water by an industry

precipitation — any form of moisture that falls to Earth from the atmosphere (rain, snow, hail, sleet)

prevailing wind — the usual wind pattern for a particular area

process — an activity we use to change natural resources in order to better meet our needs; for example, purifying water before we drink it

pull factor — a force that draws you to another place

pulp and paper — one of the main forest industries; trees are cut down, and the wood fibres from most parts of the tree are used to make paper, cardboard, and cellulose

push factor — a force that encourages you to leave a place

raw material — basic material that originates from our natural environment before being manufactured or treated

refugee — a person who flees from his or her country because factors such as war, drought, famine, and natural disasters make it too dangerous or impossible to stay

region — an area with a defined set of characteristics

relative location — the location of a place or region in relation to other places or regions (for example, northwest, downstream, two kilometres past the library)

renewable — relating to something that can be regenerated if used carefully

replanting — seedlings are planted right after the forest has been cut; these seedlings have been raised in nurseries and root in the soil quickly, helping to prevent erosion

resource — a supply of something that will help us to meet a need

reservoir — a place or area of stored water

revolution — a complete change in the way things are done, perhaps with violence or disruption

right — to have the legal title or privilege to do something

Ring of Fire — the active earthquake and volcano zone that extends from the southern tip of South America around the perimeter of the Pacific Ocean to Australia

river diversion — changing the direction and course of a river in order to meet some need, such as water for irrigation or for hydro-electric power

rural region — an area of low population density where people live mainly on farms or in the countryside

sea level — mean level of the oceans at 0 metres

selective logging — cutting down only the mature trees in a forest; younger trees are left uncut

shield — the base of an ancient mountain region where formerly high mountains have been worn away leaving a rocky, rugged landform; very old rocky regions that are the foundations of our continents

shifting cultivation — a system of farming in which fields are cultivated for a few years and then abandoned when they lose their fertility

site — the original starting point of a place, or a place with specific qualities

slip-off slope — the bank of the river where sediment falls to the bottom and builds up over time

smog — polluted air that is made up of fog and smoke or other chemical fumes

softwood — needle-leafed coniferous trees that grow in cooler climates and whose wood is relatively soft (for example, pine and spruce); used for lumber, paper, and siding

soil region — an area with similar soils

specialized agriculture — a form of farming that requires unique conditions that can only be found in specific places

specific location — a particular position on Earth, like where you are now

sprinkler irrigation — one of the main types of irrigation; water is carried by pipes to the field and sprayed onto the crops using a sprinkler head; used mainly by North American farmers

steward — someone who manages or takes care of something, such as a farmer protecting and caring for his land

strip logging — a type of logging that takes down all the trees in a 20-metre-wide path

subsistence agriculture — a type of farming that produces only enough food to support a family, with nothing left over to sell

supply — something that satisfies a want or a need

surface irrigation — one of the main types of irrigation (about 96 percent of all irrigation); water is carried in canals and ditches to the fields; farmers make small openings in the walls to let the water flow from the canals and ditches onto the fields; the openings are closed when the soil is wet; water is lost through evaporation

surplus — abundance of water; occurs in a region when more precipitation falls than can sink into the ground, or be used by plants and animals; the extra runoff water becomes running water in streams and rivers

sustain — to help protect and conserve resources so that they survive for future generations

sustainable — a practice or system that can be maintained in the future

sustainable development — using resources without using them up; being able to meet our needs and protect the environment at the same time

tailing — the waste material that has been separated from the valuable ores; it can become an environmental problem

technology — the practical use of scientific knowledge to solve problems and to meet our needs and wants

temperate forest — one of two major categories of forest; located north of the Tropic of Cancer and south of the Tropic of Capricorn; grows in climates that are cooler and less moist than in the tropical regions; growing conditions vary considerably, and these growing conditions produce deciduous forests, coniferous forests, and mixed forests

terracing — a method of farming in which fields are cut into the sides of hills to produce a series of steps or terraces; stone walls hold the soil in place; farmers control when water passes to the next lower terrace

time zone — one of 24 regions having a one-hour difference in time from the next zone

topographic map — a map that shows the natural features of Earth's surface, such as hills, valley, rivers, lakes, and so on

topography — the surface features of a place, including hills, valleys, rivers, lakes, and so on

traditional technology — the use of tools and methods developed far in the past with little change over time

trellis drainage pattern — the rectangular river drainage pattern that forms where the tributaries flow perpendicular to the main branch of the river

tributary — a river or stream that flows into a larger river or stream

tropical forest — one of two main categories of forest; located between the tropics of Cancer and Capricorn, on both sides of the equator; gets 2000 millimetres of rainfall or more each year; has temperatures usually above 27 °C; grows thick and lush trees reaching 45 metres above the ground; contain 40 to 50 percent of Earth's plant and animal species

underground mining — a method of mining used where the ore is far below the surface; shafts and tunnels are used to cut through the rock to reach the ore

urban and regional planning — the area of study that considers future needs and growth, and plans how to organize our spaces effectively

urban region — an area of high-density population; a city or a town

user-defined region — an area determined by a special service or product

valley — feature of the land that is U-shaped or V-shaped and created by the work of running water, moving ice, or the movement of land areas along faults

vegetation region — an area that shares the same major vegetation types

volcano — a landform caused by magma escaping from below Earth's crust

weather — the condition of the air over a place for a short period of time; includes short-term changes in the temperature and precipitation

Western Cordillera — mountain ranges in western Canada, from the Rockies in the east to the Insular mountains of the coastal islands

wetland — lowland area that has plenty of water, such as a swamp, marsh, bog, lagoon, and river delta

wilderness region — an area with no human population

wind — movement of air across Earth's surface; the air movements that bring daily weather to your area

Index

Visual and Text Credits

This page constitutes an extension of the copyright page. We have made every effort to trace the ownership of all copyrighted material and to secure permission from copyright holders. In the event of any question arising as to the use of any material, we will be pleased to make the necessary corrections in future printings.

Front Cover: (mountains) © Vinicius Tupinamba/Shutterstock Images, **(forest)** © iStockphoto.com/AVTG

Unit 1 Opener. Page 2: (top) NASA/National Space Science Data Center, (centre) Lew French, (bottom) © 2008 Jupiterimages Corporation **Page 3:** (top) © 2008 Jupiterimages Corporation, (centre, l.) M. Gaden, GLFC, (centre, r.) © 2008 Jupiterimages Corporation, (bottom l.) Photodisc/Getty Images, (bottom r.) © Patrick Henry Photography/ www.PatrickHenryPhotography.com

Chapter 1. 1.1: NASA/National Space Science Data Center **1.2:** V. Last, Geographical Visual Aids **1.3:** AP Photo/Achmad Ibrahim **1.10:** © 2008 Jupiterimages Corporation **1.11:** Seth Goldfarb/Photonica/Getty Images **1.12:** Photodisc/Getty Images **1.13:** © John Sylvester/Alamy **1.14:** (top, l.) CP Photo/Richard Lam **1.14:** (top, r.) Tim Boyle/Getty Images **1.14:** (centre) © 2008 Jupiterimages Corporation **1.14:** (bottom) AP Photo **1.16:** CP Photo/Ryan Remiorz **1.17:** (left) © Olga Skalkina/Shutterstock Images **1.17:** (middle, t.) © Corel **1.17:** (middle, centre, l.) © kavram/Shutterstock Images **1.17:** (middle, centre, r.) CP Photo Archives/Jonathan Hayward **1.17:** (middle, b.) © Corel **1.17:** (right) © Dvoretskiy Igor Vladimirovich/Shutterstock Images **1.18:** V. Last, Geographical Visual Aids **1.20:** (left) Thomas Kitchin & Victoria Hurst/First Light **1.20:** (right) Library and Archives Canada, Acc. No. 1946-110-1. Gift of Mrs. J. B. Jardine **1.21:** © Dario Diament/Shutterstock Images

Chapter 2. 2.1: © foxie/Shutterstock Images **2.4:** © Corel **2.5:** Gavin Brown/Shutterstock Images **2.6:** S. Meltzer/ PhotoLink/Photodisc/Getty Images **2.7:** © Alexander Kolomietz/Shutterstock Images **2.9:** (top, l.) © M. Dariush/ Shutterstock Images **2.9:** (top, r.) © 2008 Jupiterimages Corporation **2.9:** (centre) © V. J. Matthew/Shutterstock **2.9:** (bottom) Lew French **2.11:** © Dmytro Korolov/ Shutterstock Images **2.14:** (top, l.) © 2008 Jupiterimages Corporation **2.14:** (top, r.) AP/Manish Swarup **2.14:** (bottom) © Corel **2.17:** (left) Alan Marsh/First Light **2.17:** (right) © ElenaElisseeva/Shutterstock Images **2.19:** © Graca Victoria/ Shutterstock Images **2.23:** V. Last, Geographical Visual Aids **2.25:** Stuart O'Sullivan/Taxi/Getty Images **2.26:** © Dan Breckwoldt/Shutterstock Images **2.29:** V. Last, Geographical Visual Aids **2.32:** Dick Hemingway **2.33:** Liu Jin/AFP/Getty Images **2.34:** Bruce Weaver/AFP/Getty Images **2.35:** Jerry Grayson/Helifilms Australia PTY Ltd./Getty Images **2.36:** NOAA/Satellite and Information Service **2.38:** © 2008 Jupiterimages Corporation **2.39:** Motordigitaal/Shutterstock Images **2.40:** V. Last, Geographical Visual Aids

Chapter 3. 3.2: Gary Weber/AFP/Getty Images **3.4:** CP Photo/AP Photo/Fabrizio Villa **3.5:** © Andrew McDonough/ Shutterstock **3.6:** Lew French **3.7:** David McNew/Getty Images **3.8:** © kavram/Shutterstock Images **3.9:** © V. Last, Geographical Visual Aids **3.17:** Travel Excellence/Alamy **3.18:** AP Photo/Ben Margot **3.19:** Courtesy of Kirstin Schwass and Morton Way Public School, Brampton Ontario **3.20:** CP Photo/AP Photo/Trevor Collens **3.21:** © 2008 Jupiterimages Corporation **3.22:** © Focus Strategic Communications Inc. **3.23:** (right) CP Photo/AP Photo/Michael Probst **3.23:** (left) Courtesy of Easy-Glider AG **3.24:** Andre Jenny/Alamy **3.25:** Lew French **3.26:** © Focus Strategic Communications Inc. **3.27:** CP Photo/*Toronto Star*/Salvatore Sacco **3.28:** William Albert Allard/National Geographic Images **3.29:** © 2008 Jupiterimages Corporation **3.31:** Ruben Sprich/Reuters/Landov **3.32:** Courtesy of VIA Rail Canada **3.33:** Will & Deni McIntyre/Stone/Getty Images **3.34:** Courtesy of Wallenius Wilhelmsen Logistics **3.35:** Greg Wood/AFP/Getty Images **3.36:** CP Photo/AP Photo/George Ruhe **3.39:** CP Photo/Larry MacDougal **3.40:** Oote Boe/GalileoPix/Digital Railroad, Inc. **3.42:** CP Photo/*Chicoutimi Le Quotidien*/Steve Tremblay **3.43:** Courtesy of Alcoa (Alcoa in Australia) **3.46:** © 2008 Jupiterimages Corporation **3.47:** © 2008 Jupiterimages Corporation **3.49:** Johner/Johner Images/Getty Images **3.50:** Bob Daemmrich/PhotoEdit, Inc.

Chapter 4. 4.5: Adapted with permission of Robert A. Rhode, www.globalwarmingart.com **4.6:** Data sourced from National Inventory Report, 1990–2004, Greenhouse Gas Sources and Sinks in Canada, Annex 8: Canada's Greenhouse Gas Emission Tables, 1990–2004. (2008). Environment Canada's *Information on Greenhouse Gas Sources and Sinks* [Online]. Available: http://www.ec.gc.ca/pdb/ghg/inventory_report/2004_report/ ta8_2_e.cfm. Cited 2008 March 12. **4.7:** Jaime Reina/AFP/Getty Images **4.8:** (top) M. Gaden, GLFC **4.8:** (inset) T. Lawrence, GLFC **4.12:** Fisheries and Oceans Canada **4.13:** G. Peck/Ivy Images **4.14:** © 2008 Jupiterimages Corporation **4.15:** (top, l.) © fenghui/Shutterstock Images **4.15:** (top, r.) © Tatiana Morozova/Shutterstock Images **4.15:** (bottom, l.) © Merryl McNaughton/Shutterstock Images **4.15:** (bottom, r.) Daniel J. Cox/Photographer's Choice/Getty Images **4.16, 4.17:** © 2008 Jupiterimages Corporation **4.19:** Hager/Robert Harding World Imagery/Getty Images **4.20:** Art Wolfe/Stone/Getty Images

4.21: Image Science and Analysis Laboratory, NASA–Johnson Space Center. *The Gateway to Astronaut Photography of Earth.* **4.22:** Patrick Hertzog/AFP/Getty Images **4.23:** © Patrick Henry Photography/<www.PatrickHenryPhotography.com> **4.24:** Courtesy of the Toronto Zoo Page 85: Literacy Tip, Canada's Forests, A Fine Balance, © Natural Resources Canada

Chapter 5. 5.1: © Jhaz Photography/Shutterstock Images **5.2:** ©Tony Campbell/Shutterstock **5.3:** Ami Vitale/Getty Images **5.4:** B. Lynne Milgram, Ph.D. **5.5:** © Bryan & Cherry Alexander **5.6:** L. MacDougal/First Light **5.7:** © F. Jack Jackson/Alamy **5.8:** © Bruce Cooper/Lew French **5.9:** © Corel **5.11:** CP/Pavel Rahman **5.12:** CP/Kevin Frayer **5.13:** Franke Keating/First Light **5.14:** The Canadian Press **5.15:** © Sally Scott/Shutterstock Images **5.16:** © 2007 Jupiterimages Corporation **5.17:** © Bruce Cooper/Lew French **5.19:** © MaxFX/Shutterstock Images **5.20:** Photodisc/Getty Images **5.22:** Photodisc/Getty Images **5.24, 5.25:** adapted from Statistics Canada pub., *Waste Management Industry Survey, Business and Government Sectors, 2002*, Catalogue 16F0023XIE, p. 14, http://www.statcan.ca/bsolc?catno=16F0023X **5.27:** Candace Feit, *The New York Times*/Redux (altered with permission of Redux Pictures) **5.29:** © Bob Turner/Alamy **5.30:** CP Photo **5.31:** CP/Lars Hagberg **5.32:** Steve Vidler/Image State/Jupiterimages Corporation **5.33:** © Vankina/Shutterstock Images **5.34:** © Jim Mills/Shutterstock Images **5.35:** Courtesy of Conservation Halton **5.36:** © Lew French **5.37:** © Howard Sandler/Shutterstock Images

Unit 2 Opener. Pages 118–119: (top) © V. Last, Geographical Visual Aids **Page 119:** (centre) Bernard Grilly/Stone/Getty Images, (bottom) Robert Van Der Hilst/Stone/Getty Images

Chapter 6. 6.1: NASA/JSC/GPN-2000-001097 **6.6:** AFP/Getty Images **6.7:** © *Journal-Courier*/Clayton Stalter/The Image Works **6.8:** Paul Chesley/Stone/Getty Images **6.9:** © V. Last, Geographical Visual Aids **6.11:** © V. Last, Geographical Visual Aids **6.12:** Todd Korol/Aurora/Getty Images **6.13:** © J. N. Burnett **6.14:** Christer Fredriksson/Lonely Planet Images/Getty Images **6.19:** John Sylvester/First Light **6.20:** John Dunn/National Geographic/Getty Images **6.22:** © 2007 Jupiterimages Corporation **6.24:** Bryan & Cherry Alexander/First Light **6.26:** Reproduced with the permission of the Minister of Public Works and Government Services Canada, 2007, and courtesy of Natural Resources Canada. **6.27:** © 2007 Jupiterimages Corporation **6.29:** Hart House, Permanent Collection

Chapter 7. 7.1: © Dainis Derics/Shutterstock Images **7.10:** NOAA Photo Library, NOAA Central Library; OAR/ERL/National Severe Storms Laboratory (NSSL) **7.11:** © Craig Hansen/Shutterstock Images **7.14:** Ron Elmy/First Light **7.15:** T. Kitchin/First Light **7.16:** Michael Gilbert/Photo Researchers, Inc. **7.17:** © Maksym Gorpenyuk/Shutterstock Images **7.19:** Reuters/Landov **7.20:** Sustainable Development Committee and Principal Chris Lees of Cochrane High School, Cochrane AB **7.23:** (1) Doug Allan/Oxford Scientific/Jupiterimages **7.23:** (2), (3), (4), (5) © Robert Waldock **7.23:** (6) © JTB Photo/Digital Railroad **7.23:** (7) © Norman Price/Alamy **7.23:** (8) Bruno Morandi/ Robert Harding World Imagery/Getty Images **7.23:** (9) Maria Stenzel/National Geographic Image Collection **7.23:** (10) Ariadne Van Zandbergen/Lonely Planet Images/Getty Images **7.23:** (11) © Ladi Kirn/Alamy

7.24: © Luchschen/Shutterstock Images **7.26:** Courtesy of Assoc. Prof. M. R. McDonald/Dept. of Plant Agriculture, Ontario Agricultural College **7.27:** © 2008 Jupiterimages Corporation

Chapter 8. 8.5: © Alan Gignoux/Alamy **8.6:** © Laurin Rinder/Shutterstock Images **8.9:** Reproduced with the permission of the Earth Sciences Sector of Natural Resources Canada, 2008 **8.10:** Image courtesy of the Image Science & Analysis Laboratory, NASA Johnson Space Center/Mission STS067, Roll 703D, Frame 93 **8.11:** CP Photo/*Charlottetown Guardian*/Brian McInnis **8.12:** © J. David Andrews/Masterfile www.masterfile.com **8.14:** Jessamine Hetty/Workbook Stock/Jupiterimages Corporation **8.16:** Gavin Hellier/Robert Harding/Jupiterimages Corporation

Chapter 9. 9.3: Robert Van Der Hilst/Stone/Getty Images **9.5:** Robert Van Der Hilst/Riser/Getty Images **9.7:** Skip Brown/National Geographic Image Collection **9.8:** Al Harvey/The Slide Farm **9.10:** © Andrew Park/Shutterstock Images **9.11:** adapted from Statistics Canada CANSIM Database <http://cansim2.statcan.ca> table 002-0027 **9.12:** © Dirk Herzog/Shutterstock Images **9.13:** B. Lynne Milgram, Ph.D. **9.14:** Bernard Grilly/Stone/Getty Images **9.15:** B. Lynne Milgram, Ph.D. **9.17:** James Strachan/Stone/Getty Images **9.18:** Andy Sacks/Stone/Getty Images **9.19:** Jerry Alexander/Stone/Getty Images **9.20:** B. Lynne Milgram, Ph.D. **9.21:** CP Photo/Jacques Boissinot **9.24:** © Alexei Novikov/Shutterstock Images

Unit 3 Opener. Pages 198–199: (top) Jaime Villaseca/The Image Bank/Getty Images **Page 199:** (centre) © Lowell Georgia/Corbis

Chapter 10. 10.2: (left) CP Photo/Larry MacDougal **10.2:** (centre) © frank ungrad/Shutterstock Images **10.2:** (right) © MaxFX/Shutterstock Images **10.6:** (all) Courtesy of the National Cotton Council of America **10.8:** Walter Bibikow/Jon Arnold Travel/Photolibrary **10.9:** data sourced from (1) Energy Information Administration (EIA). (June 2004). *International Energy Annual 2002*. Product # DOE/EIA-0219(2002). (2) EIA. (May 2007). *International Energy Outlook 2007*. Product #DOE/EIA-0404(2007). **10.10:** sourced from United Nations Development Programme. (1998). *Human Development Report 1998 Overview*. Excerpt used also available Online: www.globalissues.org/TradeRelated/Consumption.asp **10.11:** Tony Freeman/PhotoEdit, Inc. **10.12:** Excerpted from Basic facts about recycling. (2007). *Recycling International* [Online]. Available: http://www.recyclinginternational.com/basicfacts/index.aspx Cited 2007 Dec. 6. Reprinted with permission of Recycling International. **10.13:** David Young-Wolff/PhotoEdit, Inc. **10.14:** © Jennifer Farrell **10.15:** Chad Ehlers/Stock Connection/Jupiter Images Corporation **10.20, 10.21, 10.22:** Victor Englebert/Time & Life Pictures/Getty Images **10.23:** © Ben Wicks Estate

Chapter 11. 11.1: (oil) Paul Rapson/SPL/PubliPhoto **11.1:** (salt), (potash hill) © 2008 Jupiterimages Corporation **11.1:** (copper wire) © Chris Harvey/Shutterstock Images **11.1:** (gravel) © Marko Vesel/Shutterstock Images **11.1:** (sand) © Ramzi Hachicho/Shutterstock Images **11.1:** (gold bar) © Sebastian Kaulitzki/Shutterstock Images **11.1:** (coal) © pixelman/Shutterstock Images

11.7: © Hans Blohm/Masterfile, www.masterfile.com **11.9:** Jeff Green/*Frontenac News* **11.11:** Photo by Jiri Hermann courtesy Diavik Diamond Mines Inc. **11.13:** D. Johnston/Ivy Images **11.14:** Wellington County Museum and Archives: Slide 13201 Limestone Quarry, Guelph Township, 25 September 1976. Photographer Gordon Couling. **11.15:** Bill Lowry/Ivy Images **11.16:** referenced from Nikiforuk, A. (2007 Jan. 15). Mythoilogy. Written for ASPO Canada [Online]. Available: http://aspocanada.ca/mythoilogy-2.html. Cited 2008 March 13. **11.17a, 11.17b:** adapted from Statistics Canada publication, *Canada's Mineral Production Preliminary Estimates 2006*, Catalogue 26-202-XIB, Released Date: June 6, 2007 http://www.statcan.ca/english/freepub/26-202-XIB/26-202-XIB2007000.pdf **11:19** referenced from (1) Canada's diamond rush. (2007 Sept.). *CBC News* [Online]. Available: http://www.cbc.ca/news/background/diamonds/. Cited 2008 March 13. (2) Canada: A diamond producing nation. (2007 June 19). *Natural Resources Canada* [Online]. Available: http://www.nrcan.gc.ca/ms/diam/index_e.htm. Cited 2008 March 13. **11.20:** © Courtenay Keenan, Instructor, Diamond Cutting and Polishing, Aurora College, Yellowknife Campus, Yellowknife, NT **11.21:** © Diaphor La Phototheque/Photolibrary **11.22:** Larry Macdougal/First Light

Chapter 12. 12.1: © dbimages/Alamy **12.10,12.11:** © 2008 Jupiterimages Corporation **12.12:** © blickwinkel/Alamy **12.15:** © Sherman Hines/Masterfile, www.masterfile.com **12.16:** Jaime Villaseca/The Image Bank/Getty Images **12.18:** © Troy & Mary Parlee/Index Stock Imagery/Photolibrary **12.20:** © Keith Dannemiller/Corbis **12.22:** David R. Frazier/Photo Researchers/First Light **12.23:** Michael Stuparyk/*Toronto Star* **12.26:** Peter Essick/Aurora/Getty Images **12.27:** © 2008 Jupiterimages Corporation **Page 260:** (Table, "Percentage of Wood...") sourced from: 5.1 Net Merchantable Volume of Roundwood Harvested by Category and Province/Territory, 1940–2006. (2007 Sept. 18). *National Forestry Database Program*, Canada [Online]. Available: http://nfdp.ccfm.org/compendium/ data/2007_10/tables/com51e.htm. Cited 2008 March 13.

Chapter 13. 13.1: Doug Hamilton/First Light **13.8:** (top) © Tony Hertz/Alamy **13.8:** (centre) © J. Lawrence/Imagestate/Jupiterimages Corporation **13.8:** (bottom) Mick Rock/Cephas Picture Library/Photolibrary **13.10:** B. Lynne Milgram, Ph.D. **13.11:** Courtesy of the Department of the Interior, The Bureau of Reclamation, U.S. Government **13.14:** © Gueorgui Pinkhassov/Magnum Photos **13.16:** Courtesy of the Ontario Power Generation Corp **13.17:** Water Heroes Story. (2007). *Great Lakes Kids* [Online]. Available: http://www.on.ec.gc.ca/greatlakeskids/heroes-story6-e.html#content. Cited 2008 March 6. © Her Majesty the Queen in Right of Canada, Environment Canada 2007. All rights reserved. Reproduced with the permission of the Minister of Public Works and Government Services Canada, 2007; this reproduction is not an official version of the Work, nor has it been made in affiliation with or with the endorsement of Environment Canada. **13.19:** Reproduced with permission of Global Wind Energy Council (GWEC), http://www.gwec.net/ **13.20:** David Nunuk/First Light **13.24:** © 2008 Jupiterimages Corporation **13.27:** © Lowell Georgia/Corbis **13.28:** © Rolf Hicker, Rolf Hicker Photography **13.29:** sourced from: Commercial/Landings/Seafisheries/Tables for Atlantic Regions–Quantities, for 1990–2006. (2007 Sept. 12). *Fisheries and Oceans Canada, Statistical Services* [Online]. Available: http://www.dfo-mpo.gc.ca/communic/statistics/commercial/landings/seafisheries/index_e.htm. Cited 2008 March 13. **13.31:** Tom Kitchin & Victoria Hurst

Chapter 14. 14.1: © Photodisc **14.3:** Art Gallery of Ontario **14.4:** excerpted and adapted with permission from: John Slykhuis/*Georgina Advocate* **14.5:** © egd/Shutterstock Images **14.9:** Bill Ivy/Ivy Images **14.10:** (top) © Alex Neauville/Shutterstock Images **14.10:** (2nd from top) © manfredxy/Shutterstock Images **14.10:** (3rd from top) © 2008 Jupiterimages Corporation **14.10:** (bottom) CP Photo/AP/Leslie Mazoch **14.12:** Bill Ivy/Ivy Images **14.13:** Rene Johnston/*Toronto Star* **14.14:** David Young-Wolff/Photo Edit, Inc. **14.15:** © Kameleon007/istockphoto.com **14.16:** © Syracuse Newspapers/Randi Anglin/The Image Works **14.17:** CP Photo/Adrian Wyld **14.19:** sourced from: ITOPF's Oil Tanker Spill Information: Numbers and Amounts Spilt(Table 1). (2007). *The International Tanker Owners Pollution Federation Ltd. (ITOPF)* [Online]. Available: http://www.itopf.com/information-services/data-and-statistics/statistics/. Cited 2008 March 13.